History
of the
Llynfi Valley

History
of the
Llynfi Valley

Brinley Richards M.A.

Bridgend Library and Information Service
Gwasanaeth Llyfrgell a Gwybodaeth Pen-y-bont ar Ogwr

First published by D. Brown & Sons Ltd 1982
This edition specially produced by
Cedric Chivers Ltd, Trowbridge, Wiltshire
for the publishers
Bridgend Library and Information Service
Gwasanaeth Llyfrgell a Gwybodaeth Pen-y-bont ar Ogwr

© Bridgend Library and Information Service
Gwasanaeth Llyfrgell a Gwybodaeth Pen-y-bont ar Ogwr 2008

ISBN Hardback 978-1-872430-28-7
ISBN Paperback 978-1-872430-29-4

Printed in Great Britain by
Cromwell Press, Trowbridge, Wiltshire

Contents

LITERATURE

Publishers' Note

Brinley Richards handed me his completed manuscript for printing just eleven days before his tragic death at Interlaken, Switzerland, on 18th September, 1981. I first met him in late August and saw him only three times, yet he has made a greater impression on me than almost anyone else I have ever met—both through his arresting personality and through the remarkably knowledgeable and interesting volume he miraculously left behind him.

Our Company, D. Brown and Sons Ltd. of Cowbridge and Bridgend, Glamorgan, took over the responsibility of not only printing, but publishing, this remarkable volume and it has been our endeavour to make the book a fitting memorial to Brinley. To this end we have expanded the illustrative content some four times to a total of 167 old photographs, maps and line drawings, many of which have never been published before.

We have tried to illuminate the text wherever possible and in the search have been helped over many weeks by 'that local collector of manuscripts' (as Brinley disarmingly describes him in his *Introduction*), John Lyons. Without John Lyons the volume could never have appeared in its present form, for not only did he produce himself a large proportion of the more unusual photographs, maps and documents in the book, but he provided the local historical knowledge to make their captioning meaningful and interesting to the present-day reader.

Another who has been of inestimable help in proof-reading and providing photographs and information is Norah Isaac, formerly of Caerau, while Professor Stephen Williams of Swansea University, Meirion Davies of Bridgend (who also compiled the Index), May Brown of Cowbridge and Gwynfryn Richards (the author's brother) also read a complete proof. Gill John of Maesteg Library, David Pearce of the Mid Glamorgan County Library, Bridgend, Patricia Moore of the Glamorgan Archive Service, Richard Keen and John Lewis of the National Museum of Wales, John Bevan and Derrick Jenkins of the National Folk Museum, Donald Moore of the National Library of Wales and Arthur Flint (an expert on the Duffryn-Llynvi tramroad) have all been of particular help.

We are grateful to the Llynfi Valley Historical Society (of which Brinley was a former President) for readily agreeing to distribute his book in the Valley on our behalf.

We would also like to thank the following for providing photographs and other information: Glyn Ball (Maesteg), Howard Balston (*Glamorgan Gazette*), Carmel Chapel Deacons (Maesteg), Richard David (The *Old House*, Llangynwyd), D. Davies (*Ty'r Llwyni*), B. Gage (Cynonville), Jane Isaac (Maesteg), L. Jones (Maesteg), the Llynfi Valley Historical Society, Maesteg Cricket Club, J. Morgan (Cymer), Paris House (Maesteg), G. Thomas (Maesteg). This has truly been a co-operative effort!

Finally, we thank Mrs. Muriel Richards for her continual support during these difficult months.

R. D. Whitaker M.A.
February, 1982

Publisher's Note, New Edition

Bridgend Library and Information Service is delighted to be able to make this publication available again. Many excellent books have appeared on specific aspects of the history of the area during the quarter of a century since it was first published, but Brinley Richards' work remains the only modern attempt at a comprehensive general history of the Llynfi Valley. This reprint will make the results of his extensive research easily available to a new generation of readers and, we are sure, stimulate renewed interest in the heritage of the valley.

We would like to express our thanks to the Llynfi Valley Historical Society for their support in this venture, and in particular to Mr Cyril Phillips of Maesteg for his painstaking work in drawing up a revised and expanded index.

We would also like to thank Mr Randall Richards of Ynys Mon, and Keith Brown & Sons Ltd of Cowbridge, for permission to reprint the book. Mr Richards has also asked that we draw attention again to the invaluable help and support Brinley received from his brother the Very Reverend Gwynfryn Richards when working on the original edition.

Lesley Milne
Reference and Local Studies Librarian
April 2008

Foreword

(Emeritus Professor STEPHEN J. WILLIAMS, M.A., D.Litt., Swansea)

Readers of this remarkable book will, early in their reading, glean that the author has outstanding qualities as a writer, and that he is an extensively-read scholar and local historian. They will realise that it could not have been written without sound research extending over very many years and a background of long acquaintance with the life and history of Maesteg and its environs. The author, however, gives no indication of the influences and forces that prompted him to write it. Indeed, with natural modesty, he says nothing about himself directly, and when the matter in hand obliges him to refer to himself, he does so in the third person. It is never 'I', but 'the writer of these notes' (or rarely, '. . . of this book'). He writes of the achievements and publications of 'the Rev. Gwynfryn Richards' who became the Dean of Bangor; but omits to say that he is the author's own brother!

A few facts concerning Mr. Brinley Richards himself do come to light on reading the work, viz., that he is a native of Nantyffyllon, that he is exceedingly proud of the culture of his own locality and that the versatility of his treatment of it comes from a variety of sources.

His family background accounts for his deep interest in Welsh literary culture — an interest that led him to participate in literary activities. His association with the National Eisteddfod paved the way to the fame he acquired when he won the coveted prize of the 'Chair' in 1951 for his 'Awdl' (a long poem with traditional, intricate metrical forms). His many publications and long service have recently gained for him the National Eisteddfod's highest honour — that of 'Cymrawd' ('Fellow'). It is no wonder that he writes so learnedly about the literary tradition in this volume. His chief Bardic Honour was his election to serve as Archdruid (1972-4).

Mr. Richards's ability to trace the history of local government must be attributed to his membership of the Maesteg U.D.C. for more than 42 years (including the office of Chairman four times — a record)! His observations on the social and industrial life of Mid Glamorgan are the fruit of this and other public services.

His thorough knowledge of the history of religious institutions, especially in the Maesteg area, is well exemplified in this book. Here interest is combined with deep religious convictions. His various services to the Welsh Congregational Union were acknowledged when he was elected President for 1964.

The many references to legal and technical matters in this history came easily to him after his training in law, and subsequent practice as solicitor for very many years until his recent retirement.

Mr. Richards's gift of an extraordinary memory must have been an invaluable asset to him in all his spheres of activity: as solicitor, lecturer, raconteur, poet, historian and writer. His attention to detail, which is a feature of all his writing, probably owes something to his professional training. It has played an important part in critical treatises of 'detection', such as his examination of the Cefn Ydfa romantic story, or his re-appraisal of aspects of the Iolo Morganwg controversy.

The wide scope of his interest is shown in the nature of his literary publications, such as poetry, biography, essays, criticism (including adjudications), local history, church history and traditional legend. The honour bestowed upon him by the University of Wales, by the award of the honorary degree of M.A., was well deserved.

Despite the diversity of his published works they display a unity of purpose and zest for living. This latest book of his may prove to be his *magnum opus*, but the unpredictability of 'Brinli' (by which form of his name he is known in bardic circles, as well as to his close personal friends) precludes such speculation. This volume will undoubtedly be welcomed by his 'own people' and by all who find pleasure and enrichment in reading a fresh contribution to recording the story of life in Wales.

Postscript

Some two months after the above Foreword was written came the tragic news of Brinley's sudden death on 18 September in Interlaken while he and Mrs. Richards were on holiday. The reference (in the last paragraph of the Foreword) to his 'unpredictability' has therefore by now acquired a sad connotation which was inconceivable when the word was written.

Many worthy tributes have been paid to the life and work of this lovable Welshman. Such expressions of admiration and esteem will help to bring sweetness to the memory of his passing, above all to his wife, Muriel, and to his brother whose counsel he valued so highly. An outstanding son of the Llynfi Valley and of Wales, he will be long remembered.

October 1981   *S.J.W.*

Introduction

In the Cardiff Free Library there is a copy-book with an undated note on the cover by David Jones of Wallington stating that he, David Jones, had written a history of the Parish of Llangynwyd at some length and had sent the same to T. C. Evans, Llangynwyd, better known as Cadrawd, who, in turn, had lent the MS to Rhys D. Morgan (ap Lleurwg), Maesteg. The note asserts that R.D.M. had extracted the principal parts out of it, and with some additions, had used the material for a lecture to the Literary Institute at Maesteg. This was about 1880. This lecture, based on David Jones's history of the Parish and revised viciously by a person calling himself 'Gomer Morganwg, B.B.D. of Tir yr Iarll', is the one contained in the copy book at the Cardiff Library. We have no knowledge of the whereabouts of David Jones's original essay.

Several attempts have subsequently been made to gather information regarding the development of the district. In November 1946, the Maesteg Rotary Club held a meeting to devise ways and means of collecting records and other information regarding industry, education, music, politics, sport, religion and the social life of the Llynfi Valley from Caerau to Llangynwyd. Officers were elected but no tangible evidence remains of the result of these activities.

In 1887, Cadrawd published his *History of Llangynwyd Parish*. It still remains the most authoritative and comprehensive book written to date on that subject, although other local historians have added substantially to our knowledge of the past. Thomas Morgan, better known as Llyfnwy, emigrated to America, where he died in 1910, whilst David Davies, known locally as 'the historian', died in 1966. We are also indebted to Frederic Evans, the youngest son of Cadrawd, who later wrote under the name of Michael Gareth Llewelyn, for his informative book, *Tir Iarll*, published in 1912 when he was only 22 years of age.

In attempting to bring the history up to date, one is faced with the difficulty of deciding how much to quote from the above-mentioned volumes as they have been out of print for many years. A history of the valley would be incomplete without reiterating some of the facts which they contain. It is hoped to avoid repeating more than is necessary.

Our literary past has been dealt with by the well-known Welsh scholar, Professor Griffith John Williams (1892-1963). Much controversy arose over his attempt to debunk the story of the romance of the Maid of Cefn Ydfa with which we hope to deal later in this volume. However, Professor

1   Thomas Christopher Evans (Cadrawd), 1846-1918

Williams agrees that the literary tradition of Glamorgan is superior to that of any other County of Wales, with the possible exception of the former Denbighshire, and that the focal point or centre of the Glamorgan tradition for many centuries was Llangynwyd.

The task of attempting to write the history of the Llynfi Valley has its advantages and disadvantages. One advantage is the fact that it is such a compact valley stretching south from Caerau for about 6 or 7 miles to the point at which the Llynfi river joins the Ogmore river near Tondu and thereafter loses its identity and name. The river flows in a south easterly direction and leaves Tir Iarll near the small village of Coetrehen. The valley can boast of a rich and colourful history much earlier than the industrial revolution of the nineteenth century. In this respect, no other valley in Glamorgan can favourably compete with it.

2 The Author as Chairman of Maesteg U.D.C. welcoming the Rt. Hon James Griffiths, Secretary of State for Wales. Also in the welcoming party were (*left to right*) Mr Laity (local Health Insurance Office), D C Watkins, R Mordecai (part of head), J J Jones, Emlyn Druce (Assistant Clerk), Llew Thomas (partly covered) and Stanley Lewis

In addition, it is doubtful whether any other Glamorgan valley of comparable size and population has been the scene of so much social activity up to the present day. It is true that a rich history linked with the present-day social activity can provide an abundance of data for the purpose of compiling a volume of local history, yet, on the other hand, it can induce a headache in having to decide how to compress that information into the size of a readable and saleable volume.

In many respects, life in the valleys of South Wales has followed the usual pattern — being first agricultural, then industrial followed by depression and migration, and ultimately by a new type of industrial revival.

It is hoped to deal with the available material objectively without foisting upon the reader the opinions of the writer. The personal views of the author would require another volume of a different nature!

The writer was privileged to have been born in Nantyffyllon. His father was a miner for over 50 years and had previously worked at the Llynfi Iron Works, where the writer's paternal grandfather was employed as a baller over a hundred years ago. The writer himself has spent the whole of his professional life as a solicitor in the Llynfi Valley, thereby coming in almost daily contact with every stratum of local society. His membership of the Maesteg U.D.C. for over 42 years helped to provide him with data that could possibly have escaped those who have to rely on the printed or written word only.

On occasions, when he was chairman of that Authority, it fell to his lot to give civic receptions to various bodies and distinguished visitors. The picture painted was always a favourable one and led guests to believe that they were being welcomed to the finest valley in Wales! However, it is assumed that readers of this volume will require an objective account, warts and all, free from personal prejudices.

When material was first being gathered, the writer lost two valuable friends, namely Donald B. Jones, who died aged 54 in May 1970, the assistant editor of the *Glamorgan Gazette* and previously of the *Glamorgan Advertiser*, and Victor Hampson-Jones, who died in July 1977, an extra-mural lecturer under the University of Wales. The former possessed a wealth of knowledge of the present-day life of this valley. He was an outstanding journalist and could easily have made his mark in Fleet Street. The latter was a profound scholar of strong convictions. The untimely departure of these two meant the loss of much valuable material for this volume.

It is encouraging to lovers of our traditions to know that a local Historical Society was formed in June 1979. Judging by its present enthusiasm, it will be of immense help in preserving and collating much local history that would otherwise have been lost for ever. We are also glad to note that a similar society, *Afan Uchaf*, has been established, under the enlightened leadership of the Rev. Roger Lee Brown, in the upper part of the Afan Valley of which he was Vicar until 1980 when he moved to Tongwynlais. Argoed Afan was once within the Manor of Tir Iarll and the Parish of Llangynwyd, but remained a distinctive unit for centuries.

There is reason to believe that many former residents of the district would welcome an up-to-date account of the valley of their birth. Maesteg natives are known to be clannish. In 1930 as many as 350 former residents of the Maesteg valley attended a reunion at Bethlehem, Pennsylvania. The following year at Lake Oriel, 18 miles north of Scranton, 600 old Maestegians and friends attended a Cymanfa Ganu. They came from Bethlehem, Philadelphia, Wilksbarre, Scranton (all in Pennsylvania), Albany (New York), California and elsewhere.

It is realised that we cannot live on traditions, but at the same time they can be an incentive and an inspiration. It would be a sad situation if we had no roots of which we could be proud.

A bibliography has been prepared of all known books, booklets, articles and pamphlets relating to the Llynfi valley, however tenuous the references to the valley may appear in some of them. A further list has been prepared of all known literature, published or unpublished, written by persons connected with the district, either by birth or residence, temporary or otherwise, on subjects of a general nature.*

In all this the writer has received much helpful information from that local collector of manuscripts, John Lyons, and from bibliographies mentioned in the two lists referred to above. These lists are obviously incomplete as further relevant information continues to appear from time to time. Incidentally, John Lyons, who has learnt Welsh, is a direct descendant of John Yorath (1775-1843) known as Jac y Gôf, the first blacksmith at the Maesteg Iron Works. Cadrawd refers to him in his *History of Llangynwyd*, whilst three *in memoriam* stanzas (*englynion*) appeared in *Yr Haul* in 1843.

Lord Acton once said that true history was not a burden on the memory but an illumination of the mind. It is hoped that the reading of this volume will not involve too wearisome a task and that a glimpse of the past of this valley which we love so much will not be without its reward. As the volume is almost entirely a one-man effort, the author will be solely responsible for all the omissions, limitations and errors that a perusal of the book will be bound to reveal.

The writer feels deeply indebted to Dr. Stephen J. Williams for his most generous foreword. Encouragement from a person of his status is greatly appreciated.

My main thanks are due to my wife for acquiescing to her husband devoting so much time to the preparation of this work at the expense of home duties of a more practical nature. It is my privilege to dedicate this volume to her.

Publishers' Note: This list was compiled by the author and presented to Maesteg Library.

Fig. 1 The Llynfi Valley

The Llynfi Valley

As this volume deals almost exclusively with this valley, it becomes necessary to convey to non-residents some idea of the geography of the district.

The whole area was formerly in the Parish of Llangynwyd and an integral part of Tir Iarll. By to-day, the only means of transport throughout the whole of the valley is by road.

In travelling north from Bridgend for 3 or 4 miles, we reach the point where the rivers Llynfi and Ogmore merge. A mile to the north is the picturesque village of Coetrehen, but although it is in the Llynfi Valley, it seems to have more in common, socially and otherwise, with Tondu and Bridgend rather than with Maesteg. Prior to the reorganisation of local government in 1974, it was governed locally by the Penybont R.D.C., and not by the Maesteg U.D.C.

The village does not appear to have any exceptional historical associations. One claim to fame is the fact that the Rev. Samuel Jones, who was deprived of his living in Llangynwyd in 1662, had used a thatched building, Cildeudy, in Coetrehen as a place of worship after his eviction. Iolo

3   Cildeudy, Coetrehen

Morganwg, in his writings, refers to eisteddfodau held at 'Pont y Goetre Hen Inn' in the mid-eighteenth century. The original village was a row of houses called Oak Terrace, each house having 2 bedrooms and 2 living rooms with outside sanitation and front gardens. Behind these houses was a watercourse which had once fed the Tondu Iron Works. There is only one public house in the village, the Nicholls Arms, built at the time the valley railway was constructed. There has been much building development in the meantime. English appears to have been the sole language of the village and of public worship, both at the local Methodist Chapel and the Anglican Church.

As we proceed about a mile north from Coetrehen, we pass the site (to our left) of the demolished Round House, formerly the eighteenth century Cefn

4   Round House, former Cefn Ydfa Lodge, photographed in 1939, now demolished

Ydfa Lodge. It was a white washed cottage called *Corn Hwch* (the horn of a sow). Llyfnwy maintained that the name was ridiculous as no sow had a horn! Some thought that the name was *Caer Ynwch* as there was a similar place-name near Dolgellau. Others thought it was *Corn Iwrch*, the horn of a roebuck or of a deer. In any case, the name appears to be a corruption. The

5   (*Opposite*) This aerial photograph, taken Oct 1971, shows the main Bridgend to Maesteg road with associated houses, including the Round House (Corn Hwch Lodge), Gelli Las signal box, Llynfi Power Station in operation and connecting rail network. Bottom right hand shows Shwt village, with Tŷ Isaf farm near the Power Station. Due to road improvements and Power Station closure, many of these buildings no longer exist

building itself was demolished in 1972. On the opposite side of the River Llynfi, below the road level, there is a homely village bearing the quaint name of Shwt, and if we follow the road through the village, we ascend the Moelgiliau Mountain and reach the village of Betws. The old houses have been swamped by the number of comparatively new Council houses.

The old Church at Betws was looked upon by some authorities as a half-way house for monks who used to travel from Tintern Abbey to St. David's Cathedral in Pembrokeshire. A Chapel, known as *Y City Fawr*, was erected in Betws in 1722 by Protestant Dissenters classified as Presbyterians, being the followers of the Rev. Samuel Jones. The Church ultimately became Unitarian until its dissolution over a century ago. It was at Sardis Baptist Church, founded in 1839, that the famous Eisteddfod conductor and poet, Gurnos, ministered from 1882 to 1886.

6   Cabivor Hill, early 1930's

On returning to the main road and travelling further north, we pass (on our right) the Llynfi Power Station, which has now become derelict. Immediately opposite the entrance to the Power Station is the unobtrusive entrance to the road leading to Cefn Ydfa, without any directive sign. On the hill on the horizon immediately facing the traveller, the tower of Llangynwyd Church comes into view. To our right, on the east side of the Llynfi River, we can see the Cwmdu viaduct in the District known as *Y Darren*, once a favourite spot for picnics. On this site stands *Gelli Eblig*, the birthplace of the Rev. Evan Griffiths, to whom reference is later made in this volume.

After passing through the villages of Pontrhydycyff (rhyming with 'beef) and Cwmfelin (earlier known as Cwm-y-felin), we reach Cerdin Square, from which point one can branch off to the left to the south west to reach Llangynwyd village after climbing a rather steep hill for nearly a mile. As we climb the hill, we can see to our right the beautiful Sychbant valley, the

7 General view, Sychbant Valley, *c.*1906-8

venue of many picnics in the past and the site of Graig Fach, where Calvinistic Methodism got a foothold in the latter part of the eighteenth century.

On returning to the main raod at Cerdin Square and proceeding north at right angles, we enter the town of Maesteg. It was formerly known as *Y Llwyni*, being the name of a local farm which disappeared many years ago. Maesteg has been described as a saucer-like area, as the valley at this point opens out. It is 420 feet above sea level, and to-day, its two main streets are wide and spacious. It is the principal town of the Llynfi Valley, which first developed with the growth of the two iron works, then with coal mining and tinplate works. According to *Kelly's Directory of South Wales*, 1906, Maesteg is 198 miles from London, 28 miles from Cardiff and 8 miles north west of Bridgend.

Continuing along the main road northwards for a mile or so, we come to Nantyffyllon, formerly called *Tywith*, and earlier still *Nantyffyrlling* or *Nantyffyrling*. The two mountains, *Y Garn Wen* and *Pwll-yr-iwrch*, stand as eternal sentinels above the activities of the village below. David Bowen (Cynwyd), in his essay on the geology of the valley (*Y Berllan*, 1869) states that the name *Y Garn Wen* arose possibly owing to the fact that scores of tons of greyish white stones remained loose on its slopes.

8   General view of Maesteg, *c.*1908, with working collieries in the background

9   Homfray Street, Nantyfyllon, and occupants *c.*1900

Immediately adjacent to the north of Nantyffyllon, and to the west of the Llynfi River was a wooded area formerly called Tynycoed. It later became known as Tyderwen because of an oak tree on the right of the entrance gate to Tyderwen House, a mansion built by the Cambrian Iron Company (the New Iron Works). The trees of this wooded area were uprooted by oxen. The upper part of Nantyffyllon on the east side of the Llynfi River was formerly called Spelters as it was the site of the first spelter works in the valley at the dawn of the Industrial Revolution. It is bounded by *Mynydd y Dyffryn* to the left and by *Y Darren Pannau* to the right.

North of Spelters, at the top of the Llynfi Valley, we have the populous village of Caerau, which grew rapidly at the end of the last century. When

10   Caerau Library and railway bridge (demolished 1981) with *Moel y Dyffryn* in the background

the Maesteg U.D.C. was formed under the Local Government Act, 1894, Caerau was non-existent, and there was no Caerau Ward. It was in April, 1903, owing to the rapid increase in population and industrial growth that Caerau Ward was added to the then three existing Wards. It was in March, 1898 that the Caerau Post Office was opened, although there was a branch office kept by a Shadrach Lewis in Spelters over a century ago.

Caerau is guarded by the two mountains, *Mynydd y Caerau* and *Y Foel Fawr*. The name 'Caerau' can be construed as the 'Place of Cairns'. The view from the summit (1,823 feet) is magnificent, and on a clear day, the Bristol Channel, Barry Island and even Caldey, near Tenby, can be seen. An inter-valley road leads northwards over the Caerau mountain to Cymer, branching west to the Afan Valley and east to the Rhondda Valley after passing through Abergwynfi, being about 2 miles north of Cymer.

11 Rural view of Cymer in the 1950's looking down the valley towards the former
Gelli Woollen Mill

The Llynfi Valley was formerly connected by rail with Cymer and the Afan
Valley by means of a tunnel (now closed) between Caerau and Cymer. It was
driven through the *Moel Trawsnant* Mountain and took 3 years to complete,
the foreman of the works being Stephen Lewis of Maesteg. During the construction of the tunnel, workmen's huts were erected on land which later
became the site of the Caerau Road houses. The Caerau railway station was
not opened until April 1901. In his *Track Layout Diagrams* (Section 51),
dealing with the Port Talbot and Cymer railway branches, R. A. Cooke
provides us with maps of Collieries, including those in the Maesteg area. His
Diagrams (Section 49) relate to the Llynfi Valley. We are told that the
Nantyffyllon-Cymer railway line was opened in 1878, the Cymer-
Abergwynfi line on 22 March 1886 and the Blaengwynfi-Blaencwm
(Rhondda) line in 1890 through another tunnel since closed. The last train
from Caerau to Cymer Afan ran on 25 June 1970, all traffic from Bridgend
upwards having ceased that year.

Another access route to the Afan Valley was a railway line (now closed)
formerly known as the Port Talbot Railway (P.T.R.). It ran from Port
Talbot through the village of Bryn, formerly known as Bryntroedgam or
Bryn-troed-y-garn, reaching Maesteg therefrom by means of a tunnel. The
first train ran through this tunnel on 14 February 1898. R. A. Cooke states
that the same line had been extended to Llety Brongu by 1 September 1897.
Here again the road has replaced the railway line, the passenger line from
Maesteg, through Bryn, to Port Talbot having closed on 11 September
1933.

12   The last goods train to run on the PTR line at Neath Road Station, 1964

The source of the River Llynfi is on *Mynydd y Caerau* at a spot called by Cadrawd *Coed-cae-ffyrch*. The river is fed by many rivulets. D. R. Waldin, a native of the valley who died aged 89 in 1933, could remember the river being joined by a tributary then known as *Nant-y-pistyll du* or *Cil-ffrwd*, near Blaenllynfi Cottages where the Caerau Square now appears. The wooden bridge was replaced by a modern structure in 1906. The main river was fed by springs from Blaencaerau, Nyth y Frân, Nant-cil-ffrwd, Dyffryn, Nant-y-ffyrlling in the upper part of the valley. Water was pumped into the Nantycrynwydd Pond, Maesteg, later called Bryant's Pond (now drained and built over) to supply the Llynfi Iron Works. Other streams to the south of Maesteg included Nantybwbach and Heolfain, whilst Nant-y-cerdin, fed by waters from Cwm Sychbant, supplied the Llwydarth Tinplate Works.

D. R. Waldin could remember seeing housewives clean vegetables in the river as the water was so clear. They also took their washing to the river, lighting a fire on the banks and laying the clothes on bushes to dry in the sun. The river contained eels, trout, sewin and salmon weighing up to 20 lb.

The fact that the valley contained such beautiful names as Ysguborwen, Cwm-nant-y-gwiail, Cwrt-y-mwnws as well as those mentioned above, indicates that our forefathers had an imagination that should put to shame those responsible for some of the colourless (and sometimes snobbish) names foisted upon us in recent times. Although the residents of the Cae Tincer

Estate at Garth objected to the name presumably on social grounds, the name was merely a revival of the name by which the former field was known. The occupiers had complained that the name 'Cae Tincer' implied that they lived like gypsies, and consequently the Maesteg Council agreed to their petition to give the site a more respectable name — Oakwood Estate.

2. The Earliest Times

How far back can we trace our past? Archaeologists tell us that there are still traces of the Roman and Norman occupation in the valley. According to R. D. Morgan (ap Lleurwg), Maesteg, a party of antiquarians led by David Jones, Wallington had discovered one of several Roman camps and a camping ground of two Legions in a field called Parc Tynycwm, near Llangynwyd village. There can still be seen traces of a Roman road from Bryncyneiron mountain reaching across the intervening valley to ascend the brow of Garnwen mountain and to traverse the ridge to Cymer. C. J. Evans (Cadrawd's son) informs us that earthworks at Mynydd Baeden, near Cefn Ydfa, were probably constructed about 20 centuries ago to resist the advance of the Romans. There is still evidence of a Roman camp at Rhyd Blaen-y-Cwm.

Judging by the number of tumuli, entrenchments and encampments found on the hilltops near Llangynwyd, it appears clear that the area was inhabited from time immemorial and was a centre of Celtic culture and Christianity. The famous mound on Margam mountain, called *Twmpath Diwlith* was once classed as one of the seven wonders of Glamorgan because it was popularly believed that dew never fell upon it. One explanation given for the name was that it was derived from the two words *Duw* and *llith*, and meant the Mound of the Lesson of God. It was so called, we are told, because a priest stood once a year on the boundary between Margam and Llangynwyd parishes, and from the mound read a lesson from the Book of Homilies while, according to custom, the local inhabitants 'beat the parish bounds'!

According to Sir Cyril and Lady Fox, (*Bulletin, Board of Celtic Studies*, I, p. 66) the *Twmpath Diwlith* was opened by Dr. R. E. Mortimer Wheeler in 1921, disclosing a simple burial in a cist. Both have given us much information (in 1934) regarding the forts and farms on Margam Mountain and the *Bulwarcau* (Roman) camps and also the Bodvoc Stone. There were four groups of earthworks in each of which the site of a pair of buildings was apparent. It suggested separate shelters for man and beast. The *Bulwarcau*, like the other forts, is regarded as sub-Roman, and was probably in use in

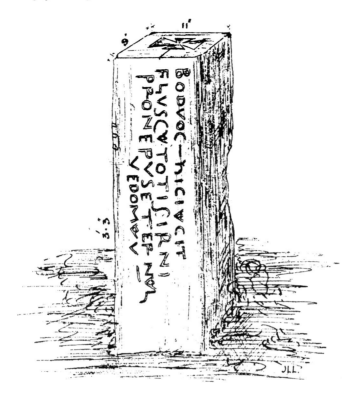

Bodvoc Stone
Mynydd Margam

13 Line illustration of the Bodvoc Stone taken from the Cardiff Naturalists'
Society *Report and Transactions* 1894-95

the sixth century when Bodvoc died. Later it ceased to function and farmers
settled there, modifying its defences to suit their peaceful purposes.

The Bodvoc Stone inscription is in Roman capitals. Translated, it means:
'(The stone of) Bodvoc; here lies the son of CATOTIGIRNUS, great
grandson of Eternalis Vedomavus' — a record of three generations of a royal
or princely Celtic dynasty with some Roman traditions. The character of the
lettering suggests that the stone was set up about A.D. 550. We are told that
Bodvoc was probably a British chieftain killed in battle against the Danish
or Norse sea-rovers. A plaster cast of the original stone (about 3½ feet high)
was taken to the Welsh National Museum about 1939. Dr. Thomas
Richards, formerly of Maesteg, stated that the eminent Celtic scholar, Sir
John Rhŷs, had found a similar name in Gaul.

In an article in the *Observer*, 16 March 1930, reference was made to the
proposal to remove the Bodvoc Stone from its remote location (on Margam

Mountain between Maesteg and Port Talbot) to Margam Abbey. The inscribed stone or pillar had been the object of many pilgrimages by organised school parties and antiquarians.

Tradition also provides us with the story of a meeting of the Tir Iarll bards at this spot on Margam Mountain and of the finding of a newly-born child on the green grass. The child was brought up by Rhys Goch ap Rhiccert and became a renowned literary figure called *Ieuan Fawr ap y Diwlith* because he was discovered on the mound. However far back our valley history can be traced, we must reach for the salt cellar when we read that Llyfnwy suggested that it was at Llangynwyd that the legendary King Arthur fell!

The Sychbant Stone

Some years ago Mr. Peter Thomas, son of Dr. Ralph Thomas, Maesteg, rescued from the mud of Sychbant farmyard, Llangynwyd, a stone which the experts state is a fragment of an early Christian monument, probably a cross, dating back to the eleventh or twelfth century. It can be seen at Bron-y-garn, Maesteg, the home of Dr. Ralph Thomas where it is used as a flower bed. An article on the stone written by J. M. Lewis of the Medieval and

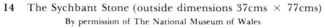

14   The Sychbant Stone (outside dimensions 37cms × 77cms)
By permission of The National Museum of Wales

Later Archaeological Department of the Welsh National Museum appeared in the 1980 volume of *Archaeologia Cambrensis*, CXXIX.

The article gives minute details of the stone and suggests the presence of a standing cross at Llangynwyd Church. In the absence of contrary evidence, it could be regarded, for the present, as the most likely original site of the stone.

Mr. Glynne Ball, Llangynwyd, has referred us to an earlier article by W. F. Grimes in the same journal (Vol. LXXXVII 1932), dealing with a stone axe acquired by purchase through information supplied by the late Roderick G. Williams, then of Bridgend. It had been found about 1917 above the cutting at the Caerau end of the former Caerau-Cymer G.W.R. tunnel. The site, now part of the Caerau Park, was under cultivation as allotments at the time the stone axe was found. The stone is a shapely implement of flint and was found 18 in. below the surface. At one time it was used as a shovel cleaner yet the axe appears undamaged. It is 117 mm. long and 49 mm. at the edge with a maximum thickness of 24 mm.

The author of the article suggests that it belongs to the Early Bronze Age.

3. Tir Iarll

The area known as Tir Iarll was called Maes Mawr before the coming of the Normans. It was also anciently known as 'Llangunith'—a variation of 'Llangynwyd' when it was ruled by Welsh lords who claimed descent from Einion ap Collwyn. It was so described in the Calendar of Inquisition in the 35th year of the reign of Edward I.

Professor G. J. Williams states in his *Traddodiad Llenyddol Morgannwg* (The Literary Tradition of Glamorgan, p. 32) that it was towards the end of the thirteenth century that the district became known as Tir Iarll (The Earl's Land) after Richard de Clare, or perhaps his son, Gilbert, had possessed the lordship. It is named as such in Professor William Rees's map of Wales in the fourteenth century, and consisted of four parishes— Llangynwyd, Betws, Margam and Kenfig. There was an old saying: *Pobl y Betws* (the people of Betws), *deiliaid Margam* (the tenants of Margam) and *gwŷr yr Hen Blwyf* (the men of the Old Parish). In 1349 there were 585 Welsh tenants in Tir Iarll.

However, it is generally agreed by historians that the Earl in question was the Norman, Robert Fitzhamon, Earl of Gloucester, of the eleventh century. Tir Iarll, in all, contained 41,854 acres. On the dissolution of the

Fig. 2 Cut-out from Professor William Rees' map of Wales in the fourteenth
century showing the area known as 'Tir Iarll' (The Earl's Land). Note the locations
of Llangynwyd village and its former castle, Castell Coch

monasteries by Henry VIII, the Margam Estate, part of Tir Iarll, was sold in
two lots at Westminster to the Mansel family, one in 1540 for £983 and the
other in 1543 for £642. There were further acquisitions of adjoining lands by
the Mansels in 1546, 1557 and the early seventeenth century. Incidentally,

C. R. M. Talbot, M.P., the Squire of Margam and landowner in Maesteg, who died in 1890, had sufficient estate derived from his ancestors to enable him to bequeath to his eldest daughter, Emily Charlotte Talbot, his landed property then valued at £2,000,000 sterling and his G.W.R. stock valued at £1,000,000. To his daughter, Olive, an invalid and a major benefactor of the Anglican Church in Wales, he gave £800,000 and his London and North Western Stock and to Mrs. Fletcher, his third daughter, he gave the residue of his railway stock valued at £1,000,000. Andrew Fletcher, the latter's son, then aged nine, was originally due to succeed to the estates, but the entail had been severed earlier and discretionary powers given to Emily Charlotte Talbot, the eldest daughter, to make what arrangements she could please with him. The estate of this eldest daughter was sworn at over £6,000,000 in 1918.

Much helpful information regarding Tir Iarll can be gleaned from *Tir Iarll* (Frederic Evans) and from scholarly treatises by writers like J. Beverley Smith, Michael Altschul and others in *Glamorgan County History*, Vol. III and writers in other countless publications.

4. Llangynwyd Castle

Although much has been written by Cadrawd, Frederic Evans and others regarding this castle, it was thought that a resumé of that history with further information that has come to light in the meantime would be needed to give a fuller account of the past.

The remains of the castle, called Castell Coch, a quarter of a mile west of Llangynwyd village, had for centuries disappeared. Mainly through the efforts of Cadrawd and his sons in 1906, excavations proved the existence of the castle, which had been once part of the dominions of Robert of Caen, Earl of Gloucester. The remains of the portcullis and moat can be seen, whilst the walls show that Sutton stone was used in the erection of the castle.

It was built by Robert Fitzhamon to confirm and to tighten his grip over the Glamorgan uplands. In his article on 'The Castles of Glamorgan and Gower' (*Glamorgan County History*, vol. III) Mr. Douglas B. Hague states that at only 7 or 8 sites are there remains of motte-and-bailey castles, and of these, only Cardiff, Llangynwyd and Y Gaer, St. Nicholas, were complete. The majority of Glamorgan castles had their origin in the twelfth century, their plans being based on a motte or a castle ring-work and bailey. The well-defended site of Llangynwyd Castle was carefully chosen. It was most impressive as a castle mound and bailey, worthy to be the seat of the chief lord. It was so described by Sir J. E. Lloyd in his *History of Wales*, when its

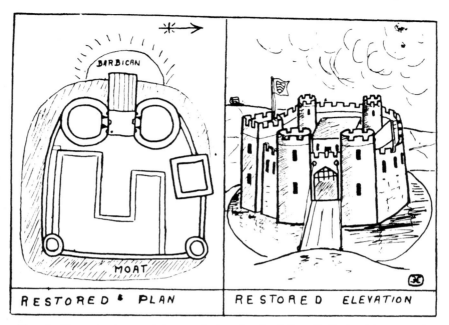

Fig. 3 Ground plan and 'restored elevations' of Castell Coch, Llangynwyd,
reproduced from 'Tir Iarll' by Frederic Evans, published 1912

condition (in 1262) was said to be much damaged by war, the castle having
been attacked by Llywelyn ap Gruffudd, the last Prince of Wales, during
the occupancy of Earl Richard de Clare, whose son, Gilbert, married the
daughter of Edward I.

The castle was set in a sheltered valley at the confluence of two small
streams and could have accommodated all the administrative buildings
needed for the centre of a lordship. Some dressed stones of the entrance
passage survive. Others were used in the farm buildings occupying the
extreme south-west part of the bailey. A detailed description of the castle is
given in Mr. Douglas B. Hague's article previously referred to.

The Margam Charters refer to a bailiff in the castle of *Llanguned*
(Llangynwyd) A.D. 1246. According to the Patent Rolls (1262), Henry III
gave orders to Humphrey de Bohun to take charge of certain castles owned
by the Earl of Clare (then a minor) in South Wales. One of those mentioned
was *Llangonyth* (Llangynwyd). The castle had been completely rebuilt after
the attack of Llywelyn ap Gruffudd in 1257. It ultimately passed to
Mortimer, Earl of March, but in 1307 Hugh le Despenser seized the castle
from Mortimer after the death of Edward I.

Edward II came as a fugitive to Llangynwyd in 1327 under the impression
that the castle was still in the hands of his friends, the Despensers. When he
found that it had been recaptured by Mortimer tradition says that he took
refuge near Gelli Lenor (Gelli Eleanor) farm, Llangynwyd, only to be

murdered later at Berkeley Castle. Much information hereon is contained in *Tir Iarll* (Frederic Evans) and *Edward II in Glamorgan* (1904) by the Rev. John Griffiths, curate of Llangynwyd, 1907-14.

Mr. Tom Evans, a former occupier and owner of Gelli Lenor, knew of the tradition that the King was reputed to have hidden in a tree near the farm building when his enemies searched the farm. He could remember seeing the stump of the tree where the stone now stands. His grandfather had cut down the tree by mistake. At the request of Miss Emily Charlotte Talbot, Margam, a stone in front of the farm was removed to the spot where the tree had grown. There was some doubt as to whether Edward II had actually stayed at the farm. Tom Evans thought that he had possibly called at the farm when he discovered that his enemies were in possession of the castle.

In his *Tir Iarll* Frederic Evans states that Edmund Mortimer, the third Earl of March, and son of the second Earl and the Countess Philippa (daughter of the first Earl of Salisbury), was born at the Castle on 1 February 1351. He married Philippa, daughter of Lionel, Duke of Clarence, son of Edward III. His grandson, another Mortimer, claimed the English throne in the reign of Henry IV.

It was at the time of the occupancy of the castle by Philippa, Countess of March, that the famous garter scene took place at the Court of Edward III in 1347, resulting in the institution of the most ancient and honourable Order of the Garter. The Order is restricted to 25 members outside the Royal Family and the Knights are appointed through the personal favour of the Sovereign. It is interesting to note that the only Welsh Knight of that most exclusive Order is Sir Cennydd Traherne, some of whose ancestors lie buried in Llangynwyd Churchyard.

In his *History of Glamorgan Antiquities*, Rhys Amheurug (Rice Merrick) refers to Castell Coch (Llangynwyd Castle) as one of the seven castles in the hills of Glamorgan. In reply to a questionnaire sent by Edward Lhuyd (1660-1709), a Mr. Jenkins of Llangynwyd refers to the ruins of an old castle not far from Llangynwyd Church, whilst the Rev. John Hutton, the then Vicar, mentions the 'ruins of a little castle called Castell y Lhan'.

It appears that during the Owen Glyndŵr rebellion the men of Tir Iarll, known for their intense love of their home land and its traditions, joined forces with the rebels. Presumably it was at this time that the castle was captured from its English oppressors and razed to the ground, leaving little trace of its former existence.

5. The Lordship of Glamorgan

The Norman invasion of Glamorgan, by sea from the south-west of England, took place between 1087 and 1100. The invaded area was incorporated into the Marcher Lordship of Glamorgan. The area between the

Rivers Neath and Tawe was occupied by the Normans, but Tir Iarll remained in Welsh hands, especially the upland districts.

In an article on Llangynwyd Castle (*Transactions of the Port Talbot Historical Society*, No. 1, Vol. II, 1969), T. C. Williams tells us that after the Norman Conquest, Welsh customs were respected and carefully preserved within the Norman administrative structure. It substituted a strong central government for a weak tribal overlordship. For many years Glamorgan was independent of the rest of Wales and had developed local government of its own prior to the Norman Conquest. Hywel Dda had not included the shire within his domains. The Normans found in Glamorgan an independent Welsh state governed by a Welsh prince on tribal and patriarchal lines following the system outlined in the laws of Hywel.

Fitzhamon was allowed to assume the supreme lordship of Glamorgan and exercised sovereign rights within the shire, unfettered by outside interference. He appointed his own sheriff, maintained his own chancery and great seal, established his own courts from which there was no appeal, held his great council of tenants and benefited from feudal incidents such as fines, wardships and escheats in the shire. The courts were held in the open air, and Glamorgan was a kingdom within a kingdom. The courts decided all property disputes and maintained the lord's peace.

On the death of a tenant seised of free land, the lord was to have the tenant's best beast. A fee was payable for alienation by the tenant and any former or recent purchaser of freehold within the lordship had to pay 6 shillings and 8 pence for entry. The goods and 'cattelle' of a felon, as well as treasure trove, belonged to the lord. The legal document agreed by jurors gives details of payment by tenants, of the appointment and duties of bailiffs, the rights of tenants, and common of pasturage and herbage. Bailiffs had to secure for the lord 'one vayne (vein) of sea cole' under the common. On the death of the lord, the tenant had to pay a 'myse' within 5 years. The rent of 'avowry' was payable according to old custom.

In his 'History of Antiquities of Glamorgan' (*The Glamorgan County Handbook and Industrial Review*, 1967-70, reprinted from *Glamorgan Forests*), Professor Glanmor Williams states that Fitzhamon not only succeeded in overthrowing the old kingdom of Morgannwg, then stretching from the River Rhymni to the River Tawe, but in usurping the rights of the former Welsh rulers. For the following four centuries Fitzhamon and his successors were to rule Glamorgan as the frontier or marcher lordship of Glamorgan. However, Professor William Rees tells us that Welshries like Castell-nedd (Neath) and Llangynwyd, not under the authority of the castle, had kept the Welsh way of life better that the others (*South Wales and the Marches, 1284-1415*).

Fitzhamon's successor, Robert, Earl of Gloucester, tried to come to terms with the valley farmers who were allowed to retain their local customs and native culture. Robert was succeeded by his son, William, but the people of Glamorgan, under Ifor Bach, rebelled successfully against the introduction of the Norman feudal system and insisted upon maintaining and preserving the Welshries of the Glamorgan valleys, which included Tir Iarll. Ultimately, Tir Iarll became part of the dominions of Gilbert de Clare, who died in 1229, leaving no male heir. On the partition of the de Clare inheritance, Hugh Despenser the Younger, who had married Gilbert's eldest sister, Eleanor, was given, *inter alia*, the lordship of Glamorgan, thus ending the dominance of the de Clare family among the marcher lords of Wales. It resulted in more efficient government, replacing the loosely-knit activities of the previous years.

Under the de Clares, separate courts for Englishries and Welshries existed in the lands controlled by them, and those included Tir Iarll. They were independent of royal control. In his essay 'The Marcher Lords of Glamorgan', 1317-1485 (*Glamorgan County History*, Vol. III), T. B. Pugh states that Hugh Despenser the Younger was intensely unpopular with the Welsh. In 1321 the whole of the lordship of Glamorgan was overrun and devastated and Despenser became exiled. However, Edward II subdued the Welsh marcher lords in 1322 and for the last 4 years of his reign, Despenser was the real ruler of England. He recovered the lordship of Glamorgan by fraud, violence and lavish royal grants. He ruled over almost the whole of South Wales.

In the Roger Mortimer revolution of 1326, the government of the Despensers collapsed. Edward II, accompanied by Hugh Despenser the Younger, fled to South Wales and sheltered for some days at Neath Abbey. It was during this time that Edward II visited Gelli Lenor. Despenser was betrayed by the Welsh and captured near Llantrisant. He was executed at Hereford, his father having previously been executed at Bristol. Edward II abdicated in 1327.

The Despenser lords again ruled Glamorgan between 1337 and 1400 but their possessions were ultimately seized by the Crown and the male line of the family extinguished in 1413.

Without troubling the reader with details of the devolution of the lordship over the succeeding centuries, it can be stated that the lordship of Tir Iarll became ultimately vested in Thomas, Viscount Windsor, who sold it to Herbert Mackworth of the Gnoll, Neath, and who, in turn, sold it to a H. Grant, passing thereafter to his devisee. In the P.O. Directory of Monmouthshire and South Wales, 1871, Henry Jeffreys Bushby and Charles Evan Thomas, of the Gnoll family, are named as lords of the manor.

Although manorial rights were abolished in 1925, the nominal right to be called a lord of the manor of Tir Iarll still exists. It was considered saleable, just like a house or freehold land, and was not a hereditary title. The title became attractive to foreigners as the manor was one of the biggest in Wales, dating back to the Norman Conquest. A native of Nantyffyllon, Oswald D. Lucas, a Cardiff auctioneer, bought the title some years ago to prevent it being sold to a Pittsburgh newspaper proprietor who had intended to offer it as a first prize in a competition. Details of the purchase were given by Jayne Isaac in the centenary issue of the *Glamorgan Gazette*.

There are no monetary privileges or ownership rights attached to the present lordship of the manor, except an entitlement to all acorns on Caerau mountain, although oak trees have long since disappeared therefrom! The lord of the manor had the right to graze goats where Commercial Street (the main street of the valley) now stands. If he owned a mill, he could compel local farmers to bring their corn to the mill. He was also entitled to the wrecks on part of the Aberafan beach, and had the right to appoint a coroner and an honorary steward.

6. Local Revolts

As we have already seen, the Welsh communities (the Welshries) recognised only the most tenuous obligations of dependence upon their Norman overlords. The Welsh preserved their pastoral way of living with its characteristic, social and personal independence. There is clear evidence in the second half of the twelfth century that the Welsh of *Blaenau Morgannwg* (the uplands of Glamorgan), stoutly resisted the Lord of Glamorgan who exercised feudal lordship over them. They remained unreconciled to the Norman conquerors.

They supported the aspirations of the Welsh princes, among whom were Yr Arglwydd Rhys (The Lord Rhys — 1155-97) and Llywelyn Fawr (Llywelyn the Great — 1194-1240), to whose men the Margam monks were made to pay tribute. Llywelyn ap Gruffudd, the last Welsh prince (1247-1282) received much support from Madog ap Llywelyn of Tir Iarll. In 1316, the Welsh community of the lordship of Glamorgan, which included Tir Iarll, under the leadership of Llywelyn Bren, rebelled again owing to the ransoms imposed upon them and other causes of disaffection. The Welsh of Glamorgan from the barren upland regions became engaged in the revolt, which was defeated in 1316. Llywelyn Bren and his family, including his brother, Madog Fychan of Tir Iarll, were taken to the Tower of London for perpetual punishment. Casnodyn, a fourteenth-century poet and a native of Cil-fai (Kilvey), wrote an elegy to Madog who lived in Llangynwyd and who was a steward of Tir Iarll under Arglwydd Morgannwg (the Lord of Glamorgan). The poem indicates that Madog was a powerful man who provided a new social basis for the renaissance of Welsh poetry. The poem describes Madog's savage onslaught upon the English in battle.

Madog Fychan and his son, Owain ap Madog, were ultimately given lands, and soon regained their position of eminence in Tir Iarll. Most of the leading rebels were released before 1317.

Hugh Despenser, then Lord of Morgannwg, caused Llywelyn Bren to be brought to Cardiff where he was hanged, beheaded and quartered. His mutilated body was buried at Greyfriars. This added to the hatred of the Despensers and resulted in the uniting of the Welsh leaders. Further details can be found in articles by Beverley Smith and Michael Altschal in *Glamorgan County History*, Vol. III.

The support given in Tir Iarll to the revolt of Owain Glyndwr was understandable.

Before leaving the subject of local revolts we venture to refer to Einion ap Collwyn of Tir Iarll, who is reputed to have taken a leading part in bringing the Normans into Glamorgan, including Tir Iarll. He was an ancestor of Sir Cennydd Traherne, the present and highly-respected Lord Lieutenant of Glamorgan, who regards him as a traitor. However, Prof. Ceri W. Lewis, in his article on the Literary Tradition of Glamorgan (*Glamorgan County History* III, p. 502), states that there is no consistency in the various traditions concerning the part which Einion ap Collwyn is alleged to have played in enticing the Normans back to Glamorgan so that they could defeat Iestyn ap Gwrgant and drive the latter from his inheritance. It was widely held that it was the act of studied treachery which won for him the appellation of 'Einion the Traitor', an act for which he was rewarded by the Normans, according to the antiquary, John Leland, by being granted the Uplands as his inheritance.

Prof. Ceri W. Lewis states that some of the details recorded in these traditions were probably apocryphal.

7. Llangynwyd

There have been several variations in the name of this Parish.

Prof. William Rees gives the name *Llangunith* in his fourteenth century map. In 1560, John ap Morgan was the Vicar of *Langunwode* and Sir Hugh Meredith, in 1608, was Vicar of *Llan-gynoud*. Edward Lhuyd (1660-1709) also, in Part III of his *Parochialia*, mentions *Llangonud-fawr*. In a Court action brought in 1613, *Llangonwood* is quoted.

We are told that Samuel Jones became vicar of *Llangonwyd* in 1657. In 1706, Thomas Edmunds called himself vicar of *Llangynwyd*. The G.W.R. named the village railway station as *Llangonoyd*, taken from the 1771 Registry of the Consistory Court of Llandaff.

Various documents from 1573 onwards mention *Llangonoid* or *Llangonyd*. However, Iolo Morganwg's copy of the inscription on the gravestone of Wil Hopcyn, the poet (1700-1741), uses the modern form, *Llangynwyd*.

As the Rev. R. Pendril Llewelyn, who was Vicar of Llangynwyd from 1841 to 1891, was always known as the Vicar of Llangynwyd, and as the

15 Woman carrying pitchers probably photographed at Llangynwyd Village, *c*.1910. Note the thatched cottages in the background

Church is dedicated to St. Cynwyd, there would be no point in further considering the variations that would seem to be spurious.

Yr Hen Blwyf (The Old Parish)

The valley is still referred to by this name and a facetious explanation of the origin of the term has been given by our local historians. Cadrawd says that there was a tradition, probably invented by a local wag, that a local carpenter had been asked to make a coffin for a man aged 28. As he was puzzled as to how to inscribe 28 on the coffin plate, he resolved the difficulty by inscribing thereon 7777, being four sevens, thereby leading people to believe that the deceased was aged 7777.

However, Cadrawd thought that a far more feasible origin for the term was the fact that the Parish was once co-extensive with the larger and older Lordship of Llangynwyd.

8. The Early Rural Scene

The *Blaeneudir* (Uplands) of Glamorgan were desolate and sparsely-populated, and were entirely agricultural. The thickly-wooded valleys, including the Llynfi Valley, and bleak moorland were broken only by a few scattered sheep farms and an occasional hamlet. The concealed riches had not then been explored by the industrial revolution.

Leland surveyed the Parish of Llangynwyd at the command of Henry VIII in 1530. He wrote: 'The third lordship is *Tiryarlthe* and is mountainous and less fruitful than the other two lordships. It hath in divers places good pastures and plenty of wood in *Dyffryn Lleueny*. The valley is 3 miles by north from Margam.'

The farms in the immediate surrounding districts give some idea of the nature of the landscape and of the fauna of those times — *Penhydd* (the hill of the hart), *Twyn-yr-hydd* (the hill of the stag), *Llwyn-y-brain* (the grove of the crows), *Pant-y-moch* (the plain of the wild boar), *Cil-carw* (the retreat of the deer), *Nant-y-bwch* (the stream of the buck), *Twyn-y-barcud* (the hillock of the kite), *Pant-y-fleiddiast* (the plain of wolf bitch) whilst *Pwll-yr-iwrch* mountain overlooking Nantyffyllon reminds us of the home of the roebuck.

The woodland association is all the more evident by such names as *Nant-y-fedw* (birch), *Cwm Cerdin* (rowan or mountain ash), *Gwernllwyn* (alder), and *Pantyscawen* (elder).

Corn and oats were the main products of the lowlands — with sheep farming on the hills. Wil Hopcyn, the famous local poet of the first half of the eighteenth century, was known as *Wil Goch o wlad y geirchen* (red-haired Wil of the land of oats). Cadrawd informs us that *bara gwenith* (wheatbread) was a luxury unknown to the poor even in the eighteenth century. *Bara ceirch* (oatcakes) was the staple food generally. The chief crops were wheat, barley, oats, corn, potatoes and pasturage.

The custom was to prepare broth in a cauldron suspended above a wood fire with plenty of *bara haidd* (barley bread) or *bara ceirch* (oatcakes) at hand. Wooden spoons were used, each member of the family having carved his or her initials on the handle. Knives and forks were unknown and the master or servant used his pocket knife at the dinner table.

Cadrawd in his *History of Llangynwyd* has quoted from the diaries of the Rev. John Parry, Vicar of Llangynwyd from 1790 to 1829, giving details of the cost of living and of the wages paid at the time.

Edward Lhuyd (1660-1709), the keeper of the Ashmolean Museum at Oxford and considered to be the greatest Welsh scholar of his day, sent a questionnaire to the gentry and clergy of Wales with the object of compiling a natural history of Wales. Four thousand copies of the Parochial Queries were printed and three sent to each parish in Wales. Lhuyd spent two months in Cowbridge in 1697-8. A Mr. Jenkins of Llangynwyd and the then vicar, the Rev. John Hutton, went to considerable trouble in replying to the queries, and details are given in Lhuyd's *Parochialia*.

According to Mr. Jenkins, the Parish of *Llangonud-fawr* was about 7 miles in length and 3 in breadth, with about 600 inhabitants. Half-a-mile west of the castle (which was then in ruins) was an old entrenchment called *Bwlwarca*. A common called *Mynydd y Cayra* (Caerau) belonged to the lordship of Tir Iarll. The valley contained a great precipice called *Tarren y Garth* (now called *Y Darren*). At a place called *tor y keurig* (Tor-cerrig) there was a spring that cured gout and 'all aches' and people gathered thereat yearly in May. One of the tributaries of the *Llynfi vawr* was called *Nantffirlling*.

The produce of the parish, according to Mr. Jenkins, consisted of barley, 'oates with some wheat and pease'. The cattle, horses, sheep and hogs were 'without number'. The air was healthy and sharp and the parish contained many people from seventy-five to ninety years of age. The horses, though small, were good in their kind but liable in winter to cold and want of grass. There were numerous springs, some near the tops of the mountains. Most parts of the parish had quarries of stone and 'cole' mines. The water that came down from the 'cole' turned the stones into 'a kind of orange colour'.

The rivers contained 'trouts, lampens and eles' and in winter 'salmon and chevins besides artificial flie wormes called ye slow taylor'. In May and June the red 'flie' gathered on fern, followed by the 'grashopper'. Quite common was a small bird in the shape of a 'Merlyn of a darke grey colour, the tipps of the wings white, short leggs, seldom seen unless late in the evening in the woods, makes a noise somewhat like a Rayle'.

The Rev. John Hutton, in reply to the same questionnaire, tells us that *Llangynwyd* or *Llangonwyd* was a little village with a Church dedicated to St. Cynwyd and seven or eight houses. It was situated in the Hundred of Newcastle and contained 500 inhabitants (Mr. Jenkins had stated 600). The peculiar feasts or wakes were held on 28 September. The parish was partly corn ground and partly pasture. However, 'wheate, barley, oates and some pease were sown' and use was made of lime and dung 'indifferently stowed with Cattell, horses, sheepe and hogs'. Some inhabitants lived to the age of eighty or ninety years. The people were of middle stature and of good complexion. There were many little springs and a good store of 'good King Coale' and quarries of stone. Few houses were built in the valley itself. They were mainly on the mountains or on the slopes.

According to Clark in his *Genealogies of Glamorgan*, almost all the gentry in the county hailed at one time or another from Llangynwyd, but with few exceptions none of them ever lived within its bounds for 300 years or more. The local people were called *Gwŷr Llangynwyd, tlawd a balch* (the men of Llangynwyd, poor and proud).

Edward Lhuyd also sought information as to the names of rivers and rivulets in the respective valleys. Mr. Jenkins, previously referred to, stated: 'The Llynfi vawr rises in the north part of the Parish and receives severall Rivuletts in the higher hamlett as Nantffirlling, Nant y Sarn, Nant Clwyd and then passes to Cwmdu and midle hamlett where it received Hemmi Kerdin, Nant y felin and Nant Gwyn.'

Nantffirlling presumably refers to the district now known as Nantyffyllon. In his *History of the Llangynwyd Parish*, Cadrawd interprets the name as 'the brook of dark recesses' whilst his son, C. J. Evans, in his *Place Names of Glamorgan* (1908) translates it as 'the brook of gloomy recesses'.

Hutton also names three brooks or rivulets that join the main river — Nantffyrlling, Nant Cerdin and Nant Rhyd Halog. Mr. Oswald D. Lucas reminds us that in a survey of 'Tiryarlle' dated 10 November 1588, a 'Res Apowell' is shown to be the tenant of 'Forest Nant Ffirlloige on the River Llyffin', which he held of the Lord of the Manor of Tir Iarll at a rent of eight pence.

The Parish Registers show that William, son of Edward Thomas of 'Nantyffyrlling' by Margaret, his wife, was baptised 24 December 1811. 'Ffyrlling' is the Welsh for 'farthing', although the natives of the district used the other term 'ffyrling'. 'Y ffyrling eithaf' means 'the last farthing'. A map dated 1839 prepared for the Tithe Commissioners by Edward Neale, Surveyor, Laleston, shows Nantyffyrlling Farm.

In his *Geiriadur Lleol o Blwyf Llangynwyd* (Topographical Dictionary of Llangynwyd Parish), a prize essay at a Maesteg Eisteddfod in 1870, Llyfnwy calls the farm Nantyffyrlling, but asserts that the proper name was *Nant y Ffyllong*, that is, *Nant y Tywyllwch* (brook of darkness). In a map of the Llynvi and Rhondda Valleys Mineral District published in the *Proceedings of the South Wales Institute of Engineers*, 1874, Nantyffyllon is referred to as Nant-y-fferlyn.

Title deeds to some houses in the district in 1859 indicate that they were built on land described as part of 'Nantyfirlling' Farm whilst the deeds of other houses show that in 1875 the houses formed part of the Nantyffyrllyn Estate. There is no doubt that the residents of the district in the latter half of the last century called the place Nantyffyrling. The writer has met people who could remember their parents calling the place as such. Daniel R. Waldin, previously referred to, could remember the place being called by that name. He maintained that there were healing virtues in the brook and a tradition that a person who had benefited from them had tossed a farthing into the brook as a token of gratitude for his recovery, hence the name Nantyffyrling.

In an eisteddfod held at Salem (B) Nantyffyllon (then called Spelters) in 1856, Thomas Morgan (Llyfnwy) was acclaimed winner of a prize for an essay on 'The Origins and Development of Industries in Maesteg'. The essay refers to the village as Nantyffyrling. In another eisteddfod held in the same Chapel in January, 1858, David Henry (Myrddin Wyllt) then of Maesteg, won a prize for a Welsh poem on the Llynfi Valley. In the poem there is a reference to Nantyffyrling. One can only conclude that the name used in documents was either Nantyffyrllyn or Nantyffyrlling, but that orally in the last century, the place was called Nantyffyrling. As such names refer to a farthing, one can only assume that there is some substance in the old tradition of someone expressing his gratitude for the recovery of health. Farthings and halfpence were first coined in 1210 during the reign of Henry III.

During the last century, Nantyffyllon was also known as Tywith, which was the name on the railway station. It is no longer referred to by that name.

In his volume *Glamorganshire Place Names* (1901), the Rev. Thomas Morgan states that Maesteg was probably known as Llwyni from a farmhouse so named on the side of Pwll-yr-iwrch Mountain. At an eisteddfod held in Maesteg in 1839, Nathan Dyfed suggested that the name *Llwyni* should be changed to *Llyfnwy*. According to the Rev. Morgan, the suggested name never became popular enough to catch on. However, several local literary and musical figures subsequently assumed bardic titles such as *Dewi Glan Llyfnwy, Telorydd Llyfnwy, Cerddor Llyfnwy, Llinos Llyfnwy, Mair Llyfnwy, Dewi Llyfnwy* — and *Llyfnwy* himself.

9. Llynfi Valley Farms and Houses

In his *Geiriadur Lleol o Blwyf Llangynwyd* (Topographical Dictionary of the Parish of Llangynwyd), Llyfnwy lists all the valley farms with details as to acreage, ownership and history, together with notes on the derivation of some of the farm names. Cadrawd published in serial form his *Llangynwyd Parish Place-Names*, whilst Dr. William Rees has provided us with his *Fourteenth Century Map of Wales*. These three publications contain much helpful information regarding all the local farms. Almost all, if not all, of these farms and buildings existed before the Industrial Revolution. Some of them disappeared as its consequence.

Castell y Wiwer (The Squirrel's Castle), near Coetrehen, was demolished when the tramroad from Maesteg to Porthcawl was built in 1827. Berthlwyd Farm was demolished when Coegnant Colliery was sunk nearly a century ago. The ancestors of William Griffiths, locally known as Squire Griffiths, had occupied the farm for about three centuries. Daniel R. Waldin could remember an old lady who was born at this farm.

Three ancient farm houses after which the town of Maesteg ('Fair Meadow') was named are no longer extant. They were Maesteg Uchaf, Maesteg Ganol and Maesteg Isaf. The ruins of the first-named adjoin the Maesteg cricket field at the rear of Church Street, Maesteg. The second-named was buried under the Oakwood colliery tip which was cleared to make room for factories, whilst the third-named was about 100 yards to the south of Maesteg Ganol Farm. Llwyni Farm was probably under the tip of what was later known as No. 9 Level in Maesteg. 'Llwyni' was the name used for Maesteg by the old residents of the valley.

According to Daniel R. Waldin, a shepherd occupied Tŷ'r Bugail under the slopes of Darren y Pannau, a mountain overlooking Caerau. On the opposite side of the River Llynfi was Nyth y Frân, a quarter of a mile below Blaencaerau farmhouse. Ton-y-cwd Farm was in the centre of Ton-y-cwd Row in the Spelters district of Caerau, whilst Tŷ-gwyn-bach Farm in the same area became converted into a dwellinghouse. On the eastern side of the river overlooking Maesteg was Cae Chwarel, now in ruins, whilst adjoining the new road from Nantyffyllon to Maesteg was the old Dyffryn Madog Farm which was demolished to make room for housing development. Llwynderw School, Maesteg was built on a site formerly occupied for centuries by Tycandryll Farm. Aberddwynant Farm was buried beneath the coal tips of Cwmdu.

Tom Evans, late of Gelli Lenor, Llangynwyd, states that eight or nine farms had been almost completely submerged as the result of the march of industry. However, the consequent increase in population meant the need for more farming produce, much to the advantage of the local farmer.

A general idea of the antiquity of the local farms can be gathered from the fact that Rhys ap Rhys Fychan, the great-grandfather of one of the best-known poets of Tir Iarll, Rhys Brydydd, who lived in the fifteenth century, occupied Gadlys and Brynllywarch Farms. His descendants owned Maescadlawr and 'Keven Baydan' Farms. The father of Rhys Brydydd at one time lived at 'Keven y grydfa' (Cefn Ydfa).

The Margam Charters of the thirteenth and fourteenth centuries refer to several local farms — Llwyngwladys, Cae-mab-Ifor, Gelli Eleanor (and not Gelli Lenor), Maescadlawr, Bryn Cynan, Caeremi, Bryn Dafydd (Defaid?). In Dr. William Rees's map of the fourteenth century we can locate Nant y Crynwyth, Gelli Ceran (Gelli Seron?), Gelli Lenor, Llwynglades (Llwyngwladus) and Pentre.

There is evidence of the sale of 'Kelleseron' (Gelli Seron?) on 23 April 1390 in the reign of Richard II. 'Lloyne Glades' (Llwyngwladus) and 'Garnllwyd' are mentioned in 1520, during the reign of Henry VIII. There is reference to a grant of the tenement known as 'Cwmkeron in the demesne of Tir Iarll' by Llyson ap Jevan to Llywelyn ap Griffith of Llangonoyd on 1 May 1539.

To Mr. Glynne Ball we are indebted for producing a photostat copy of the Manorial Survey of the Parishes of Betws (24 farms) and Llangynwyd (73 farms) taken in 1570. Among the Betws Parish farms situated in the Llynfi Valley we find: Come duy (Cwmdu), llodre brangye (Llety Brongu), Kon horday (Cynhordy), Kelly heyre (Gelli Hir), Bryn llowdarche (Bryn-llywarch), Coytre Hene (Coetrehen) — occupied by Morganus ap Hoell and Lewis ap Jevan.

Among those named in the Llangynwyd Parish we find — Syche bant (Sychbant), y gyllvach (Y Gilfach), y gilfach yssa (Y Gilfach Isaf), ty ny wayn (Tynywaun), llowayn gladys (Llwyngwladus), mays y llan (Maesyllan), llawdarth (Llwydarth), blaen llyffin (Blaenllynfi), y llowney (Y Llwyni), Dyffryn llyffin (Dyffryn Llynfi), y garn wen, Come Dee (Cwmdu), blaen y come Dee (Blaencwmdu), Torr y vron (Toryfron), y gadlis (Y Gadlys), bryn y vro (Bryn-y-fro), Kelly ziron (Gelli Seron), nant y firling (a tenement occupied by Thomas Wylym), Pentrye (Pentre), bryn llyffryth (Bryn Llefrith), Kaer quarell (Cae'r Chwarel), forest Nant-firlling (Nantyffyllon Forest), lloyn daries (Llwyndyrus), llyffney (Llynfi), Forest cayr wen (Garnwen Forest), Mays Teg (Maesteg), and the garthe.

There are grounds for believing that the proper name of the valley should be *Llyfni* and not *Llynfi*. In early references, the *f* (or *ff*) invariably precedes the *n* in the name.

Further manorial surveys made in 1570, 1588, 1630 and 1666 provide helpful information regarding the number of tenements and their occupants in the Parish of Llangynwyd. The forest lands were held mainly by copyhold and not freehold tenure, though some were held by lease. The area included mixed arable pasture and underwood.

When Rhys Amheurug (Rice Merrick), who died in 1586, visited Llangynwyd, he listed several farms he had visited—'Nant-y-dylles' (the home of Madog Fychan) and the homes of the descendants of Rhys Goch ap Rhiccert ab Einion ap Collwyn—Llwydarth, 'Gadlis', Bryn Llywarch, 'Maes Cad Llawr', 'Keven y grydfa' and 'Keven Baydan'.

Most of the old farms of Llangynwyd were connected with 'penceirddiaid Tir Iarll' (the chief bards of Tir Iarll).

Edward Lhuyd in his *Parochialia* refers to Nant y Gilvach, 'Nant kerdyn', Llwydarth, 'Gadlis', Brynllywarch and 'Maes Cad Llawr'. There is still uncertainty as to the persons whose names are perpetuated in Brynllywarch, Cae-mab-Ifor (locally called Caebifor), Hendre Owain, Llwyngwladus and Neuadd Domos.

By the end of the last century, the principal ground landlords in the valley were the Dunraven, Margam, Coetrehen, Dyffryn, Nolton, Cwrt Colman, Merthyr Mawr, Blosse, Mackworth and Greenmeadow Estates. To this list must be added North's Navigation Collieries (1889) Ltd., who became the principal landowners before the collieries became nationalised. A plan of the Dunraven Estate was prepared by Edward Thomas of Margam in 1778, whilst an inventory of the local properties owned by North's is available.

As Gelly Farm, Cymer (famous for its hounds), was at one time within the Parish of Llangynwyd, it is interesting to note that in 1928 it became occupied for the first time since the days of Queen Elizabeth I by someone other than a member of the Gelly family of Jenkins.

Cadrawd prepared a helpful chart, *Nodau Clustiau Defaid Tir Iarll* (Tir Iarll sheep earmarks), indicating the earmarks of sheep in the Parishes of Llangynwyd, Betws and Margam, and listing 133 farms. The farm names show how imaginative our ancestors were in their choice of names.

Owing to limitations of space, only a brief reference can be made to a few of these farms.

Bryn Cynan is named after Cynan, the son of St. Cynwyd, to whom Llangynwyd Church is dedicated.

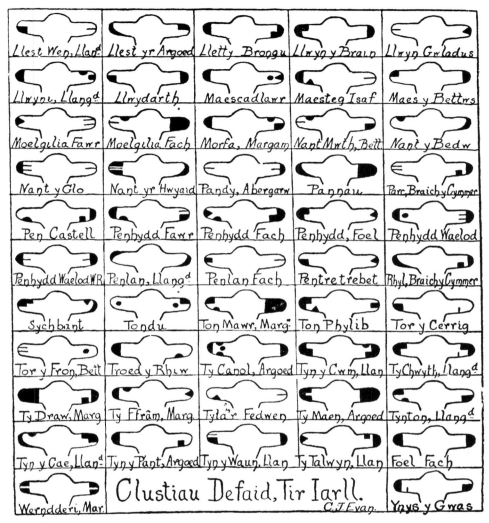

16 Part of Cadrawd's comprehensive chart of the ear marks of sheep in Tir Iarll

Bryn Llywarch. Next to Cefn Ydfa, this is possibly the best-known farm in the Llynfi Valley, if not in Glamorgan. It housed the first Nonconformist Academy in Wales, the forerunner of the former Carmarthen Presbyterian College and other Nonconformist colleges in Wales. The Academy was opened by the Rev. Samuel Jones, who was deprived of his living in Llangynwyd for refusing to conform to the requirements of the Act of Uniformity, 1662. He died in 1697. The main room in which he taught his students remains intact after three centuries, but the stone roof has been replaced by slate.

17   Bryn Llywarch farmhouse, Llangynwyd (see also plate 70)

18   Cefn Ydfa Farm. The lady is Mrs Catherine Maddocks who died 1922 aged 79
     years; her husband, Morgan, had died 25 May 1907 aged 82 years

Cefn Ydfa is famous for its association with the romance of the Maid of Cefn Ydfa. In his Topography of the Parish of Llangynwyd (1872), Llyfnwy states that the mansion and farmhouse had been in the possession of the Mackworth family for about 150 years after the death of the Maid in 1727 — the daughter of Anthony Maddocks, by his second marriage, having married a member of that family.

Llyfnwy attributes the name, Cefn Ydfa, to the suitability of the land for growing corn ($\mathring{y}d$). Rhys D. Morgan, Maesteg, disagreed. The former Vicar, the Rev. R. Pendril Llewelyn, was of the opinion that it meant 'the ridge of wailing' (udfa), upon the assumption that it was formerly the site of a great battle.

The mansion itself has been in ruins since the last century. Mr. Graham V. Hill of Porthcawl has made extensive inquiries into the history of the mansion and the farmhouse and has supplied us with a copy of a very interesting article published by Mr. Roscoe Howells in *Welsh Farm News*, 12 August 1961. It was based on information obtained from records at the offices of Messrs. J. C. Llewelin & Co., Solicitors, of Newport, Gwent. According to this article, the Cefn Ydfa estate at the time of the marriage-settlement dated 3 May 1725, made between the Maid's mother and Anthony Maddocks, consisted of the house in which the former lived, one bakehouse, one barn, a cow-house, two orchards, one garden and tenements of land of about 50 acres. The mansion (in ruins and beyond repair) and the farmhouse are two separate buildings.

19 Cefn Ydfa mansion in ruins, *c*.1905

By 1973 both the mansion and the farmhouse were derelict. In 1974 the buildings were bought by Mr. Eugene Kococ, a Ukrainian, who, at considerable expense, has made the farmhouse attractive and habitable. He is keenly interested in the historical and romantic background of the mansion and farm, and most anxious to preserve the inherent character of the buildings. Any visitor would be charmed with the two ancient fireplaces that were in use when the Maid and her mother occupied the place. The welcome given to visitors is most affable and sincere. The ruined mansion and the renovated farmhouse are situated about 2 miles to the south of Llangynwyd and can be approached from the main Maesteg-Bridgend road by means of a rather narrow, steep lane from a point directly opposite the entrance to the former Llynfi Power Station. On reaching Cefn Ydfa, one has the feeling of being 'far from the madding crowd' although the place has a commanding view of the valley.

We have seen that the father of the famous Tir Iarll poet, Rhys Brydydd, who flourished in the fifteenth century, lived at Cefn Ydfa.

Gadlys, Llangynwyd was originally a manor-house occupied by the Vaughan family, who were stewards of Tir Iarll during the Tudor period. When Pitt, in the reign of George III, levied tax on windows, several of the windows were walled up. This explains why so many of the valley farms had such small windows. At the beginning of the last century, any dwelling-house with more than seven windows paid a heavy tax on light. The wealth

20   Gadlys Farm, Llangynwyd

21 Gelli Lenor Farm, reproduced from 'Glamorganshire' by J H Wade M.A.,
published 1914

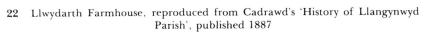

22 Llwydarth Farmhouse, reproduced from Cadrawd's 'History of Llangynwyd
Parish', published 1887

of the occupants was estimated, not by the number of his servants or horses, but by the number of glass windows in his abode.

Gelli Lenor. It appears that the rent demands from the Margam Estate up to 1896 referred to the farm as Gelli Eleanor, the female name being favoured by the Despensers and the de Clares. A map prepared in 1839 by Edward Neale of 'Lalestone' for the Tithe Commissioners gives the farm name as 'Gelli Lenor Farm' (Tŷ Gelly Eleanor). The fact that it is linked with Edward II indicates that it existed in the fourteenth century. Tom Evans, the former occupant and owner, who died about 1975 at an advanced age, told the writer of this volume that the farm was at least 800 years old. He could trace his ancestors on his mother's side for 300 years and his paternal ancestors 500 years.

Llwydarth, Maesteg is said to have been occupied from at least the twelfth century. It is famous as the home of the Powell family, including Antoni Powell, who was at one time steward to the Mansels of Margam, and the author of *The History of the Kings of Britain*. His great-grandfather, Siôn Goch, and his grandfather, Hywel ap Siôn Goch, both lived at Llwydarth.

Llwydarth was famous for its hospitality. Dafydd Benwyn, a Tir Iarll poet who flourished in the latter half of the sixteenth century, wrote five stanzas (*englynion*) in praise of the good time visitors received at Llwydarth:

> A'th fir, a'th gwrw a'th fawredd,
> A thi yn fwyn, a'th hen fedd.

(Where greatness and gentleness were accompanied by liquid hospitality such as mead or beer).

As Llwydarth could boast of ten to twenty windows and was considered a substantial house for the élite to live in, the occupants, including Antoni Powel, became known as the 'ten-shilling-tax people'.

The Powell family was also noted for its public service and patronage of the bards. Thomas Powell was Under-sheriff to Sir Rice Mansel in 1554, Antoni Powell himself was Under-sheriff to Sir Thomas Mansel in 1604, whilst Thomas Powell of Coetrehen was Sheriff of Glamorgan in 1673 and Edward Powell of Tondu was Sheriff in 1667. Further details of the Powell family are contained in the chapter on the literary tradition of the Llynfi Valley. Suffice to say now that the horizontal tombstone of the Powell family is the last you pass on your left as you are about to enter Llangynwyd Church. It clearly shows, after nearly four centuries of exposure to the elements, the coat of arms of the Powell family and also the date of death (1618) of Antoni Powell.

Maes Cadrod (or Maes Cadrawd). It is named after another son of St. Cynwyd, who was the son of Cynfelyn, a chieftain of North Britain. The fact that Cynwyd was known to be the father of at least five sons proves that saints in those days were not celibates.

Sychbant Farm, Llangynwyd, was lately owned by the Forestry Commission, who decided to sell in 1977 owing to vandalism during its non-occupancy. It was owned during the latter half of the eighteenth century by a Rees Howells, who allowed the farm to be used for religious meetings by the local Welsh Presbyterians and for whom he built a Chapel called 'Y Graig Fach' on his land. When he fell out with them, he allowed Independents (Congregationalists) to use the Chapel, but under his will the Chapel reverted to the Presbyterians. It was the first meeting-place of the Welsh Calvinistic Methodists (Presbyterians) in the valley.

Nant-y-crynwydd, Maesteg, is considered one of the oldest tenements in the valley. It is situated on the site of the Llynvi Iron Works, near what was known as Bryant's Pond and almost adjacent to the Maesteg R.F.C. ground. It can be located as Nant y Crynwyth on Dr. William Rees's map of the fourteenth century. The Margam Charters refer to a quit-claim before St. Luke's Day, 1401, in respect of Nant-y-crynwyth. A Margam MS shows that this tenement was released by 'John Thomas ap Hoell' of Llantwit to 'Jevan ap Madoc of Bettws' on 10 March 1547, in the reign of Edward VI. According to tradition, Cromwell's soldiers called at this house on their way to Margam. Llyfnwy tells us that the early Calvinistic Methodists worshipped thereat — with five laymen, including John Maddock of Blaenllynfi Farm, Caerau, in charge.

During the last century the Iron Works constable lived at this house. It had a stone staircase, unique oak beams devoid of dry rot, and had a triple chimney. Much controversy was aroused in 1979 when it became known that the Ogwr Borough Council proposed to demolish the house and also the adjoining corn stores of the Llynvi Iron Works. It was thought by conservationists that the buildings were of historical interest. They were on land which the local authority desired to develop as a recreational centre. The corn stores, used for grain storage for pit ponies, was formerly the blast engine-house of the Llynvi Iron Works and is the only reminder of the iron industry of Maesteg in the nineteenth century. Both buildings were owned by the N.C.B., and later by the Ogwr Borough Council. The authorities ultimately yielded to the protests, which were supported by the Association of Industrial Archaeologists, who considered the former blast engine-house in particular to be of importance historically and architecturally, provided the top of the building were removed and it made waterproof.

The Welsh Office decided in June 1981, to schedule the building as an ancient monument and to give it increased protection against the possibility of demolition or alteration.

The Ogwr Council has agreed to restore the building (which was roofless) with a pitched and slated roof. The masonry is being cleaned and as many as possible of the original features will be retained. It will be incorporated into the design of the new sports centre. We are told that it is the last blast engine-house of its kind in Wales. The Historic Buildings Council have agreed to pay £44,000 (the largest grant ever made by them) to cover half the estimated £88,000 cost of restoration. The work is in progress at the time of the writing of these notes.

The two oldest occupied houses in the valley are in the village of Llangynwyd.

The Old House. This old tavern dates back to at least the time of the Abbey of the Blessed Virgin at Margam and is immediately to the south of the old Llangynwyd churchyard. It used to be the scene of Gwyl Mabsant celebrations centuries ago on 29 September each year. Historians maintain that it was probably built for pilgrims on their way to the church. David Davies, in his book, *Tŷ'r Llwyni*, p. 48, says that the Old House was the headquarters of the Women's Section of *Clwb yr Hen Gymry* (the Club of the Ancient Welsh) who paraded annually through the town. The minstrel harpist was John Thomas, the father of the famous harpist, Pencerdd Gwalia. The conductor of the Aberafan Town Band, Bleddyn(?) Jones, the author of the song 'Young Margam Bando Boys', was the band conductor. The dancing was to the accompaniment of the Swansea hornpipe. The tavern was also reputed to be the meeting place of the bards of Tir Iarll.

23   Early 20th century view of *The Old House*, Llangynwyd, showing the horse-mount that was replaced in 1927 by the Wil Hopcyn memorial (see the almost identical later view in plate 36)

The tavern has recently been restored and the roof re-thatched at considerable expense. Previously the roof had been thatched in accordance with the English square method but the recent thatching has resulted in the eaves being of the traditional Welsh forked pattern. The old oak beams and the old mantelpiece in the licensed rooms, together with the Saxon arch, as well as the thatched roof, are an added attraction. This is where Wil Hopcyn is reputed to have sung many of his songs over two-and-a-half centuries ago.

The Corner House is immediately west of the Churchyard and at right angles to the Old House. It was formerly the parish tithe barn, the tithes being payable in kind, and laid out on the appointed day. Wil Hopcyn is said to have sung his songs in this building as well. In 1761-62 two Welsh Circulating Charity Schools, promoted by the Rev. Griffith Jones, Llanddowror, were successively held at the inn, one attended by 26 pupils and the other by 30. The tavern has been re-adapted from time to time to assume its more modern appearance. Like the Old House, it has an old-world atmosphere, both houses being a decided attraction to tourists.

It is a matter of gratification that the village of Llangynwyd has been allowed to retain its original features with the help of a Conservation Order to protect it from massive building development that would shatter the dreams of all those who have any respect for the past. It is interesting to note that the first house on your right as you enter the village from the Maesteg direction is named *Llonydd*, indicating peace and contentment.

24   *The Corner House* Inn, early twentieth century

When C. R. M. Talbot, M.P., laid the foundation stone of the Maesteg Town Hall in 1880, he said: 'Seventy years ago, this valley was a desolate place as the only living inhabitants were an old oak tree and a venerable raven.' This was surely an exaggeration when we remember the number of valley farms extant at the beginning of the last century, and the fact that in replies to queries by Edward Lhuyd at the end of the seventeenth century, the Rev. J. Hutton, vicar of Llangynwyd, stated that the valley contained 500 inhabitants whilst a Mr. Jenkins of Llangynwyd, in reply to the same queries, gave the number as 600. However, in his essay on the origin and development of industries in the Llynfi Valley, Llyfnwy stated that in or about 1820 there were only about six or seven houses from Cwm Cerdin (at the foot of Llangynwyd) to Blaenllynfi, at the top of the valley. Presumably the occupants of the farms brought the number up to 500 or 600.

Incidentally, it is not difficult to go back over 300 years with the help of only a few links. Hundreds in the valley to-day can remember the Rev. William H. Thomas, the esteemed minister of Tabor C.M. Church, Maesteg, who died in 1933. He could claim to have been a co-preacher with the celebrated Edward Matthews, Ewenny, at a certain religious festival. Edward Matthews was born in St. Athan in 1813 and was thirteen years of age when the famous Iolo Morganwg died. Iolo himself has recorded having had a chat with a milkmaid at St. Fagan's whose grandfather could remember Cromwell's soldiers fighting the Battle of St. Fagan's in 1648. Many, like the writer of these notes, can remember the Rev. W. H. Thomas, who could remember Edward Matthews, who could remember Iolo Morganwg (who lived at Flemingston — 3 miles from Matthews's home), whilst Iolo could remember the milkmaid whose grandfather could remember Cromwell's soldiers in St. Fagan's in 1648!

10. Llynfi Valley Wells

Cadrawd has listed 10 wells in the valley:

1. *Ffynnon Gynwyd* in Llangynwyd village.
2. *Ffynnon Fair*, one of that name being 300 yards from the Church, and the other on Dyffryn Llynfi Farm, 3 miles to the north of Llangynwyd near the old Colliers' Arms in Dyffryn Road, Caerau.
3. *Ffynnon Wrgan* on Llwyni Farm, probably named after Gwrgant, prince of Glamorgan.

4. *Ffynnon Rhydhalog* near Cae-mab-Ifor Farm, Llangynwyd. There was a legend that the waters remained foul during the time two quarrelsome women lived in the area.

5. *Ffynnon Ffos* on Ffos Farm near Cwmdu Colliery.

6. *Ffynnon Iago* on a small farm near Cwmcerwyn Fach Farm.

7. *Ffynnon Wysgar* on Gadlys Farm, Llangynwyd.

8. *Ffynnon y Gilfach* on Gilfach Mountain, near Llangynwyd.

9. *Ffynnon y Gilfach Isaf* nearby.

10. *Ffynnon yr Ysfa* on the hill leading from Maesteg to Llangynwyd in the Alma area.

In a series of articles in the *Glamorgan Advertiser* in the twenties, Daniel R. Waldin referred to the following healing wells of the valley:

1. *Ffynnon y Caerau* which was noted for its healing powers and was praised by Bardd y Spelters (The Poet of Spelters) in a poem:

Mae'n gwella'r gravel a'r gwynegon,
A Duw a ŵyr pa beth yn rhagor.

(It cures gravel trouble and rheumatism and God only knows what else). Visitors used to drop a pin in the well as a token of thanks.

2. *Ffynnon Ddrewllyd* (the Sulphur Well) near Dyffryn Farm, Caerau, and referred to by Cadrawd as Ffynnon Fair. The well emitted a strong smell. Copper coins dropped into the well would turn yellow.

3. *Ffynnon Fair* (St. Mary's Well) near the old Colliers' Arms, Dyffryn Road, Caerau, where the Mission Hall is to-day.

4. *Pistyll Ton-y-cwd* (The Well of Ton-y-cwd), Caerau, had great strengthening powers.

5. *Pistyll Tŷ'n y Coed*, where Tonna Road, Caerau is to-day, also had like powers. Broken limbs were bathed in the well.

6. *Pistyll Tŷ'n y Deri* was formerly the main water-supply for the upper part of Nantyffyllon.

7. *Ffynnon Ffyrllyn* between Penylan Farm and Garnwen Farm, Nantyffyllon. Daniel R. Waldin, who was born in 1844, could remember seeing trout in several pools in the brook. It was noted for its healing powers. As previously mentioned, it was a custom to drop a farthing (ffyrlling or ffyrling) into the water in thanks for a cure. The well was called Ffynnon Ffyrlling until the postal and educational authorities became a power and then called it Nantyffyllon.

8. *Ffynnon Torgwili* on the brow of the hill beyond Cwmdu, near St. John's Colliery.

It is not known how many of these wells still serve their purpose.

11. Iolo Morganwg's Visit

The great antiquarian, poet and scholar, Iolo Morganwg (1747-1826), was a constant visitor to Tir Iarll, particularly Llangynwyd. He claimed to be a descendant of Rhys Goch ap Rhiccert of the famous bardic pedigree of Tir Iarll. He knew of Llangynwyd as the centre of the literary activities of the province and used to visit the old farms of Gadlys, Bryn Llywarch, Cefn Ydfa and Maescadlawr, where his bardic ancestors lived. He knew of the old *cwndidwyr* (carol writers) of the sixteenth century and the local County families (including the Powells of Llwydarth) who took pride in the old cultural life of the valley.

In his diary he records a visit to Llangynwyd in June 1796. It was 'a village of about ten or twelve houses surrounding a handsome and spacious church that has a good school at its western end'. The school was given rent-free to an approved schoolmaster. Iolo had read in the Church and the churchyard numerous tombs and monuments, many of which were in Welsh but a far greater number in English. He noted the gravestones of about fifty people who had lived until eighty or upwards, one of them reading thus: Jane Jenkins, died 21 January 1774 A.D., 110. The Parish Register (p. 91) disclosed that a Gwenllian Lewis, 'the old woman of Talgarth' (in the Garth district) aged 113, was buried 7 February, 1799.

Iolo had been told in Llangynwyd that several aged 100 and upwards, had been buried in the churchyard without gravestones. He called Llangynwyd a 'salubrious village' — not greatly exposed to 'keen skies'. The force and edge of rough and sharp winds were blunted ere they reached the village. The land was of the best kind of mountain soil, dry, healthy and

25   Iolo Morganwg, from Elijah Waring's 'Recollections and Anecdotes' of the bard, published 1850

fertile enough to produce plenty of all sorts of corn. At hand there was plenty of coal. The place was for one who wished to be out of the way of the world, and a traveller would experience 'fine air and cheerful views'. If he would content himself with wholesome Welsh mountain fare, drink often from the fine mountain streams that served him for a mirror, and hear often a Welsh Bard and a Welsh harp, he would stand a fair chance of living to the age of Jane Jenkins.

The above is Iolo Morganwg's description of *mwynder Morgannwg* (the gentleness or suavity of Glamorgan) and particularly of the parish of Llangynwyd.

12. The Cwm-y-felin Druidical Society

Iolo Morganwg asserted that there was a *Cymdeithas Ddirgel o Ddwy-fundodiaid Derwyddol* (a secret druidical society of Unitarians) in Cwm-y-felin in the sixteenth century. It was known as *Cymdeithas Gwŷr Cwm-y-felin* (the Society of the Men of Cwm-y-felin). Antoni Powell of Llwydarth who died in 1618, and his nephew, Watcyn Powell, were stated to be the first members. Iolo maintained that the Society flourished in the valleys of Glamorgan in the days of his youth.

Cwm-y-felin is described as being in Betws, Tir Iarll. A part of the Llynfi Valley between Maesteg and Llangynwyd is called Cwmfelin, being a quarter of a mile to the South of Llwydarth, the old home of Antoni Powell. It is only about a mile from the boundary of the Parish of Betws, which is also in Tir Iarll. Cwmfelin was formerly known as Cwm-y-felin. Indeed, the Parish Registers show that a seven months old child of Rees D. of Cwm-y-felin was buried on 13 February 1800 and that a Jane Lewelyn of Cwm-y-felin in the Cwmdu Hamlet was buried on 25 January 1801. Neighbouring farms such as Llety Brongu and Blaencwmdu were in the Parish of Betws.

As there was an old mill about a mile from Llwydarth, it would not appear unreasonable to assume that it was somewhere in this area that the Society in question met.

Professor Griffith John Williams attributes the history of the Society to the fertile imagination of Iolo Morganwg. It can be stated with confidence that so far as his published works are concerned, Professor Williams has not produced any factual evidence to prove that such a Society did not exist or could not have existed. His opinion is based on his general suspicions of the writings of Iolo, and we now know to what extent the Professor had changed his attitude towards him during the latter years of his life. In the end he came to admit in a public lecture in 1962, a few months before he died, that there was an element of truth in everything that Iolo Morganwg wrote.

13. The Parish Registers

Unfortunately, the local Parish Registers do not take us back further than 1662 when the Rev. Samuel Jones was deprived of his living. Possibly the deposed Vicar could have taken the pre-1662 registers with him. Gomer Morgannwg states that Vicar Pendril Llewelyn was of that opinion. However, Gomer Morgannwg, who cannot be considered as a reliable witness, maintained that it was the King's messenger and spies who took possession of all books and Church papers in 1662. The writer of these notes feels indebted to the Rev. M. J. Mainwaring, former Vicar of Llangynwyd, for his characteristic courtesy and kindness in allowing access to the post-1662 registers.

Excerpts have been published by Cadrawd in his History of the district. The ages of several whose deaths are recorded are not mentioned in the registers. The burial of the 'old man of Pontrhydycyff' on 19 April 1797 is recorded but his age is not given. An illegitimate daughter was christened as *filia reputata* and an illegitimate son as *filius reputatus*. Filius (son) is mentioned for the last time on 11 December 1778. From 1767 to 1782, there is a record of the christening of children from twenty well-known local farms and of the burial of the residents of over fifty equally well-known local farms.

Between 1782 and 1800, five deaths from smallpox are recorded, several from 'a decline as it is thought' and also from dropsy. John Williams, 'the stoutest man in the neighbourhood' was buried 9 September 1799. Watkin, son of Watkin Richard by Ann, his intended wife, was baptized 27 September, 1802, 'but the said Watkin Richard died while the Bannes were going'.

There are several references to a 'base son' and an 'imputed daughter'. The unusual name of Xantippe (wife of Socrates) survived in the same family for over 200 years, and one bearing that Christian name was a valued next-door neighbour of the writer's parents.

14. Local Customs

In his volume (in Welsh) on Iolo Morganwg (pp. 38-40), Professor Griffith John Williams quotes Iolo's list of over fifty customs and festivals in vogue in his days in Glamorgan, 'the most old-fashioned County of Wales'. In another document, Iolo gives details of scores of additional customs with yet a further list wherein he describes the nature of the fare provided at such festivals. As Iolo knew Llangynwyd very well, it can be assumed that most of these customs and festivals prevailed in the district.

Cadrawd states that the ploughman's custom of singing while ploughing with oxen persisted until the middle of the last century. He and other collectors of folklore had spoken to elderly people who could remember the customs and the songs. The oxen were objects of endearment to the ploughman and were the subject of a special ceremony on the feast of the Epiphany. Much information hereon had been provided earlier by John Howells of St. Athan's.

Many of the customs are mentioned by Cadrawd and his son, Frederic Evans, in their respective publications. Unfortunately, owing to the decline of the Welsh language, the many examples of colloquial words and expressions have lost their impact and meaning and interest.

Cadrawd gives us details of the Court Leet, which ceased to exist about a century ago. It met twice a year and consisted of the representatives of the Lord of the Manor. It was customary to appoint a constable each for Llangynwyd and Betws and a reeve, who owned land in the Parish, to collect the chief rent &c., which was about £50, collected every six years.

The Court Leet was a Court of Record for punishing offences against the Crown. It settled disputes regarding boundaries, fences, trespassers &c. A jury of twenty-four persons was sworn, the expenses being defrayed by the Lord of the Manor.

It was customary for the young people of the district to meet at a farm-house to peel rushes. The long white centres, which remained after the peeling, were placed in a frying pan full of tallow. The pan was placed on the fire and the 'strips of pith' were twined until they were well covered. When cooled, they were ready for use. Thousands of these were made on the 'peeling night' ready for the winter.

Other customs not noted in Cadrawd's volume include the provision in the eighties and the nineties of the last century at Llangynwyd of a church-warden's claypipe and a pair of carpet slippers for the weekend stay of the visiting preacher for the 'cwrdde mawr' (annual preaching festival) at the old Methodist Chapel later transformed into a dwelling-house.

The Parish Clerk was entitled to a tax of 2d. per hearth or fireplace. The office has long been extinct. Thomas Williams, successor to Cadrawd's father, Thomas Evan, was the last to collect his dues.

When a person took over a farm, the adjoining farmers in turn helped him for a week. This would be called 'diwrnod o breimin' or 'diwrnod o gyfar'. This custom appears to have disappeared, but we are told that help is still given in respect of sheep-shearing and threshing.

Most taverns brewed their own beer. There were complaints that the beer was weak and not up to the standard required by law. Shwned (Jennet) of the Cerdin (Cross) Inn was known for the weakness of her beer, especially her hot drinks. This caused her brother, Gruffydd y teiliwr (tailor) of the famous literary family of Brynfro, Llangynwyd, to write a satirical *triban* (poem) to her. Mead, or beer, called *cwrw bach*, was brewed for financial gain. Invited friends, who paid for the drink, joined in the drinking and consequent merriment.

The *Ffest Clwb* (Club Feast) was an annual feast held at Llangynwyd until the end of the last century. The custom spread to various other public houses in the valley, particularly the Swan Hotel, Maesteg. Members wore top hats, and with draped staves, moved in procession to a service in the Parish Church. The obvious attraction was the feast that followed in the long room of the public house, where goose, turkey, pork and beef were on the menu, with *pwdin 'falau* (apple dumpling) to follow. A ceremonial quaffing jug containing a gallon of beer was passed round the members during the *ffest* (feast).

In an Exhibition staged at Maesteg during the celebrations of the Festival of Britain, 1951 and opened by H. A. Marquand, the then Minister of Health, among the items then exhibited were an old oak dresser made by a local craftsman about 200 years earlier, a *pedwran* used by farmers to measure wheat and oats, and made out of fine staves, a love spoon, a goffering iron to iron the frill in caps used under the Welsh hats, a brass pan used for warming milk for cheese-making or the making of clotted cream, a candle box to hold short rush candles, and later, tallow candles, a brass ladle for ladling soup and porridge, a brass warming pan which was filled with hot cinders and placed in the bed, a salmon spear, a rolling pin, a potato masher and a cake-slicer usually given as a wedding present, a sampler made of wool 200 years earlier, a *peithynen*, being the wooden book of bards cut on staves, an oak bellows, a toasting fork, and an oak cradle.

Nos Twco 'Falau—'Ducking Apple Night'—fell on All Hallows Eve. According to age-long custom a large tub was filled with water and children were invited to catch with their teeth the floating apples, or when blind-folded, to prod the apples with a fork. The writer of these notes can remember such occasions in Nantyffyllon.

Calennig was a custom of children collecting pennies from neighbours before dawn on New Year's Day. The children had as an emblem an apple or an orange stuck upon a tripod or three hazel sticks and decorated with holly or mistletoe, with dried ears of oats or barley together with a coating of white flour to resemble snow. The children sang traditional songs in groups outside the houses. All would be over by noon.

Y Plygain or *Canu Cwndidau* (Carol singing). Prior to 1752 the church was lit up about 4 a.m. to 5 a.m. on the old Christmas morning, being twelve days later than the present Christmas, for a religious service including carol singing. The service was called *Y Plygain*, the word in its earlier forms, *pylgain* and *pylgaint*, being derived from the Latin *pulli cantus*, 'cockcrow'.

Cadrawd tells us that as late as 1865, a form of 'Candle-mass' was held at each dissenting place of worship at Llangynwyd. The chapel would be lit by about seventy candles, given and decorated by the ladies of the church.

26 and **27**
The *Calennig*
(New Year's gift)

Sometimes, each worshipper would bring his or her candle. The idea was that candle-lighting at Christmas was a symbol of the coming of the Light of the World. A prayer-meeting would be held and carols sung. The custom has persisted to a lesser extent in the valley, but without the candles. In the mid-nineteenth century, Christmas morning services were held at 7 a.m. at Carmel Congregational Church, Maesteg. The favourite hymn sung was:

> Dyma fore haedda'i garu,
>   Dyma fore haedda glod;
> Dyma fore tra rhagorol,
>   Dyma fore gora' 'rio'd.

(This is the best ever morning that deserves to be loved and praised). Other churches, e.g. Ebenezer (C), Garth, Maesteg, followed the custom in recent years.

An idea of the carols can be gleaned from the volume *Hen Gwndidau*, 1910, edited by the Rev. Lemuel J. Hopkin-James and Cadrawd. The *cwndidau* (carols) were in reality Welsh sermons in song in the Gwentian dialect by forty-two bards of Tir Iarll of the Tudor period. At a later date local poets wrote new carols on the traditional themes. In the last century, young people met after the service to partake of *cyflaith* (treacle toffee) available in the larger farm-houses.

Gwylnos was a religious service at the home of the departed the night before the funeral. It resembled an Irish wake and was a relic of pre-Protestant times. Mourners and friends gathered in the room containing the open coffin of the deceased. In a much overcrowded and unventilated room, the scriptures were read and prayers offered for the dead. Mournful hymns in the minor key were sung. The father of the writer of these notes could remember such *gwylnosau* in Nantyffyllon, when the hymns sung were 'Ai marw rhaid i mi?' (Must I die?) and 'Mae 'nghyfeillion adre'n myned' (My friends are departing hence). A *gwylnos* was held in Grove Street, Nantyffyllon, during the early days of the writer of these notes, but the practice has long ceased to exist. In his reminiscences (*Cyn Cof Gennyf a Wedyn*), the Rev W. G. Glasnant Jones, a former minister of Siloh Welsh Congregational Church, Nantyffyllon (1901-1906), states that he nearly found himself in hell-fire locally for suggesting that a room which contained the body of a typhoid victim was not suitable for holding a *gwylnos*.

Gŵyl Mabsant was originally, in Catholic times, a religious ceremony preceding the day of the Saint to whom the Parish Church was dedicated. In Llangynwyd it was held on 29 September each year. The religious ceremony was later discarded and the day devoted to eating, drinking, dancing and merry-making, and very often to debauchery. It formerly included the singing of *tribannau* (typical Glamorgan verses) to the accompaniment of the harp. Cadrawd has given us excerpts from the diary of the Rev. J. Parry, a former Vicar of Llangynwyd (1790-1829), recording payments to his servants to enable them to attend. By 1873, Gŵyl Mabsant had disappeared locally, and even twenty years earlier in Breconshire and Monmouthshire.

James O'Brien, Port Talbot, writing on Gŵyl Mabsant in the *Transactions of the Aberafan and Margam District Historical Society* (Vol. 1, 1928), states that some modern writers considered that the pleasure fairs of today were a development of the social side of the Mabsant. It was even more likely that the annual tea-parties which had become so popular a feature of church life in South Wales had their origin in the *medd a pasti* (mead and pies) of those times.

Mari Lwyd. The main actor wore the skull of a horse, cleaned and polished to resemble ivory, decked with ribands and draped in white cloth (calico or linen) falling loosely over the body of the bearer and reaching the ground. Cadrawd tells us that the eyes were made of the bottoms of two black bottles rimmed with white paint. The cocked and pointed ears were of the black felt of an old bowler hat or of black leather. The mane was of plaited ribbons of brilliant hue and the head generally was decorated with rosettes.

Tom Jones, Trealaw, writing in *Y Darian*, 29 July 1926, states that acting the Mari Lwyd was common in almost every parish and village in Glamorgan and Gwent in the mid-nineteenth century, particularly 1859-75, and occasionally thereafter. A little prior to 1926, the custom was enacted throughout the Rhondda Valley as well as in Llangynwyd and various places on the outskirts of Cardiff.

During the last century the custom was merely the extension of Christmas celebrations without any religious significance. 'Mari' would be accompanied by about half a dozen merrymakers with lanterns. Those inside would respond in turn to each verse sung by the Mari Lwyd company outside. It was a test for the ready rhymester, within and without. The opening verse would invariably be:

> Wel dyma ni'n dwad
> Gyfeillion diniwad
>   I 'mofyn am gennad i ganu

(Here we come, genial friends, to ask for permission to sing).

The replies from within would have to be in the same metre. When the responses would cease, Mari and the company would be invited inside to partake of the home-brewed drink and cakes readily provided. It seems that Llangynwyd is now one of the few places where the custom has survived up to recent times.

Dr. Iorwerth C. Peate suggests that 'Mari' in 'Mari Lwyd' came from the English 'mare' which was in 'nightmare', being a female monster supposed to settle upon people and pound them to suffocation. To support this contention, Dr. Peate reminds us that the mediaeval pronunciation of the word 'mare' in English was 'mari'. The adjective 'lwyd' bore its ordinary meaning of 'grey'.

28 and 29 The *Mari Lwyd* at
Llangynwyd *c.* 1880

30 and 31   The draped and
undraped skull of the Mari Lwyd.

Frederic Evans contended that 'Meri Lwyd' and not 'Mari Lwyd' was the correct name and that the custom was the vestige of an old religious mystery play of the Middle Ages. The name 'Meri Lwyd' seemed a corruption of the English 'Merry' whilst 'Lude' came from the latin 'ludere'—to play. The latter word appeared in words such as 'prelude' and 'interlude', and the term 'merry' was often used to describe such mediaeval 'interludes'. Frederic Evans thought that possibly the original play depicted the flight to Egypt, which would appear to be an appropriate theme between Christmas and the New Year.

Limitations of space prevent us from giving details of the many other interpretations by such people as Sir Thomas Hughes, the Rev. W. Roberts (Nefydd), David Jones (Wallington), Wirt Sykes, Charles Redwood (friend of Carlyle), Marie Trevelyan, and D. Rhys Phillips whilst the subject is also discussed by Trefor M. Owen in his *Welsh Folk Customs* and by Cadrawd in his *History of Llangynwyd* and in his articles in the *Cardiff Times*.

Gŵyl y Cwltrin (The Cooltrin Feast). Cadrawd tells us that this festival usually coupled with Gŵyl Mabsant, ceased to exist in the mid nineteenth century. The object was to hold to public ridicule husbands and wives who had quarrelled and had fought each other during the previous year. The custom appeared to resemble the ducking stool for scolding wives in parts of England. A detailed account of the ceremony is given by Cadrawd in his History of the valley.

Y Gaseg Fedi (Harvest Mare) was a custom whereby a handful of corn that had been ungarnered by the reapers was carefully plaited. According to Cadrawd, all the reapers, at a certain distance, would aim their sickles with the object of cutting down the plaited sheaf and then struggle for the scattered corn. The winner had to carry it dry to the centre of the farmhouse table on which the harvest dinner would be laid. On his way to the farmhouse he was waylaid by maidservants, each with a pail of water, with the object of sousing the corn and its bearer. If the man arrived dry, he would be the hero of the harvest dinner.

Up to about 1880, the hiring of male and female servants took place every six months on the first Wednesday after the Old May day and on the first Wednesday after All Hallows' tide. Cadrawd tells us that these days were called 'Mercher Amodau' (Covenant Wednesdays) when terms were agreed upon between master and servant. In consideration of the master paying a shilling to the servant, the bargain was clinched until the agreed term of service had expired.

We are told that in the earlier years the Churchwardens paid out of the Church-rate funds one shilling per bell to provide beer for bell-ringers on New Year's Eve. The overseers of the hamlet paid to the local huntsmen £1 in beer for every fox killed, whilst 5/- was paid by the overseers for killing a polecat, 1d. each for all rooks killed and 2d. for killing a carrion crow.

15. Local Superstitions

Both Cadrawd and his son, Frederic Evans, have in their respective books given an account of local folklore. Cadrawd was successful at the Aberdare National Eisteddfod, 1885, with a comprehensive collection of the folklore of Glamorgan.

We are now conversant with the details of *y toili* (phantom funeral) and apparitions resulting in death — and also signs of the supernatural. Many authors have referred to the *cannwyll gorff* (corpse candle) as an omen of death, being a light which passed along noiselessly at night from the house of death to the grave.

Presumably the omens of death in the Llangynwyd district were also experienced in other parts of South Wales, as evinced in old folk songs, e.g., the crowing of cocks before midnight, the howling of dogs at night, or the crowing of hen birds. Other examples are the birth of twins to a cow or mare, the ticking sounds of a death watch, the blossoming of fruit trees at unseasonable times of the year, or the beating of screech owls against the window of a sick room.

If the cut hair of a person would not kindle into a flame when placed upon a fire, it would indicate that a shorn person would die within that year. It was a custom by the wisest old men on New Year's Night to sit up all night in the church porch. A voice from beneath the altar table would announce the names of those who would die in the coming year. On All Hallows Eve a disembowelled spirit was supposed to be seated on every stile and cross road. Those born after dark and before midnight were supposed to be gifted with second sight or the faculty of seeing and hearing signs of death.

If an owl were heard hooting in the night from one of the yews in the churchyard, it was a sign that an unmarried girl from Llangynwyd had lost her virginity. To see a single crow in the morning would bring ill-luck. To see two crows together would bring luck. If a magpie crossed one's path in the morning, it presaged an evil day.

Cadrawd and Frederic Evans have given details of the legends regarding the maid of Gelli Lenor and *Ysbryd y Pentre* (The Ghost of Pentre Farm, Llangynwyd).

We have also been given instances of the curing of whooping-cough by cutting off the hair from the back of the head of a child sufferer, placing it between two pieces of bread and butter and giving it to a dog sent out of the house.

Christenings were usually performed at the home of the infant's parents and the water after the christening was thrown over the leek bed in the garden to ensure luck for the child. Washing hands in water after another was considered unlucky and butter made by a red-haired woman was reputed to become unwholesome in a few days. Many other customs are described by Cadrawd in the *Cardiff Times*, 1 January 1916.

Among superstitions that have persisted until this day is that connected with the falling of a picture from a wall without a break in the cord attached to the nail in the wall. This was a sign of approaching death in the family. In having a bath after a day's work at the coal face, some miners would purposely omit to wash their backs as they thought it would soften or weaken their spines. The writer of these notes has heard of the belief that excessive eating of tomatoes induced cancer.

In an address to the Aberafan and Margam Historical Society on 'The Folklore of the District', Martin Phillips refers to the bewitching of cattle at Llangynwyd. A witch, by a curse and sign, would cause a cow to yield water instead of milk because the owner had refused a piece of cream cheese to the witch. The farmer consulted a local conjuror who advised him to get the witch to undo the witchcraft and, after certain cabalistic ceremonies, the witch restored the milk to the cow. The lecturer also stated that Morgan Jones, Gelli Lenor, of the eighteenth century was proficient in black art and magic and possessed the power of charming. He is said to have commanded the Devil to carry water in a sieve (to be kept full) from a brook and to make a rope from dry slippery sand.

There were similar legends regarding Croes Efa, a cottage near Llangynwyd and of ghosts at Cefn Ydfa and Llangynwyd Church on New Year's night. The Rev. Edmund Jones (c.1760) of Pontypool tells the story of the wife of a preacher at Llangynwyd seeing an apparition of a man who told her to remove certain things from the barn and cast them into the river. Her husband thought that it was his own father who had been excommunicated by him.

16. Llangynwyd Church

At one time the Parish of Llangynwyd extended north 11 miles from Coetrehen to Abergwynfi and was one of the most important parishes in Glamorgan. With urban development new parishes were carved out. Now it covers Llangynwyd and Maesteg and was recently extended to Bryn.

The focal point of the Parish was St. Cynwyd's Church, revered by the people of the valley. There still remains a general desire to have children christened in the old Church, to be married thereat and to be buried in the old churchyard. Formerly local landowners (but not their wives or children) were buried within the walls of the Church.

Professor Glanmor Williams tells us (*Glamorgan County History*, Vol. III, p. 143) that although the Statute of Mortmain prevented the transfer of property to clerics without express royal permission, Margam got

32 and **33**   Llangynwyd Church before and after the 1893 restoration

into disfavour shortly before 1353 when it secured the appropriation of the Church at Llangynwyd without royal licence. The Abbey was later pardoned for this transgression. Appropriation meant the transfer to the Abbey of the bulk of tithes and other income of parish churches. When Margam Abbey was dissolved in 1537, the connection with Llangynwyd Church was severed and the advowson passed to the Mansels. It was only in 1866 that the patronage became vested in the Bishops of Llandaff.

Tithes payable to the Church were instituted by the Normans. When the Cistercian Abbey at Margam assumed the advowson of Llangynwyd Church, it received the revenues of the Parish and appointed a vicar to minister to the people. The vicar usually received a third of the revenues as a stipend.

The Church is mentioned in a Charter of 1128 confirming the possessions of the see of Llandaff. The advowson of Llangynwyd Church with an acre of land was granted to Margam Abbey by William de la Zouche, Lord of Glamorgan, and his wife in 1331. On 28 June 1351, Edward III presented a William Sampson to the living of the Church.

Mr. Glynne Ball has drawn our attention to a *Court of Langunyth* document of 1258, sealed by the Bishop of Llandaff (W. de Rodenoure), the Archdeacon of Llandaff and William Scurlag, constable of Langunyth (Llangynwyd), whereby Ieuan ap Gweyr and his three sons undertook not to depasture cattle at Llangeinor and elsewhere and promised to act like brothers to the monks — with an arrangement that if their cattle were liable to be impounded for trespass, they would pay one half penny per head if they prevented the impounding thereof, under penalty of excommunication and interdiction by the Bishop of Llandaff and forfeiture of church sepulture. In 1413, the Abbot of Margam and the Bishop of Llandaff were summoned to Rome by Pope John XXIII to settle a dispute regarding the appropriation of the Church.

The early Church had the right of sanctuary. In 1477, Ieuan Glas took sanctuary in Llangynwyd Church. Residents were required to keep watch to prevent his escape for a requisite period of forty days. The parishioners were fined 100 shillings for allowing him to escape. However, Bishop Smith of Llandaff exempted the Margam Abbey tenants from payment of the fine as all Cistercian lands were exempt from taxation.

The Church is within the walled graveyard called *yr hen fynwent* (the old churchyard) which contains the old church school room at the north-west. Many thousands have been buried in the churchyard. *Y fynwent newydd* (the new churchyard) was opened and dedicated in 1859, with a narrow road between the two. At the first burial in the new churchyard, the then Vicar, the Rev. R. Pendril Llewelyn, stood inside the boundary of the old churchyard whilst the interment took place in the new ground across the road. It was the Vicar's solution to the problem that the new ground had not then been consecrated although legally sanctioned. As this new churchyard became rapidly filled, a further extension was consecrated by the then

34 View of Llangynwyd *c.*1910 with children playing marbles in the foreground
and the Church in the centre of the village within the walled graveyard

Bishop of Llandaff (Timothy Rees) on 24 May 1933 and even that further
extension is becoming increasingly inadequate.

The Church itself was founded in the sixth century during the age of
saints, e.g., Teilo, Illtud, Dewi, Dyfrig, Beuno. Professor E. G. Bowen tells
us that there appears to be general agreement among scholars that the sites
of ancient churches dedicated to Celtic saints were originally established by
the Saint himself or by one of his immediate disciples. A map indicating
such sites shows not only the places visited by a particular saint but also the
limits of his *patria* or territory in which his name is venerated.

The stone socket of a wooden cross appears to be all that remains of the
original structure and can be seen in the wall above the entrance.

The rood in the Church became famous as an attraction to pilgrims.
Several Tir Iarll poets sang the praises of this pre-Reformation relic. The
Church also contains a staircase leading to the old gallery, some centuries-
old seats and a sun-dial built in the wall on the left side of the porch. The
baptismal font belongs to the fourteenth or fifteenth century. The painted
panels of the reredos includes one which depicts St. Dyfrig who died in
612 A.D. The east stained-glass window depicts the Ascension and was fixed
in 1893.

The Church was rebuilt in the thirteenth century and has since been
restored several times. The square tower is of the fifteenth century and was
completely restored in 1893 at a cost to Miss Olive Talbot of Margam of
£3,000 (big money at the time). R. D. Morgan (ap Lleurwg), Maesteg, states

that there was a square memorial stone within the wall of the Church, bearing certain initials and also the dates 1596, 1608 and 1616. He had also seen a broken coffin shaped stone in the churchyard bearing the inscription TM 1624 (being Thomas Maddock) and MT (being Morgan Thomas, his son) and dated 15 November, 1683.

In the safe are housed pieces of old church plate dating from 1576, being a silver cup and two alms dishes of pewter. The communion cup is said to have been one of the first from which the laity were allowed to drink. Items not herein included owing to lack of space are given by Cadrawd in his *History of the Parish of Llangynwyd*, containing a detailed description of the interior of the Church. Similar descriptions are given in guide books available for visitors.

Also in the safe is the parish register containing the original entry of the marriage of Ann Thomas, the Maid of Cefn Ydfa, and Anthony Maddocks on 4 May 1725. The grave of the Maid is in the chancel of the Church, the old memorial stone having been replaced in 1893 by a tablet of marble and brass. This was accomplished mainly through the efforts of Cadrawd and T. H. Thomas of Cardiff known as Arlunydd Penygarn. Wheat and sycamore leaves are woven into the design of the tablet. Inside the tower are the original tombstones that once rested on the grave of the Maid and also above the grave of her poet lover in the churchyard.

We can thank Iolo Morganwg for having copied in good time the inscription on the gravestone of the poet. A replica of the old stone was erected above his grave under the yew tree in the old churchyard in 1927 through the efforts of the Maesteg Cymrodorion Society.

On the original gravestone of Wil Hopcyn, who died in 1741, we find the *englyn* (stanza) and couplet:

> Dyma'r lle gole gwelwch — 'rwy'n gorwedd
> Dan gaerau pob tristwch;
> Os tirion, chwi ystyriwch
> Llug â llên llawen a'n llwch.

> Nid yw'r hollfyd hyfryd hedd
> A'i fwriad ond oferedd.

These lines refer to the vanity and the emptiness of all human designs and accomplishments.

Cadrawd has given details of the inscriptions on the gravestones of the Powell family of Llwydarth, the Cwmrisga family of the Maddocks, the Cefn Ydfa family, the Prices of Tynewydd. The three tombs of the Powell family can be seen on the western side of the porch. According to tradition, they are the resting place of Ieuan Fawr ab y Diwlith and Rhys Goch ap Rhiccert, who flourished about the thirteenth century, but of this there is no certainty. An tombstone unopened for about 200 years is inscribed:

Good friend, for Jesus' sake forbear
To dig the dust enclosed here;
Blest be the man that spares these stones,
And woe to him that moves my bones.

Near the tower on the south side is buried the Rev. Evan Phillips, curate of the Parish, who died 11 September 1783, aged 34. On the front panel of

35   Memorial gravestone of the poet Wil Hopcyn

the gravestone is a verse by the famous preacher, the Rev. David Jones, Llangan. Another tombstone is that of the Rev. T. J. Williams (Myddfai), who was a local curate for six months and who died 25 March 1854, aged 36. Islwyn, the greatest poet and literary figure of Monmouthshire in the last century wrote a lengthy elegy to him.

In the centre of the old churchyard can be seen the grave of Thomas Evan, parish clerk of Llangynwyd, who died 30 December 1877, aged seventy-six years. The englyn (stanza) on his tombstone reminds us that the one who had prepared the last resting place for a multitude of people had himself been reduced to eternal silence.

Thomas Evan's son, Cadrawd, is buried nearby, his grave being marked with a Celtic cross with Celtic lettering thereon. His sons and two daughters are buried nearby. The most famous tombstone is that of the Rev. Samuel Jones, Brynllywarch, adjoining the path immediately to the south of the Church and about a dozen yards from the porch. He died in 1697. It was after much effort that the original inscription on the tombstone of Mrs. Jones, who died in 1676, was deciphered. In 1883 a committee under the chairmanship of the Rev. Isaac Evans, Llangynwyd, was set up to arrange a suitable memorial. A few yards nearer the porch lie the remains of the Rev. T. Llynfi Davies, a well known poet, theologian and chronicler of the eisteddfodic background of the Llynfi Valley during the early twentieth century. His M.A. degree was awarded for a thesis (now at the Maesteg County Library) on the Bardic Order of the fifteenth century.

Also buried in the old churchyard is Vernon Hartshorn, the local M.P., who was Lord Privy Seal at the time of his sudden death in 1931, having pre- viously been Postmaster General and a member of the Simon Commission on India. J. R. Clynes and C. R. Attlee (the then future Prime Minister) attended his funeral. Near his grave is that of Pastor Stephen Jeffreys, the famous evangelist and a native of Nantyffyllon, of whom details are given in the chapter on Religion.

The Bells of Llangynwyd Church

The bells were first hung in 1730 and were six in number. The largest, with the lowest note, is called the Tenor Bell and the smallest is called the Treble. The names of either the churchwardens or the vicar are recorded on four of the bells, whilst the third bell tells us that 'Abr Rodhall of Gloucester cast us all'. The largest bell weights 9 cwts. with a diameter of several feet. The sixth, or Tenor Bell, bears the couplet:

> I to the Church the living call
> And to the grave do summon all.

It appears that the first and second bells cracked and had to be re-cast in 1786. This explains the different dates and names of makers recorded on them. The bells are hung 40 feet up the tower and are unseen by the ringers. They were re-hung in 1953 at a cost of £490 and re-dedicated on 29 June, 1954 by the Archdeacon of Margam, the Ven. Lawrence Thomas.

Wil Hopcyn (1700-1741), the local poet wrote:

> Caru'r wyf ar hirnos gaea
> Sain peroriaeth sŵn y clycha;
> Rhain sy'n addas rhwng mynydda—
> Wych chwiorydd, chwech yn chwara.

(I like to hear the sound of the bells during the long winter nights. The six of them, splendid sisters, are suitable for a mountainous district).

Recently, on special occasions, a band of ringers was engaged. In October 1977, the curate of Llangynwyd, the Rev. John Richards, got together a new team of about a dozen, under the able tutorship of Dr. Lyn Jones, Maesteg, an experienced bellringer and an expert in campanology. Members met every Monday evening, beginning during the 1978-79 winter, and after much practice for six months, the volunteers succeeded in getting the bells to ring on Sundays to the delight of a wide area of listeners.

We are assured that the present band of ringers are determined that the Llangynwyd Church bells will never again be silenced.

A plaque commemorating the 250th of the anniversary of the hanging of the bells was dedicated by the Assistant Bishop of Llandaff (The Right Rev. David Reece) at the Harvest services of the Church in October 1980. The plaque, in ceramics in a wooden base, was donated by Mr. Keith Hall, Head of the Ceramics Department of the School of Home Economics at Llandaff.

17. The Cefn Ydfa Romance

Despite the attractions of the quaint village of Llangynwyd and the historical and cultural associations of the old Church, the district has become a tourist attraction because it is the setting of one of the best-known and best-publicised romances in Welsh history. Of the three romances connected with the area—the Maids of Tŷtalwyn, the Maid of Gelli Lenor and the Maid of Cefn Ydfa, the last named is infinitely the best known.

The story of the romance can be stated briefly. The Maid of Cefn Ydfa came from a local family influential on both sides. Her mother's brother, the Rev. Rees Price, Tynton, Llangeinor succeeded the Rev. Samuel Jones (who died in 1697) as the tutor at the Brynllywarch Academy. He was the father of that eminent eighteenth-century Welshman, Dr. Richard Price, F.R.S., who was consequently a first cousin to the Maid of Cefn Ydfa, although he was only four years old when the Maid died. When Richard

36 Memorial cross to Wil Hopcyn in Llangynwyd between the Church and *The Old House* (right background)

Price received the Freedom of the City of London, the citation ran: 'No living man is a greater authority on the principles of revenue. He has not his equal as an arithmetician in Europe and he has cast a new light upon the principles of civil government.' On one historic occasion, he and George Washington were the only persons to receive an honorary doctorate from Yale University. His nephew, his sister's son, William Morgan, F.R.S. (1750-1833), the famous actuary, was born at Bridgend. Incidentally, he was the great-grandfather of the well known novelist, Evelyn Waugh.

To return to the Maid. She was the only child, and consequently heiress to her parents' possessions. Her ambitious mother wanted her daughter to marry someone of the same social status. Wil Hopcyn, the local rhymester, was occasionally employed as a thatcher and plasterer at the Cefn Ydfa mansion, and as he was of humorous bent with ready wit, the Maid fell in love with him.

The mother wanted her to marry Anthony Maddocks, a local solicitor, who lived at an adjoining farm, Cwm-yr-isga. She forbade her daughter to see her true lover. According to tradition, the Maid was imprisoned in her bedroom (or in a cellar under the mansion) to prevent her from seeing Wil Hopcyn. Tradition also tells us that the Maid wrote to her lover with her own blood on a dry sycamore leaf. It was maintained that about this time the poet wrote the most famous of old Welsh love songs, 'Bugeilio'r Gwenith Gwyn', testifying that he, Wil Hopcyn, was the one fostering the ripening wheat whilst the harvesting was assigned to someone else.

According to the marriage settlement, signed on 3 May 1725, a day before the Maid's marriage to Anthony Maddocks, the latter was to receive a large portion of the Cefn Ydfa estate. The marriage is recorded in the parish register.

The Maid continued to pine for her true lover, Wil Hopcyn. We are told that the poet, who was then working at his trade in Bristol, had dreamt that Anthony Maddocks had died and that the Maid was accordingly free to marry him. He hastened to Llangynwyd only to find the Maid on her deathbed. She died in his arms when her husband was out hunting.

Wil Hopcyn remained single until his death in 1741. Anthony Maddocks married another young heiress within a few months of the death of the Maid. In 1743 be became Under-sheriff to Matthew Deere of Ash Hall, Ystradowen near Cowbridge and acted likewise to Richard Jenkins, Marlas, in 1750.

37   Reduction of a post-card of The Maid of Cefn Ydfa, original size 8″ × 5″,
        produced in 1927 by 'The Wil Hopcyn Memorial Committee'

With the Compliments of
The Wil Hopcyn Memorial Committee
(1927).

THE MAID OF CEFN YDFA.
("Y GWENITH GWYN.")

The above is the nucleus of the story, although there are understandable variations in the details, the romance having depended to some extent on oral tradition for at least two centuries.

The popularity of the romance has been widespread in Wales. In his booklet, *The Cupid* (1869), Thomas Morgan (Llyfnwy), a local historian, gives the traditional story and includes poetic effusions by Dewi Glan Llyfnwy, Maesteg, Llewelyn Griffiths (Glan Afan) and others. In a volume called *Y Berllan* (The Orchard), 1869, containing the successful composi-tions of an Eisteddfod held in Carmel, Maesteg, there appears a lengthy poem to Cefn Ydfa by the well known local poet, Rhydderch ap Morgan (a former minister of Bethesda Church, Llangynwyd), a love song to the Maid by a Taibach poet, Gwilym Glan Ffrwd, and a translation by Mrs. Pendril Llewelyn, wife of the Vicar, of the famous love song 'Bugeilio'r Gwenith Gwyn' attributed to Wil Hopcyn.

The romance has been the subject of *pryddestau* (lengthy poems), lyrics, and *englynion* (stanzas) by some of the best-known poets of Wales, such as Ceiriog, Mynyddog, Dyfed, Wil Ifan, A. G. Prys-Jones, T. Llynfi Davies, Dr. Pan Jones, and D. Onllwyn Brace. Operas were composed by Dr. Joseph Parry and Dr. Haydn Morris. Ap Madoc (1844-1916), a native of Maesteg, wrote the libretto of 'The Maid of Cefn Ydfa', the music having been composed by J. J. Mason, Mus. Doc. of Wilksbarre, U.S.A. It was per-formed many times before Welsh communities in the U.S.A. As recently as 1980 at the National Eisteddfod of Wales held at Gowerton, a new play, 'Y Gwenith Gwyn', written by Rhisiart Arwel, was performed by Cwmni Theatr Cymru at the Grand Theatre, Swansea, whilst a record number of 4,000 tickets were sold in advance for the Company's production of 'White Wheat' by Rhisiart Arwel in July 1980, in Bangor. It is a musical play based on the story of the Cefn Ydfa romance in which the traditional and modern stand side by side — and is a translation of the play by the same author, who is a classical guitarist from Cardiff.

The Welsh version of a novel on the subject, written by Isaac Craigfryn Hughes in 1873, reached its fifth edition. In 1979 a new English edition of the same novel was published. Other novels have been written by Dr. Geraint Dyfnallt Owen, Frederic Evans (writing as Michael Gareth Llewelyn) and others, with a number of plays, films and also references in a host of periodicals.

According to a report in the *Western Mail* in the last century the per-formance at Treorchy of a drama on the Cefn Ydfa romance by J. Bonfyl Davies, based on 'the old story beloved by the South Wales Welshman', was 'a gratifying success'. There were also many performances of a drama written jointly by Frederic Evans and Dr. Emrys Jones (son of the Rev. Iorwerth Jones, Bethania, Maesteg) on the same subject. Indeed, during the period of industrial depression in the thirties, this play brought in £400 to help local charities. In 1975, the play 'Sonnet for a Summer's Day' on the same theme, written by Vivian Paget, was performed many times in South Wales by the Bridgend Castle Players.

In 1927 the Maesteg Cymrodorion Society commemorated the bi-centenary of the death of the Maid of Cefn Ydfa. Thousands gathered at Llangynwyd for that purpose. The old tombstone above the grave of Wil Hopcyn was replaced by a replica thereof, whilst the memorial cross on the Square was a new one commemorating the romance with the words of Dyfed, the then Archdruid of Wales—'Cofiwn Adfyd Cefn Ydfa' (We remember the tragedy of Cefn Ydfa). On the memorial were inscribed the names of the worthies of Tir Iarll—Wil Hopcyn, Siôn Bradford, Twm Ifan Prys, Lewis Hopcyn, Dafydd Nicolas, Richard Price, Samuel Jones, Cadrawd, Llyfnwy, Ceulanydd and Christopher Williams.

A commemorative booklet was published, edited by the Rev. William Edwards, M.A., Caerau, giving the traditional story of the romance, with special reference to the poetry of Wil Hopcyn, the author of 'Bugeilio'r Gwenith Gwyn'. The booklet infuriated Professor Griffith John Williams, an outstanding and profound Welsh scholar, and prompted him to write two biting articles to the Welsh periodical *Y Llenor* (Winter, 1927 and Spring 1928) expressing surprise that the people of Maesteg and district should have believed such nonsense. He contended that there was no actual proof that Wil Hopcyn had composed even a single verse, that there was no foundation for the story of the romance and that Wil Hopcyn was not the author of 'Bugeilio'r Gwenith Gwyn'. In fact, he went as far as to suggest that the originator of the modern story was Mrs. Pendril Llewelyn, wife of the Vicar of Llangynwyd, who first mentioned the matter in a letter written to *The Cambrian*, a Swansea paper, in 1845.

These allegations were refuted by Frederic Evans in the *Western Mail* at the time. Matters remained quiescent until 1969, over forty years later, when Mrs. Elizabeth Williams, the widow of the Professor, published in *Glamorgan Historian*, edited by Mr. Stewart Williams, an English translation of her late husband's two articles in *Y Llenor*. The object, presumably, was to remind people of Maesteg that the whole affair was a fabrication after all.

This led to further research work and resulted in the publication in 1977 of a book in Welsh called *Wil Hopcyn a'r Ferch o Gefn Ydfa* (Wil Hopcyn and the Maid of Cefn Ydfa)* which attempted to show that Wil Hopcyn was a well-known and popular poet in his day, that there were positive grounds for believing in the genuineness of the story and that there was also evidence to connect Wil Hopcyn with the famous love song.

Publishers' Note: The author was Brinley Richards.

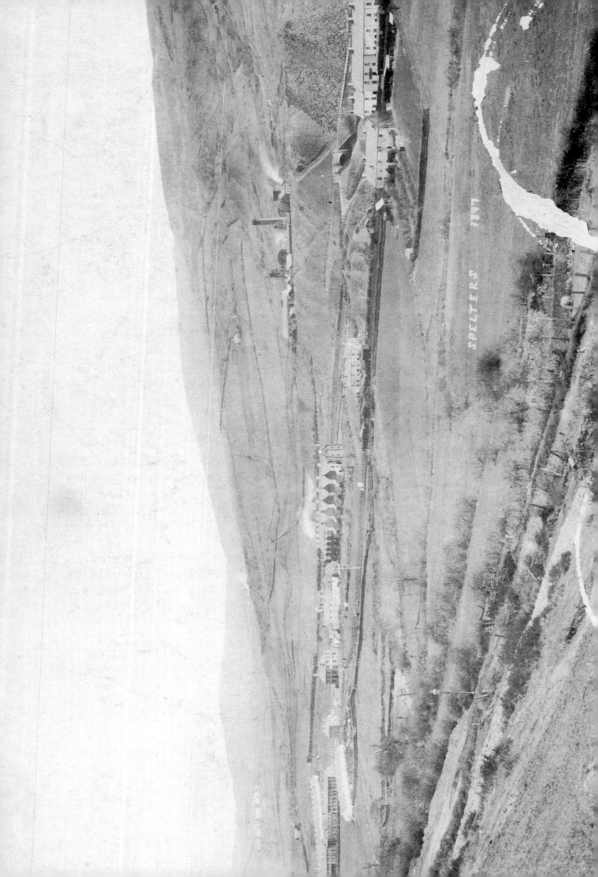

SPELTERS 1897

All this is important to the people of the Llynfi Valley, as Cefn Ydfa is still the most-visited private building in the valley. Comparatively recently as many as 300 people in one day visited the farmhouse and the mansion ruins. Parties from all over Wales call there from time to time. All those tourists who visit Llangynwyd for the first time invariably ask to see the grave of the Maid of Cefn Ydfa in the Church chancel and the grave of Wil Hopcyn under the old yew tree. No written history of the Church, whether in book or pamphlet form, omits reference to the romance.

The people of the Llynfi Valley understandably want to assure visitors, for reasons apart from sentimentality, that there are positive grounds for believing in the authenticity of the story and that they are not pursuing a phantasy. The critics who have attempted to debunk the story have never lived in the valley and have entirely ignored the strong oral tradition of the district. Prejudice was created by the fact that the much maligned Iolo Morganwg was one of those responsible for attributing the famous love song to Wil Hopcyn. Further evidence has come to light in the meantime confirming the genuineness of the story of the romance but limitations of space compel us to deal more fully with the matter elsewhere.

18. The Pre-Industrial Revolution Period

The tendency is to consider the twenties of the last century as the starting point of the Industrial Revolution in the Llynfi Valley. It was then that James H. Allen opened the Spelter Works in the district now called Caerau. In the same decade, the Maesteg Iron Works, known as 'Yr Hen Waith' (The Old Works) began to operate.

Mr. Martin Phillips, Port Talbot, reminds us that the Llwyni property, together with that of Brynrhyg and Cwrt-y-mwnws, all on the east side of the River Llynfi in the Maesteg area, were acquired by a Company trading as the Maesteg Iron Works Co., who commenced operations in 1826, when industry developed on a large scale in the valley.

However, there is evidence of industrial activity centuries earlier. Some old place names indicate early mining, e.g., Rhyd y Gefeiliau (The Ford of the Smithies), Cil y Gofiaid (The Retreat of the Smiths) and Cwm-nant-y-glo (Coal Brook Dale).

The Margam monks mined local coal and iron in the mid thirteenth century. In a Margam Charter of 1516 the Abbot of Margam gave

38 (*Opposite*) This magnificent 1897 view shows (left to right) Ton Coed Row (built 1935), Caerau Colliery (just completed) peeping over the hill, and Coegnant Colliery in its heyday, close to the site of the Spelter (zinc) Works

permission to a person 'to dig for coals'. As early as the sixteenth century George Owen drew up a clear description of the South Wales coalfield. It was found among his papers after his death and published later in the *Cambrian Register*.

Professor William Rees states in his *Industry before the Industrial Revolution* that Henry VIII appointed a Commission in 1534 to search for metals. Peter, son of Almain, a German metal expert, was commissioned to make the survey. Most of the sites were located at Merthyr and Llangynwyd.

The earliest available dated document relating to coal mining is a survey of 'Tiryarlle' dated 1588, which states that 'Ievan ap Ievan ap William of Fforest Kaerwen holdyth by a newe lease the ffree working of the cole pittes, being under the Comyn at the yerelye rent of two shillings and six pence' (*Margam MSS and Clarke's Cartae*). The fact that coal and iron ore have been worked in the Llynfi Valley from early times is confirmed by Sir John Stradling of St. Donat's Castle in a poem written in 1620. He presumably includes the valley in his description:

> And in Glamorgan's hilly partes
> Coal great lie doth abound;
> For goodness and for plenty too
> It's equal ne'er was found.

Coal was being mined on the Common of Caerau in Tir Iarll in 1597. Later, in the same century, the upper seams of the hill country of Llangynwyd were being exploited to yield 'ring of cole' but advance into the Llynfi Valley came about only in the eighteenth century. Ironstone in the adjoining areas of Bryn and Pont Ynys Afan (in the Afan Valley) had been discovered before 1633.

There is evidence of early iron ore working in the valley. In his *Coalfield of South Wales* F. Moses states that the remains of an ancient iron smelting furnace had been found near Cwmdu on the east side of the River Llynfi. This was confirmed by James Barrow, a celebrated mining engineer of Maesteg. On the discovery of an early iron furnace during an excavation in the 1860's for the Cwmdu Tramway, a silver coin of the Queen Elizabeth I period was found on the site.

A survey dated 1650 refers to coal in the Llangynwyd Parish and states 'there is coal under Forest or Brombil, the Lord's land'. On 22 January 1682, a Henry John of Brynrhyg Farm was killed through coal 'falling upon him' at Llwyni.

In 1697 the Rev. John Hutton, Vicar of Llangynwyd (1662-1705), stated in reply to the Parochial Queries of Edward Lhuyd: 'Here is a good store of good ring (soft) coale and also quarries of stone'. Another correspondent, a Mr. Jenkins, informed Lhuyd in the same year that most parts of the Parish had quarries of stone and 'cole mines'.

It is recorded in a survey of the Manor of Tiryarlle, dated 1700, that 'Thomas Rees Esq. holdeth by grant all manner of veines of coale now known, or which may be found, upon any of the lord's lands within the said manor at ye yearly rent of two shillings and six pence'. This survey can be seen at the Cardiff Central Library.

Professor William Rees states that a forge at Aberafan recorded a list of ironworks compiled in 1737. One with a capacity of 150 tons a year was established by a lease granted by Thomas, Lord Mansel to Philip Jenkins of Llangynwyd and held by him until 1746. It is known that there were iron works at Taibach in 1750.

The Cae'r Defaid seam on the Pwll-yr-iwrch side to the east of the River Llynfi was the biggest then discovered. It was worked for scores of years. People carried coal, called *glo Caedefaid*, to adjoining areas as far as Llanilltud Fawr (Llantwit Major) in 1750 and later. David Bowen (Cynwyd), Maesteg knew an old man who had carried (or carted) coal to Margam about 1789.

In 1772 John Bedford of Worcester (and later of Cefn Cribwr) agreed with Llewelyn David of Llwyni and Brynrhyg Farms for the supply of iron ore which was already being worked on his land. A copy of the Indenture dated 7 October 1772 shows that David agreed to supply for 100 years coal at 16/- a wey of 100 sacks, each of 2 cwts, i.e., a wey of 10 tons for delivery by cart or other means at the works. Fuller details are given in Volume I, page 3 of Professor Rees's volume.

Early mining prior to the major onslaught of the Industrial Revolution was limited to surface outcrops. For centuries the house-coal was sufficient to supply a wide area. The larger houses in the Vale of Glamorgan usually obtained a year's supply. The practice was to store the coal in fields near the workings in winter, ready for delivery when the roads became passable.

The shafts were sunk to a depth of 20 to 40 feet. If it became difficult to operate with naked lights, the shaft was abandoned and a new one opened. There was room for only one collier at each of these pits and the coal was brought up in a basket by means of a ladder. Coal was sold at 3d a sack irrespective of size and weight. A troop of donkeys under the care of a boy, or even a woman, brought empty sacks to the pit. The sacks were then filled and delivered to the purchaser's door on payment of a small gratuity. When Iolo Morganwg visited Llangynwyd in 1796, he recorded that there was plenty of coal at hand.

In 1798, Thomas Jones, a currier from Abergavenny, and his two brothers came to the valley in search of a site for an ironworks. Thomas Jones obtained from Llewelyn David, who was operating a small coal level on his land, a lease of the farm for £100 a year, together with three sacks of coal weekly in the winter and two sacks each week in the summer. Thomas Jones scoured the streams for iron ore but without result. Four years later he acquired Brynrhyg Farm with the intention of working the minerals on a larger scale, but without success.

It was in 1824 that Dyffryn Llynfi house-coal was first sold. Mr. Hopkins, Cwrt-y-mwnws, Maesteg, and Mr. Griffiths, Coegnant, Spelters, refused to sell to strangers all the coal then mined as they thought that the supply would have been exhausted in a short time. Ultimately, coal and iron ore mining became organised on a more technical and commercial basis, thus superseding the levels, pits, coke-ovens and tramways of the primitive past.

19. Flannel Mills

Although remote areas such as Llangynwyd were heavily wooded in 1800, a few people other than farmers lived in the valley even before that time. Professor Glanmor Williams in *Glamorgan County History*, vol. IV, p. 111, mentions a court case involving the forcible abduction of fifteen-year-old Gwenllian, daughter and heiress of Thomas Griffiths of Betws, in February 1594. The abductor, who compelled the heiress to marry him, was a Llangynwyd tailor named John David Griffiths.

Mr. Moelwyn I. Williams in his essay in the same volume on 'The Economic and Social History of Glamorgan' (1660-1760) states that the uplands of Glamorgan, including Llangynwyd, had their weavers and tuckers. In the Parish of Llangynwyd, Evan Maddock, a weaver, owned looms valued at £1.5.0 and 'two stones of wooll' worth 10/-'. He possessed cattle, sheep and a working horse and implements of husbandry worth 6/8. When he died in 1704, his estate was valued at £23. 2. 0.

There was a flannel mill at Croeserw, Cymer, in the parish of Llangynwyd prior to the nineteenth century. An apprenticeship deed, dated 1 May 1784, stipulated a term of three years for the apprentice, Thomas Griffiths, to a weaver, Evan Hopkin, at Llangynwyd. Griffiths agreed not to commit fornication nor to marry within three years. He was not to play at cards or at dice tables or play any other 'unlawful games', which would cause the master any loss. He would have to obtain the master's licence to buy or sell. The document forbade him from frequenting taverns or playhouses or to absent himself from his master's service unlawfully. The master, who paid £4, agreed to instruct the apprentice in the art of a weaver and provide him with sufficient meat, drink, washing and lodging. during the three years. The apprentice's father was to provide sufficient 'apparall' for his son.

Cadrawd tells us in 1887 that the Talyfedw Mill, a woollen factory in Cwmfelin, three quarters of a mile south of Llangynwyd, was functioning up to the forties of the last century. It was destroyed by its then proprietor, John Joseph, who had suffered financial loss as the result of the stoppage of the Maesteg Iron Works (the Old Works) and the failure of the Neath Brewery Co. After the departure of Mr. Joseph from Talyfedw, the premises were adapted as a brewery and later as a chemical works. After they had been idle for several years, the then owner of the Cwmfelin woollen factory,

39 Showing site and scant ruins of Croeserw Woollen Mill (bottom left below the Seven Arches Bridge)

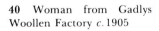

40 Woman from Gadlys Woollen Factory *c.* 1905

John Jones, came to terms with the Llwydarth Tinplate Co. regarding a water supply to the Company and consequently removed his plant to Talyfedw which ultimately became known as the Gadlys Woollen Factory.

The factory was later owned by Evan Rees (1857-1923) and the products sold locally and at the Bridgend market. The factory had only four female employees when it closed. Mr. David Davies, Maesteg, wrote in 1949 that the factory had then no roof and was merely a relic of the past. He added that a mill near the Pontrhydycyff viaduct was still on its feet, the wheel and chute having been seen on the site two years earlier.

There was also a flannel mill at Gelly, Cymer, at the close of the eighteenth century, and another at Maesteg Isaf, but Cadrawd tells us in 1887 that they had then been idle 'for many years'. The only mill within the Parish in 1887 was the one in Pontrhydycyff.

The writer is indebted to Mr. Glynne Ball for drawing his attention to early manorial surveys of Tir Iarll. The 1570 survey refers to 'Melyn Tull y Vedw' (Talyfedw Mill) held by letters patent by Thomas ap Thomas. It is the only mill shown in the 1570 and 1588 surveys, and was in a stream which once formed part of the defence of the castle. It was here that the tenants used to grind their corn. In the 1630 survey, it is called 'Milin Tal y Fedw' and is described as 'indifferently repayred'. The same survey showed that Rees Powel (brother of Thomas Powel) owned one water mill and one 'Welsh acre' of underwoods and rough ground belonging to the mill. Again, it is the only mill recorded in the 1666 survey. It was obviously not a flannel mill at the time. The manorial surveys indicate that by 1689, a third mill was in operation at Croeserw, Cymer, according to the will of Thomas Griffiths preserved among records of the Llandaff Diocesan Court.

The late William Thomas, Barry, born in Maesteg in 1876, the youngest brother of Dr. D. Vaughan Thomas, the musician, informed the writer that his great-grandfather, known as Siencyn y Felin, was buried at Llangynwyd near Wil Hopcyn's grave. One could deduce from this fact that he was a local miller, taking us back easily to the eighteenth century.

According to D. R. Waldin (previously referred to) there were in 1871 grinding mills turning corn into flour at (1) Gelly, Cymer, (2) Melin Maesteg (Maesteg Mill, opposite the lower end of Heolfain, Garth), (3) Melin Cwm Cerdin, 300 yards from the Llynfi River, and (4) Melin Pontrhydycyff, worked by a water wheel.

20. The Iron Industry

At an Eisteddfod held at Salem Baptist Chapel, Spelters (later called Nanty-ffyllon) in February 1857, Thomas Morgan (Llyfnwy) of Alma Banks, Maesteg, was awarded a prize for an essay on 'Dechreuad a Chynnydd

Gweithiau Maesteg' (The Origin and Progress of Industry in Maesteg).
Most, if not all, subsequent writers have based their accounts of our early
industrial history up to 1857 on this very informative essay which has been
out of print for many years. To Thomas Morgan we are indebted for much
of the information hereinafter contained up to 1857.

We have already seen in the chapter on the pre-industrial period that
Llewelyn David of Llwyni Farm had in 1798 granted a lease to Thomas
Jones of Abergavenny to operate a small coal level on his land called Llwyni
and Brynrhyg. However, the lease itself, dated 29 August 1799, for ninety-
nine years from 29 September 1799, was from Llewelyn David to William
Barrow & Co. One can only gather that there was an understanding
between William Barrow and Thomas Jones, both of the same town, as we
are told that Thomas Jones took over from William Barrow in December,
1801.

Thomas Jones constructed a pond above the leased land. He thought that
by releasing the water of the pond, the surface of the acquired land below
would be removed, thus disclosing the coal underneath. This primitive
experiment proved a failure and Jones was later adjudged a bankrupt.
However he had previously arranged to have the lease vested in the name of
his brother, Charles. Thomas Jones went to London in 1824 to form a
company, but before an agreement was signed, after waiting 26 years, he
died suddenly, leaving Charles to take over. He also died suddenly, and the
third brother, William, completed the deal.

Despite opposition from three valley colliers, the Company leased Cwrt-y-
mwnws Farm, Maesteg, on the east side of the River Llynfi, for ninety-nine
years at a ground rent of £105 per annum, although several levels in search
of coal had been previously opened on the adjoining land. These levels were
16 to 18 yards deep and workmen descended into them in baskets controlled
by ropes.

A Llynfi Valley railway map (London, 1859) contains references to four
local Iron Works: (1) Maesteg Works (*Yr Hen Waith*, the Old Works),
(2) Llynvi Vale Iron Works (*Y Gwaith Newydd*— the New Works), (3) Garth
Iron Works and (4) Tondu Iron Works— as well as a Spelter Works at the
top of the valley.

21. The Maesteg Iron Works

These Works were erected on the east side of the Llynfi River in the area
now identified as between South Parade and Crown Road, Maesteg. In May
1826, clay was cut to provide bricks for the construction of the Works.
Various 'patches' were opened to quarry for iron ore, the first being at Cwm-
nant-y-gwiail, near the spot where the Crown Hotel now stands. By 1827,

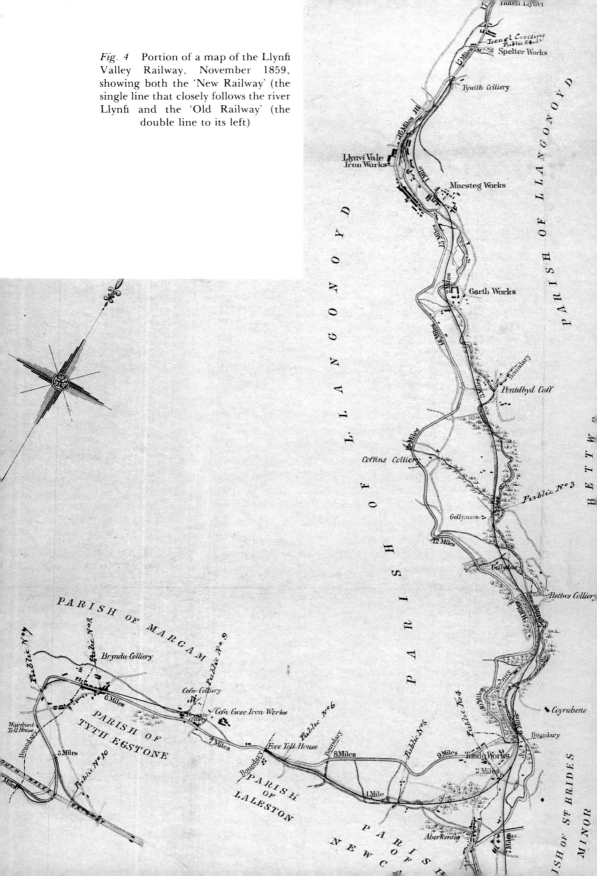

Fig. 4 Portion of a map of the Llynfi Valley Railway, November 1859, showing both the 'New Railway' (the single line that closely follows the river Llynfi and the 'Old Railway' (the double line to its left)

41   Old Ironworks Bridge, Castle Street, Maesteg, demolished 1952

42   Maesteg Iron Works Casting House, 1970, shortly before its disappearance

foundations for two blast-furnaces were being laid. In 1828 the first blast-furnace was completed and 'blown in' and coke ovens were in use. This was the time iron-smelting commenced in the valley. In 1831, the second blast-furnace began to operate, and by 1844 the engine-house and the third blast-furnace had been erected.

In an article, 'Family Party of Five': *A Journal of a Trip to Glamorgan*, Esther Phillips Williams of Cowley, near Oxford, describes in 1836 the process of iron-making at night at the Maesteg Iron Works. Iron ore and coal were dug from various seams in the adjoining mountain. The source of limestone required for fusion was some miles away. The authoress saw coal burnt into coke and ironstone roasted to free it from clay. Residents were within hearing distance of the hissing noise caused by the explosion of the steam-engine as it belched forth into the blazing furnaces of the Works.

In 1836 the Works provided pillars for the new Bridgend Market, as well as rails, rail chairs and plates. The wages of a skilled workman came to £1 a week. In 1846 a new foundry was opened to make shears for the proposed Llynfi Valley railway line, producing 700 to 1,000 shears daily.

Owing to depression in the trade, the Company became insolvent in 1847. It was also alleged that the heavy subsidising of the Neath Brewery Co. had contributed to the Company's failure. In 1847 the furnaces were 'blown out'. Most of the employees obtained work at the Llynvi Iron Works (the New Works). The particulars of sale of the Maesteg Works listed the following assets: 3 blast-furnaces and cast houses, 2 blast-engines, 3 refineries, foundry for chairs, steam-engine and 2 cupolas, 2 winding-engines and 70 coke-ovens.

After the bankruptcy proceedings, a new partnership, R. P. Lemon & Co., re-opened the works in 1851, with a Mr. Buckland as manager of 81 coke ovens besides the 3 blast furnaces. At its peak the Maesteg Iron Works employed 500 to 600 workmen. In 1856 it had 15 levels in production. Mr. Buckland was looked upon as a benefactor as he gave £2 a week towards the poor.

After working spasmodically from 1860 onwards, the works were sold to the Llynvi, Tondu and Ogmore Coal and Iron Co. with which the Brogdens were connected. By 1873 the last furnace had been 'blown out', never again to be re-lit. However, the mineral resources were fully exploited to supply the Llynvi Iron Works (the New Works), as, in 1872, the two undertakings were owned by the Brogdens.

22. The Llynvi Iron Works (the New Works)

In 1830 William Griffiths of Coegnant leased to James H. Allen of Neath 285 acres of land in the upper part of the valley for ninety-nine years at £250 per annum plus a royalty of 6d a ton for ironstone. Allen first opened two levels, one on the mountain side and the other at Tywith (later called Nantyffyllon) known as Lefel y Gwter.

In his essay on 'The Geology of the Llynfi Valley (*Y Berllan*, 1869), David Bowen (Cynwyd) tells us that workmen discovered in the black-band seam, between two rocks in the Spelters level, a live frog of ordinary size. It hopped out of its craggy cell, but, on being exposed to the air, died almost immediately.

On the land leased by William Griffiths, James H. Allen proceeded to build four furnaces and a calciner for the production of spelter (zinc). It was at this time that the pollution of the River Llynfi began. The works were near Metcalf Street, Caerau (then called Spelters). Spelter or zinc ore was brought from Porthcawl to the Llynfi Valley, where there was plenty of timber and coal for smelting. The zinc was then returned to Porthcawl for shipping.

Allen observed that the valley was rich enough in minerals to support a second iron works. He formed a partnership which acquired fifty-three acres of N•ntycrynwydd Farm, Maesteg, on which the works were built. Apart from land which the partnership had leased at Tŷ-gwyn-bach, Tywith, from Mr. Treharne of Coetrehen, land was bought at Nant-y-ffyrling (later called Nantyffyllon) from William Thomas of Maescadlawr Farm, Llangynwyd, and at Garnwen (Nantyffyrling) from Lord Adare. In 1837 the partnership paid a man £40 to report on the possibilities of industrial development in the valley but unfortunately the money was spent on drink. In 1839 C. R. M. Talbot leased to the partnership 260 acres for ninety-nine years at £71 per annum plus mineral royalties of 7d a ton. Ultimately Allen sold his Spelter works and his Coegnant lease to the partnership for £25,000.

In 1838 C. R. M. Talbot cut the first sod for the building of the new Iron Works, then called the Llynvi Vale Iron Works. The first furnace was 'blown in' on 12 October, 1839, the second in 1840, the third in 1846 and the fourth in 1850.

A Joint Stock Company was formed in 1844 and the Works became known as the Llynvi Iron Company. On 17 June 1845 the foundation stone of the Forge Works was laid and the Forge undertaking commenced operations on 10 February 1846. The weekly wages bill was then £1,000. In 1852 the Company was re-formed and called the Llynvi Vale Iron Co. with a capital of £120,000. The weekly output in 1853 from the three furnaces was 400 tons.

By 1856 the Company controlled 4 blast-furnaces, 28 puddling furnaces, 2 squeezers, 2 pair of rolls, 4 mills and their requisites, 10 steam engines, 14 levels on Garnwen Mountain and 12 at Coegnant, 2 patches, 9 smithies employing about 20 workmen and 3 carpenters' shops with 14 workmen. The brickyard manufactured 17,000 bricks weekly. There were also a pattern-make shop employing 5 workmen, 107 coke furnaces and over 100 horses. In all, about 1,500 men and women were employed.

43 Taken from the Illustrated London News of July 15th 1858 this magnificent print shows the following (left to right) Llynfi Iron Works (Gwaith Newydd) with the blast engine-house (Corn Stores), Nant-y-Crynwydd Farm, Bryant's Pond (Works Reservoir). In the background are Cavan Row (formerly Cambrian Row), Talbot Terrace (formerly Puddler's Row), Zoar Chapel, Castle Hotel, Plasnewydd House; in the foreground are Llynfi Lodge (formerly Bowrington Lodge), with the New Works School (formerly Bowrington School) adjacent

In 1866 the Company's capital was increased to £300,000 and the name changed to the Llynvi Coal and Iron Co. Ltd. Despite the intervening industrial depression there were still 4 blast furnaces, 54 puddling furnaces and 6 mills operating in 1871. In 1872 all the assets of the Maesteg and Llynvi Iron Works were sold to the Brogden syndicate and included in the assets of the new Company, called the Llynvi, Tondu and Ogmore Coal and Iron Company, with a capital of £550,000 and with Alexander Brogden as Chairman. It still controlled 7 furnaces in Maesteg. The national coal strike of 1873 resulted in the liquidation of the Brogden Company.

In 1878 a receiver was appointed and he reconstructed the Company under yet another name, the Llynvi and Tondu Coal and Iron Co. Ltd. It opened two collieries — Park Slip, Tondu, and Coegnant, Nantyffyllon. This Company ultimately failed in 1886 and iron-making in the Llynfi Valley came to an end that year. Unemployed iron workers set up a relief fund and were allowed to pick coal from the tips. On 14 April 1886, it was reported that 250 tons of iron rails were lying at the Llynvi Works, being 16 lbs. to 20 lbs. to the yard and £3.5.0. a ton. All this was bought by a Mr. Buckley of Walsall, Stafford. After 1870 iron was replaced by steel for making sheets for tinplating and galvanising, the Iron Works having failed to modernise to meet competition.

In 1889 North's Navigation Collieries (1889) Ltd. took over what was left of the iron industry for £250,000 and thereafter concentrated on coal production.

There is hardly any trace to-day of the Maesteg Iron Works (the Old Works), but the numerous tips on the slopes of Garnwen Mountain, where men and women had dug for coal and iron ore over a century ago for the Llynvi Iron Works (the New Works) still tower above the Maesteg Park to the north of the Maesteg Hospital, although some of the lower tips facing the Park are now being removed to make room for housing and other developments. The green coating of nature that hitherto adorned the landscape had helped to offset the otherwise drab reminder of the past. The site of the Llynvi Works and particularly of the Forge can be seen to advantage by looking down at the valley from the verge of the Maesteg Park. A derelict railway line (the former P.T.R.) separates it from the Maesteg R.F.C. football ground. The corn stores and the adjoining derelict buildings, including Nant-y-crwydd, were allowed to remain through the efforts of conservationists, local and national. Nant-y-crwydd, however was demolished in 1981.

Incidentally, Garnwen Mountain supplied fire-clay for the making of bricks, and also surrendered its loose stones on its rocky summit for the Llynvi Works and for the building of houses for the workmen. In 1856 there were 14 levels and 1 pit in production on Mynydd-y-Garnwen.

44　This early coloured sketch of *c.* 1865 shows the three enormous blast furnaces of the Troedyrhiw Garth Iron Works (opened 1847), with the engine-house extreme right. The Works were situated on the site of the present Maesteg Celtic Social Club. The lifts between the furnaces were each capable of thirty trips an hour, moving four tons of material each trip. The platforms were suspended by two of the company's patent galvanised wire ropes. On the left Llwydarth Cottages can just be seen. *Artist unknown.*

23. Tondu Iron Works

In 1846 Sir Robert Price owned these works. Much of the ore used was obtained at the Bryndefaid Farm on Garth Mountain. It was conveyed to an old weigh-house at Llwyndyrus Farm, Llangynwyd, and taken therefrom to Tondu. Sir Robert sold his controlling interest, including his interest in the Llynvi Iron Works, to Messrs. John Brogden & Co. of Sale, Manchester, in 1853. In 1863, they took out a new lease of Cae-cwarel and Tywith on the slopes of Pwll-yr-iwrch Mountain, and raised much coal. The Brogdens controlled the works for ten years with James Barrow as the mining engineer of the Company. After approximately eight years a receiver, John Joseph Smith, was appointed. Two years later he floated a new company, the Llynvi & Tondu Co. Ltd. The venture was bought by Norths in 1889 and modernised, but it failed and was closed in 1896. It appears that few men from the Llynfi Valley worked at the Tondu Iron Works.

24. Garth Iron Works

Two furnaces were 'blown in' by Messrs. Malins and Rawlinson on Easter Monday, 17 April 1847. The works engineer was a Mr. Stanton. The undertaking was mainly designed by Lewis A. Williams, the Company's mining engineer and surveyor. The site of the works was about half a mile south of Maesteg Isaf Farm. There were also 30 coke ovens, an engine house, 27 houses for workmen and 2 engines. In all, 9 levels were opened. A third furnace was built but never 'blown in' as the Company became bankrupt in the fifties of the last century. The officials were blamed, as some were found carrying 2 or 3 bottles of wine to work. There were also deficiencies in the weighing scales. The furnaces were 'blown out' and never re-lit. The site is now occupied by the Celtic Social Club and has been converted into playing fields. Incidentally, the Parish Rate Book for 1849 discloses the existence of the Galvanised Iron Co. at Garth, naming the owners as John Cole, David Francis and William Francis.

In 1856 Messrs. Sheppard & Matthews built a blast furnace at Ffos Farm, near Cwmdu, half a mile to the east of Maesteg Isaf Farm. The undertaking included four levels and several coke ovens. The works closed after a few months owing to financial difficulties and came into the hands of R. P. Lemon & Co., who also fell on bad times and became insolvent. The engines were removed to Pontardawe.

In all, 20 blast furnaces were built along the tramway line running through the valley between 1826 and 1861. They included 3 at the Maesteg (Old) Iron Works, 4 at the Llynvi (New) Iron Works, 3 at Garth, 1 at Ffos (near Cwmdu) and 2 at Tondu.

Much helpful information is contained in an article by Henry John on 'The Iron Industry of Maesteg in the nineteenth century' (*The Journal of the S.E. Wales Industrial Archaeological Society*, Vol. 2, No. 2) in which the author also acknowledges his indebtedness to Arthur J. Flint, Caerphilly. There was also an interesting article on the Maesteg Iron Industry, 'From making Iron to making Saints' in *The Dragon*, the magazine of the Steel Company of Wales. Facts relating to the Industry are also given in Cadrawd's *History of the Parish of Llangynwyd, 1887*. An informative account of 'John Brogden & Sons, Industrial Pioneers in Mid Glamorgan' written by Leonard S. Higgins, Porthcawl, appeared in *Glamorgan Historian*, Vol. 10, 1974, giving details of their involvement in the Llynfi Valley industrial scene.

Since writing this chapter, a useful account of the industrial past of the valley by Dr. Graham Humphreys, a native of Maesteg, has appeared in the commemorative booklet published in May 1981 on the occasion of the centenary celebrations of the opening of the Maesteg Town Hall.

25. The Llynfi Valley Tramroad, Railway &c.

In 1816 a plan prepared by Pinkerton and Allen, Civil Engineers, was published by Samuel Bartley, Carmarthen, indicating an intended line of tramroad from the Turnpike Road leading from Ewenny to Neath along 'Blaen Llanvy in the Parish of Llangenoyd through the several of Coyty Lower, Coyty Higher, St. Bride's Minor, Llaleston and Llangenoyd'. The 'deposited' original is in the Glamorgan Record Office, refce: 'Q/DP 17'.

However, it was obvious that the Llynfi Valley could not develop commercially without an outlet to the sea for the coal and iron produced therein. The original intention was to construct a tramroad from Spelters (later developed as Caerau) to Aberogwr beyond Bridgend. This did not materialise owing to the objection of Sir John Nicholl, M.P., of Merthyr Mawr, a shareholder in the venture. He contended that the proposed tramroad would adversely affect the amenities of his home. It was consequently diverted to reach Pwll-y-cawl (Porthcawl) via Tondu, a distance of nearly 17 miles. It was intended to connect with the sea the iron works and collieries at Maesteg, the iron and brickworks and collieries at Tregunter Park, near Cefn Cribwr and the limestone quarries at Cornelly.

The tramroad was constructed under a private Act of Parliament of 1825 because the people living on the coast did not want the inconvenience caused by the smelting of the iron ore brought from Cornwall. So it was decided to have the smelting done inland in the Llynfi Valley where the raw materials were to hand.

From the Spelters terminus, near the present Caerau Square, the tramroad proceeded south through Nantyffyllon, (then called Tywith), along the Forge, being the site of the Llynvi Iron Works, passing the site now known as the Maesteg Football Field, along Commercial Street (then known as Bowrington Street), and then on to Llwyndyrys, Greenmeadow, Cornhwch (the Cefn Ydfa Lodge), Coetrehen, Kenfig Hill, 'Smokey Cot' Weighbridge, Pyle, Nottage and finally to Porthcawl Docks, which were built by 1828. The cost, approximately £60,000, was found from the original capital. The name given to the tramroad was The Duffryn Llynvi and Porthcawl Railway. The engineer was John Hodgkinson, from Newport, Monmouthshire.

Building operations commenced in 1826 and the line was opened for traffic in 1828. The trams in trains were horse-drawn but the public were allowed to use the road, subject to certain regulations. Sometimes an enterprising workman would purchase a tram and horse in order to trade along the tramway to Aberkenfig and Porthcawl and Stormy. Private trams were used by common carriers. The tramroad formed the principal link between Maesteg and the outer world.

It remained as such until 1855 when Acts had been passed to transform it into a railway operated by steam locomotive engines from Tywith to Bridgend and Porthcawl. The first sod was cut in 1858 and the railway officially opened in 1861. It had been constructed under the direct control of James Brogden, the old tramroad being transferred for £92,520. The new railway ran from Spelters to Tondu and the old tramroad to Porthcawl became derelict. Spelter or zinc ore for smelting was brought in ships from Cornwall and carried along the old railway track to the Llynfi Valley — where there was an abundance of timber and coal.

The railway line became available for passengers in 1864. The cost of travelling in open trucks to Porthcawl was a penny per person. The

45   Schedule of tolls payable on the Llynvi Valley Railway

passengers were often entertained in song by local characters such as Shoni Puddler of John Street, Nantyffyllon. These excursions, however primitive, caused much enjoyment and merriment in what was otherwise a drab life.

The Great Western Railway took over control in 1873, and in the same decade the railway line was extended through a tunnel to Cymer and Abergwynfi. It was finally closed in June 1970.

An exhibition catalogue prepared by the Kenfig Hill and District Music and Art Society in 1968 states that a book describing the tramroad and the events in its history was then in course of preparation by the Society. The catalogue contains a helpful map of 'The Duffryn Llynvi and Porthcawl Railway and The Bridgend Railway, 1825-1860'. All papers resulting from the thorough researches of the Society have been handed to the National Museum of Wales.

In August 1969 a plaque was unveiled at the Porthcawl Slipway by Mr. John Blundell on behalf of the Society commemorating the restoration (or re-discovery) of the track of the railway (1825-1860). Another plaque was unveiled by Sir Cennydd Traherne in April 1970 on a wall at Quarella Road, Bridgend, at the terminus of the Bridgend Railway, a horse-drawn tramroad which ran for 5 miles through Aberkenfig to join the Duffryn Llynvi and Porthcawl Railway at Cwm Ffoes (Ffos). The project and research work had been carried out by a group of twenty members of the Kenfig Hill and District Society led by Mr. Arthur J. Flint and Mr. Bryn James and known as the 'Tramroaders'. Helpful information is provided by Mr. Flint in his article on the railway in *Morgannwg*, Vol. XIII, 1969.

In September 1971, during the Maesteg Civic Week, through the efforts of the Maesteg Historical and Preservation Society, led by the brothers Dr. Lyn and Trefor Jones, acting jointly with the sister Society from Kenfig Hill, a plaque set in a stone structure adjoining the Maesteg car park was unveiled by the Maesteg Council Chairman (Councillor Dilwyn Jones). Mr. A. J. Flint presented the Maesteg Council with a set of maps of the project and maps showing how the terminus had been located at Spelters (Caerau). The site of the plaque was chosen as more people were likely to see it in the town centre than on the actual site of the terminus near the present Caerau Square.

To remind us of our industrial past, the brothers Lyn and Trefor Jones rescued from a Swindon scrap yard and restored a Pannier tank railway engine, which was later used occasionally for trips for children in aid of local charities.

As Porthcawl had become inadequate to handle all the coal from the valley (north of Cwmdu) and was developing as a seaside resort, it became necessary to have an outlet to Port Talbot. By an Act of Parliament in 1894 a new railway was sanctioned. A dock on a nine-acre site was to be built at Port Talbot and connected with the Llynfi Valley by means of what became later known as the Port Talbot Railway (P.T.R.). The railway line began to operate in 1898 and carried 2,000 to 3,000 passengers in the first week. A profit of £2,000 was made in the first year, whilst the expenditure in 1912 was only a third of the income. However, only 6% of the income came from passenger traffic.

The Port Talbot Docks were completed in 1901. After the first World War, the P.T.R. amalgamated with the Great Western Railway, but owing to the industrial depression of the thirties, when coal exports were halved, passenger service from Maesteg to the Garw Valley ceased on 12 September 1932 thereby closing Cwmdu, Llety Brongu and Betws stations to passengers. The service to Port Talbot, via Bryn, ceased in September 1933.

An informative book on the Port Talbot Railway was published by Mr. S. Richards of Norwich early in 1978, whilst much information can be

46   Maesteg Castle Street (old) Station *c.*1892, when the fountain froze. Fourth from left is William Akehurts who was stationmaster for over 50 years from 1861

47   Llety Brongu Station in 1949

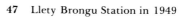

gleaned from *The Railways of Mid-Glamorgan*, part of an M.A. thesis by Thomas Bevan of Bridgend written in 1928.

Incidentally, as far back as 1865, Thomas C. Watkins of Nantyffyllon won a prize at an Aberafan eisteddfod for an essay on the proposed railway from Aberafan to Mynydd y Caerau, Cwmcorrwg and Maesteg.

26. The Truck Shop

One undesirable feature of the iron industry was the truck shop system. The employees were customers of the Company shops by compulsion, and very often by threat. The system was initiated fifteen years after the men had been paid regularly in cash. They were expected to take their paper money to the shop.

Sometimes the workman had to wait nine weeks before being paid and had only the Company shop from which to draw goods. The account was settled by deducting it from his wages and the balance paid to the workman. These shops traded in groceries, drapery, footware, ironmongery, meat, and other domestic goods.

48   Sir Robert Price's old Company Shop and buildings. Situated on top of Derllwyn Hill, Tondu, near the Dyffryn Llynvi-Porthcawl tram line

Very often after pay day (usually a Saturday) work was not resumed until the following Tuesday or Wednesday or sometimes for a week. Intemperate workmen exchanged goods for beer in the overcrowded public houses and there would be much street fighting.

If a young man had no money to get married, he induced the Vicar of the Parish, then the Rev. R. Pendril Llewelyn, to accept, in place of fees, goods drawn on account in the truck shop, the passbook being left with the Vicar. The bridegroom would give notice that the shop book was lost and that if it were found and presented at the shop, it was to be retained — with no goods supplied to the finder.

There were three Company shops, one owned by the Maesteg Iron Works (the Old Works), situated near the Coetrehen Arms in the district called Garnlwyd. The other two were owned by the Llynfi Iron Works (the New Works), one being at the rear of the Cambrian Inn in the area known as the Forge, and the other higher up the valley near Coegnant Colliery in the Spelters district. It appears that for a short period a truck shop operated at the top of Brick Row, Maesteg, for the employees of the Llwydarth Tinplate Works.

There was much agitation against the system. A William Howells opened a shop at the lower end of Commercial Street and fought for freedom for workman and trader. However the fight was unequal and he emigrated to the U.S.A.

In 1842, four local petitions were submitted to Parliament. They were included in the 28th Report of the Select Committee of the House of Commons on 30 May of that year. The first petition in favour of the abolition of the truck shop system was signed by 120 persons. The second, in the name of a Mr. Farrand, was signed by eighty-four 'workmen of Maesteg'.

The second petition was signed by John Hopkins, Thomas Price, and John Rees. The petitioners stated that they had heard with regret that an honourable member of the House (presumably Dr. John Bowring) had been 'down this neighbourhood' to seek evidence to prove that the local workmen were in favour of the 'truck system' and had learned with sorrow that both companies (i.e., the Maesteg and Llynvi Iron Works) had drawn up petitions to the House of Commons stating that they were 9 miles from any market and that the truck shops were considered a great accommodation rather than a baneful curse. The petitioners prayed for the total extirpation of 'this tyrannical system'. All those employees who had signed the petition in favour of the system had done so from fear of being expelled from the works, and many had been compelled to do so in absolute opposition to their own convictions. By doing so, they had violated a most sacred principle of justice and morality.

The petitioners averred that although there was no local market, they could buy their goods locally 15% cheaper than at the truck shops. Even if they could not get their necessities locally, they would prefer to have the produce of their hard labour in their own hands, with liberty to make use of the nearest and cheapest market. This they demanded as of their own right. They considered the truck shops as a most crying evil and earnestly requested the House to pass immediately a more stringent measure 'to put down for ever this abominable system'.

On the other hand, the two petitions in favour of payment in goods instead of money bore 198 and 125 signatures respectively — 323 in all.

The first petition, signed 25 May 1842, was in the name of Dr. John Bowring and was submitted on behalf of the workmen employed by the Cambrian Iron and Spelter Co. at their works at Maesteg. It was signed by Thomas Fearn, David Sims, and Lewis Lewis. It stated that the petitioners had for several years been supplied with provisions and other necessities from the Company's shop at the Works and that the Works were 9 miles away from the nearest town. The district was at first thinly inhabited and destitute of shops of any kind. It was unable to supply the wants of so many people suddenly collected together. Supplies from the Company's stores at the Works were indispensable for the support and comfort of the employees. The benefit of the stores continued to be felt in the salutary check and protection afforded against high charges of speculators and the introduction of inferior quality goods.

The petitioners had heard with feelings of great alarm of the charges about to be submitted to the Committee, tending to influence the House so as to bridge or altogether deprive the petitioners of the advantages they then enjoyed by causing a stoppage of the shop supplies or otherwise causing a greater difficulty in obtaining them. The petitioners, 'fully impressed of the falsity and perfectly convinced of the utter groundlessness of such charges', prayed to be heard by being allowed to produce evidence in defence of the present mode of payment which they justly esteemed in their case to be a privilege and an advantage.

The second petition in favour of the truck shop system was signed by workmen employed at the Maesteg Iron Works (the Old Works).

Mr. David Davies, in his book *Tŷ'r Llwyni*, quotes from a report in *The Cambrian*, 2 October 1846, the rapturous welcome given to Dr. Bowring when he visited Maesteg in 1846. He was presented with a silver salver by workmen, tradesmen and others interested in the prosperity of the Llynfi Valley. The salver was inscribed with these words: 'A testimonial of their esteem and gratitude for the indefatigable exertions in obtaining means of communication with the locality by locomotive and also for having led the way to free trade in this district by abolishing the truck act system at the Llynvi Iron Works.'

If Dr. Bowring had abolished the system at his Llynvi Iron Works, we can only conclude that although he had sponsored a petition for its retention in 1842, he had changed his mind by 1845-46. The Maesteg people would hardly have presented him with a silver salver had he adhered to his previous intention to support the system.

What became of the four petitions to Parliament in 1842? We can only conclude that no action was taken at the time.

We recall that the Truck Act of 1831 enacted that hired artificers were to be paid in current coin. There was to be no stipulation in the hiring agreement as to the manner in which wages should be expended. The Act declared payment in goods to be illegal. However, it was not until the passing of the Truck Amendment Act, 1887, that the provisions of the 1831 Act were extended to apply not merely to artificers, but also to any workmen as defined by the Employers and Workmen Act, 1875 — and they included labourers, servants in husbandry, journeymen, artificers, handcraftsmen, miners, and others engaged in manual labour. It was in 1887 that the truck shop system for *all* manual workers became illegal.

Did Dr. Bowring actually abolish the system voluntarily in his own Works? It was certainly in operation up to 1849 when he severed his connection with the Llynvi Works. We are told that the Company shops were finally dismantled about 1870-71. The utensils, including the big flour bins, were taken to the Bowrington shop at Bridgend, but the smaller ones were for some years in Ferrier's shop next to the Castle Hotel, Maesteg. At that time the Maesteg Iron Works had been closed for many years whilst the Llynvi Iron Works (formerly owned by Dr. Bowring) was then languishing. It was obvious that the trade recession had affected the Company shops.

In any case, the abolition of the system led to the day of the small shopkeeper, who could bid for a fairer share in the prosperity and business life of the valley.

27. New Societies

The coming of industries to the valley gave rise to a spate of various societies. The only Order of truly Welsh origin was that of the Iforiaid (Ivorites) founded in Wrexham in 1836. It had much influence and popularity in Mid Glamorgan. Its publications in the fifties of the last century contained many articles on the principles of the Society and detailed reports of the lodge meetings. The Order derived its name from Ifor Hael (Ivor the Generous), who was an ancestor of Lord Tredegar. Unity, love and truth were the avowed basic principles, together with the fostering of the use of the Welsh language.

An essay on the principles of the Ivorites by John Thomas of Cwmafan was awarded a prize at an Ivorites' Eisteddfod on 23 June 1853, held in the Market Place, Aberafan, and attended by 3,000 to 4,000 people. The works at Aberafan, Cwmafan and Taibach were idle for the day. Professor Glanmor Williams has written an informative account of Friendly Societies in Glamorgan (*B.B.C.S.*, November 1959) whilst D. T. Eaton, in his account of local Friendly Societies, mentions the Loyal Order of Alfreds (English and Welsh) of the Loyal Streams of Love, Lodge No. 37 of the Cwmafan District in 1887.

At Llangynwyd there was a Friendly Society of Women and on its behalf the then Vicar, the Rev. John Parry (treasurer), William Parry (Clerk of the Parish of Newcastle) and William David of the Old House, Llangynwyd entered into a bond for £200 with John Wood (Clerk of the Peace of the County of Glamorgan) in 1812 to keep the rules of the Society.

The Swan Inn, Maesteg, was the headquarters of the local branch of the 'Order of True Ivorites'. Members of 'Lles y Corff' (The Physical Benefit) of the Order assembled annually, and the procession would leave the Swan Inn for Carmel Welsh Congregational Church, Maesteg, to attend a service conducted by the minister, the Rev. William Morgan. The procession was often joined by the Aberafan Lodge which included about eighty women members. The women, marching two abreast, were dressed in the colourful regalia of the Order — with beaver hats, green shawls and pink ribands. The loyal toasts were much in evidence.

The Newton Nottage Lodge of Porthcawl boasted 240 lady members in 1848. Members paid 1/- a month and 1/- extra on the death of a husband or member. The sum of £10 was paid to a member on a death in his family.

As far back as 15 September 1838, amended rules for the 'good order and government' of the 'Benefit Society of Gentlemen, Farmers, Tradesmen and Others' were agreed upon at a general meeting under the auspices of the Maesteg Iron Works and held at the Coetrehen Arms, then occupied by a William Richards. The Society was established on 20 June 1827, in the eighth year of the reign of George IV. The amended rules were sworn by William Davies (Secretary) on 28 December 1838, before a Justice of the Peace. The rules governed the sickness fund for the maintenance and mutual relief of members in sickness, old age and infirmity. In order to establish a Raising Fund, each member had to pay 1/4d every four weeks and 2d for the use of the rooms, fire and candles.

The Benefit Society held its annual meetings at the Coetrehen Arms, and they were followed by sumptuous dinners. However, after an annual meeting on 5 July 1843, the members had to return home dinnerless owing to the depression in the iron trade and the consequent reduction in wages together with 'the obnoxious Truck Act'.

The *Cardiff and Merthyr Guardian* of 12 September 1846 reports a procession of three female clubs in the valley. One proceeded from the Odd-fellows Arms on Saturday, 29 August, whilst the other two took place on the following Monday from the Star Hotel and Coetrehen Arms respectively. They were numerously attended. One of these Clubs owned a house in Bowrington Street, Maesteg, in 1849. The same paper also reported that five new benefit societies had been established within the valley during the previous twelve months. Thomas Morgan (Llyfnwy) stated in 1856 that twenty-four such societies had been formed in Maesteg.

49   The Coetrehen Arms, Garnlwyd, photographed in the early years of this
century

The societies invariably met at the local public houses. The 'Llygad y
Dydd' Society met at the Red Cow Inn, Maesteg. The 'Grand United Order
of Oddfellows' met at the Dunraven Hotel, Bridgend and the 'Royal Order
of the Hampton Lodge' at the Swan Hotel, Maesteg, under the leadership of
the works manager. Among other societies were the 'Ancient Order of
Foresters', which met at the White Lion Hotel, Maesteg, and of which the
Revs. W. Morgan (Carmel) and W. Watkins (Saron) were prominent
members; the Faithful Friend Society; the Ivorites; the Friend in Need; the
Druids; the R.A.O.B; the St. David's Lodge; and the Man in the Wilderness
Lodge No. 14 of the Alfred Friendly Society. The local farmers formed a
club known as Clwb y Doctor and entertained their local doctor to dinner on
Saturday nights from time to time at the Old House, Llangynwyd.

Apart from Friendly Societies, other clubs were formed in the valley, e.g.,
the Firemen's Club in 1847 for the Llynvi and Garth iron workers.

With the advent of the welfare state, the need for mutual helpfulness
became less necessary and resulted in the elimination of the Societies that
were ostensibly formed for aiding the sick and the poor. Public-house life
yielded ultimately to club life, which received its first impetus on the
opening of the Glamorganshire Working Men's Club at 14 Bridge Street,
Maesteg, on 27 January 1885.

In order to help those who wanted assistance to purchase their own
houses, the Maesteg Building Society was formed in 1857. Later we hear of
the Caerau Building Society, the Central Glamorgan Permanent Building

Society and the Llynfi Building Society. The smaller Societies have been superseded by the national ones, some of which have branch offices locally.

Insurance offices later sprang up and in 1871 there were local representatives of Companies such as the Accidental, North British and Mercantile Fire, Provincial Fire and Life, Sovereign Life and Whittington Life, apart from the better known Companies such as the Prudential, Britannic, Pearl, and Refuge. There is now no local insurance office in the Maesteg Valley. Most have been removed to Bridgend.

28. Female Labour

A feature of the early Industrial Revolution was the employment of women in arduous work at the colliery pit head. Some were of tender years. There is also evidence of women working at the coal face in the Llynfi Valley. In an article by Jayne Isaac (*Glamorgan Gazette*, 3 October 1975) we are told that women were extensively employed underground in the Afan Valley at one time, mainly for loading and hauling coal in baskets on their backs or by dragging trams along the roads. In his *History of Llangynwyd Parish*, Cadrawd tells us that when James Barrow became manager of Tychwith Colliery, owned by Brogdens, in 1864, there were always from 10 to 12 women employed underground, chiefly at the pumps and filling coal. In the early part of this century women were employed on the screens at the local collieries.

A party of trippers from Oxford visited the Maesteg Iron Works in 1836 and saw the process of iron-making. They noticed that the limestone had to be broken in pieces, the work being done by women. In fact, men, women and children — about 400 in all — were employed at the old (Maesteg) Iron Works. It is also known that women were engaged in all weather in digging for iron ore in the 'black band' seam of one of the patches near Ton-hir, between Maesteg and Bryn. They also filled, pushed and pulled trams of coal at patches nearby, and worked at the washeries and at the brickworks in upper Maesteg near the former surgery of Dr. Henry Sinclair. The bricks were baked by them in a kind of bread tin. A Mary Lanan(?) from Ireland was known as a skilled brickmaker. She also attended upon skilled masons and lived near South Parade, Maesteg.

There is a tradition that a Sarah Bowen (later Mrs. John Isaac) of Tŷ'n Cornel was the first woman checkweigher in Wales. She was the grandmother of Tudor Isaac, former Maesteg Council Surveyor. She weighed the coal at Tywith Colliery for Lord Dunraven. Tŷ'n Cornel was then a thatched cottage on the road leading from Cross Inn, (Cwmcerdin) at Cwmfelin to the Red Cow Inn. In the seventies of the last century, Sarah Bowen and a

Nancy Samuel were employed as rubbish tippers at Cwmdu. They were looked upon as knights of the yard and of the lodge at the mouth of the lower level. Even the overman (a William Llewelyn) and the master haulier (Dai o'r Garth) were subject to their control. Spitting in the lodge meant immediate expulsion. Screen work, banking, and black band cleaning were done by women.

According to Angela John (*By the Sweat of their Brow — Women Workers at the Victorian Coal Mines*, 1980), South Wales had the highest rate of women surface-workers at coal, iron, shale and clay mines. The number was halved by 1890. There were women hauliers at the Abergorki Colliery in 1880. In 1886 the Tredegar Iron & Coal Company employed over 200 women.

Women as well as men worked in the early days of Caerau Colliery. They worked a full eight-hour shift of picking coal on the screens and were paid according to the amount of coal they were able to retrieve.

However, J. Boyd Harvey, who was general manager of North's Collieries from 1889 to 1912, would not employ any women or girls in or about the local collieries.

The International Labour Organisation in 1939 declared that underground work for women was absolutely forbidden in every country, whilst the Mines and Quarries Act of 1954 was the last major mines legislation to reconfirm the ban on women miners below ground.

29. Local Tragedies

General

The Llynfi Valley can consider itself fortunate in having escaped major catastrophies that have beset other parts of Glamorgan.

It was subject to outbreaks of Asiatic cholera in 1832, 1849 and 1866, but the toll of lives was not unduly severe. It certainly caused people to become Church members, and it is on record that during the 1866 outbreak, the increase in membership of three Welsh Congregational Churches was thus: Carmel, Maesteg — 185; Soar, Maesteg — 187; Siloh, Nantyffyllon — 130.

Although the valley has never experienced great floods involving loss of life, we find that the Rev. T. Cunllo Griffiths, Maesteg, wrote a poem published in *Lloffion y Beirdd* (Gleanings of the Poets) in 1879 on 'Gorlifiad y Llyfnwy a'r Ogwr' (The Overflowing of the Rivers Llynfi and Ogmore), August, 1877. However, the district escaped the ravages of war-time bombing. It has no colour problem and anti-Semitism is unknown.

In his essay on the Geology of the Llynfi Valley (*Y Berllan*, 1869), David Bowen (Cynwyd), the Maesteg essayist, mentions a conflagration at Gwaun-y-dyffryn Level, Maesteg, in 1772. A stock of coal caught fire and the few available men failed to put out the fire. It was said that people in the Vale of Glamorgan could perceive signs of the fire as the flames had assumed such menacing proportions. In those days the event was considered a 'terrible' accident although there was no loss of life.

On 29 October 1868, at 10.40 p.m., there was a slight earthquake which affected the lower part of the Maesteg Valley. According to the *Cardiff and Neath Guardian*, 7 November 1868, the earthquake was described as a shaking or trembling of the earth. The houses were 'accompanied by a sub-terranean booming noise somewhat resembling the rumbling noise of a heavy carrier on the high road'. The shock, which lasted only a few seconds, did no damage, and there was no loss of life. The same paper referred to a similar earthquake in Ireland on 24 October, 1868, which occurred at Cork County Mallow. According to a witness at North's Offices, Maesteg, an earthquake shock took place on 27 June 1906, when the offices appeared to 'heave over'. The witness felt himself being lifted and pitched forward as if through the window. There were no casualties nor was there damage to property.

Industrial Fatalities

On 8 April, 1847, four men were killed, three of them under a 'clamp' in the Old (Maesteg) Iron Works at Maesteg and one in the New (Llynvi) Iron Works. At the Llynvi Iron Works, on another occasion, a quantity of boiling lava became separated from the load in transit and buried two men, a Welshman and an Irishman.

During the construction work on the Caerau-Cymer railway tunnel, which was completed in 1877, thirteen men lost their lives on 21 April 1876, one of them being David Hitchings, the precentor of Salem Welsh Baptist Church, Nantyffyllon. A survivor stated that he saw a man named Parsons, one of those killed, preparing the dynamite with a candle close by. It was assumed that the candle had fallen over and had ignited the fuse. Parsons and another named Weeks were blown to pieces. Only a pair of feet and a rib were found. It was stated that there was a terrible stench of rotting flesh in the tunnel for weeks after the explosion.

The most serious mining fatality was the explosion on 26 August 1892 at the Park Slip Colliery, Tondu (owned by North's Navigation Co.), a little beyond the lower reaches of the Llynfi Valley. The 110 men who died were mainly from Penyfai and Aberkenfig and included five brothers of the Lyddon family of Aberkenfig. The colliery was re-opened in 1895, closed in 1904 and re-opened again for a short period during the first World War.

Within the Llynfi Valley the losses have been comparatively slight as compared with the mining tragedies of Senghennydd, and the Rhondda. At least two valley men were killed at Senghennydd — Reuben Hughes of Maesteg and Gwilym Rees of Nantyffyllon.

THE COLLIERY DISASTER AT ABERKENFIG, SOUTH WALES.

FROM SKETCHES BY OUR SPECIAL ARTIST.

GENERAL VIEW OF NORTH'S NAVIGATION COMPANY'S COLLIERIES, INCLUDING THE PARK SLIP COLLIERY.

CARRYING AWAY THE DEAD.

THE HOME SECRETARY VISITING THE HOUSE OF HENRY WHITE.

ENTRANCE TO THE PARK SLIP COLLIERY: BRINGING UP THE LAST MAN ALIVE.

50 Extensive coverage from 'The London Illustrated News' of 3 September 1892 of the terrible Park Slip Colliery disaster of 26 August 1892 when 112 miners were killed

No. 10.—*To be retained in book for reference.*

COAL MINES REGULATION ACT, 1887.

NOTICE OF ACCIDENT.

Postal address *Coegnaut*
Maesteg

Date *June 19* 18*95*

Sir,

In terms of " The Coal Mines Regulation Act, 1887," I beg to send intimation of an accident, particulars of which are as follows :—

Date of Accident *June 19, 1895* hour *1. 0 p.m.*
Name of Colliery *Coegnaut* Name of Pit *Coegnaut*
Where situate—Parish *Llangynwyd* County *Glamorgan*
Name of Firm or Owner *North's Navigation Coy Ld*
do.   Seam or Place where accident occurred *9 ft Seam*
Thickness of Seam *6."* Mode of working *Long coal*

Names of Persons Killed or Injured.	Reputed Age.	Occupation.	Number of Hours person injured or killed had been At Work when accident occurred.	Remarks—Nature of Injuries, whether serious or slight, etc.
Thomas Lewis	*34*	*Collier*	*6*	—

Circumstances under which the accident occurred*:— *This person was in the act of filling a tram when a piece of strong clod 5.0 long & 4 ft in the widest part & running to 2. " " narrowest, & about 2 ft thick fell upon him causing such serious injuries that he died before reaching his lodgings*

* *Describe as fully as possible the causes of accident and circumstances connecting therewith. This will save correspondence.*

I am, Sir, Yours faithfully,

Signed *Jenkin Jones*
(Owner [Agent] or Manager)†

† Strike out descriptions not applicable.

To *J T Robson* Esq.
H.M. Inspector of Mines.

NOTE.—That where any personal injury results in the death of the person injured, notice of the death must also be sent to the Inspector within twenty four hours.

FORM PUBLISHED BY W. M. HUTCHINGS, LONDON

51 A typical page from the 'Explosion or Accident' book of Coegnant Colliery 1891-96 which contains horrific details of maimings and deaths from roof falls, runaway trams and winding gear in days when safety clothing was quite unknown

On 26 December 1863, there was an explosion at the Gin Pit which supplied coal for the Llynfi Iron Works. The site is now within the present Maesteg Park and all traces of the pit have disappeared, the local Council in January 1923 having decided to fill the shaft with rubbish. The men had worked with naked lights (candles) and the inquest verdict was 'Accidental Death'. Fourteen lives were lost.

In 1867 there was an explosion at Garth Pit. Although no lives were lost as no-one was working therein at the time, the pit was idle for more than a year.

On 10 January 1872, as the result of an explosion at Oakwood No. 1 Colliery, eleven lives were lost and also six pit ponies. There was a further explosion at the same colliery in 1892. Many were injured but there were no deaths. A fire occurred on 6 February 1880, at the Cae'r Defaid (No. 9 workings) but there was no loss of life. The damage to machinery was not great. As the Parish of Llangynwyd once included Cymer and Blaengwynfi it would appear relevant to refer to the sinking of the Avon Pit, Blaengwynfi. On 6 September 1880 the rope broke, hurling four Irish 'navvies' to their deaths at the bottom of the pit.

An unfortunate accident occurred on 11 June 1897 at the Garth Colliery when, as the result of over-winding, the rope became dislodged from the cap. The brakes failed and the carriage hurtled to the pit bottom, resulting in the death of nine men. The remaining occupant suffered a compound fracture of his legs. Crowds gathered at the pit-head and sang Welsh hymns, including 'O fryniau Caersalem'. On 14 November 1904, four miners were killed in an accident at Maesteg Deep Level. The colliery rider was imprisoned for three months for gross negligence. The writer of these notes knew of two Nantyffyllon families where the father and two young sons were killed separately in Coegnant Colliery accidents. Scores of individual fatal accidents occurred from time to time in the local collieries. In August 1931 three men were killed at an outcrop coal level at Caerau. When an underground miner was killed it was the custom of the remaining miners in the same district to give up work for the remainder of the day.

For the period 1856-1863, the total number of deaths in Welsh mines came to 1093. The local fatalities were:

Llynfi Iron Co.	...	...	23
Tondu (Brogdens)	...	...	11
Maesteg Iron Co.	...	...	4

Professor R. L. Galloway in his Annals of Coal Mining and Coal Trade (*Colliery Guardian*, Chapter IX) has dealt fully with the problem of explosions in South Wales.

An extensive list of fatal mining accidents in South Wales in the year ended 31 December 1884 indicates that six occurred in the Llynfi Valley.

30. Strikes, Lock-outs, etc.

From the commencement of the Industrial Revolution the workmen of the Llynfi Valley, like those in other industrial valleys of Glamorgan, had to struggle for a decent existence. The conditions of employment were primitive, depressing and oppressive, whilst the wages were anything but adequate for the work performed and for the needs of the workers' families.

There was a stoppage due to shortage of materials at the Old (Maesteg) Iron Works in 1834. The furnaces were 'blown out' and were idle for thirteen weeks. There was a further stoppage due to financial troubles from 1847 to 1851, and many workmen found work at the Llynfi Iron Works (the New Iron Works).

In 1853 there was a thirteen-weeks' strike of miners against the imposition of the Company truck shop system, and two furnaces were 'blown out'. It is recorded that there were five or six 'blacklegs' but although fifteen to twenty policemen were called in, there were no incidents. Needless to say, there was no strike pay.

Alexander Dalziel has written of the colliers' strike in South Wales in 1872, its causes, progress and settlement, whilst Richard and Michael Keen have written of 'The Coal War in South Wales, 1893' (*Glamorgan Historian*, Vol. 10, 1974).

In 1873 there was a national strike of miners who were then led by Thomas Halliday. Alexander Brogden, M.P., one of the coalowners, withdrew from the Coalowners' Association, paying a heavy penalty for doing so. After a strike lasting three months, the demands of the men were granted. In 1880, 120 miners at the Maesteg Deep Colliery went on strike to claim 1/3d a ton for the coal produced, whilst the management offered 1/2d a ton. The strike was short-lived. After the sinking of the Caerau Steam Coal Pits to the six-feet seam of steam coal, a dispute arose over the price list, and resulted in a strike lasting twenty-two months.

A local strike (or perhaps a lock-out) of Llynfi Valley miners occurred on 1 November 1895 and lasted about three weeks. There was a further strike regarding wages and conditions from 31 March to 1 September 1898. Miners became very embittered as there was an attempt to starve them into submission. Some of the local colliery managers scoured the South Wales coalfield to ensure that no striker would obtain employment elsewhere. This led to some strikers resorting to the use of a false name when signing the register at the newly-found place of employment. There is reference to this strike by Lawrence John Williams in *Morgannwg*, 1965. On 29 October 1910 a further strike was declared — in the year of the Cambrian strike and the Tonypandy riots — and lasted eight weeks. In 1912 there was an extended strike resulting in much local hardship and the setting up of canteens in Chapel vestries.

The Llynfi Valley felt the full impact of the national coal strike of 1921.

After the first World War it became obvious that there would be a recession in the coal industry. Early in 1921, approximately 400 miners received notices to terminate their employment. As they had been dismissed, they became entitled to unemployment benefit. The remaining miners who came out on strike later in the year were denied such benefit. The coalowners had announced that the terms of the Sankey Award would make them bankrupt. They demanded an increase in hours and lower wages for the miners. The miners resisted by calling a strike which lasted three months, but were forced, owing to impoverished circumstances, to return to work on the coalowners' terms.

The circumstances of the 1926 strike, which had such a devastating effect on the economic and social life of the mining valleys, are too well known to require amplification. Briefly, it can be stated that because coal profits had tumbled, miners in 1926 were asked to accept a reduction in wages from 78/- a week to 46/- a week, being less than they were earning in 1914. In addition they were expected to work longer hours. The miners replied with A. J. Cook's slogan: 'Not a penny off the pay; not a second on the day'.

The general strike, which was declared on 4 May 1926, officially ended on 12 May although it was resumed the following day for a day or so. There was no local violence and no-one was killed. However, the miners stayed out for six months — to return defeated, crestfallen and dismayed, having lost the battle. The writer's father was not able to resume work until 3 December 1926.

52   Strikers digging coal at Oakwood Colliery *c.*1910

53 Siloh Canteen staff who operated during the strike in 1912

The strike resulted in soup kitchens, the digging of levels for house coal, mass emigration from the valley, and the singing of unemployed valley choirs in the provincial cities of England. Much has been written of the industrial depression in the mining valleys.

In 1921 the population of the Maesteg Urban Council area was approximately 30,000. In 1970 it was about 20,000, although there were at least 2,000 more houses in the urban area. When Ted Williams, the local M.P. attended a Maesteg Council meeting on 18 July 1931 to discuss the serious unemployment problem in the Llynfi Valley, it was stated that of the insurable population of 6,990, 3,715 were totally unemployed and 1,850 partially unemployed. When the local Council advertised for six labourers there were at least 800 applicants. As many as 110 applied for the position of lavatory attendant at the Maesteg Town Hall for a weekly wage of £2.6.0. In the East Ward of the Maesteg Urban Area in 1937, 85% of the male adult population were unemployed.

There was much dissension among the miners themselves over the question of trade-union membership. In the early days of Caerau colliery there was a strike over the rates of pay. Some miners who were not members of the miners' union continued to work. Those on strike, led by the miners' agent, Vernon Hartshorn, marched in force to the pit and a deputation was allowed to speak to the 'blacklegs', otherwise the colliery would have been rushed. The 'blacklegs' were forced out of the pit and paraded through the village. As it was a Monday morning, washing lines were raided and the victims were paraded in white shirts through the valley.

Miners were expected to pay their dues to the local lodge secretary of the South Wales Miners' Federation. Every three months there would be a 'show cards' meeting and a defaulter would be warned. If he had not paid after three warnings, he would be paraded in a white shirt through the valley with a band and the miners' agent leading the procession. Three miners were sent to jail for a month for their part in coercing the non-union miners, and the local sergeant at Nantyffyllon lost his 'stripes' for a breach of duty. Incidentally, he was the father of a police officer who ultimately became Chief Constable of Brighton. Those who were forced to parade in white shirts were looked upon as outcasts by the mining community. There has been no such parade in the valley for the last seventy years.

In July 1927 there was a strike of about 800 miners in the Maesteg district over the question of fifty colliery craftsmen belonging to the Craftsmen's Association. Within a few days the craftsmen agreed to join the miners' Union and the strike was ended.

In 1941 there was a short-lived local strike by young colliers who wanted their 'trumps' (being tips or extras payable by the miners with whom they worked) paid at the beginning of the working week.

In 1942 apprenticed miners published a pit boys' Charter, which included a demand of £1 a week increase in wages for all youths, adult pay for adult work and an assurance of a place for a youth at twenty-one. As the Greene Award thereon was unacceptable, there was a strike of youths in the Maesteg Valley and the adjoining valleys, but it only lasted a few days owing to lack of leadership among the boys.

The causes and results of the national coal strike from 9 January to 28 February 1974 are too well-known for reiteration. The strike ultimately caused the fall of the Heath Government. At Caerau, the safety men were withdrawn, contrary to Union instructions.

31. Housing during the Industrial Revolution

The Industrial Revolution of the last century meant an influx of workers from outside the valley. The housing situation became acute. There was no railway, no gas (let alone electricity) service, no water service, and only a crude system of sewerage. A well or pump served two or three rows of houses. Sunday water was stored on Saturdays and each house had a rain-water cask.

The houses built by the iron and colliery companies consisted of two bedrooms and two living rooms, with a stone staircase leading to one bedroom through which one had to pass to reach the other. In the middle of the last century there were, on an average, twelve occupants per cottage with weekly rents of 2/- to 3/-. One can well imagine the gross overcrowding, bad sanitation and consequent high death rate, particularly through T.B. Houses were built near the pits and pits were sunk near the houses. At one time there were eighteen lodging-houses in the valley.

Thomas Morgan (Llyfnwy) stated in 1856 that thirty years previously there were only six or seven families from Cwm Cerdin (below Llangynwyd) to Blaenllynfi (at the top of the valley). In 1851 the population had grown to 4,800 with a further increase of 3,000 by 1856.

The houses were in long rows facing each other in unimaginative uniformity, and most were shoddily built. They were small, unadorned and uncomfortable, with two or three windows and a primitive fireplace. The lavatories were at the far end of a very lengthy garden. Even in later years, Michael Gareth Llewelyn (Cadrawd's youngest son), in his book, *Sand in the Glass*, describes the houses about Nantyffyllon as 'box-shaped, plaster covered, often inconvenient and always ugly'. The parlour consisted of a cupboard containing china, ornaments (often bought at the local flannel fair), a book-case, a piano and a Bible. The enlargements of the family portraits were invariably ugly. The parlour itself was the resting place of the dead.

R. D. Morgan (ap Lleurwg) of Maesteg has described the conditions when he first saw Maesteg in 1871. He found in Bowrington Street (later Commercial Street), Maesteg, low-roofed cottages. The road was rough and irregular. The small shops were lit by candles as the local Gas Company was not registered until 1873. The shopping hours were late and the public-houses were open until midnight, resulting in much fighting. In Bowrington Street, within a distance of 200 yards, there were seventeen public-houses. Anyone could have had a licence to keep one on payment of £6 per annum. The upper bedrooms of the small, low cottages of the street were about level with the surface of the old tramroad. The Post Office was at the end of the upper part of the 'street' where London House was once situated.

On the other hand, Talbot Street, the other main shopping street, was more recently built, with leases containing a restrictive covenant to prevent public-houses being built therein.

Even as late as September 1894 the Glamorgan M.O.H. reported that the older houses were in a state of disrepair. They had no proper privy accommodation and this resulted in foul smells. There was no means of disposing of slop water. Of the two remaining lodging houses, one was about to be closed and the other was declared unfit. There were open, untrapped privies over culverts, and box drains were attached to about 200 houses, mainly in Nantyffyllon.

At the opening of the Maesteg Iron Works in 1828, company houses such as South Parade, Crown Row, Shoemakers Row, Cwmdu Street and a part of Castle Street, all in Maesteg, were built. Tŷ Candryll (where Llwynderw School now stands) was also built, as well as Plasnewydd Mansion, in 1832 for a Mr. Buckland, the then manager of the Works. Ton-y-cwd Row in Spelters (Caerau) was built around a farm of that name in 1835 to house workmen employed at the Spelter Works nearby. Metcalf Street, in the same area, was built about the same time and for the same purpose. It was named after Stephen Wright Metcalf, a director of the Llynvi Iron Works.

Before 1842 the Iron Works had built Cambrian Row in Maesteg. It was later renamed by the Llynfi Iron Works, McGregor Row, Charles Row and Cavan Row, all named after the Company's directors, 'Charles' being the name of the brother of Sir John Bowring. Talbot Terrace, in the same area, was built later by the same Company. Then, in 1845-46 there was a massive building of houses again by the same Company in Nantyffyllon, resulting in Brown Street, John Street, Union Street and Dyffryn Row. The last named was demolished ten to fifteen years ago. Brown Street was named after Francis Brown, a director of the Llynvi Works, and John Street after Sir John Bowring, one time proprietor, whilst Dyffryn Row was named after the adjacent Dyffryn Madog Farm.

When the Llwydarth Tinplate Works were opened in 1869 the Company built Brick Row, Gwenllian Terrace (named after the wife of the proprietor, David Grey (later called Gwendoline Terrace) and Olivia Terrace (named after David Grey's daughter). They were then occupied by the Company's employees.

By to-day there has been a complete transformation, and the many company houses that still remain in the valley bear witness to the industry and the sense of pride of their present private owner occupants. It would be a sad day if these modernised little palaces were to disappear from the scene. Nantyffyllon, in particular, would be deprived of much of its personality. A nostalgic link with the past would be severed.

32. Llwydarth Tinplate Works

Both Cadrawd (*History of the Parish of Llangynwyd*) and David Davies (*Tŷ'r Llwyni*) have given some details of this undertaking. The works were the result of the enterprise of David Grey, a native of Llansamlet, the mineral agent of the Llynvi Iron Works. He was aided by Thomas Thomas (Saer), a carpenter, and father of Dr. W. H. Thomas, Maesteg.

The foundation sod was cut in 1868 and work commenced in 1869. At its peak, the Company employed 500 persons with an annual pay roll of £21,000, and turned out more than 10,000 boxes of tinplate annually. The Works consisted of a forge, 12 puddling and 4 balling furnaces, 2 ponderous steam hammers, 6 rolling mills, a tinning department containing 13 patent tinning pots with an annealing and cold rolls department.

The Works became famous for its japanning processes for the adornment of tinplates, resulting in a polished surface for sheet iron and steel. This work was carried out at Rock House adjoining the site where the new Tabor C.M. Chapel was later built in Commercial Street, Maesteg.

The conditions of employment of the workmen were printed on the back of the pay dockets. The employees were liable to be fined from 2/6 to £2 for neglect of duty, late arrival or damage to property, and 10/- for drunkenness or insulting behaviour to officials or fellow workmen. The fines would be deducted from their wages.

After leaving the Company's employment, a workman lived in a company house on a day to day basis at a rent of 1/- a day. One can just imagine trade-union reaction to-day to the Company's rule 12: 'Any workman combining with others to stop the works or any department thereof, or threatening to do so in order to obtain the dismissal of any person employed therein in order to compel any such person to join any union or society, and any workman who shall threaten or molest any persons employed in such works for the purpose of compelling such person to join such union or society shall be liable to dismissal without notice.' In other words, strikes and compulsory union membership were prohibited.

Owing to the adverse effect of the McKinley tariffs, the Works closed in 1897.

33. Candle-Making and Brick-Making

There were two candle factories in the valley in the latter half of the last century, one owned by David Davies at Nantyffyllon. He was a native of Bangor, hence the reason why Bangor Terrace was so named, his factory being at the rear of the centre of that street. On his gravestone at Llangynwyd churchyard is inscribed 'Canhwyllydd' (Candle Maker). The other factory was at Cwmdu House, near Shoemakers' Row, Maesteg, and owned by a John Rees.

Brick Making

Daniel R. Waldin, previously referred to, remembered seeing a brickyard some distance higher than Brynllefrith Farm, Caerau, on the mountain slope. Clay was available near-by. Bricks from this yard were used to construct the two Coegnant pits a century ago, whilst bricks from the mountain-side near Dyffryn level, Spelters, were used to build the Caerau-Cymer tunnel. D. R. Waldin could also remember seeing the big brickyard on the

54 Daniel R. Waldin, who is mentioned frequently in this book, is second from right in the front row of this photograph taken at the Diamond Wedding of Mr and Mrs Richard Williams in 1927. The others are:
(Back Row) Benjamin Rees, Benjamin Williams, Thomas Rees, Thomas Richards, John Jenkins, Thomas Rees (Michael), Thomas George, Evan John Treharne, David Evans
(Sitting) Thomas Bowen, Joshua Richards, Richard Williams, Mrs. R Williams, Daniel R Waldin and William Treharne

site now known as 'White City', Maesteg. It belonged to the Llynvi Iron
Works. An ordnance survey map of 1876 shows a brickworks at Llwydarth
Road, Maesteg. The manager was a William Treharne.

David Davies, Maesteg, knew of a brickworks in upper Maesteg, near the
former surgery of Dr. Henry Sinclair. A large chimney stack at the top of
McGregor Row was constructed from bricks from these works. However, the
best known brickworks was at Tondu on the fringe of the lower end of the
valley. Hundreds from that area were employed, but depression in trade,
keen competition and new techniques contributed towards its final closure
in 1974-5.

D. R. Waldin further testified that there was a pottery called the
Coegnant Pottery where Coegnant House, Caerau, now stands. The work
was limited to the making of drain pipes, earthenware pipes, semi-troughs,
etc. The clay came from Staffordshire and Cornwall. The pottery closed in
the early fifties of the last century.

At one time there were two privately-owned gasworks in the valley, the
first Company having been registered in 1872, following the passing of the
Llynfi Valley Gas Act, 13 July, 1868. The surviving works was closed in 1948
following the nationalisation of the gas industry, and gas was piped in from
Port Talbot.

It was alleged that the introduction of electricity in the valley had been
impeded by the fact that some Council members and officials had a vested
interest in the local gas companies. Houses became electrically lit over sixty
years ago. However, there has been a revival of the use of gas locally,
particularly for central heating purposes.

34. The Miners

It is common knowledge that the miner's lot was a hard one. Children were
once employed in the mines for the purpose of opening and closing ventilation doors. Sometimes trams were pushed or dragged by children, and the
conditions were grim.

Ventilation was totally inadequate. Naked lights from candles and oil
lamps were used and the danger from gas and coal dust became obvious.
Few miners lived beyond fifty years of age. Much evidence of these conditions can be gleaned from the Afan Argoed Miners' Museum opened
Easter, 1975.

In 1931 an article by a J.R. in the local press describes the conditions
under which the Llynfi Valley miners worked a century earlier at the
Tŷgwynbach and Cae'r Defaid Collieries and also at the 'Black Band' mines
of Garnwen. The mines were badly ventilated, the roofs of the roads being

very low and tortuous. Only small boys could work in parts of them. Each boy had a girdle round his waist to which was attached a chain passing under the legs and attached to a cart for drawing a load through low-roofed roads.

Horses sometimes had to work three shifts consecutively and one can imagine the torture to the horses' backs when the roof was low. It was with the horses' fodder that the rats were able to reach the pit bottom. As horses are no longer used underground, the rodent population has been deprived of its sustenance. At one time about 200 pit ponies were engaged at both the Coegnant and Caerau collieries.

It was an offence for a miner to fill trams with a shovel. He had to use a 'box' for that purpose and empty the contents of the box into the tram. There was no remuneration for small coal, known as 'billy', and the miners had to provide their own tools. It was asserted by some old-timers that Park Street and the Coed houses in Maesteg were built on the proceeds of sale of small coal.

Miners had to walk to work in all sorts of weather without any outside protection from rain and sleet. The carrying of an umbrella would have appeared incongruous. The miner had to be underground in good time despite the fact that his clothing had been soaked with rain, thus exposing him to pneumonia or rheumatism by working and perspiring in damp clothes. Sometimes he would have to walk a mile or two from the pit bottom to the colliery face.

Owing to a local strike, the writer's father worked at the International Colliery, Blaengarw, from 3 December to 23 December in 1895 and walked each day thereto from his home in Nantyffyllon. During the first World War he walked each working day for several months to Cynon Colliery in the Afan Valley, having to climb Garnwen Mountain in the process of doing so. Maesteg miners in the first quarter of the twentieth century walked daily to the Garw Valley and to the Cynon, Nantybar (Dyffryn Rhondda), Bryn and Cwmdu (St. John's) pits. A Nantyffyllon miner known as Twm Bach Nêt was known to have walked to a Blaengwynfi colliery at least five or six miles away after an overnight snowstorm that prevented even the local Blaengwynfi miners from leaving their homes. It meant scaling the Caerau-Cymer mountain in 3 feet of snow. He returned home on foot the same morning under the same conditions. Another miner would walk to Neath from Spelters (Caerau) to buy young pigs and return home on foot with the pigs and resume work on the night shift on the same day.

It is understandable why miners did not want their sons to follow them in the same occupation, for in winter months they saw daylight on Saturdays and Sundays only. Until the passing of the Eight Hours a Day Act before the first World War, miners worked ten hours a day for the first five days of the week and worked until 2 p.m. on Saturdays.

On the passing of the Workmen's Compensation Act, jurisdiction in respect of miners' compensation claims was vested in County Courts and

much acrimony arose over the interpretation of the phrase in the Act —
'during the course of his employment'. The judgments of Judge Bryn
Roberts, a former North Wales M.P., who dealt with Maesteg cases at the
Bridgend County Court, aroused much resentment among the miners. A
strict interpretation of the Act resulted in decisions that were adverse to the
interests of the miners. Demands for his removal, voiced by Mabon and
local leaders, were made throughout the South Wales coalfield. However,
the well known Welsh journalist, E. Morgan Humphries, contended that the
Judge has been wrongly blamed for giving judgments which he con-
scientiously thought were the correct ones within the provisions of the Act.

Yet, despite the squalid conditions that existed in the mines at the beginning of this century, many slate quarrymen, owing to the strike at the North
Wales quarry at Bethesda, settled in Caerau and formed a colony called
Newtown. In some special colliery occupations, e.g., that of banksman at
the pithead, the position would be held by successive generations of the
same family, covering a period of about a century.

Prior to the passing of the Minimum Wage Act before the first World
War, miners working in a hard heading where coal was difficult to hew,
were paid a mere pittance for a week of hard slogging. Diligent work,
irrespective of results, was not recognised. Parliament decreed that a
minimum wage should be paid to those whose output was low because of
difficult conditions.

W. J. Watkins, who was treasurer of the Maesteg group of miners for
thirty-five years, maintained that it was at the Tonhir level between Maesteg
and Bryn that a minimum wage for miners was first secured in Wales. For
some years, Maesteg miners received 8d a day more than the remaining

55   Typical underground conditions — Croker's Double

miners of Wales. W. J. Watkins attributed the credit for this to Vernon Hartshorn, the then miners agent, who was considered one of the out-standing miners' leaders of the century. Yet, during the depression years, the minimum weekly wage for a collier was £2.14.0. and that of a colliery labourer £2.6.0.

For nearly a half of the present century, pneumoconiosis and silicosis had not been defined. Lack of breath was attributed to *mociant* (asthma). Under the Industrial Injuries Act, tribunals were set up after the 2nd World War to deal, *inter alia*, with appeals against disallowance of death benefit to deceased miners' families. Very often, on the evidence of an X-ray plate, a miner was certified as a 100% sufferer from silicosis or pneumoconiosis, called industrial diseases, whilst a post-mortem examination on the same miner indicated that the incidence of either disease was negligible and did not materially contribute towards the cause of death. The miners' dependents felt frustrated and robbed of a benefit to which they under-standably thought they were entitled.

It was shortly before the last World War, and also during the War, that miners realised they could earn more money whilst working less slavishly, with the result that many left the mines for the Royal Ordnance Factory at Bridgend.

Oil lamps are no longer used at the collieries and this has meant doing away with jobs reserved for the oldest miners, i.e., *rhoi tân* (re-lighting), at the pit bottom, lamps that had run out of fuel or had blown out by accident. The provision of the modern safety-lamp has helped to eliminate the industrial disease of nystagmus caused by poor light. The biggest offence which a miner could commit formerly was the changing of numbers on someone else's filled trams so that he could be paid for the labour of a fellow miner.

The lot of the miner has been eased by the provision of pithead baths, canteens, first-aid measures, rescue stations and the replacing of timber by steel. With the advent of mechanical coal-cutting and conveyors and modern mining methods, output has doubled with a reduced labour force. Fatal accidents have been almost eliminated. Underground roadways and workings have been enlarged and improved.

With the advent of the nationalisation of the mines in 1947, provisions were made for safer and better working conditions, including the improve-ment of efficiency, at the Maesteg collieries, in the No. 2 Area of the South Wales Division of the N.C.B. Improved safety gear has been fitted to winding engines. In order to eliminate coal dust, 70,000 samples in the No. 2 Area were analysed in one year. The coal is transported from the colliery face by rubber belt conveyors for loading into trams at the pit bottom. A central repair shop has been set up to recondition thousands of yards of conveyor belting and also a stockyard for timber to service the local collieries. The former Rescue Station is now a training centre for mining recruits, and includes a model coal face.

Electricity has replaced steam to effect economy. The linking of air supplies of Caerau and Coegnant Collieries meant much saving. Most sidings have been relaid.

In 1957 a modern washery plant was opened near the site of the old Maesteg Deep Colliery. It had a washing capacity of 250 tons per hour, being 2,000 tons per shift. It cost £400,000.

35. The Coal Industry Potential

According to past reports of the bright prospects of the coal industry in the Llynfi Valley, it could reasonably be anticipated that coal mining would continue for centuries. Yet the high rate of output of later years made such a prospect appear exaggerated and almost naive.

In his essay on the geology of the valley (*Y Berllan*, 1869), David Bowen (Cynwyd) states that despite geological faults in the 1,200 acres then owned by Messrs. Brogden & Sons at Garth, Cwmdu and Tywith (later known as Nantyffyllon), 600 tons could be raised daily for 380 years before the supply would be exhausted. The Oakwood Colliery site of 574 acres at Maesteg, owned by W. & D. Davis, could produce 600 tons daily for 180 years. Mr. Vivian, M.P. had fifteen years earlier stated in Parliament that South Wales could continue to supply coal for 2,000 years at the rate then existing. Mr. Bowen stated that only part of the valley had then been developed (in 1869) and that the potential of the undeveloped parts could be tremendous. This was even before the advent of Col. North in 1889. It was then only 9 a.m. in the industrial life of the valley.

The essayist also stated that the valley contained much iron ore, the thickness of the seams being 6 feet 3 ins., to which could be added the black band seam of 5 feet 10 ins., making a total of 12 feet 1 ins. If 3 tons could produce 1 ton of iron, and as the Llynvi Works had four blast furnaces, making 200 tons of iron weekly, then assuming a sufficiency of supply of iron ore, it would take 255 years of smelting to exhaust the supply.

Daniel R. Waldin (previously referred to) has supplied us with details of 22 seams in the Pwll-yr-iwrch Mountain to the east of the Llynvi River and overlooking Nantyffyllon. Many of these seams, he stated, extended to the Garnwen Mountain immediately opposite. Early in 1882, a 6 feet seam of coal was discovered at the Coegnant Colliery sunk by the Llynvi Coal & Iron Co. Ltd. In August of the same year, a 9 feet seam had been struck at the same pit. Within a few months, three very valuable and workable seams of coal had been discovered that would result in employment for 800 to 1,000 miners.

Even as recently as 7 August 1930, a new slant driven by the Bryn Navigation Colliery controlled by Messrs. Baldwins Ltd. was officially opened and the first journey of trams laden with 15 tons was drawn out. The slant had been driven 1,232 yards into the middle of the lower seams of steam coal which was found to be of the best quality. At that time about 9,000 men were employed at the Company's collieries, and it was hoped that 700 to 800 men would be employed at the slant when fully developed. Many employees would be from the Llynfi Valley, a mile or two away. At the time of the writing of these notes there is no visible trace of this new slant which was closed in 1963. The site has since been well landscaped to remove the scars.

In 1952 Mr. Minhinnick, Area 2 General Manager of the N.C.B., estimated that the remaining reserves of coal in the Llynfi Valley were about 80 million tons.

36. The Coal Industry Development

At one time in the last century there were 33 levels working coal and ores. There were 9 separate seams of coal and ironstone. The last of these closed many years ago. The last ironstone (black band) level (near Cwmdu) was abandoned 27 November 1884, presaging the end of the Llynvi Iron Works.

Among coal levels closed were Penylan (opened 1881), Garnwen (closed 1903), Tonyfron (1907), Llety Brongu (1907), No. 3 Dyffryn and Tygwynbach (1908), New Brynllywarch (1911), Ton Hir (1919). Others included Gwernllwyn, Mountain, Tondu Drift, Washbourne Level, Brithdir (6 feet Level), Coetrehen, Celtic Lower, Dyffryn (near Lock's Level), No. 13 Level (near Brynllefrith), Exeter (under Y Darren), Lefel Noah (opposite the present Caerau Surgery), Blaenllynfi (near the present Caerau Library), Rickett's Level (behind the present Caerau Road), Level Waun Rydd, and Coffin's Colliery (site of present Paper Mills).

The pit depths in feet of the collieries where shafts were sunk were as follows: Oakwood, Maesteg (900); Gin Pit (328) and Dyffryn Madog (554), the Gin Pit being on the site of the present Maesteg Park and the Dyffryn Madog adjoining the Llynvi Works; Garth Merthyr (1,120); Coegnant, Caerau (1,121); Caerau Steam Coal Pits (1,066); St. John's, Cwmdu, North Pit (1,135) and Caerau House Coal Pit (530).

During the twenties of this century the Llynfi Valley collieries produced over a million tons of coal annually.

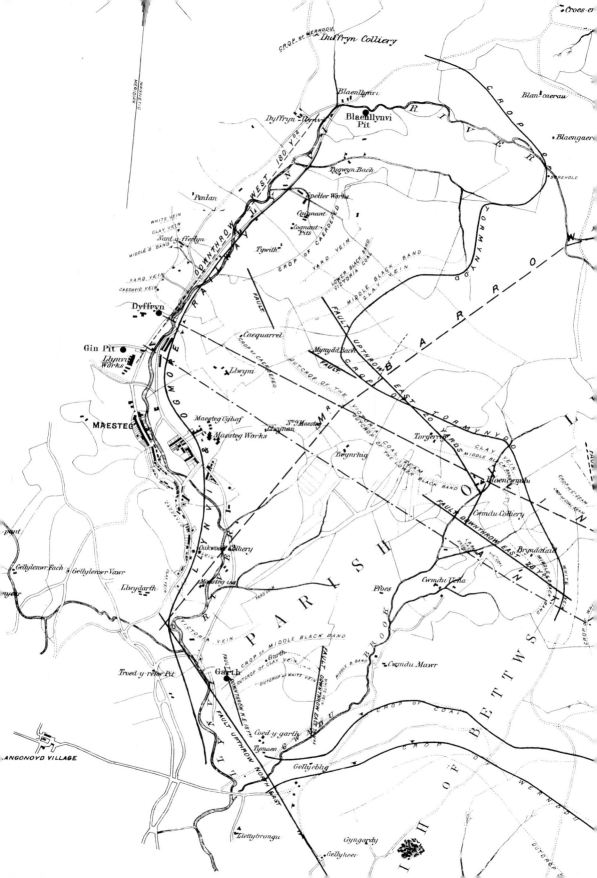

56   CAPTAINS OF INDUSTRY
John Brogden (*left*), founder of the firm of John Brogden and Sons (died 1869), and
his eldest son, James, born 1832, who came to Tondu in 1860 as junior partner in
the firm to superintend the Company's property

A rare print (*left*) of Colonel North, founder of North's Navigation Company, with
his friend and business associate Mr John Joseph Smith who was the receiver at the
ill-fated Tondu and Llynfi Iron Company (*see* Section 23) and later joined North's
Navigation Co.
Reproduced from 'A History of the Pioneers of the Welsh Coalfield' by Elizabeth
Phillips, published 1925

Fig. 5   (Opposite) Portion of an 1874 Map of the 'Llynvi and Rhondda Valley
Mineral District' from the South Wales Institute of Engineers' *Transactions* Vol IX
(1874 and 1876)

57   Oakwood Colliery *c.*1908 with Bridgend Road in background. In left background are Tai Candrill houses, now the site of Llwynderw School

Hereunder are details of the best known local collieries now closed:

1846. Tywith Colliery and black band level opened by a company from Tondu and later leased by J. Brogden & Sons in 1863. It was closed to make room for the sinking of Coegnant Colliery and was the only works at the time where workmen were paid in cash and not under the truck shop system.

1864. Oakwood (known as Pwll Dafis). W. Davis, Bridgend, had purchased from Col. Turbervill a small pit previously sunk by Charles Sheppard, and also minerals under Llwydarth Farm, Maesteg. In 1868 he opened a large colliery called Maesteg Merthyr Colliery, later called Oakwood. It was situated alongside the street now called Bethania Street, Maesteg, and was closed in 1928. The land has since been levelled and has become a building site.

1863. Brogden & Sons obtained a lease of Blaen Cwmdu and Ffos Farms and a railway was constructed from Cwmdu to Garth to meet the Llynfi Valley railway at Pontrhydycyff. A drift was driven into the land under the supervision of David Grey on behalf of the Brogden Company and was known as No. 9 Colliery, otherwise known as Cae'r Defaid Colliery. It was opend in 1863. The site is approximately half a mile to the north-west of the present Maesteg Cemetery. Much coal was raised but after the sinking of St. John's Colliery, the drift was closed in 1908 by the then owners, Messrs. North's. It had a haulage rope three miles long.

The Gin Pit. A shaft was sunk in the fifties of the last century, the site being within the present Maesteg Park. It is best remembered for the explosion in 1863, when fourteen lives were lost. The pit was finally closed 1877-78. The shaft was finally filled in by order of the Maesteg Council in 1923, leaving no trace of the former pit. Elegies to the lost men were composed by two local poets — Richard Hopkins (son of the Rev. Thomas Hopkins, Bethania) and Benjamin Benjamin (Y Bardd Coch).

1864. Garth Pit. J. Brogden & Sons bought Garth Fach and Cwmdu Canol Farms and sank this pit in 1865. The sinking operations were supervised by James Barrow, who was later President of the South Wales Institute of Engineers. He was also mineral agent to the Margam Estate. In 1867 there was an explosion but no-one was hurt. It resulted in the closure of the colliery for a year. About 1880 the pit was idle for another year but in 1882 it was sunk to a depth of 250 yards, 3 seams being worked. In addition there were 60 coke ovens producing 1,000 tons of coke weekly. Fuel for the speed trials of the Mauritania was supplied from its 2 feet 9 ins. seam. It was after the sinking of Oakwood and Garth Pits that the village of Garth developed. Garth Pit closed in 1930 when it employed 616 men.

Maesteg Deep was first called Moffatt's Level (after an Iron Works' Director), then Cwrtymwnws and later Maesteg Deep. It was a drift mine to work the 2 feet 9 ins. seam. Its coals became famous throughout the world and were used for railway engines and ships. It was the oldest of the 7 collieries owned by North's in the twenties of this century. Owing to the exhaustion of resources, it closed in 1929 when 171 men were rendered unemployed.

58 Garth Colliery, general view, *c.*1912-14

59   This general view of Caerau, *c.*1912, shows Caerau Colliery top right in operation

60   Caerau Colliery: demolition of South Pit Winder stack in 1958. The North Pit Winder stack (behind) was pulled down in 1960

1893. Caerau Colliery. After the shafts were sunk the colliery opened four years later (in 1897), attracting workmen from North and West Wales, Gwent and Forest of Dean. About 200 pit ponies were used. In 1904 Messrs. North built a power-house at Caerau and became the pioneers of the use of electricity in the South Wales coalfield in place of steam and compressed air. The Caerau collieries were equipped with the first mechanical screening plant in the coalfield. The Caerau miners held the record for productivity in the South Wales coalfield in 1913.

In 1906 a third pit was sunk to a depth of 176 yards to tap the house coal seam, which was between 18 ins. and 2 feet high. Miners had to lie on their sides to hew the coal. The colliery closed in 1925. When the other two pits closed in 1977 the 430 miners employed thereat were transferred to Coegnant and St. John's Colliery.

In 1917, despite the number of miners serving in the first World War, those employed locally were:

Cedfyw ...	...	56	Ton Hir ...	...	180
Bryn ...	...	675	Maesteg Deep	...	614
Blaencorrwg	...	100	St. John's	...	638
Corrwg Vale	...	150	Caerau ...	...	2,300
Coetrehen	...	500	Coegnant	...	1,900

37. The Coal Industry Decline

Since 1977 only two collieries have operated throughout the valley — Coegnant and St. John's, whilst the future of the former is very much in doubt. Had it not been for the threatened strike of miners in 1981 against colliery closures, it is more than likely that Coegnant would have been closed even earlier. We are indebted to Mr. Verdun Price, secretary of Coegnant Lodge and a member of the South Wales Executive of the N.U.M., for the following details, published by the N.C.B.

Coegnant Colliery at which the writer of these notes worked for nearly eighteen months. The first pit was sunk by the Cambrian Iron Co. When it was dismantled the boilers were taken to the Blaenllynfi level at Caerau. It was in 1882 that the pits, as we know them to-day, were sunk by the Llynvi and Tondu Iron Co. They were equipped to deal with a daily output of 3,000 tons of coal. According to a recent N.C.B. publication supplied to us by Mr. Verdun Price, this pit produces an average annual output of about 100,000 tons of semi-coking coal from its lower 9 feet seam. It is taken to the Maesteg central washery where it is blended into coking 'mixtures' for

61 *(Opposite)* Eighty-one year-old David Jones of Nantyffyllon and the doomed Coegnant Colliery where he worked for 51 years. The photograph shows the Colliery pond with, in the backgound, the South Pit and North Pit Headgear and Winder Houses, the Power House and colliery workshops and storage yard

supply to the steel industry. As the consequence of geological faults and difficulties, about 100 workmen were transferred to nearby St. John's Colliery in 1976. In December 1980 a new colliery face named Y2 commenced operations at Coegnant, at a cost of £1,500,000, after the old Y1 face had hit a severe geological fault. By the end of March 1981 the colliery output had almost doubled. The lodge officials pressed for the opening of a new face to make the pit more viable. In April 1981 the N.C.B. agreed to invest a further £500,000 to open up a still further face called Y3. Owing to roofing difficulties, and despite the workmen's efforts, the pit had lost £850,000 in the three months ending March 1981. The coal is of top quality and is blended with the St. John's coal. It is suitable for domestic, power-station or cooking use. At the time of writing, the future is still in the balance despite the praise given to the workmen by the N.C.B.*

*Publishers' Note: An announcement of closure was made in November 1981.

62 St John's Colliery, showing the railway sidings which connected with the Port Talbot Railway

St. John's Colliery, Cwmdu would be the sole remaining colliery in the valley if the threat to Coegnant Colliery materialises. It overlooks Maesteg a mile or so on the east side of the River Llynfi. It comprises two shafts cut down into the deeper workings of the old Cwmdu Colliery in 1908-1910. The object was to obtain access to the reserves of high quality coke coals which lay in the five seams below the older colliery's working levels. In the current mining programme there are 13 miles of underground roadways and almost 5 miles of high speed belt conveyors in daily use. In 1950, 840 men were employed, with an annual output of 230,000 tons. The average output per coal face worker per shift in the four coal faces currently working was 59 cwts.

In 1968 it was announced that there were in the valley enormous reserves of coking and bituminous coal for which there was a big demand. At that time the local pits were supplying half a million tons of top quality coking coal a year to the Steel Company of Wales at Port Talbot. Schemes for the further mechanisation of the remaining collieries were then being initiated. One enterprise by St. John's Colliery at a cost of £400,000 involved driving into two seams, each containing a million tons of coal. The colliery itself was paying for most of the scheme out of its major revenue account. It was then hoped to increase the output per man from 35 cwts. to 45 cwts.

63   'Pamela' at Maesteg Washery, 1975

38. The Outlook

To what extent did the much-trumpeted potential future of the coal industry in the valley materialise?

At one time there were 11,000 members of the South Wales Miners' Federation in the Maesteg District alone.

In May 1928 the Secretary for Mines listed 118 South Wales coal-mines that had been abandoned during the previous three years, and of those, fifteen were in or about the Llynfi Valley. That year (1928), North's employed 4,962 men and there were seven small levels (soon abandoned) employing 85 men.

Prior to the last World War, only three collieries remained in the valley: Caerau, Coegnant and St. John's. In 1953 nearly 3,000 were employed by the three, producing 10,000 to 12,000 tons per day of first grade steam coal. As we have seen, Caerau Colliery was finally closed on 26 August, 1977 and its 430 workmen offered alternative employment at the two remaining collieries, Coegnant and St. John's. At the time of the closure some of the older miners thought that tremendous reserves of coal had been left

64 Many scenes from the feature film 'Blue Scar' made in 1947 were shot in Coegnant Colliery. Here director Gill Craigie explains a point to a group of miners, with the star, Emrys Jones, far right

untapped and asserted that there were 6 square miles of coal in the Gelli
Deg seam from Caerau towards Glyncorrwg, Neath and the Rhondda. It
appeared that, in the main, geological difficulties accounted for the closure.

In 1978 the two remaining collieries employed 1,500 men. By the end of
1979, 570 were employed at Coegnant and 750 at St. John's. In addition,
many hundreds of miners from the valley were employed in collieries outside
the district. At the beginning of this century there were over twenty mines in
the adjacent Afan Valley. Here are details of some of the pit closures:
Nantewlaeth, Cymer (1948); Bryn (1963-64); Dyffryn Rhondda, Afan
Valley (1966-67); Cefn Coed, Dulais Valley (1968-69); Avon, Blaengwynfi
(1969-70); South Pit, Glyncorrwg (1970-71). Dyffryn Rhondda was closed
after £6,000,000 had been spent a few years earlier in sinking the shaft
deeper and after the pit had been substantially modernised.

In 1979, Ian Isaac, Secretary of the St. John's Lodge of the N.U.M., published an essay on the decline of the mining industry in Maesteg, giving
details of the decline in manpower and coal production in the local pits
since 1889. In the meantime, owing to depression in trade, the importation
of foreign coal at a cheaper price than it can be produced in this country,
the possible run-down of the Port Talbot Steel Works, the best customers of
the local pits, and other well-known factors, make the future of the coal
industry in the valley anything but promising.

If the last colliery in the valley were finally closed, then only the scars
would remain of an industry that had put the district on the map in the
industrial world and had given employment and a livelihood, however
scanty in the past, to thousands of our people for a century.

In the past, abandoned pits and levels were allowed to remain to
desecrate the countryside, with the former proprietors taking no further
steps to remove the scars that they had created after reaping their profits. It
is a welcome sign that land reclamation schemes are now being evolved by
the Mid Glamorgan County Council, to landscape waste colliery tips and
provide suitable drainage. The scheme was to be financed jointly by the
County Council and the Welsh Office, which had agreed to give an 85%
grant. Since 1975, financial difficulties have impeded the progress of this
worthy project.

39. Ownership of the Collieries

North's Navigation Collieries (1889) Ltd. was formed with a capital of
£450,000. The undertaking took over control of the Park Slip Colliery, the
Wyndham and Tynewydd Collieries in the Ogmore Valley, The Tondu Iron
Works, the No. 9 Level at Maesteg, Maesteg Deep and Coegnant Collieries.

Two new pits were opened at St. John's, Cwmdu, to a depth of 385 yards, and a private railway, a mile long, was constructed to join the P.T.R. The Company owned 9,000 to 10,000 acres, mainly in the Llynfi Valley. It was later that the Caerau collieries were sunk. In the late twenties of this century, North's controlled seven collieries in the valley — three at Caerau, two at Coegnant and two at St. John's.

The quality of the coal ranked with the best produced in the Welsh coalfield, having high calorific power. It was exported to French, Mediterranean and South American markets. In addition, North's were the biggest producers of the best house-coal in the South Wales coalfield. Lysberg Ltd., the sole agents for North's, controlled 2,000,000 tons of coal per annum.

In 1916 Lord Rhondda, H. Seymour Berry (later Lord Buckland), and others, purchased the shares of North's at £2 a share. In 1921 the Company purchased 229,085 of 10/- ordinary shares of the Celtic Collieries Ltd. by a cash payment of 6/- per share and the issue of one North's fully paid

65   Elders' Navigation Collieries Staff Photograph, 2 September 1905.
(Back row) S H Futers, F Howells, G Thomas, J Hamley, P Allen, S Stephens (Surface Manager), W S Wardlaw (Manager), C A Baker (Chief Mechanical Engineer), W Jones, G R Jones, J Davies, D Evans, A Avramovitch
(Middle row) T Williams, T Mullins, D Jones, J Llewellyn, R Jones, T Samuel, J Jones, O Griffiths, E Thomas, D Brace, J Thomas, G Davies, W Walters, W Baines, J G Lewis
(Front row) D Richards, W J Sutton, T H Williams, G A Paterson, B Rees, W Jones, G Whittington, W Williams, D W Thomas, W J Jones, N Grey, O W Jones, M Evans, W Thomas, E Williams

ordinary share for each Celtic share. The Celtic shares had been previously bought in 1914 from the Elder Dempster Co. Ltd. with which Sir Alfred Jones (the 'Banana King') had been associated.

In March 1919, 2,400,000 additional ordinary shares were created. The authorised capital in 1923 was £1,250,000 in shares of 5/-. The Board of Directors included H. Seymour Berry, Sir D. R. Llewelyn, Sir Leonard Llewelyn, and Viscountess Rhondda.

Ultimately the undertaking became merged with the Powell Dyffryn Group from 1935 to the time of the nationalisation of the mines in 1947.

40. North's Chief Officials

J. Boyd Harvey was appointed the first general manager of the collieries and works in the Llynfi Valley and at Tondu. D. Sims Rees was the mining agent. During this time coke-ovens and engineering and wagon works were erected in Tondu. Contracts were made for the supply of Caerau and Coegnant coal for the Admiralty. In 1902 a central power station for generating electricity was erected at the Maesteg ovens.

In the same year, J. P. Gibbon succeeded D. Sims Rees and, on the resignation of J. Boyd Harvey in 1912, the dual position of general manager and mining agent was ultimately filled by J. W. Hutchinson, J. P. Gibbon having retired in 1914. J. W. Hutchinson was succeeded by Rees Rees as general manager and agent in 1921, the former having become a consulting engineer at Bridgend. It is interesting to note that D. M. Rees, the son of Rees Rees and a school contemporary of the writer of these notes, was manager of the Caerau Colliery at one time and ended up as head of Area No. 2 of the N.C.B.

In 1916 David Davies, manager of Coegnant Colliery, was appointed J. W. Hutchinson's assistant and in 1920 Jenkin Jones, the then manager of St. John's Colliery, was appointed second agent. In 1922 Joshua Davies was appointed assistant general manager and, on the retirement of Rees Rees, became general manager. He was later appointed to the Board of Directors.

During 1938-45 F. Stacey, manager of St. John's, served as agent under Joshua Davies and in 1945 G. A. Watson took charge, followed by A. T. Minhinnick in 1947, when the latter became area general manager. When nationalisation came into effect on 1 January 1947, the local pits became part of Area No. 2 of the N.C.B. with G. A. Watson, A. T. Minhinnick, Lister Walker, Donald Davies and W. B. Cleaver successively in control.

41. Pioneers of Industry in the Llynfi Valley

Although pioneers like John Bedford, William and James Barrow, the Jones brothers of Abergavenny, James H. Allen, Sir Robert Price, the Brogdens, Sheppard, Malins and Rawlinson deserve special mention, limitations of space will only allow us to refer to one each for the iron, tinplate and coal industries. Probably the three best known of these industrial pioneers were Sir John Bowring (iron), David Grey (tinplate) and Colonel North (coal).

(a) Sir John Bowring

He was born at Larkbeare, near Exeter, on 17 October 1792 and died in October, 1872 at the age of eighty. From the profuse *Times* obituary we glean most of the undermentioned facts. A detailed account of his background and activities appeared in the *Illustrated London News*, 1 December 1860.

At the age of fourteen Bowring became attached for four years to his father's woollen business of preparing coarse woollens for export to China and Spain. His employment involved visits to Spain, Russia, Sweden, Finland and Germany.

66   Sir John Bowring, from his obituary in 'The Illustrated London News'
of 1 December 1860

In 1828, he was commissioned by the Chancellor of the Exchequer to report on the public accounts of Holland, and later on those of France. He was appointed Commissioner to inquire into the state of records of births and deaths in extra-parochial places, involving the examination of more than 7,000 volumes. In 1832 he became Secretary to the Commission for the reform of Public Accounts and presented two volumes of valuable reports. He and Sir Henry Parnell jointly wrote the Reports of the Exchequer affecting the law of public accounts. Together with Lord Clarendon, the Commercial Commissioners to France and their French counterparts, he examined the tariffs of France and England with a view to extending commercial relations between the two countries.

He was also sent on commercial missions to Egypt, Syria, Lombardy, Tuscany, Rome, Belgium and Switzerland and assisted in the formation of the Manchester League, which helped to abolish the Corn Laws. He wrote a large part of the Joseph Hume report on import duties.

He entered Parliament as M.P. for Kilmarnock Boroughs in 1834. Later, he became M.P. for Bolton from 1841 to 1849. Through his friendship with Lord Palmerston he was appointed British Chief Superintendent of Trade in China and Governor of Hong Kong. He returned to England in 1859. His last public office was in 1861 in Italy, to report on commercial relations.

When Bowring was M.P. for Bolton he invested his fortune in the Llynvi Iron Works, which he abandoned in 1849. *The Cambrian* of 2 October, 1846 reports a tumultuous welcome given to him by his Maesteg workmen, who pulled his carriage by rope for 5 miles to Maesteg. A local band played 'See the Conquering Hero Comes' and he was presented with a silver salver inscribed with a message of thanks for having abolished the truck system at the Llynvi Iron Works, although there is evidence of its existence in later years, and of Bowring's petition in 1842 for its continuance, as we have already seen.

In 1847 Bowring and his brother, Charles, travelled from Bridgend to Maesteg with £1,000 in wages due to the workmen. Near Cwm-nant-gwyn, they were waylaid by two men and were ordered at pistol point to deliver the money or be shot. They yielded the lot and the horse was shot dead. One of the felons was caught at Margam and the other at Taibach and were sentenced to transportation for life. Almost all the money was retrieved. Bowring had made a fortune twice and had lost both.

In the early seventies of the last century, Maesteg had only just ceased to be called Bowrington. Commercial Street, the present main shopping street of Maesteg, was earlier known as Bowring Street and later as Bowrington Street. It later became divided into Commercial Street, Rock Street and Bethania Street. The lower part of Nantyffyllon was called Upper Bowrington. To show the influence of the Bowring family—John Street, Nantyffyllon, was named after Sir John, and Charles Row, Maesteg, was named after his brother, Charles. Llynfi Lodge was once known as Bowrington Lodge and Llynfi Court (now demolished), near Llynfi Lodge, known as

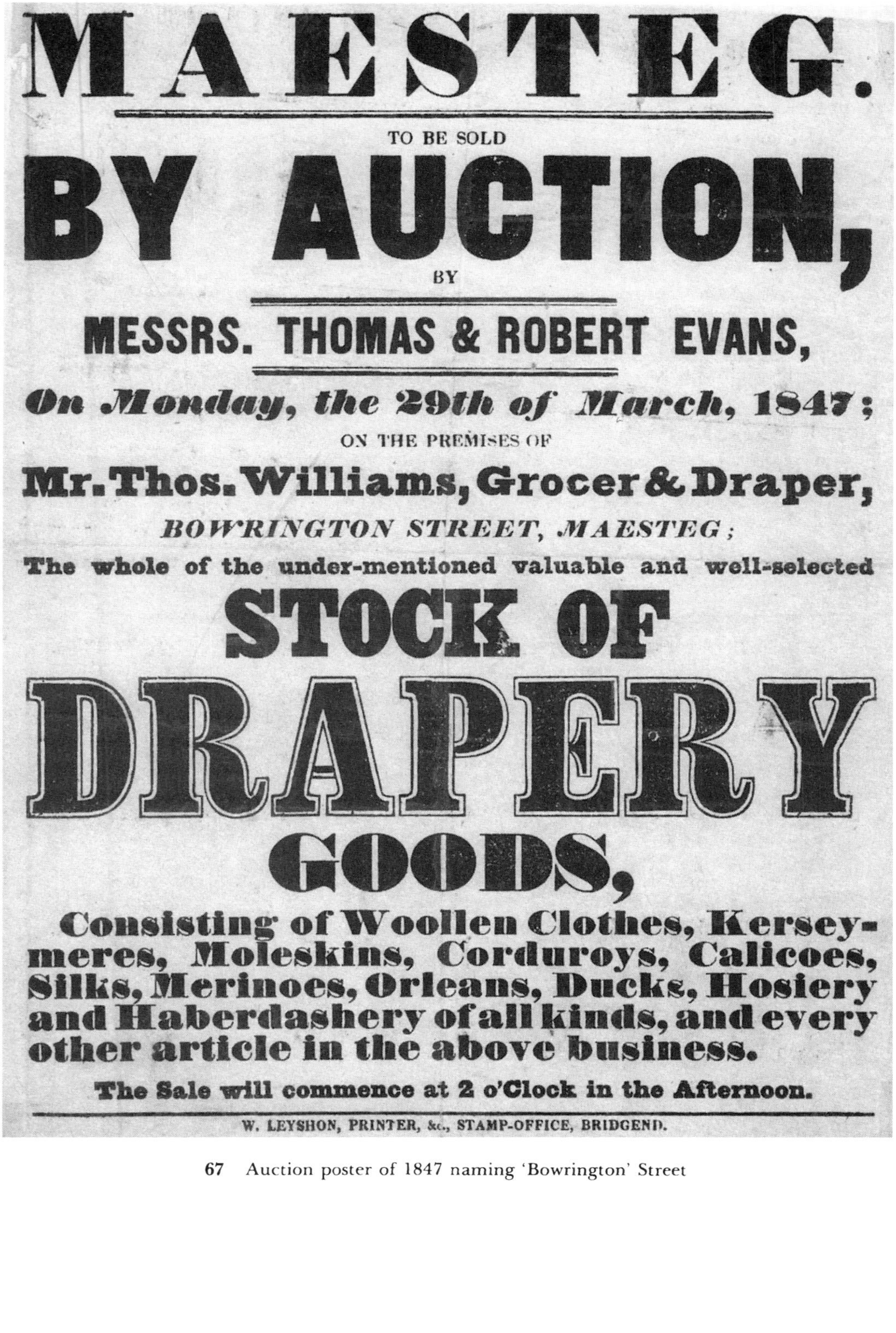

MAESTEG.

TO BE SOLD

BY AUCTION,

BY

MESSRS. THOMAS & ROBERT EVANS,

On Monday, the 29th of March, 1847;

ON THE PREMISES OF

Mr. Thos. Williams, Grocer & Draper,

BOWRINGTON STREET, MAESTEG;

The whole of the under-mentioned valuable and well-selected

STOCK OF

DRAPERY

GOODS,

Consisting of Woollen Clothes, Kersey-meres, Moleskins, Corduroys, Calicoes, Silks, Merinoes, Orleans, Ducks, Hosiery and Haberdashery of all kinds, and every other article in the above business.

The Sale will commence at 2 o'Clock in the Afternoon.

W. LEYSHON, PRINTER, &c., STAMP-OFFICE, BRIDGEND.

67 Auction poster of 1847 naming 'Bowrington' Street

Bowrington Court. There was a Bowrington Arms near Bethania Church, Maesteg.

(b) *David Grey (1833-1906)*

He was mainly responsible for the opening of the Llwydarth Tinplate Works in the Cwmfelin area, south of Maesteg, in 1869. A native of Llansamlet and educated at the Swansea Normal College, he was articled about 1855-56 to Messrs. R. P. Lemon & Co., who were colliery owners in the Llynfi Valley prior to the take-over by North's. Until 1869 he was mining enginer to the then Llynvi Vale Iron Co. and supervised the sinking of the Dyffryn Madog and Gin Pits (1858) and the No. 9 Level (1863). He had also been a director of a tinplate works at Cardiff and Milan (Italy).

Although the tinplate works at Cwmfelin were started on a small scale, about 500 were ultimately employed when trade was at its peak, resulting in the opening of Troed-y-rhiw Garth railway station and the building of Olivia Terrace, Gwendoline Terrace and Brick Row for employees on a site adjoining the works. An account of the progress of the works is given elsewhere.

David Grey was married at Llangynwyd Church and became deeply involved in the social, religious and industrial life of the valley. His wife died in Milan where he was then engaged in the tinplate industry. He was an elder of Libanus Welsh M.C. Church at Garth, and a candidate in a famous County Council election in Maesteg in 1888 when County Councils were first created. He also provided a library and a hall for his workmen.

(c) *Colonel John T. North*

The Colonel was born in 1830 in Leeds and, after an apprenticeship to a machinery manufacturer, he was sent to Peru. His invention for the condensation of sea-water for domestic purposes brought him some money with which he bought an island in Chile, where, during his twenty years' stay, he discovered deposits of saltpetre. He became known as the 'Nitrate King', and made a fortune out of his discovery.

He was a lover of sport and owned racehorses. His greyhound, Fullerton, won the Waterloo Cup three times. He was also well known as a boxing promoter and was reputed to have shared the favours of Lily Langtry (the 'Jersey Lily') with the then Prince of Wales.

On the advice of T. Forster Brown he bought the collieries and iron works of the ailing Llynvi Iron and Coal Company for £350,000, and concentrated exclusively on coal. A syndicate was formed and became known as North's Navigation Collieries (1889) Ltd. with a capital of £450,000. The pits, within twenty-three years, had paid £2,364,447 to the shareholders.

"Goreu arf, a darf derfysg,
I wr fo doeth, yw arf dysg"

THE

COLONEL NORTH

MEMORIAL HALL,

MAESTEG.

LAYING THE FOUNDATION STONES

Monday, May 3rd, 1897, at 10.30 a.m.,

BY

Mrs. J. T. NORTH & CAPTAIN HARRY NORTH.

DIRECTOR OF CEREMONIES:—

D. SIMS REES Esq., M.E.

68 Pages one (reduced) and two of the official programme of 3 May 1897 for the laying of the foundation stone of the Colonel North Memorial Hall, Maesteg

On his visit to Maesteg in 1889, Col. North was given a warm welcome. He received an illuminated address, and in response he gave £500 to the workmen of Maesteg and £250 to his Tondu workmen. At Maesteg, the gift was used towards the provision of a local library, and in Tondu it was paid to a relief fund which had been set up following a pit explosion. Col. North also gave each workman a shilling on the occasion of a Queen Victoria Jubilee celebration.

He died of an apoplectic fit while presiding over a company meeting in London in 1896. On his death, local open air meetings were held to express condolence with his family. On 3 May 1897 the foundation-stone of the Colonel North Memorial Hall was laid at the Maesteg town centre by the Colonel's widow and son, and officially opened by J. Boyd Harvey, General Manager of North's, on 6 March 1899. A painting of the Colonel was presented to the Hall, which is now used as an amusement centre.

42. The Present Industrial Situation

After the running down of the coal industry the valley had to rely on other industries to sustain its existence. There was much concern about the employment situtation. Sir Stafford Cripps, then President of the Board of Trade, and Mrs. Barbara Castle, M.P. of his department, visited Maesteg in October 1946. Minutes and press reports of Maesteg Council meetings refer to the efforts made to attract new industries by providing factory space and houses for key workers of the incoming factories.

Thousands from the Llynfi Valley were included in the 30,000 employees engaged at the peak period of the Bridgend Royal Ordnance Factory during the second World War. The site is now occupied by the Bridgend Trading Estate, where many valley people are still employed.

The Llynfi Power Station, to the south of Llangynwyd and adjoining the main Maesteg-Bridgend Road, was commissioned in 1943, and took only nine months to build. It was closed in 1977.

As far back as 26 May 1966, the *Western Mail* reported that about 1,000 persons from the Llynfi Valley were employed by the Steel Company of Wales at Port Talbot. Owing to depression in trade, re-organisation and redundancies, that number has been considerably reduced.

The Bridgend Paper Mills, commissioned in 1946, began to operate in 1950. Although it was sited in the Penybont R.D.C. area, it was actually in the Llynfi Valley. It was built at a cost of £1,250,000 near the Llynfi Power Station on the banks of the River Llynfi, a mile or two lower than Llangynwyd. In the first production year (1951), 250 employees, mainly

69 Llynfi Power Station photographed *c.*1950 during the second phase of building. Note the wartime camouflage still on the cooling-tower and the absence of any council housing in Betws

70 Bridgend Paper Mills, Brynllywrach (*see* Plate 17) is the white farmhouse immediately behind the mill complex

from the Maesteg area, produced 6,500 tons of tissue-paper from three paper-making machines. It was then anticipated that by 1968, more than 35,000 tons of tissue paper would be produced from five paper making machines, as well as more than 10,000,000 toilet rolls and kitchen towelling rolls per annum by the converting machine installed in 1962. In 1963 there were about 600 employees and, after several mergers, the undertaking became known as the British Tissues (Bridgend) Ltd. in 1968. Half is owned by Smith & Nephew, and the other half by the Finnish paper-making firm of Nokia.

By the end of August 1980, owing to high fuel costs and the industrial depression generally, the number of employees had been reduced to approximately 1000.

Apart from the above-mentioned factories, it was reported in 1969 that six new factories had been opened since 1945. Some have closed down in the meantime, including the Progress Drilling Machine Co. Ltd., built in 1953 with 140 employees manufacturing vices, drilling and grinding machines. Some of the machines were shewn in the French Industrial Exhibition at Toronto. The factory was closed in 1958 and 170 employees became redundant.

The factory owned by Multimetal Products (Maesteg) Ltd. was opened in 1968 at the rear of the Forge Industrial Estate. It specialised in metal pressings and metal fabrication. Unfortunately, this factory has also closed.

Fairfield Aquaria was built by Constructacor Ltd. in May 1968, the aim being to cater for tropical fish enthusiasts with the Company purchasing all sundries and fish and plants direct. The venture was short lived.

Llynfi Valley employees were also affected by the closure of the Metal Plastics Factory between Caerau and Cymer.

In 1961 Hazell, Watson & Viney Ltd. opened a book-binding factory at Cymer at which there were employees from the Maesteg district. By 1968 an original staff of ten had been increased to 250. New specialised binding equipment was installed, making the factory one of the most modern of its kind. Books so produced included the Encyclopaedia Britannica, Chambers' Encyclopaedia, Children's Britannica, road books, atlases and mail order catalogues. The firm became part of the British Printing Corporation. The closure of this factory had sad consequences.

Apart from the Port Talbot Steel Works, the Bridgend Paper Mills and the Bridgend Trading Estate, the scope for employment became restricted to the two industrial estates in the valley.

43. The Ewenny Road Factory Site

This site, under the Oakwood Colliery tip, was levelled in 1947 to make room for factories. It was ultimately occupied by (1) Louis Edwards & Co. Ltd. (2) Revlon International Ltd. (formerly the Fountain Perfume Factory) and (3) Silent Channel Products.

(1) *Louis Edwards & Co. Ltd.*, the Athenia Works, Maesteg, clothing and gown manufacturers. The firm has been based in London since 1896 and commenced manufacturing in South Wales in 1945 at the Nantyffyllon Library and the Garth Library. In 1947 they moved into a purpose-built factory at Ewenny Road, Maesteg, the present site, producing, in the main, ladies' and children's frocks for multiple stores, including Marks and

71   Battle of Britain queen, Miss Elizabeth Thomas, at Louis Edwards' factory
1951

Spencer. In 1949 about 300, mostly women, were employed. A big extension of the works was announced in 1964. Apart from a few key staff officials, local labour only was employed. The managing director, Sidney Edwards, died in September, 1964. Owing to depression in trade and lack of orders, the number of employees was reduced to 130 by August 1980. The last remaining 30 production workers were made redundant in January 1981, following the collapse of the parent group, leaving only 6 to remain to wind up its affairs, the Company being in the hands of a liquidator. However, by March 1981, a new dress factory was opened in the same building and 30 former employees recruited by a new firm from Cwmbran specialising in ties and sportswear. The firm had chosen Maesteg as so many skilled workers had become available on the closure of the Louis Edwards Factory. Presumably there will be further developments by the time these notes are published.

(2) *Revlon International Corporation* claimed to be the world's largest cosmetic company selling through retail outlets. Production was commenced at the Maesteg Plant in June 1950, the first sales to the domestic market being made in November of that year. Exporting commenced in the spring of 1951. After taking over the site from the Progress Drilling Factory, the Company aimed at occupying about 200,000 square feet by the end of 1969.

The Company has exported to 83 different markets outside Maesteg, the main customers being the E.E.C. (Common Market) countries in Europe. From 1965 to 1968 an increase in trade of 80% has been achieved.

72   Aerial view of Revlon's Maesteg plant

Approximately 1,300 different products and shades have been manufactured at Maesteg, involving 6,000 varying components and 800 types of raw materials. Maesteg was the site of the first Revlon factory in Britain. The work-force increased from 400 (in 1962) to about 700 in 1969. By August 1980 the number had increased to 950, but in that month the *Western Mail* sounded a warning that up to 250 workers would be laid off with a possible alternative of a three-day-week at the factory. Since then there has been a considerable reduction in the number of employees.

According to a report by Jayne Isaac in the *Glamorgan Gazette*, 9 July 1981, Revlon, previously the biggest employer in the Llynfi Valley, had announced that they intended to axe 370 jobs (mainly female), leaving only 350 between Maesteg and Port Talbot. There would be negotiations regarding redundancy payments. Although big profits had been made in the past, the Company had lost two million pounds in Maesteg, despite the fact that Maesteg was an efficient and economic factory. Revlon's only other European factory was at Lille in France. In the event of further recession it would be more difficult and expensive to close the factory in France as that country had stricter laws regarding redundancy. Yet the Company states that it fully intends to remain in Maesteg.

(3) *Silent Channel Products* produced rubber-sealing strip and rubber components for the motor industry. Of the production at Maesteg, 65% was exported. The work force in August 1980 was 230, but trade depression has affected the factory in the meantime.

In the same month, 23 men were employed at the old Drill Hall by Technical Tooling Ltd., Technical Pressing Ltd. and O. & M. Filters Ltd. The work consisted of toolmaking and precision engineering.

44. The Forge Factory Site

Midcast Numerical Controls (Wales) Ltd. was formed in 1968, and engaged in the production of component parts for air frame manufacture, including the Concorde, and other engineering industries. In 1980 the factory was fulfilling a new contract for Boeing of Seattle, making fixed leading-edge ribs for the new Boeing 757 for 1981, besides manufacturing parts for the Chinook helicopter and making wing parts for the European airbus. The Company secured contracts from Marconi and British Aerospace. In 1980 about 140 were employed locally. A helpful article by Jayne Isaac on the nature of the work performed locally appeared in the *Glamorgan Gazette*, 17 March 1977. The same weekly paper informed us in its issue of 18 April 1981 that on board the craft of the American Space Shuttle in its historic maiden flight into outer space that month, were major structural components manufactured in the Maesteg factory. They included the floor and walls of the experimental laboratory platform carried by the spacecraft. The order to date was worth £150,000, with the prospect of providing that amount of work again.

Vitafoam Ltd. commenced production locally on 22 July 1968, its head-quarters being at Middleton, Manchester. The work consists of converting loaves of polyether into suitable sizes for use in the upholstery and allied trades, serving beyond South Wales. The products vary from solid rubber mouldings, mainly for the car industry, to latex foam for cushioning. There were 63 employees by August, 1980.

WBC Bookbinders Ltd. (formerly Western Book Company Ltd) commenced operations at the Garth Library and later removed to the Forge site. The number of employees had increased to 76 by August, 1980. The Company has felt the impact of the general recession in trade and also of keen competition, as British publishers find it cheaper to have books bound overseas, but is now doing well.

System Hydraulics (Maesteg) Ltd. In August 1980, 36 men were employed locally, the nature of the work being hydraulic pipe-work installation and maintenance.

Porcelain of Italy Ltd. exports jewellery accessories to America, Canada, Europe and Japan. The work includes the making of bird models for the Royal Society for the Protection of Birds, and Shakespearean models for the Royal Shakespeare Company. There were about 50 employees in August, 1980.

Mastercraft Ltd., part of the Christie-Tyler Group, set up on the Forge site in 1976. The work is limited to manufacturing solid wood furniture, such as antique reproduction pieces, pine tables, dressers and chairs. In 1980 about 50 men were employed there.

Eton Electricals (D.R.) Ltd. moved to Dyffryn Rhondda from High Wycombe. The work consists of manufacturing small transformers and coils for the electronic and electrical industry. Owing to overcrowding at Dyffryn Rhondda old colliery site, the Forge factory was used for storage only until ready for production. In all, about 90 were employed in 1980.

Despite efforts to maintain at full strength the Ewenny and Forge factory sites, the numbers employed there, even at their peak, would be inadequate compensation for the loss in manpower involved in the running down of the coal industry in the valley. The Maesteg U.D.C. in 1969 made an outline application for industrial development on a 47-acre site at Heolfain, Garth. An interim report, dated 9 December 1969, to the Development Control sub-committee, indicated that a site at Spelters, Caerau, was more suitable than the one suggested for Heolfain.

Two factories were built on what was called the Tonna Road site between Nantyffyllon and Caerau about five years ago. Mastercraft Ltd. occupied one and the other was taken over by Eton Electricals (D.R.) Ltd. Prospects of development have not materialised. In fact, Mastercraft announced in July 1981 the closure of their works, thereby creating about 40 redundancies.

As the present industrial situation is in such a state of flux, there could be further developments, generally, by the time these notes are printed.

In March 1981 a new Maesteg Job Centre was opened in Commercial Street by the then Chairman of the Mid Glamorgan County Council, Councillor Vernon Hart, Caerau. It was disclosed in a *Glamorgan Gazette* report of 26 March 1981 that the local unemployment rate was close on 20%, compared with an average of 13.9% for Ogwr, 13.5% for Wales and 14.4% for Mid Glamorgan. There were 1,412 unemployed adults consisting of 888 men and 524 women, as well as 128 young people aged between 16 and 18.

The new Centre is linked by computer to centres throughout Britain, and vacancies from the whole country can be displayed in Maesteg. The office is run by a manager and 3 trained counsellors. In the first six weeks of its existence the average rate of callers was over 300 a week.

Recruitment at the Theros and Silent Channel Factories on the Ewenny Road Factory Site resulted in 130 new jobs by July 1981 although it has far from balanced the loss of 400 jobs at the Llynfi Power Station and another 400 on the closure of Caerau Colliery in 1977.

A further article by Jayne Isaac (*Glamorgan Gazette*, 23 July 1981), states that the Theros Factory, which by then had occupied the old Louis Edwards premises for four months, having started with a handful of former Louis Edwards employees had increased the staff to 110. They aimed at employing 140 by the end of August 1981.

The wedding of the Prince of Wales gave a fillip to their business. They received orders for 20,000 blouses of the 'Lady Diana Look' from top fashion companies, keeping 25 women busy for twelve weeks. They are currently producing 6,000 garments a week for a number of stores and customers all over Britain.

The Welsh Porcelain Co. Ltd., which first began to operate as a large modern factory five years ago as Porcelain of Italy Ltd. (previously referred to) on the Forge Industrial Site, assumed its present name three years ago. For the royal wedding occasion they produced 2,500 hand-painted commemorative bells crowned with the Prince of Wales feathers at £36.95 each. Building work is to start shortly on a large two-storey extension of the factory, which, in July 1981, employed 86. It hopes to expand the workforce before the end of the year as it has work in hand for the next three years. The firm appears unaffected by the general trade recession.

Another firm that benefited from the royal wedding was the Badge Factory at the old Drill Hall, Ewenny Road, Maesteg—owned by Bristol Button Badge Co., but with a Maesteg workforce. They made and sold all over Britain over 80,000 acetate-covered lapel badges to commemorate the wedding. At the request of the Maesteg Community Council, they made a special medallion for every valley school-child under sixteen.

45. Education

The late Professor Evan J. Jones has reminded us that the Council of the Lateran (1179) decreed that every cathedral should provide free schools for clerks and the poor. This applied to Wales but there is no direct evidence to show that that policy was carried out.

The task of the parish priest was to secure the early education of the children, which included the Lord's Prayer, the Creeds and the Salutation of the Virgin Mary. The scholars were invariably clerics. The monks were the historians and authors of many theological and philosophical works and translations from Latin into Welsh. The *Annales of Margam* became well known, but many precious documents were lost on the dissolution of the monasteries. Iorwerth Fynglwyd, whose son, Rhisiart, lived at Llangynwyd, sang to the glories of Margam Abbey in the early sixteenth century.

In the Middle Ages the parish priest, the monk, the friar and the masters of schools all contributed their share in educating the people. There were treatises in Welsh on theology, philosophy, astrology, botany and medicine as well as Welsh versions of the works of Greek and Latin authors. Wales then participated in the intellectual life of Western Europe.

After the Rev. Samuel Jones was deprived of his living as Vicar of Llangynwyd for refusing to conform to the requirements of the Act of Uniformity, 1662, he ultimately established a Nonconformist academy at Brynllywarch Farm, Llangynwyd. Students from noted local families were taught Greek and Latin and Logic, but mathematics was excluded as it had a tendency to create atheists! After the death of the Rev. Samuel Jones in 1697 the influence of the Academy waned and ultimately ceased.

In the early eighteenth century, superstition and ignorance prevailed, and the main interests were in running, jumping, playing football and bando. Sundays were spent in games, fighting, cock-fighting and drunkenness. Gŵyl Mabsant had lost its religious significance.

Bishop Lloyd said in 1662 that Glamorgan was 'utterly destitute in schools'. However, unendowed schools began to appear in places like

73 '. . . .fighting, cockfighting and drunkenness. . . .'

Margam and Llangynwyd. On 21 January 1714, William Lewis, curate of Margam, was able to inform the Society for the Promotion of Christian Knowledge (known as S.P.C.K.), founded in 1699, that there was hardly a parish in that part of the country where there was not a private school for teaching children to read.

In his treatise 'Religion and Education in Glamorgan, 1660-*c*.1775' (*Glamorgan County History*, Vol. IV, p. 434), Canon E. T. Davies states that a Welsh Trust was formed in 1672 to set up schools. In 1675, 15 attended at Betws whilst 196 Welsh religious books were distributed in Llangynwyd 'with Leckwith and Tragans'. The system flourished until 1681.

Between 1738 and 1777 the Welsh Circulating Schools, a movement founded by Griffith Jones, Rector of Llanddowror, provided free religious education to the children of the poorer classes. The schools opened in the winter months in a given district. Children were taught to read the Bible and the Prayer Book and were given instruction in the Catechism. Subjects like arithmetic, husbandry, sewing, needlework were eschewed. In Welsh districts the medium of instruction was Welsh. The aim was purely religious.

The schools were held in parish churches, farms and cottages. The local incumbent or curate usually invited the school to the district and was responsible for seeing that the school was conducted in accordance with the rules of the promoter. Quarterly reports were sent to Llanddowror and

Canon E. T. Davies quotes testimonies regarding the beneficial effect on the spiritual life of the local Churches.

A list of the schools was issued annually in *Welch Piety*. Up to the death of Griffith Jones (1761), the schools were held in about 300 districts in Glamorgan. Details were given of the number attending these schools.

Between 1740 and 1773 schools were held at Llangynwyd, Betws, Bryn, Penhydd-waelod (Bryn), Baeden Chapel, Tynycwm, Gilfach, Troed-y-rhiw, Corner House, Llwyngwladus Farm, (all of Llangynwyd), Farteg Fawr (Bryn), Ffynnon Iago (Margam Mountain), Drysiog Farm (between Bryn and Maesteg), Pontrhydycyff, and Gelli Eblyg. At Llangynwyd in 1740, 69 attended, whilst 60 attended at Bryn (1747-1748). The attendance at the other schools ranged from 23 to 55. Schools were also held at Cwmdu, Garnlwyd and Nant-y-crynwydd, Maesteg. Dafydd William of Llandeilo Talybont, the hymn-writer, kept a school at the Goetre and Farteg Fawr Farms, Bryn, for a few years from 1764.

Despite these heroic efforts Thomas Morgan (Llyfnwy) tells us that a document dated 1771 at Llandaff showed that of thirteen parishioners in the valley at that time, only two could write their names.

Prior to the industrial revolution the need for the building of schools hardly existed. About four or five years after the first blast furnace of the Maesteg (Old) Iron Works had begun to operate in 1828, two houses in South Parade, Maesteg, then recently built, were used as a school. In 1841, the Company built a school where the Salvation Army Hall in Castle Street,

74   Salvation Army Hall, Castle Street, site of Maesteg (Old) Ironworks School

Maesteg, now stands. A Mr. Protheroe from Pembrokeshire was the school-master, and the Iron Works employees paid weekly towards his salary. The main object was to teach the three 'r's.

The school was visited in March 1847 by a Government Commissioner, R. R. W. Lingen, M.A., Fellow of Balliol College, Oxford, assisted by David Williams of St. David's College, Lampeter, who prepared the detailed reports on the local schools. There were 184 scholars at this school when the Commissioner called. The school was held in a spacious room used for divine service. On one side was a pulpit and reading-desk and on the opposite side a raised gallery. The intervening space and the two other ends of the room were used for class teaching. The report stated that the school contrasted favourably with the workmen's schools at Michaelston (Cwmafan) and at Margam.

The Commissioner stated that the noise was deafening when he entered the school and that it was hard to conceive how anyone could learn in it. However, the master seemed to have full control over his pupils, and 'silence was immediately restored on his speaking'. At that time the school catered for children of a superior order, being the progeny of engineers and 'upper workmen' at the Works. Boys and girls occupied the same classroom and normally left school after reaching the second class.

In 1799 Vicar John Parry opened a school at Tŷ Cynwyd, Llangynwyd. It was attended by 19 children who paid up to 3/- a week per pupil. However, the National or Church of England School in the village was opened in the

75   Llangynwyd School, *c.* 1895

early forties of the last century and was visited by the same Government Commissioners on 4 March 1847. The children read Matthew XI and part of the following chapter. Six pupils were unable to say who Jesus was. They could not tell the name of John the Baptist's father nor what a 'messenger' was. They knew that Elias (Elijah) was a prophet, but only one could say who the publicans were. Sodom was a city burnt to ashes. The good news of the Gospel was about Jesus Christ and had been sent to the people and not to the angels. The children could spell some words correctly, but mis-spelt 'receive'. All but one could spell 'cleanse' and 'mourn'. The children were orderly and neat and the master appeared to be very intelligent, painstaking and apt to teach. The school appeared to be conducted 'on a good method'. The children attended irregularly, the neighbourhood being chiefly agricultural. The master had to encounter the disadvantage of the scholars knowing little English.

It had not dawned upon the authorities at that time how grossly unfair it was to subject monoglot Welsh children to critical questioning by a monoglot Englishman who was totally ignorant of their background and language. All this led to the understandable outcry of *Brad y Llyfrau Gleision* (The Treachery of the Blue Books) when the report was published. It would have been interesting to note the reaction of a monoglot Englishman to questions framed entirely in Welsh, and to ascertain how many pupils in English-speaking schools even to-day would have been able to answer the Commissioner's questions fully and correctly.

For many years Mrs. Elizabeth Evans, Cadrawd's wife, was in charge of this school. There was another Church of England School of mixed pupils at Pontrhydycyff. In 1895 it had 96 pupils. D. E. King Davies was the headmaster and Mrs. Elizabeth Evans the mistress. There was also a Church School in Spelters (Caerau) in the early days, and we find that a Miss Carson was in charge in 1875. There are now no Church Schools (except the R.C. School) in the valley. In the seventies of the last century Mrs. Sarah Gregory kept a preparatory school at 116 Bridgend Road, Maesteg.

After the Llynvi (New) Iron Works began to operate in October 1839 Bowrington School, otherwise Miss Roderick's School for Girls, was opened in 1846 at the Wesleyan Chapel in Alfred Street, Maesteg. The building consisted of a pulpit, a gallery, a pew and some benches. It was rented at 1/-a week and there were 19 scholars. The mistress sat with them at a round table on which lay some needlework. There were 9 little girls at school when the Commissioners called on 9 March 1847. The mistress, Miss Roderick, was reported to be intelligent and able to express herself correctly. She attempted to teach the Church catechism, but the parents objected. The children, whose writing was reported to be indifferent, had to provide their own books. Five were able to read Chapter VI of St. Luke's Gospel, but with difficulty. The mistress was a native of Margam and lodged with her sister during the week, returning home every week-end.

On the same day the Commissioners visited a school kept by Daniel

Williams, who had only one arm. The schoolroom was reported to be very dark, but was a good specimen of a common private-adventure school. According to the school's account book, some boys had made considerable progress in Arithmetic and wrote 'good hands'. Five of the boys could read with ease Chapter XI of St. Matthew's Gospel. One boy was 'remarkably acquainted' with the Bible.

David Davies, in an article in the *Glamorgan Advertiser* (25 July 1947) quotes a report in a Cardiff weekly under the heading 'Bowrington Schools'. It refers to a 'well-conducted school' at the top of Bowring Street in the charge of a Mr Monroe (senior) and his daughter. The school was examined at the request of the Bishop of Llandaff by the Rev. Henry Lynch Blosse, the Rev. Thomas W. Jones, perpetual curate of Maesteg, and another cleric. It was a circulating school embodying mutual tuition and receiving the approbation of the Llynvi Iron Works Company. The school contained a lending-library of about 150 books and the children were examined strictly in theology, mental arithmetic and geography. The men paid ½ d. a week for the education of any number of their children and the pupils were supplied with slates, pencils, pens, ink, copying books and ciphering books.

This school (for boys), then known as the Llynvi Works School was opened in 1845 to accommodate 400 children. The average attendance in 1895 was 154. The infants school catered for 200 children with an average attendance in 1895 of 117. A Miss Margaret Jones was the mistress.

In the *Transactions of the Honourable Society of Cymmrodorion*, 1963, Part II, there is a copy of a report by Matthew Arnold, who, in 1852, visited this school, which he described as a school established for children of the workpeople by the Llynvi Iron Company. He was much impressed and suggested a similar plan for other areas of the country. We quote his words: 'This school is not maintained by the Company, nor by the payments of children who frequent it; but a weekly deduction is made from the wages of every person employed in the Works, whether married or single, to form a fund to defray the expenses of the school, of a library and of medical attendance. Those who have families pay no more than those who have none and any number of his children may be sent to the school by the head of the family . . . The school is regarded as existing for the common benefit of all . . . The deduction (i.e., from the men's wages) is submitted to without reluctance.'

This school became the basis of the New Works School on the same site, with schoolmasters such as Messrs. Protheroe, George Emery and Worth in succession, followed by T. L. Roberts, a North Walian, until he became headmaster of the new Plasnewydd School nearby in Maesteg. The father of the writer of these notes attended the school when George Emery was the head and Miss Cole was the mistress. It was on the site now occupied by the Gateway Stores adjoining the present Maesteg car park.

A mixed British School was opened at Garth in 1874 for 200 pupils. It had an average attendance of 120 in 1895. The headmaster, Llewelyn Phillips, known as Llewelyn Bach, was noted for his short stature and his keen intellect. By 1873 there were 7 British Schools in the valley, including the Castle Street School for girls, with an average attendance in 1895 of 190, the mistress being Miss Hannah Jones. The Castle Street Infants' School, opened in 1875 for 300 children, had an average attendance of 187 in 1895 — with Mrs. Catherine Roberts as mistress.

What about the upper part of the valley? In an article in the *Glamorgan Gazette*, 29 May 1953, Jeremiah Williams, a native of Nantyffyllon, tells us of a crusade by Sir Hugh Owen (1804-81) in the 1840s to establish un-denominational schools, called British Schools, in Wales. At that time, subscription to the 39 Articles of Faith of the Anglican Church was a condition of entering any college at Oxford and of taking a degree at Cambridge.

At a conference of the Association of Welsh Congregational Churches of Glamorgan (Cymanfa Morgannwg) held at Carmel Church, Maesteg, on 23 and 24 May 1866, and reported in *Y Diwygiwr* (The Reformer), July 1866, p. 217, the conviction was expressed that British Schools (Ysgolion Brytanaidd) were the most suitable for Wales. It appealed to the Churches of all denominations to maintain unsectarian schools and to establish new ones where required. The conference looked with disfavour on the 'unprin-cipled behaviour' of nonconformists who sent their children to Church Schools in districts where there were already British Schools and declared that it was unjust for Churchmen to foist National Schools on districts where they were not in accord with the feelings and opinions of the people.

As the Company which sank the first Coegnant pit had failed because of flooding trouble, the old engine-house was converted into a school named the Spelter British School, as there was a spelter works in the district. The school was at the lower end of Metcalf Street, Caerau, and became, in turn, a library and reading-room. The engineer's house was converted into a dwellinghouse in which the said Jeremiah Williams was born.

The first mistress of the school was a Miss Crossman. It was described as an oblong room with 3 large windows. At one end stood the desk of the head mistress. At the other end a gallery for the infants was built, made up of 6 rows of seats with room for 8 children to sit closely together. There were no backs to the seats, and there was a pupil-teacher for each class. Jeremiah Williams stated that he first attended the school when he was two years of age and that the late Dr. Philip B. Ballard was once a pupil-teacher there, the headmistress being a Miss Cole.

As the premises had become unsuitable and overcrowded, the Llynvi Iron Works Company bought Old Salem Baptist Chapel building which was being vacated by the members on their removing to the new spacious Salem Chapel in 1873. The site of the school was near the former Tywith (Nantyffyllon) railway station. It was at this building that the pupils of the

The Goods which I ordered before the holidays have Not Yet come. We want many things badly.

Oct 4th

Attendance still very low. Fever increasing in prevalence.

7th

Mabon's Day. Flannel Fair, Baptists' Tea, And Foundation Stone of Church laid. Compelled to give a holiday.

Syllabus for Oct. 18th

	Reading	Writing	Arith.	Occupation	Obj Less
1st class 2nd class	Blackie's 39 to 46 Moffatt's 18 to 23	Names Dictation of Letter	Add" if 10 Sub" if 10'	Mats 4" pat" Embroidery Button sewing Hemming Knitting	Blackbird Apple Owl Herring Forms & Colors
	Word Building to page 6. & preceding every Reading Lesson from page learnt				
2nd class	Cards 13 to 18	o a s x b h k y z q	Dict" of units Blackboard add" & subt" to 7	Mats Word Building from ax, at, ed, en, em, eg, it, id in, im, ip, ig, ic	B.S. Pencil Apple Owl. Herring. Forms & Colour
	Needle Thimble & Hemming Drills				
1st class	Alphabets. Cards 3 letters Needle & Thimble Drills	m c e s	Mental to 6 Figure making "	Cubes Stick laying	Rabbit Parts of Body Butcher's Shop Doll's Kitchen articles
Babies	3rd column of alph card	1 6 7	Mental to 3.	Letter making	Ditto

76   Typical log-book page of Merthyr Colliery School Infants Department in 1895

former Spelter British School were taught until the new Nantyffyllon School became available at the end of the last century. Even at this new school, when the writer was a pupil, there were 50 to 60 pupils to each class.

Under the Education Act of 1870, re-inforced by the Act of 1880 elementary schooling became compulsory up to the age of thirteen years. The control of all British Schools (or Works Schools) was transferred to School Boards. In the Llynfi Valley the authority was known as 'The Cwmdu and Llangynwyd Higher United District School Board'. By 1880, the Maesteg and Llynvi Works Schools had become vested in this local Board and were described as being 'in excellent order and fully efficient'. Some of the Works Schools that had been closed because of local difficulties were later re-opened. One of them was the Maesteg Merthyr Colliery School at Maesteg, where the Drill Hall in Ewenny Road is now situated. It was originally opened in 1877 to provide for 344 children. In 1895, the average attendance was 256. W. R. Thomas was the headmaster, assisted by Miss Mary Ann Williams.

Hereunder are details of the Works Schools that had been transferred to the control of the School Board by 1894:

Glamorgan Iron Works Schools

(1) Maesteg Iron Works School: 543 scholars with average attendance of 328 and an annual grant of £280.

(2) Llynvi Iron Works School: 614 scholars with average attendance of 259 and annual grant of £266.12.0.

Schools of Non-ferrous Metal Industries

Spelter Works School: 312 scholars with average attendance of 261 and annual grant of £228.7.6.

Colliery Schools

Maesteg Merthyr (Oakwood): 304 scholars with average attendance of 259 and annual grant of £205.7.0.

In all there were at that time in the valley 7 British (non-sectarian) schools, 2 National (Church of England) schools and 1 Roman Catholic school.

Much helpful information is contained in an article by Leslie Wynne Evans, Cardiff, in the *Journal of the National Library of Wales*, Summer, 1967: 'School Boards and the Works Schools System after the Education Act, 1870'. The Glamorgan Record Office contains administrative records of the Glamorgan School Boards—over 300 volumes in all. The minutes of only 3 of the School Boards are missing.

Under the Education Act of 1902, known as the Balfour Act, these Boards were abolished and schools became administered by the County Councils,

77 Garth Primary School thespians, 1916

78 1923 class at Plasnewydd Primary School

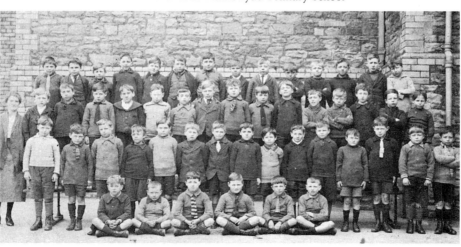

79 Nantyffyllon Infants Group V, *c.*1909
Brinley Richards is second from right in the second row; his elder brother,
Gwynfryn, fifth from right in the back row

with autonomy for County Boroughs. However, there still remained non-provided or denominational schools. As the Act stated that County Councils should not interfere with reasonable facilities for religious instruction provided by the relevant religious body, there followed a revolt by County Councils, some Welsh M.P.'s and the Passive Resistance Movement, as the Act made denominational schools maintainable by the rates.

The Education Act of 1944, known as the Butler Act, made fundamental changes in school administration. Its provisions are too recent and well-known to require reiteration. To celebrate the Festival of Wales in 1958 the Glamorgan Record Office published a booklet giving an account (pp. 17 and 18) of the changes in the administration of schools in Glamorgan. All these documents would form a basis for a very serious study of the history of school administration in Glamorgan (including the Llynfi Valley) from 1870 onwards. There are over 1000 school log books (including many from the Llynfi Valley) at the Record Office strong rooms at the County Hall at Cardiff.

(a) The Maesteg Roman Catholic School

We are indebted to Mr. Ronald P. Browne for his informative booklet published on the occasion of the centenary of this school in 1975. It was called the St. Mary's and St. Patrick's R.C. Primary School and was built in Ewenny Road, Maesteg. It is now housed in new buildings near Monica Street, Maesteg, where Mr. Browne, a former pupil, is headmaster.

In the early days the pupils were mainly children of Irish immigrants forced out of their own country by poverty and the resultant famines. When school attendance became compulsory in 1870, the third Earl of Dunraven came to the rescue by leaving £1,800 to help to provide a school. He also gave £2,400 as an endowment between Bridgend and Maesteg. The Church itself was opened at Ewenny Road in 1872 and the school in 1875, the first mistress being Miss Jane Barrett. She had 67 children from four to fourteen under her care, all taught in one room. Pupils were also drawn from the Cymer, Bryn and Llangynwyd areas. Of these 67 pupils, 12 could read creditably and 6 could write legibly. We are informed that all were backward in arithmetic.

There was much poverty, and parents were unable to pay the school fees of the children. The school log book in 1877 showed that boys of eleven years were leaving school to work at the mills. The mortality rate was very high. In 1881, 5 died of scarlet fever.

The school was financed by Government aid and inspectors visited the school from time to time. It was felt that there was religious discrimination as the valley was predominantly Protestant. The Poor Law Guardians refused to pay the fees of destitute children. However, school fees were abolished by Parliament in 1891. The average attendance in 1895 was 72, with Miss Ann White as mistress.

In 1900, there were over 130 pupils. Nine years later there were 225 pupils, of whom 70 were taught by one teacher in a room that should normally have contained 45. The need for a new school became urgent and the foundation-stone was laid (with the permission of the Abbot and Council of Douai Abbey) by J. Boyd Harvey on 18 October 1908. He also opened the new school on 1 June 1909, the contractor being Jenkin Lewis, Maesteg, and the architect E. W. Burnett. By 1922 even the new school had become overcrowded and the younger pupils had to be removed to the former school premises at the League Hall in Ewenny Road, Maesteg. The building of a new wing to the present school buildings in 1961 enabled these pupils to be re-accommodated there. By 1976 there were 240 children between five and eleven at the school—all drawn from the Maesteg area.

(b) Secondary Education

In 1900 the local School Board bought Plasnewydd House, Maesteg, the home of Captain Morris and originally built in 1832 for Mr. Buckland, manager of the Maesteg Iron Works. The building consisted of two big rooms and two small rooms on the ground floor—all suitable as classrooms. It was converted into a Higher Standard School and also housed the Pupil-Teachers' Centre for teacher trainees.

In his book, *Sand in the Glass*, Michael Gareth Llewelyn, alias Frederic Evans, states that one class in this Higher Grade School, as it was then called, had been the early training-ground of two doctors, eight schoolmasters, two lawyers, two mining engineers, one town clerk, one director of education, one estate agent, a novelist and dramatist, several farmers, competent clerks, and a registrar.

In 1911 the local School Board decided to convert the school into a Secondary School, which was opened on 8 January 1912, with G. S. Griffiths as first Headmaster. Two corrugated zinc covered buildings in the adjoining yard were used for science and art (the latter as an assembly-room and gymnasium as well). There was a staff of 8 only, including the headmaster who taught Scripture. There were more subjects than teachers with the result that the outstanding scholar and historian, later known as Dr. Tom Richards, had to teach History, Welsh and Latin. There was then no chemistry department. Although the staff appeared to be highly proficient, it was observed by cynics that, as the appointing body were in the main ardent Baptists, the staff appointed by them corresponded in allegiance to the same denomination! Incidentally, the two immediate successors of the first headmaster were also Baptists, although the domination of Baptists on the governing body had long ceased.

The school drew pupils from Blaengwynfi, Glyncorrwg, Cymer, Blaengarw, Pontycymer, and Pontyrhyl, as well as from the Llynfi Valley. Admission to the school was by scholarship examinations, written and oral. Those who sought an open scholarship did not commit themselves to entering the teaching profession and had to pay for their own text-books, whilst the 'probationary' scholars, who were so committed, got their textbooks free. There were no grants or free train or bus services, and no school prizes for which pupils could compete. There were about 120 scholars at the school when the writer was a pupil, with 10 boys and 20 girls in the first form. Those who lived a mile or two away from the school all walked. As there was a pub near every pit to attract miners, so was there a tuck-shop near the school to meet the 'needs' of the pupils.

The medium of instruction was English, even when Welsh was taught, and the morning assembly-service never included a Welsh hymn although a big percentage of pupils at that time belonged to local Welsh Chapels.

The two ultimate targets were the Oxford Local Junior and Senior examinations and if the pupils obtained sufficient passes in essential subjects in the Senior examinations, they could claim exemption from the London and Welsh matriculation examinations and thus gain admission to a University. 'O' and 'A' levels were then unknown. There were no Higher Level examinations at the school in those days. It was in 1923 that the Central Welsh Board examinations supplanted those of the Oxford Local Senior and Junior.

As the buildings had become insufficient for the fast-growing school, a new school was opened in 1923 on the Park Site, Maesteg, overlooking the town from the west side. A further wing was opened in 1929 and a sports pavilion costing £6,000 was added in 1971. Ultimately, yet a newer school was opened in Llangynwyd in 1960. As the site was near the famous Brynllywarch Farm, one cannot but express regret that the school is known as the Maesteg Senior Comprehensive School, which is as prosaic as it is unimaginative. Ysgol Brynllywarch, which would have had such historical significance, would surely have been preferable. In the naming of schools, our forefathers set an example by giving them such meaningful and charming names as Blaencaerau, Blaenllynfi, Tyderwen, Plasnewydd, Llwynderw, and Cwmfelin.

As the school at Llangynwyd catered in the main for pupils then in the Maesteg urban area, and as the school had been built outside that area, despite local objections, it was considered 'a corner of a foreign field that was for ever Llwyni'. This school became comprehensive in 1966 and is now in the Ogwr Borough area.

In 1962 a very informative brochure was published on the occasion of the 50th anniversary of the school. Another book— *Rhagor o Atgofion Cardi* (More Reminiscences of a Cardi) by Dr. Tom Richards, Bangor, the senior master at the school from 1912 to 1926, contains a lively and interesting account of his days at the school.

In all there are now in the valley 19 primary schools, including the Welsh School where the medium of instruction is Welsh. We also have the Senior

80　Maesteg Secondary School Form VI, 1948
(Standing) D R L Jones, W Richards, D B James, G Williams, T Williams,
J Howells, M Rees, T Parry, J Hayes, J Edwards, G Thomas, E Whittaker
(Sitting) M Watkins, P Lyons, J —, P Jenkins, Mr E Jones, Mr P Thomas, P Davies,
P Harris, B James, P Richards
(Front Row) S Powis, —, L Thomas, —, R James

Comprehensive School at Llangynwyd, whilst the former Maesteg Secondary School is now the Junior Comprehensive School for Girls and the former Llwynderw Schools at the lower end of Maesteg is the Junior Comprehensive School for Boys.

It would be too invidious a task to provide details of the achievements of the old pupils of these valley schools. On his visit to the area in September, 1935, Oliver F. G. Stanley, then President of the Board of Education, made complimentary references to the people of Mid Glamorgan in their pursuit of education. There are lists available of successful pupils in the Castle Street schools in Maesteg for as far back as 1879 and 1880, with details of the subjects studied under the Science and Art Department, South Kensington, for four sessions. They make formidable reading. The subjects included Physiography, Mathematics, Art, Geometry, Magnetism and Electricity, Geology, Agriculture, and Mining. It appears obvious that at that time the emphasis was on inspired teaching rather than on the provision of new school buildings.

(c) General Education and Entertainment

Although at one time many young pupils were eager to pass the 'Labour Exam' to enable them to leave school at thirteen, instead of at fourteen, in order to work underground and get pocket money, thereby attaining a state of independence and manhood, yet, generally speaking, the desire for education was intense.

Through the influence of Sir John Bowring, Managing Director of the Llynvi Iron Works, a Mechanics' Hall and Library was opened in the early forties of the last century. In 1847, he instituted a series of well-attended lectures on technical subjects.

Hundreds of 'penny readings', namely competitive musical and literary meetings, were held from the first half of the last century to at least the first quarter of the present century. One favourite competition was reading aloud an unpunctuated piece of prose called *darn heb atalnodau.* A Welsh lecture at Tabernacle Baptist Chapel, Maesteg, by the Rev. W. L. Evans on 7 October 1859 on the life and death of Socrates was extensively advertised as a 'feast for the cultured mind'.

A Literary and Debating Society was formed in Maesteg in the Autumn of 1880 at the then Post Office. The subject of one debate was 'Should the House of Lords be abolished?' A lecture on 'Early Closing' attracted 40 people. That same year, Science and Art classes were initiated under the tutorship of Philip B. Ballard, who later became well-known in the educational world. Some of the subjects taught were Agriculture, Geology, Light, Heat and Sound, Magnetism and Electricity. In January 1881 the Rev. Fred Evans, minister of Salem Baptist Church, Nantyffyllon, began a series of lectures every fortnight on the remarkable subject: *Yr Anifail fel*

Pregethwr (The Animal as a Preacher). He spoke on the fox, the beaver and the horse.

In 1881 a Coffee Tavern was opened at the Co-operative Hall, Maesteg. A quarterly subscription of 2/6 was paid by the 60 members who formed themselves into a debating society. There were debates on subjects such as 'Ought dancing to form a branch of education?' and 'Should the stage be supported?' In April 1882 'Was Napoleon a greater General than Wellington?' was debated. On 10 November that year a crowded Town Hall heard a lecture on 'The Land of the Czar'. The following year the members staged a play in the Town Hall — 'The Ticket of Leave Man'. In 1887 the Maesteg Dramatic Society performed two plays — 'Aurora Floyd' and 'Lodger or Dodger'.

In 1889 Col. North donated £500 to the valley miners for a library and reading-room and gave 200 books a year thereafter to provide a library for his workmen. The miners contributed 1d. for each £1 of their wages towards the maintenance of the local miners' libraries and institutes. Caerau Workmen's Library was opened in 1905 and among the first books presented to the library was a Bible by Dr. Harris Jones, Caerau. Dr. Hector Jones, Nantyffyllon, gave a marble clock for the billiard room.

In the first half of the present century there were 5 miners' institutes and libraries, all of which are now closed. The closed buildings at Caerau, Nantyffyllon and Cwmdu present a sad sight when the feverish activities of the past are remembered. A full account of the demise of welfare halls has been given by Hywel Francis in his article 'Survey of Miners' Institutes and Welfare Hall Libraries' (*Llafur*, Vol. 1, No. 2, May 1973, pp. 35-61). The Mid Glamorgan County Council now administers the Central Library at

81   Trustees and Committee of North's Memorial Hall and Institute, Maesteg, photographed at the Opening of Nantyfyllon Institute, Bangor Terrace, 28 August 1926

Maesteg. It was opened in 1955. The Caerau Institute is now (1981) a bingo hall with 200 to 300 attending six nights a week. Other halls are similarly used.

Limitations of space prevent us from giving an account of the hundreds of local eisteddfodau and *cyrddau diwylliadol* (mutual improvement societies) organised by the many active churches in the valley, and of the scores of distinguished lecturers who have shared with us their knowledge and culture. The Nantyffyllon Literary and Debating Society was an outstanding institution for many years and provided much needed practice for the many embryo orators of the valley.

The standard of entertainment, on the other hand, was at that time understandably primitive. In the seventies of the last century before the Town Hall was built, portable theatres visited Maesteg. They were run by people named Warren, Noakes, Johnson and Ebley, who arranged performances on the three-cornered field where the Town Hall now stands. A Sam Michael had his 'wheel of fortune' in his Crown and Feather stall. Ebley's Travelling Theatre at the Maesteg Fair performed 'Maria of the Red Barn', 'The Face at the Window' and 'East Lynne'. The early cinema, called Poole's Myroriama, gave us 'The Battle of Trafalgar'. There were regular visits by travelling shows, menageries and circuses to provide lighter relief to ease a drab and humdrum existence. One form of amusement was a competition on a raised platform at the Maesteg Fair to decide on the first to consume a basin-ful of steaming hot broth straight from the oven or cauldron. The shouts of encouragement from the partisans in the crowd formed part of the entertainment.

82   Maesteg May Day Show, 1905

At the beginning of the present century, Richard Dooner came to Maesteg and arranged for the first actual motion-pictures in the valley, the first three being of short duration. The first 'talkie'—Al Jolson in the 'Singing Fool'—was shown in his picture palace in the Maesteg market place. In 1935 Richard Dooner became President of the National Cinematograph Exhibitors Association of Great Britain and Ireland. It happened to be the year of the jubilee of King George V and Queen Mary, and he was presented to both at a silver jubilee banquet at the Guildhall, London.

He was one of the first to bring the cinema to South Wales, having started at Bristol in 1896 with an acetylene lamp for displaying slides. He died, aged 80, at Maesteg in 1950.

On 19 October 1914 the Maesteg New Theatre was opened, the proprietors being the Maesteg Property Co. Ltd. It was opened with the West End musical 'Wait and See', with ballet dances from the Russian Imperial Ballet aided by the Eight Brighton Belles, the Watteau Girls and the United Clefts. Since then the Theatre has been the scene of grand-operas, plays, variety concerts and silent films. Edward Dunstan, the famous actor, brought his Company to act a different Shakespearean play every night for a whole week. He also acted locally in 'The Wandering Jew'.

At one time there were five local cinemas—the Coliseum and the Cosy, Caerau (both now demolished) the Plaza, Maesteg (now a Country Club), the New Theatre (turned to Bingo) and the Regal, Maesteg, the sole surviving cinema.

For many years the Glamorgan County Council provided evening classes in the various schools of the valley. They have now given way to Adult Education Centres. Classes under the W.E.A. and the University were popular. In comparatively recent years (1939-1945) there were five youth centres at Caerau, Nantyffyllon, Plasnewydd School and Llwynderw School at Maesteg, and at Llangynwyd. In the meantime there has been a serious decline in their numbers and influence.

46. The Administration of the Law

It is not clear when justices of the peace were first appointed or when they began to hold Quarter Sessions in the County. Names of justices of the peace for Glamorgan were attached to the calendar of gaol delivery of the Great Sessions held at Cardiff on 27 March 1542. They had evidently acted as such before the Sessions were held. Roger Carne of Ewenny had been appointed clerk of the peace and of the crown in Glamorgan in 1539.

Prior to the last century, Court Leets were held biannually on 1 May (St. James's Day) and 29 September (St. Michael's Day). The bailiff was appointed by the Lord of the Manor.

Daniel R. Waldin, to whom we have referred so often, could remember the first lock-up prison on the site now known as Llynfi Road, Maesteg, today. It was below the level of the road and bricked inside. He could remember the old stocks in the prison, but could not recollect having seen prisoners there. The prison contained bare iron bedsteads.

For years up to the thirties of this century, police court cases were heard weekly at the overcrowded Maesteg U.D.C. offices. More accommodation became a necessity. On 10 October 1938, Sir William Jenkins, Cymer, then chairman of the Glamorgan Standing Joint Committee, which controlled the Police, opened officially the new County Police Station at Maesteg. The new Police Courts attached thereto at Station Street, were opened on the same day by Alderman John Evans, the chairman of the Glamorgan County Council. The buildings were said to be of up-to-date design and were heralded as the most modern of police stations, with a Police Court and a Juvenile Court costing, in all, £15,722. In fact they were claimed to be an architectural and constructional achievement.

In 1977 these very buildings were closed as they were considered to be inefficient for administrative purposes! The facilities, it was asserted, were not

83   County Police Court, Station Street, Maesteg

up to the required standard. The buildings were too large to be heated sufficiently and did not contain waiting rooms or consulting rooms for solicitors.

New Magistrates' Courts to serve Bridgend and the surrounding districts (including Maesteg) were officially opened by Lord Justice Edmund Davies on 18 May 1970 at a cost of £160,000. This meant that the people of the Llynfi Valley, who numbered over 20,000, were deprived of the right to be tried, even for trivial offences, in their home town.

Since April 1980, no deeds or documents can be franked at the local Post Office but must be sent to Cardiff for that purpose.

However, Llynfi Valley undefended divorce cases, previously tried at Cardiff and Swansea, can now be heard at the Bridgend County Court. The first hearing was on 8 May 1968, when Judge E. P. Wallis-Jones, sitting as a Divorce Commissioner, heard twelve undefended divorce cases.

As late as the twenties or thirties of this century, it was not unusual for magistrates to hear forty to fifty cases of drunkenness, which were usually disposed of an hour before proceeding to deal with the more serious offences. Despite the increase in drinking facilities for men, women and youths, the incidence of public drunkenness appears to be negligible. The difficulty of being consistent in regard to cases of indecent language is accentuated by the fact that all the Anglo-Saxon words which formed the basis of complaints in the past now appear uncensored in novels and plays that are considered classical and artistic.

During the depression period between the two wars the average purchase-price of a house in the Llynfi Valley was about £150. The lawyer's fee for preparing a transfer under £300 was £3.15.0. Incidentally, a big proportion of the valley houses are freehold. Single law practices have disappeared, whilst the £80 stamp on the articles of a law student is no longer required. The articled clerk is now paid substantially for learning his trade, whereas forty to fifty years ago he had to pay a substantial fee to his principal for the privilege of being articled, and be unpaid during the period of his articles.

The advent of legal aid and the extension of grounds for divorce, apart from the consequences of the arrival of the car, have extended considerably the scope of the work of the lawyers. Previous to the granting of legal aid to needy litigants, solicitors acting for impoverished wives in domestic cases had to be content with nominal fees and sometimes with nothing but a promise to pay for their services.

Earlier in the century, some Llynfi Valley ministers of the Gospel were known as makers of wills for their members and neighbours. Sometimes the amateurish and incorrect wording of those wills would lead to unfortunate consequences. This practice appears to have ceased. An echo of clerical influence can be discerned in the will of one Howell David of Llangynwyd, who, in 1729, stipulated, *inter alia*: 'First I give my soul unto my Creator . . . my body to be buried in Christian burial'. A Nantyffyllon man who died in 1901 bequeathed his cottage to his wife as long as she remained a widow and 'led a pure undefiled life' but if she re-married or 'led an impure life', she would forfeit any claim under the will. It used to be the custom in the valley to read the will of the deceased to a gathering of relatives and anticipating beneficiaries at his home immediately after the funeral. This practice has long since ceased, thereby obviating scenes occasionally caused by persons disappointed under the will.

In 1937, in a County Court case in Bridgend, an octogenarian lady from Maesteg asked to give her evidence in Welsh. His Honour Judge Clark Williams, known as a humanitarian and a highly efficient Judge, readily agreed and said that the services of an interpreter were unnecessary, as he, the Judge, the Registrar, the two barristers and two instructing solicitors on both sides and also the Defendant were Welsh-speaking. The elderly lady, who was the plaintiff, was examined and cross-examined by the respective Counsel in Welsh, and questions in Welsh were also put to her by the Judge, who was an efficient shorthand writer.

The writer of these notes has prepared wills in Welsh, and in our very mixed society, he acted in a valley divorce case where the petitioner was German, the respondent was English, the two witnesses were Dutch and Irish, respectively, whilst a Irishman and a Welshman were cited by the respondent!

A well-known law case — Thomas v. Sawkins — had its setting in Caerau during the turbulent thirties, when Communism was a force in the valley. It arose from a Communist meeting held in Caerau and attended by Sergeant Sawkins of Caerau. His right of entry was challenged by the Communist local secretary, Fred Thomas, Caerau. The Divisional Court held that the police could enter and remain at public meetings held on private premises wherever they apprehended that seditious speeches or a breach of the peace might occur (1935.2K.B.249). The case was important enough for Professor Goodhart to discuss it in an article: 'Thomas v. Sawkins — A Constitutional Innovation' (1936), 6 Cam.L.J.22.

The Glamorgan County Police was established in 1841. We are told that the early records have been lost, due to salvage drives and the flooding of the cellars of a country house where the remnants were stored during the last War. Most of the available records and exhibits can now be seen at the Police Museum at the Bridgend headquarters, established as the result of the initiative and researches of ex-Deputy Chief Constable E. R. Baker.

The former custom of having a policeman 'on the beat' was discontinued many years ago owing to economic circumstances. It has resulted in a deterioration of conduct in the valley. At one time there were only a sergeant and three P.C.'s in Nantyffyllon.

Prior to 1870 there were no local (valley) justices of the peace. In the main, they were appointed from members of county and wealthy families living outside the area, the venue of the Court being at Bridgend.

Mr. Emrys Jones, Maesteg, who returned in 1981, became the first local man to be appointed chairman of the Bridgend Bench of Magistrates.

Mr. J. Gareth Miller, a native of Maesteg and now Professor of Law at Norwich University, has written at least three volumes on legal matters that have received favourable reviews: (1) The Disciplinary Powers of Professional Bodies (2) Family Property and Financial Provisions (1974) and (3) The Machinery of Succession (1977). Mr. Roy Snape, also a native of Maesteg, has received the rare distinction as a solicitor of being first appointed Deputy Circuit Judge in 1975 and in 1979 of being promoted to be a Recorder on the Wales and Chester Circuit. His grandfather, Thomas Jones of the Three Horse Shoes Hotel, was one of the first twelve members of the Maesteg U.D.C.

When the writer of this volume qualified as a solicitor in 1930 there were six solicitors' offices in the valley, each practice manned by one solicitor only. The number has been reduced to three, each one served by several partners.

47. Local Government

Historians tell us that local government bodies were functioning in a codified way even in the days of Hywel Dda several centuries before the present parliamentary system came into being. In the main, resident farmers were the overseers of the poor of the parish in the Llynfi Valley from 1766 to 1819. According to records of vestry meetings of the hamlet of Cwmdu (part of the Parish of Llangynwyd), it was decided in 1816 that constant work should be given to paupers at 6d. a day as maintenance for those able to work and 1/- a week for each child under seven years. The minutes were signed by the then Vicar of Llangynwyd, John Parry. The Vestry minute-book, October, 1845, showed that 13 people had been excused payment of rates.

The valley was governed by the Parish Vestry but by an Order in Council, dated 5 June 1858, the Cwmdu Local Board of Health was created in accordance with the provisions of the Public Health Act, 1848. It consisted of 12 members, one-third of whom retired annually, but subject to re-election. The meetings were held bi-monthly.

At the first meeting held at the Castle Hotel, Maesteg, on 26 July 1858 under the chairmanship of the Rev. R. Pendril Llewelyn, Vicar of Llangynwyd, W. H. Buckland, Manager of the Maesteg Iron Works, was appointed chairman for the ensuing year. The first members were the Rev. R. P. Llewelyn, the Revs. Thomas Hopkins of Bethania and David Phillips (Phillips y Post) of Tabor, Charles J. Hampton of the Llynvi Iron Works, Thomas Thomas, father of Dr. W. H. Thomas, the Rev. John Jones,

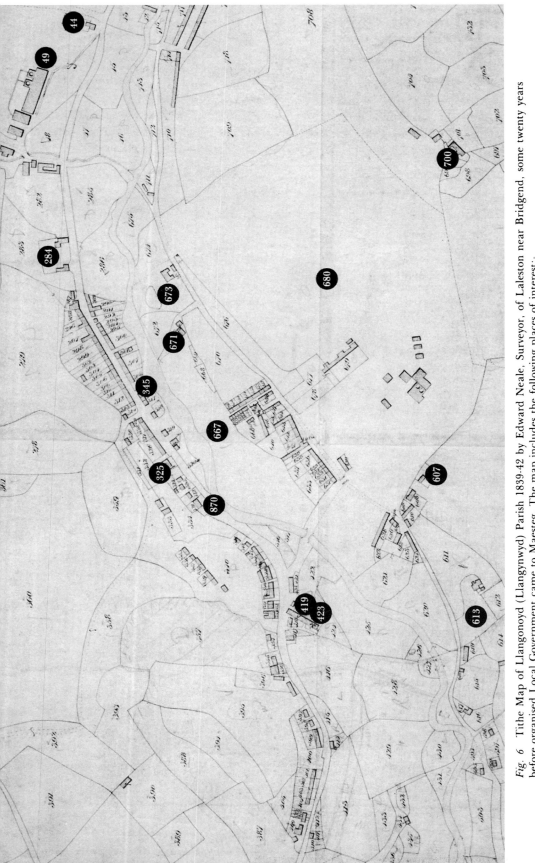

Fig. 6 Tithe Map of Llangonoyd (Llangynwyd) Parish 1839-42 by Edward Neale, Surveyor, of Laleston near Bridgend, some twenty years before organised Local Government came to Maesteg. The map includes the following places of interest:-

870 The Tram Road (now Llwydarth Road, Bethania St., Commercial St. etc). Nearby are:-

419-423 Company Row (now Maesteg Row) **325** Rock House **284** Bowrington Lodge (Llynfi Lodge) **49** Cambrian Iron Works

44 Company Shop

Near the lower road (now Bridgend Road and Castle Street) are located —

613 Clepthryf House **607** The Crown inn **680** Maesteg Iron Works

minister of Zoar Church(?), William Davies of the White Lion Hotel, William Anthony, Thomas Williams, Dr. James Lewis and W. H. Buckland.

At the first meeting Dr. James Lewis, who later became founder of the Porthcawl Rest Home, questioned the legality of the elections, but his allegations were later proved to be unfounded. It was he who first suggested providing a town hall and market place. William Powell was appointed clerk and collector of the Board at a salary of £20 per annum plus rent of £5 per annum for fire and candles for one room. The general rate was fixed at 6d. in the £1. Subsequent meetings were held at Rock Street, Maesteg. The Board immediately ordered 600 new lamps and contracted with the new local gas company for the supply of gas, as the streets were unlit at night. Water-mains were connected with the homes of the people.

In 1887 the district was extended to include the Upper Hamlet and the title of the Board was changed to the Maesteg Board of Health.

At a few vestry meetings held in Llangynwyd village in 1894 the villagers decided that they did not want to be annexed to the Maesteg Board of Health or to any other Board, but wished to remain as they were. They had never sought to be annexed to any other body. They contended that it was only a section of the Maesteg people that had opened the matter. There was also opposition from Cwmfelin and Llangynwyd, being south of the Cerdin brook, to inclusion in the Maesteg Urban area, despite the fact that it was with the higher part of the valley, including Maesteg, and not the lower part south of Llangynwyd, that there existed a close community of interest.

84 Bethania Street, Maesteg, with gas lamp, *c.* 1918

48. The Maesteg U.D.C.

By an Order in Council dated 13 September 1894, under the provisions of the Local Government Act, 1894, the Maesteg Urban District Council was formed. The district was divided into three wards, and in April 1903 divided into four wards to include Caerau. Each ward had four elected members. The area was a very compact one of 6,707 acres and included Caerau at the top end, and Nantyffyllon, Maesteg and Garth.

Maesteg is one of the most attractive mining valley towns in South Wales and is nine miles from Bridgend. Afforestation on the west side of the urban area has beautified the former barren mountains.

The first members of the Maesteg U.D.C. elected in 1894 were:-

West Ward. J. H. Thomas (brother to Dr. W. H. Thomas), Thomas Jones

85   General and Water Rate receipt of 1896, which makes nostalgic reading today!

Receipt.

MAESTEG URBAN DISTRICT COUNCIL.

No....**369**   .....*28*.....day of.....*May*.........1896.

Received of Mr...*D. H. Jones*...........Occupier (or Owner)

the sum of...*One*...Pounds,....*Eight*...Shillings, and...*Six*...Pence,

in respect of General District and Water Rates, viz.:—

	£	s.	d.
Rate made on 24th March, 1896—			
General District Rate on £..*9*...*10*......at 2/- ..		*19*	
Water Rate on £.........*19*............at 6d. ..		*9*	*6*
Previous Arrears			
TOTAL	*1*	*8*	*6*

	£	s.	d.
1st Instalment.........................			
2nd Instalment.........................			
	1	*8*	*6*

W. K. Thomas
....
COLLECTOR.

(Three Horse Shoes Hotel), T. Boucher (manager of the Maesteg Gas Works) and Thomas Rees (Garnlwyd).

East Ward. James Barrow (the mining engineer), Dr. W. H. Thomas, Evan Williams (father of Christopher Williams, the artist) and Rees Rees (Cae Chwarel).

Nantyffyllon. Dr. John Davies, J. Boyd Harvey (managing director of North's), David Davies (Liverpool House) and William Griffiths (Coegnant).

The first clerk was Robert Scale, followed in turn by E. E. Davies (1912-23), A. King-Davies (1923-1953), and T. King-Davies until the demise of the Council in 1973. The first chairman of the Maesteg U.D.C. was James Barrow. The youngest chairman was William A. Betty, Caerau (1923-24).

W. Y. Davies of the former White Lion Hotel, Maesteg, and a well known local musician, was also surveyor to the old Maesteg Local Board. The first surveyor to the Maesteg U.D.C. was W. H. Humphreys, followed by S. J. Harpur, Evan Davies, Lewis W. Jones and Tudor Isaac (until the amalgamation of local authorities in 1973). Ralph Powell was appointed the first Accountant in 1924, followed by W. T. Williams, D. E. James and G. Hutchens (until 1973).

Dr. John Davies was M.O.H. to the old Maesteg Local Board. After the formation of the Maesteg U.D.C., the Dr. Thomas family of Bron-y-garn figured prominently as M.O.H's. Dr. Ralph W. H. Thomas, who resigned in 1946, succeeded his father, Dr. T. J. Bell Thomas in 1937. Since then, four or five doctors have served in that capacity, the last of whom was Dr. H. P. Evans (until 1973).

The Maesteg Council never had a full-time Clerk or M.O.H. and it was only in 1924 that a full-time Accountant was appointed.

Apart from the M.O.H., the head of the Health Department was known by various titles, such as Inspector of Nuisances, Sanitary Inspector, or Lodging House Inspector. He was ultimately called the Public Health Officer. The last three who served in that capacity were Griffith E. Howells, D. M. Thomas and Ivor Davies (again until 1973).

The Maesteg Council was not an educational body and could only nominate representatives for school managers, governors of Grammar Schools and Swansea University Court of Governors. Most of the committees consisted of all members of the Council.

The new Council Offices were opened in Talbot Street, Maesteg in 1914.

In 1931 the Maesteg Council, under the provisions of the Local Government Act, 1929, decided to apply for the extension of its boundaries to reach as far as the outskirts of Tondu and to take in the whole of the parishes of Llangynwyd Middle and Llangynwyd Lower (part of the Penybont R.D.C. area) and Betws (Ogmore and Garw U.D.C. area). Some

86   Maesteg Town Hall and Council Chambers

87   Looking up Talbot Street from the Town Hall

of the reasons given were: (1) The two schools in Cwmfelin and Pontrhyd-ycyff, both in the Penybont R.D.C. area, were part of the Maesteg area for educational purposes; (2) Cwmfelin did its shopping mainly in the Maesteg urban area, there being a far closer affinity socially and otherwise between Cwmfelin and Maesteg rather than between Cwmfelin and the lower part of the valley; (3) Before the Maesteg Cemetery was opened, it was mainly the people of the upper part of the valley who were buried in Llangynwyd churchyard with comparatively few from Coetrehen and Aberkenfig; (4) For many years Cwmfelin was represented on the Llangynwyd Joint Burial Board which controlled the Maesteg cemetery.

In any case it came to nought, partly owing to the opposition of the Cwmfelin area itself. It did not become a reality until the amalgamation of the five local Mid Glamorgan authorities in 1973.

Council powers were further reduced in 1948 by the centralisation of services such as lighting, rating, health, maternity and child welfare, and isolation hospitals.

In 1930 the product of a 1d. rate was only £250. It increased to £1,500 by 1967, followed by much higher increases later. The biggest preceptor was the Glamorgan County Council. The product of a 6d. rate was allowed for social projects. In 1958 the Maesteg Council was awarded the Western Mail shield for being the urban area that best celebrated *Gŵyl Cymru* (the Festival of Wales) in Wales. The award was based mainly on the publication of a souvenir brochure on the history of the valley.

In the same year the centenary of local government in the valley was celebrated by a dinner in the Town Hall.

In 1970 the Council was presented with armorial bearings. Sir Cennydd Traherne, K.G., Lord Lieutenant of Glamorgan, attended a Council meeting to hand to the Chairman (Councillor E. Vivian Thomas) Letters Patent, dated 4 February 1970. The Coat of Arms bears the motto *Gorau Gweithio—Cydweithio* (The Best type of Service is Co-operation).

On the amalgamation of local authorities, Maesteg U.D.C. joined with the Councils of Ogmore & Garw, Bridgend, Penybont and Porthcawl in forming the Ogwr Borough Council. The Maesteg Council ceased to function in 1973 and the Ogwr Borough Council began to operate in 1974.

Maesteg Council had been advised by financial experts that merging with neighbouring authorities would result in financial savings through bulk-purchasing, in the sharing of major undertakings such as sewerage and lighting, and through the overall reduction of staff that a unified Council would require. As Maesteg was fast becoming a dormitory town, the local rate revenue was not very high. By amalgamation, the rates levied on big commercial undertakings in the adjoining Penybont area, including the

Fig. 7 (Overleaf) The central Llynfi Valley as depicted on the marvellously detailed Six-Inch Ordnance Survey Map of 1875-76

Maesteg Urban District Council

Armorial Bearings

Granted by Letters Patent dated 4th February, 1970

OFFICIAL DESCRIPTION.

Arms :   Or three Lozenges in pale Sable between two Flaunches indented Vert.

Crest :   On a Wreath Argent and Vert A demi-Dragon Gules armed and langued Azure supporting a Celtic Cross Or, Mantled Gules doubled Or.

INTERPRETATION.

Arms :   The background of the shield, on which the arms are borne, is known as the " field." As Maesteg means " The fair field," the heraldic field is gold. On either side of the valley in which Maesteg lies are hills and these have been symbolised by the two arcs of a circle, known as " flaunches." These are green to suggest agriculture and indented to underline the fact that they symbolise hills. The black diamonds, technically called lozenges, are used to symbolise coal. Three are shown on the shield to represent the three collieries. Caerau. Coegnant and St. John's.

Crest :   There are two devices, the arms, painted on the shield, and the crest, modelled onto the helm. It is for this reason that the helm. with its mantle, originally intended to deflect sword blows is depicted beneath the crest. The dragon supports a Celtic Cross, symbolising the Church at the head of the valley. It is fitting that a symbol of the Church should dominate not only the valley. but also the Coat of Arms.

The wreath at the base of the crest is of the Welsh colours. silver and green.

Motto :   The motto is " Gorau gweithio   cyd weithio."
                        " The best service is co-operation."

89   The last Maesteg Council, 1973
(Top Row) G Hutchens (Accountant), R Lewis (Assistant Clerk), Councillors
Glyn Devine, Danny Thomas, A Lewis (Caerau), W B Evans & Vivian Thomas,
Tudor Isaac (Surveyor), Islwyn Thomas (Councillor), G Jenkins (Assistant
   Surveyor), W J Venner (Councillor), Ivor Davies (Chief Health Inspector).
(Seated) Dr H P Evans (M.O.H.), Councillors J O Rees, D M Thomas, Brinley
Richards, M Fitzgibbon (Chairman), Edgar Lewis (Vice-Chairman), J King Davies
   (Clerk), Councillors C M Jones, W White & Jennie Gibbs.
Councillors Dilwyn Jones and Arthur Edwards missing

Paper Mills and Bridgend Trading Estate, would be available for the whole
area. Subsequent events have not justified such optimism.

Before the amalgamation, Councillors were not paid for attending
Council meetings. When the writer of these notes was chairman of the
Maesteg Council in 1950, his chairman's allowance was £25 of which £14
was spent in one evening on the occasion of a visit by a French football team.
When he was chairman for the fourth time in 1969 his allowance was £200
plus £250 in Fund B to be drawn upon, if required, but subject to the
consent of the Council. By 1972-73 it had increased to £300 with £500 in
Fund B. The local press informs us that councillors' expenses for the Ogwr
Council for the financial year 1980-81 amounted to £52,401.61. It is readily
conceded that the duties falling on councillors are much heavier, and that
attending meetings at Bridgend would of necessity involve higher
disbursements.

When the Maesteg Council ceased to exist, the local Community Council
took over some of its minor functions, but the scope of its authority is very
limited.

Administration of the Poor Law remained outside the scope of local
Councils. Before the 1601 Act, responsibility for the poor rested with the
Christian Church. Coming to modern times — as the result of the Local

Government Act, 1930, public-assistance committees supplanted boards of guardians. The Bridgend Board of Guardians was the unit for the Llynfi Valley. Under the 1930 Act the Glamorgan County Council became the unit of administration to remove the anomalies created by the nine boards of guardians that then existed in Glamorgan. The County was divided into eight assessment areas, which formed the poor law areas, in each of which there was a guardians' committee to relieve destitution. The Public Assistance Committee at Cardiff would revise the relief work and decide the scale of relief, whilst the actual administration of relief would be the work of the Guardians' committee in each area, consisting of all local county councillors and those nominated by district councils. The Bridgend Board of Guardians ceased to function on 31 March 1930. The administration of the poor law became linked with public health. The workhouse infirmary, with its taint of pauperism, was eliminated. There would be a general hospital for all.

Since 1948 there have been further important developments, including the setting up of the Ministry of Health and Social Security. The facts are too well-known to need reiteration.

The Llangynwyd Joint Burial Board was formed in 1870, and the Maesteg Cemetery was opened in 1881 at a cost of £2,500. The original area, consisting of 4 acres, has been much extended in the meantime. The Burial Board originally included representatives from the Glyncorrwg Parish and the Llangynwyd Middle Parish, as well as those from the district which later became known as the Maesteg U.D.C. area. As the Maesteg U.D.C. ultimately became the sole remaining authority attached to the Board, the administration of the Maesteg cemetery became vested in the surveyor's department of the Maesteg Council. The marked increase in the number of cremations has materially affected the need for much extended space for normal burials.

In 1969 the Margam Crematorium was opened to cater for the needs of the adjoining local authorities, including the Maesteg U.D.C. The site is the one on which the National Eisteddfod Pavilion was erected in 1966.

49. The Glamorgan County Council

Prior to 1888 the County was governed by County magistrates who met in Quarter Sessions. The first Glamorgan County Council election in Maesteg was a memorable one, the two candidates being Dr. John Davies and David Grey of the Llwydarth Tinplate Works, the nominee of Dr. W. H. Thomas. The bitterness was reflected in the election song *Y Cardi Clic* (The Cardi

Clique) sung in the streets of Maesteg by William Bevan of the Railway Inn, Maesteg, a David Grey supporter, with the aid of a bell announcing *Ding dong bell uwch bedd y Cardi Clic* (Ding dong bell above the grave of the Cardi clique). The Cardi mentioned in the lampoon (found in Cadrawd's handwriting) was the Liberal candidate, Dr. John Davies. The election result was:-

Dr. John Davies   662

David Grey   509

The scenes at the declaration of the poll were tumultuous.

Dr. Davies was elected an Alderman of the Council at its first meeting held at the Gwyn Hall, Neath, in January 1889. At that time, elections were decided locally by allegiance to a particular doctor rather than by allegiance to a particular party.

Up to 1910 the whole urban area had only one representative on the Glamorgan County Council, but that year the area was split in two—the Caerau Ward (consisting of Caerau and Nantyffyllon) and the Maesteg Ward (consisting of the East and West Wards of Maesteg). When the sitting member for Maesteg (E. E. Davies) was elected an Alderman in 1912 the Maesteg urban area for the first time had three County Councillors.

John Evans, Nantyffyllon, became chairman of the County Finance Committee from 1929 to 1938 and became chairman of the Council for two years from 1938, ultimately becoming M.P. for the Ogmore Division from 1945 to 1950.

After much controversy, the County Council was split into three sections in 1973—Glamorgan South, Mid Glamorgan and West Glamorgan. The earlier proposal was that the County area be divided into two areas— Glamorgan East and Glamorgan West. The Mid Glamorgan area includes the Llynfi Valley and extends as far north as the Rhymney area, formerly part of the Monmouthshire County Council area. In 1980, Vernon Hart of Caerau, a former member of the Maesteg Council, was elected chairman of the Mid Glamorgan County Council. He had previously been elected the first chairman of the Maesteg Community Council in 1974. Councillor Philip Squire of Tondu, a former Chairman of the Penybont R.D.C. and of the Glamorgan County Council, became the first Chairman of the Mid Glamorgan County Council.

50. Population

The rate of the decline in population has slowed down in recent years.

About 800 people lived in the Parish of Llangynwyd in 1801. The inhabited houses numbered 146, with 5 uninhabited. There were 160

90 Neath Road, Maesteg *c.*1908

families and 392 persons were engaged in farming. The whole Llangynwyd
Parish in 1871 consisted of 15,460 acres with a population of 8,944. It was
divided into three hamlets, and in 1875, according to Worrall's Directory,
5836 lived in Cwmdu (which included Maesteg), 526 in Llangynwyd Lower
and 428 in Llangynwyd Middle. In 1801 it also included part of Betws and
also Baeden and Afan Argoed.

Owing to the decline of the iron industry, before the sinking of the coal
mines, it was reported in the local paper on 13 May 1881 that many valley
residents were leaving for America.

Here are some census figures for the Maesteg U.D.C. area: *1901* – 15,012:
1911 – 24,977; *1921* – 28,196: *1931* – 29,502: *1951* – 23,141; *1961* – 21,625;
1971 – 20,971.

These figures do not include those living in Cwmfelin and Llangynwyd,
which formed part of the Penybont R.D.C. area.

There are in the County Record Office at Cardiff strip film records of the
1851 census of all families in Glamorgan. Each family is listed, giving the
age, occupation and date and place of birth of each person. Details are also
now available at the Mid Glamorgan County Library, Coed Parc, Bridgend.

51. Valley Services

The Llynfi Valley is served by three reservoirs: (1) at the Red Cow, Maesteg,
for the south and central parts of the town; (2) at Brynmawr, for the

Salisbury Road and Neath Road district and the Maesteg Park Estate; and
(3) at Caerau, for the northern part including Nantyffyllon. The authority
controlling water supplies is the Mid Glamorgan Water Board established in
1921. The constituent authorities were Penybont R.D.C., Ogmore & Garw
U.D.C., Maesteg U.D.C. together with the Cowbridge Borough and Rural
Councils. They were later joined by the Bridgend and Porthcawl U.D.C.'s.

The main pumping station is at Schwyll, near Ewenny, Bridgend, opened
in 1932. By a system of booster pumps, water can be transported from
Schwyll to the higher levels of the mining valleys, when the local upland
sources are badly affected by dry weather.

The South Wales Electricity Board supplies electricity to the valley. Before
the industry was nationalised, the responsibility rested with the Maesteg
Council, who obtained electricity in bulk supply from North's. The system
worked well, as all complaints were dealt with immediately without
resorting to the tortuous process and resulting delay caused by remote
control, resulting in increased cost to the consumer.

The valley can boast of three parks: (1) Caerau (12 acres); (2) Maesteg
(20 acres presented to the Maesteg Council in the twenties by the Margam
Estate) and (3) Garth (10 acres).

The Maesteg Post Office was officially opened by Ted Williams, M.P., on
11 August 1938. That year saw the opening of the Maesteg swimming-pool
at a cost of £8,000, the contractors being Owen E. Jones Ltd. It was converted into an enclosed swimming-pool in 1969 at a cost of £80,000, the
main contractors being Andrew Scott Ltd. — with several sub-contractors.
The County Council paid £10,000 towards the cost. There is a main pool
(5 feet 9 ins.) and one (3 feet) for learners.

A new Fire Station, in place of the old one adjoining the Maesteg 'bus
station, was opened in December 1974 at a cost of £112,000 at Coegnant
Road, Caerau. Incidentally, the Maesteg Council bought the building,
formerly used as offices for North's collieries, for £8,500 in 1971.

The valley has three hospitals: (1) The Maesteg General Hospital,
originally built during the first World War through local voluntary effort. It
includes a maternity unit (in place of the former Maternity Home at
Llwydarth Road, Maesteg) and other facilities provided through the
activities of the local Hospital League of Friends; (2) The Llynfi Hospital
(formerly the Maesteg Isolation Hospital, opened in 1903) and since 1974
occupied mainly by geriatic patients), and (3) Hyfrydol, near the former
Cwmdu Library, Garth, for elderly patients. Those needing surgical
treatment go the Bridgend General Hospital.

91 and 92   General view of the Celtic Colliery early 1900's, later redeveloped as the
Celtic Welfare Park, Maesteg (below)

93   Maesteg Welfare Park Workmen, April 1931

94   Caerau Welfare Park – opening of New Pavilion by Mr Joshua Davies, M.E.,
21 April 1934

95   Cottage Hospital, Maesteg, *c*.1915. Directly behind is 'Ty Patch'—old iron
workings area

In 1925 the Maesteg General Hospital's annual income was only about
£1,000, mainly contributed by the local miners, supplemented by the
proceeds of concerts and carnivals. In February 1938 the Vernon Hartshorn
Memorial Children's Ward was opened by Lady Gillett. In recent years the
local Hospital League of Friends has collected many thousands of pounds,
mainly by means of an annual fete held at the Maesteg Park, in order to
implement the National Health Service and provide additional facilities
such as a rest room, a lift, a new entrance hall and waiting room, mainly at
the Maesteg General Hospital.

By 1968 about 1,000 dwellings had been constructed by the Maesteg U.D.C.
since the War, apart from the 492 houses privately built. Many hundreds
have been built since then, the main estates being the Tudor Estate at
Caerau (named after Tudor Isaac, the then Maesteg Council surveyor) and
consisting of 128 houses adjoining Dyffryn Farm, Caerau, the Cae Tinker
Estate at Garth, built on the old Cae Tinker field with 188 dwellings at a
total cost of £430,000, the Parc Housing Estate of 74 houses, the Ystrad
Celyn Estate near Gelli Lenor Farm, verging on Llangynwyd, being
privately built houses, the housing estates at the rear of Tonna Road,
Caerau and at Heolfain.

In the early thirties, private street-works charges were abolished locally to
relieve frontagers in private streets from having to pay road charges, as some
of the private roads were in an atrocious condition. The Council also constructed a new road, called Heol Tywith, leading from Nantyffyllon to

Caerau and has provided playing fields, including the one at South Parade, Maesteg, and a new football field and pavilion at Caerau Park.

The town of Maesteg is an excellent shopping centre with an indoor and open market and also a spacious free car park. The market has always remained open on Good Fridays despite many arguments among Councillors for and against opening on that day. The main streets are wide and attractive, and thousands from adjoining areas do their shopping in the town. Owing to the increase in 'bus fares and the absence of trains, the local Chamber of Trade has arranged a free 'bus service for them every Friday. It has also been mainly responsible for the trade fairs at the local Town Hall. Since the amalgamation of the Mid Glamorgan local authorities in 1973, special shelves have been fixed in the cellars of Glanogwr, the former home of the Bridgend U.D.C. to house the minutes, documents and maps of that local authority up to the time of its dissolution. In 1952 a list of ledgers, reports and minute-books of the Cwmdu Local Board, including the minutes of the first year of the Maesteg U.D.C. (1895-96), was prepared by the County Record Office. The list included details of minute-books and documents of the Llangynwyd Joint Burial Board, the building contract and report of progress relating to the Maesteg Isolation Hospital, the account-book of the Maesteg Town Hall Committee, the rate-books of the hamlets of Llangynwyd and Cwmdu for periods between 1839 and 1876, the Vestry minute-book (1889-1894) and valuation lists (1891-96) for the Llangynwyd Parish as well as the first edition of ten 25-in. ordnance survey plans and a schedule of deeds and documents relating to premises mortgaged (1869-82) to the Llynfi Permanent Building Society.

The documents relating to the Maesteg U.D.C. are now in safe custody at the County Record Office, Cardiff, available for research by local government students of the future.

What has been written hitherto is merely factual. A different kind of volume would be required to do justice (if that can be done) to the various colourful and original characters and dedicated leaders that have dominated and refreshed the local scene in the last fifty years.

Before leaving the scene of local government, perhaps it would be appropriate to refer to the Welsh Office, with which every local authority in Wales has to deal, and to Donald George McPherson in particular. In 1969 he was Chairman of the Welsh Board of Health (until the Welsh takeover) and became Permanent Undersecretary of State at the Welsh Office.

He was born in 1914, the son of George and Catherine McPherson, his mother being the daughter of Mr. and Mrs. Philip Jones, Alma House, Maesteg, and his father being the son of William McPherson, a local colliery manager. He was called to the Bar (Gray's Inn) in 1937. Among his many public appointments were: Chief Examiner of the Board of Inland Revenue, 1940; Principal of the Administrative Department, 1942; Assistant Secretary to the Board of Inland Revenue, 1950; Member of the Taxation Commission in Ceylon, 1955; Establishment Officer, U.K. Atomic Energy

Authority, 1959-61; Secretary, War Damage Commission, 1961-65; United
Nations Adviser on Taxation in Cyprus, 1963; Secretary, Royal Mint,
1966-67; Assistant Secretary, Ministry of Health, 1967-69.

Mr. Peter Thomas, Q.C., M.P., Secretary of State for Wales, and Mr.
Gwilym Prys Davies, Chairman of the Welsh Hospitals Board, took part at
his memorial service at St. John's Church, Cardiff, on 19 October 1973,
whilst Sir Hywel W. Evans, Permanent Secretary at the Welsh Office, gave
the address.

Paul Loveluck of the Welsh Office is a Maesteg product, having entered
the administrative grade of the Home Civil Service as Assistant Principal at
the Board of Trade in London in 1963, becoming Private Secretary to the
Permanent Secretary and becoming a Principal in 1968. He was transferred
to the Welsh Office in Cardiff in 1968 and later became Assistant Secretary
at that Office. The Press Officer to the Secretary of State is Elfed Bowen, a
native of Maesteg.

Among the journalists who reported meetings of the Maesteg U.D.C. were
Donald B. Jones (referred to in the introduction), David Williams, who
became Press Officer to Ian Smith, Prime Minister of Rhodesia, and is a
descendant of Isaac Howells *(Perdonydd y Dyffryn)* referred to in the
chapter on Music; Alan Protheroe, Head of the B.B.C. News Service;
Iorwerth Lewis, who was Editor of *The Herald of Wales*, and D. Prosser,
retired Lobby Correspondent of the *Western Mail*. Finally, whilst still on
local government, it is a Maesteg boy, Philip Williams, of the Ferrier
Williams family, who is the Secretary to the Metropolitan Borough of the
West Midlands and also a Member of the Council of the Law Society.

52. The Political Scene

Undoubtedly the greatest statesman produced by Tir Iarll was Richard
Price, Tynton, Llangeinor (1723-1791), the son of the Rev. Rees Price
(successor to the Rev. Samuel Jones at the Brynllywarch Academy) and first
cousin to the Maid of Cefn Ydfa. However, he left the district at an early age
and his fame rests on his activities after he migrated to London, where he
lies buried in Bunhill Fields.

(a) Parliamentary

The constituency which includes the Llynfi Valley was formerly known as
the Mid Glamorgan Division but on the reorganisation of boundaries, the
valley became included in the newly-formed Ogmore Division in 1918. Here
are the names of the M.P.'s since 1830:

96   Richard Price,
Tynton, Llangeinor, 1723-1791

Mid Glamorgan

C. R. M. Talbot (1830-1890)	Liberal
S. T. Evans (1890-1910)	,,
F. W. Gibbins (part of 1910 only)	,,
J. Hugh Edwards (1910-1918)	,,

Ogmore

Vernon Hartshorn (1918-1931)	Labour
Ted Williams (1931-1946)	,,
John Evans (1946-1950)	,,
Walter E. Padley (1950-1979)	,,
Ray Powell (1979-)	,,

C. R. M. Talbot, the Squire of Margam, became the father of the House of Commons. According to an apocryphal story, he made one short speech — to complain of the draught from an open window near his seat! However, when a student at Oriel College, Oxford, he gained a first-class honours degree in mathematics.

Samuel T. Evans, a grocer's son from Skewen, was an outstanding lawyer. In 1908 he became Recorder of Swansea and Solicitor General. On being appointed President of the then Probate Divorce and Admiralty Division of the High Court, he resigned his seat in 1910. During the first World War he became President of the newly set up Prize Court and was recognised as an authority on International Law. In 1895 he had been opposed by J. E. Vaughan of Rheola, Neath, and later by Godfrey Williams, Squire of Aberpergwm, who became less noted for his political speeches than for an

unfortunate incident when he became suddenly incontinent whilst addressing an election meeting at Pontrhydyfen! Sir Samuel was never opposed by a
Socialist.

When the suffragette movement was at its height, Sir Samuel, as he was
later known, was prevented from speaking at Bethania Welsh Baptist
Chapel at Maesteg by a group of suffragettes led by a Miss Guythorpe. As an
uncompromising radical, he was known to have refused to stand to honour a
royal toast.

F. W. Gibbins, Neath, was a Quaker. The hurly-burly of Parliamentary
life was not to his liking and after some months in Parliament he stood down
for the second general election held in 1910. He was succeeded by J. Hugh
Edwards, who was an entertaining speaker and a devout follower of Lloyd
George.

In the first election in 1910, the result was as follows:

F. W. Gibbins (Liberal)	8,920
Vernon Hartshorn (Labour)	6,210

In the second election in the same year the figures were:

John Hugh Edwards (Liberal)	7,624
Vernon Hartshorn (Labour)	6,102

At the time, Vernon Hartshorn declared: 'The Labour party in Mid
Glamorgan is faced with the dead weight of generations of Liberal tradition
and prejudice. We have to overcome the hostility of a couple of hundred
Nonconformist ministers . . . but we shall go on'.

This was the period when the Independent Labour Party was beginning
to make its influence felt, and it was against the wishes of Lib-Lab. leaders,
including the Rev. William Saunders, Pontycymer, that Vernon Hartshorn
decided to contest the seat.

In 1918 Hartshorn was returned unopposed as the first M.P. for the
newly-created Ogmore Division. His political progress had followed the
usual pattern then in the South Wales coalfield—miners' lodge secretary,
then miners' agent and ultimately an M.P. He was later unopposed a few
times.

When he died in 1931 three local men were nominated to succeed him as
M.P., and as the seat was claimed to be a miners' seat, the miners themselves were the voters. The result of the first ballot was:

Ted Williams	4,477
Evan Williams	3,843
John Evans	3,255

In the second ballot the figures were:

Ted Williams	6,654
Evan Williams	6,364

Ted Williams consequently became the miners' nominee and the official Labour candidate, and in a by-election on 19 May 1931 the result was:

Ted Williams	19,356
J. R. Campbell (Com.)	5,219

During the last War, Ted Williams became Minister of Information, and was later appointed High Commissioner of Australia, thereby vacating the seat. Evan Williams, who had succeeded Vernon Hartshorn as miners' agent, had left Maesteg for Cardiff in 1934 and the succession fell to John Evans. Evan Williams was then area secretary for South Wales of the N.U.M.

The miners' official nominee for the vacant seat was D. R. Llewelyn, who had beaten Arthur D. Edwards, Caerau, by approximately 4,000 votes to nearly 3,000 votes. Of the 74 delegates of the constituency Labour Party at the nomination meeting, 43 voted for John Evans and 31 for D. R. Llewelyn. The former was consequently adopted.

John Evans was elected M.P. in a by-election in 1946, his opponent being Trefor Morgan, who stood as a Nationalist candidate. The voting figures were:

John Evans	13,632
Trefor Morgan	7,947

It was unfortunate for John Evans that he was 71 years of age when his opportunity came to enter Parliament. He had been a member of the Maesteg U.D.C. for 21 years and chairman of that body twice. We have already referred to his service on the Glamorgan County Council. He had also been chairman of the County Standing Joint Committee and of the County Education Committee, and had also served on the Royal Commission on National Health Insurance under the chairmanship of Sir Andrew Rae Duncan. When he was nominated candidate in 1946 one of the conditions laid down was that he should give up his membership of the Glamorgan County Council.

In October 1949, at a nomination meeting of the Ogmore Labour Party, John Evans was not re-nominated. Walter Padley polled 84 votes, D. R. Llewelyn 72 votes and John Evans 37 votes. Walter Padley became the official nominee and in the General Election of February 1950, in a four-cornered contest, he polled 35,836 votes with Raymond Gower (Conservative, who later became M.P. for the Barry Division) coming second with 9,791 votes.

Shortly after his non-selection, John Evans announced his retirement and moved to Tongwynlais, near Cardiff. In 1952 he re-entered the County Council by defeating the sitting member for the Castell Coch ward, but was himself defeated three years later by the one he had unseated.

As an outsider, Walter Padley was fortunate in securing one of the safest seats in Wales, if not in Britain. He was the only Ogmore M.P. who did not live in the constituency. Although he had attended to many private complaints from his constituents and matters raised by the constituency local authorities, and had been Chairman of the Labour Party, he was subject to much local and national press criticism in regard to his Parliamentary duties. The fact that he was re-elected with big majorities each time indicates the strength of the loyalty of the constituency to the Labour Party irrespective of the identity of the standard bearer.

The Conservative Party was the only Party to oppose him at each election, as the other parties realised the futility of contesting such a Labour stronghold. In the October elections of 1959 there was merely a straight fight between the sitting member and the Conservative (T. O. Ewart-Jones) in a one-sided contest.

When Walter Padley retired in 1979, Ray Powell, who had previously acted as his election agent, was nominated to succeed him and at the General Election of May 1979, he was elected M.P. with a majority of 16,087, having polled 29,867 votes. The Ogmore Division has since its formation in 1918 been represented by a Labour member and there does not appear any immediate prospect of a change in political allegiance.

There was much bitterness at one time between Tories and Liberals in the Newcastle Division (Tondu and Aberkenfig) which included Pontrhydycyff and Llangynwyd. Sir Thomas Hughes, a Liberal, had been a member of the Glamorgan County Council for seventeen years. The seat was once contested by Lynch Blosse of Coetrehen House, and it appears that the General Manager of North's Collieries had instructed his officials to persuade miners to vote Tory. Some of these officials had threatened widows with a stoppage of their Christmas gifts if they voted Liberal. Sir T. J. Hughes had a majority of 470.

(b) The County Council

After the Maesteg Urban area had been divided into two districts for the purpose of County Council representation, the top ward seat, consisting of Caerau and Nantyffyllon, was won for Labour by John Evans in 1913. The defeated candidate was the Rev. D. Bryniog Thomas, minister of Seion Welsh Congregational Church, Caerau, who presumably stood as a Liberal. The ward has been represented by Labour ever since.

The lower division, consisting of the East and West wards, has changed its political allegiance from time to time. After Labour had wrested the seat from the Liberals in 1919 the seat was held by a well-known business man, D. E. Lockyer, standing as an Independent, from 1928 to 1934. From then on it was held for Labour until Jennie Gibbs won the seat for the Liberals in 1967 and was re-elected in 1970. On the re-organisation of local government in 1973 the top ward continued to be represented by Labour, but the East and West wards became represented by two members, one Labour and one

Liberal (Jennie Gibbs), who has also contested the Parliamentary seat twice. Jennie Gibbs retained the seat until 1981.

A significant factor to-day is the loss of interest in local elections. The fact that the Mid Glamorgan County area extends as far as the Rhymney Valley with the constituent areas appearing to know little about each other — and the electors knowing far less — has contributed towards this state of indifference. This is reflected locally. In a by-election in the Caerau Ward in March 1981, for membership of the Maesteg Community Council, only one-tenth of the electorate took the trouble to vote.

(c) The Maesteg U.D.C.

The Council membership was 16, representing 4 wards. It became Labour-controlled for the first time in 1919, and Labour maintained control until 1973 when the Council became merged in the Ogwr Borough Council.

Two Communist members, one for Caerau and the other for Nantyffyllon each served a term of three years from 1933 to 1936, the member for Nantyffyllon (Dick Davies) having died on nomination day for re-election. Another Communist member (Mel Thomas), some years later, represented Nantyffyllon for three years. For over forty-two years the writer of this volume was an Independent member for Nantyffyllon, and for many years after 1948 he was the only Independent member of the Council. The highest number of Independents at any given time after 1919 was 5. In 1973, when the Council ceased to exist, there were 14 Labour councillors, 1 Independent and 1 Liberal. Previously, for a short period, there had been another Liberal Councillor and one representing the British Legion. The writer can remember 4 lady councillors.

In 1932 the Council adopted a seniority rule whereby a non-Labour member could become chairman of the Council. This rule was breached for the last year of its existence. However, from 1919 to 1973, no-one but a member of the ruling party was allowed to be chairman of any Council committee, of which there were about a dozen. The writer of this volume was once elected a member of the Pigeons Sub-committee to decide whether Council tenants should be allowed to keep pigeons!

The writer can testify that during his tenure of office, he was unaware of any case of bribery that could be levelled against any member of the Council. This would not exclude the possibility of a certain amount of nepotism.

(d) Politics Generally

The struggles of the workers of the valley to secure better working and living conditions have been mentioned in our chapter on the miners. The first miners' agent in the early un-organised days was David Beynon who took a prominent part in local affairs and who died in the early twenties of this century. He was followed by Vernon Hartshorn—of whom we write separately.

The Independent Labour Party (I.L.P.) was a driving force at the beginning of the century, and there was much conflict between the movement and the Churches as indicated in our chapter on Religion. The senior ministers of the valley were Liberals, whilst the younger element in the first quarter of the century were inclined towards Socialism. In 1909 the Rev. C. P. Thomas, Zion Baptist Church, Maesteg, read a paper on 'Socialism and the Churches' to the local Free Church Council. He was sympathetic to Socialism in its relation to poverty and unemployment. It appears that opinions differed at the meeting. The Rev. J. M. Lewis, Tabernacle Welsh Baptist Church, Maesteg, was an avowed Socialist.

In an address to the Free Church Council in 1909, Councillor John Howells, Garth, Maesteg, asked what was to be the attitude of the Free Churches towards Socialism. He stated that there was no quarrel on the question of equality of opportunity. The Churches and Socialists should unite in fighting for reform, as our fellow-men had bodies to feed and clothe, as well as souls to save. He thought that Christian Socialism was the best, but qualified his support for the Eight Hours a Day Act by saying that if the additional spare time was to be spent in public houses, then it would have been far better for men and their families if the Act had not been passed.

In recent years, the tendency of the Welsh-speaking ministers of the valley has been to ally themselves with Plaid Cymru.

The pre 1914-18 War legislation by the Asquithian Government, spurred on by Lloyd George, was considered inadequate, although it produced the Old Age Pensions Act, the Eight Hours a Day Act, the Minimum Wage Act, the National Insurance Act, and the Workmen's Compensation Act. The I.L.P. held weekly meetings at the Good Templars Hall, Alfred Street, Maesteg, and regular open-air meetings at the various public squares in the valley. There was a literature stall at the Maesteg market-place every Saturday where *The Labour Leader* and *The Clarion* were sold. Economics classes were held on Sunday afternoons, much to the dismay of the local Churches.

Politics to these self-denying pioneers, who were subject to much derision, was a matter of conviction for which they and their families had to suffer. After the battles had been won and the Labour Party had gained control over the public affairs of the valley, there came a desire by some aspirants in scholastic circles to join the band-wagon in preparation for headship appointments. Such a course also became useful for local government appointments.

In all parliamentary and local elections, every Labour candidate would be indebted to the women's section of the Party in the respective wards, as they were the most effective means of scooping in votes for their candidate. No other candidate had the semblance of a local organisation in the valley.

Some of the bitterest political battles were fought during the depression period between the two World Wars. The strikes of 1921 and 1926 resulted in hunger marches. One of the leaders was Idris Cox, a native of Garth, Maesteg, and West Wales organiser of the Communist Party of Great Britain for eleven years. He was later transferred to London headquarters and became editor of the *Daily Worker*. He had also been Communist candidate for Rhondda East. On 5 September 1931, contingents from Caerau and Rhondda formed a hunger march, which was broken up by mounted police in Bristol. Idris Cox led a march on a small scale to London in 1930, and a much larger one numbering 375 on 14 October 1932. It was estimated that there were 150 to 200 Communist recruits in the Llynfi Valley in the mid-twenties.

Idris Cox was the product of the Nonconformist Sunday School. His father, Luke Cox, whom the writer knew, was a native of Bristol and had learnt Welsh. He was for many years the secretary of Ebenezer Welsh Congregational Church, Garth. The son wrote his reminiscences, *Story of a Welsh Rebel*, in 1970.

The enmity between the Labour Party and the Communist Party in the thirties was intense, especially in local election contests. The writer of this volume remembers chairing a very acrimonious public debate at a packed meeting in the Nantyffyllon New Hall between John Evans and Idris Cox. When Vernon Hartshorn, M.P. died in 1931, the official newspaper of the Communist Party referred to his death in bold headlines — 'A Rat Passes'. Much use was made of this by the Labour Party in the subsequent bye-election.

The Communist Party has long ceased to be an effective political force in the valley. It last contested a parliamentary election in the Ogmore Division on 23 February 1950 when it polled 1,619 votes out of a total vote of 47,859, despite having a competent local candidate. It no longer contests local elections in the valley. The main opposition now comes from the Conservative Party and Plaid Cymru. Neither party won a seat on the Maesteg U.D.C. Up to recently, the gap between the Labour Party and the opposition parties on the Ogwr Council (with 57 members) was narrow, but it was widened as the result of the last Borough Council elections. Of the Mid Glamorgan County Council membership of 85, the Conservatives hold 3 seats and Plaid Cymru 9.

The referendum on Welsh autonomy held on 1 March, 1980 caused but little local enthusiasm, despite the fact that Michael Foot and other Labour M.P.'s — Ted Rowlands and Brynmor John — had addressed a meeting at the Maesteg Town Hall in favour of devolution.

Limitations of space prevent us from naming the many famous politicians who have spoken in the Llynfi Valley. A former Council colleague assured the writer that Lloyd George, in his early days, had spoken in Maesteg. All

the prominent Communists, including Harry Pollitt, Willie Gallacher, Tom
Mann, Arthur Horner, Walton Newbold, D. N. Pritt, and J. R. Campbell
have spoken locally, whilst A. J. Cook and all the South Wales Miners'
leaders were familiar figures. Vernon Hartshorn was a regular speaker for
many years. The visiting Labour leaders have been legion, and included
J. H. Thomas, Emanuel Shinwell, James Maxton, and Hugh Dalton.

The best known figures of Plaid Cymru, including Saunders Lewis,
Kitchener Davis and Gwynfor Evans, have also spoken at the Town Hall.
When the Liberal Party was the dominant party in Wales, Sir Samuel Evans
(then S. T. Evans), the local M.P., was a regular speaker.

The Llynfi Valley was the birthplace of Sir Rhys Hopkin Morris, the son
of the Rev. John Morris of Seion Welsh Congregational Church, Caerau,
and the brothers, Sir William Beddoe Rees and John Tudor Rees, the sons
of Isaac Rees, secretary of Bethel Baptist Church, Maesteg. All three were
Liberals. Sir Rhys Hopkin Morris was successively M.P. for Cardiganshire, a
London Stipendiary Magistrate, Head of the Welsh B.B.C. services and
M.P. for Carmarthenshire from 1945 until his death in 1956. An appreciation of his life and service was published by T. J. Evans, Carmarthen, with a
foreword by Viscount Samuel. In 1979, a more detailed volume (in Welsh)
was published jointly by the Rev. D. Ben Rees and John Emanuel, who
shared the prize at the Cardigan National Eisteddfod of 1976. Sir Beddoe
Rees, an architect and later a company director, was M.P. for Bristol South
from 1922 to 1929 and kept in close contact with the Llynfi Valley,
particularly regarding Welsh cultural matters such as the Tir Iarll
Eisteddfod. His brother, Tudor, became a County Court Judge after serving
as M.P. for Barnstaple. Another local product, D. Emlyn Thomas, who was
an assistant to Vernon Hartshorn at Maesteg, became a Labour Member
(M.P.) for the Aberdare Division. He specialised in compensation matters in
the mining industry.

As Cymer was once in the Parish of Llangynwyd, it would be relevant to
refer to Sir William Jenkins, who became M.P. for the Neath Division in
1922 and retained his seat until his death in 1945. He was born in Cymer
and spent his lifetime there. He became miners' agent for the Western
District in 1906 and for the Afan Valley in 1913, and later was a member of
the Executive Council of the South Wales Miners Federation. In addition to
having been thrice chairman of the Glyncorrwg U.D.C., he was elected to
the Glamorgan County Council in 1907, becoming chairman in 1920. From
1919 to 1945 he was chairman of the County Education Committee and of
the Glamorgan Standing Joint Committee and was chairman of the
Executive of the County Councils Association during the jubilee year of the
County Councils. For many years he was deacon and precentor of Hebron
Welsh Congregational Church, Cymer.

53. Vernon Hartshorn (1872-1931)

97   Vernon Hartshorn, 1872-1931

An informative account of his career was published by Peter Stead in *Glamorgan Historian*, Vol. 6, 1969 and many profuse obituaries appeared in *The Times* and many other newspapers at the time of his death.

He was born in Pantywaun, Risca, and worked for ten years at the Abercarn and Risca Collieries, and later as a surface worker at the Cardiff Docks. After becoming a checkweigher he was elected an I.L.P. member of the Risca Council at the age of twenty-nine. In 1905 he became miners' agent to the Maesteg district of 5,000 miners, and within three years he was chosen Chairman of the Maesteg U.D.C.

His stand in the Cambrian Combine dispute of 1911 helped to bring about the Minimum Wage Act. That year he topped the poll for executive membership of the Miners, Federation of Great Britain. He became a critic of Mabon and Brace and some other older leaders, but in disgust, he later resigned his position with the South Wales Miners Federation and the parent body, because power was passing into the hands of A. J. Cook, whose militancy he disliked.

During the 1914-18 War, Hartshorn had stressed the need for productivity in the mines and had served on the Coal Controllers' Advisory Committee and on the Coal Trade Organisation Committee. He also sat on the commission of inquiry into industrial unrest in 1917. *The Times* called him 'the most powerful personality in the present miners' movement' and D. A. Thomas (later Lord Rhondda) considered him as 'the man who really

SOUTH WALES MINERS' FEDERATION.

TO THE MEMBERS OF THE MAESTEG DISTRICT.

As I have not yet completed the New Lists, I am issuing this Circular as a guide those Daywagemen who formerly worked on the 1877 Standard.

The First Column shows the old 1877 Standard rates; the Second Column shows the corresponding New 1915 Standard rates; and the Third Column shows the present wage including the 30.83 per cent., which is the present percentage on the 1915 Standard.

All Workmen on the Afternoon and Night Shifts are entitled to a Bonus Turn for each week since July 21st.

The Stokers, in addition to the Bonus Turn, are entitled to an advance of 6.6d. per day for every day worked since July 13th.

All Surfacemen are entitled to at least 5/- plus percentage since July 21st.

The Night and Afternoon Shift Hauliers should receive the same wage as the Day Hauliers since July 21st.

Lamplighters underground are entitled to 5/- plus percentage from July 21st.

The recent advance of 12½ per cent. on the New Standard must be paid back to August 21st, that is to say, for weeks ending Aug. 28th, Sept. 4th and Sept. 11th.

Any Collier who has been on the Minimum during those weeks and has received only 8/8 per day, will be entitled to a further 11d. per day, to make him up to the Present Minimum of 9/7 per day.

The Advanced Rates to Colliers' Assistants should be paid from Aug. 21st.

Any Workman not being paid according to above statement should at once report to his Lodge Secretary.

LIST OF DAYWAGE RATES.

Old Rate 1877 Standard.		New Rate 1915 Standard.		New Rate Plus 30·83 per cent.		Old Rate 1877 Standard.		New Rate 1915 Standard.		New Rate Plus 30·83 per cent.	
s	d	s	d	s	d	s	d	s	d	s	d
1	8	2	3½	3	0	4	4	5	11½	7	9½
2	0	2	9	3	7	4	5	6	1	7	11
2	6	3	5	4	6	4	6	6	2	8	1
3	0	4	1½	5	4½	4	9	6	6½	8	6½
3	6	5	0	6	6½	5	0	6	10½	9	0
3	8	5	0½	6	7	5	3	7	2½	9	5
3	9	5	2	6	9	5	4	7	4	9	7
3	10	5	3	6	10½	5	6	7	6½	9	10½
4	0	5	6	7	2	5	9	7	11	10	4
4	1	5	7½	7	4	6	0	8	3	10	9½
4	2	5	8½	7	6						

The lowest rate a Collier can pay his Assistant while the percentage is at its present figure, is as follows—

Between	14 and 15 years of age	..	..	2/11½	per day.
,,	15 ,, 16 ,, ,,	..	..	3/5½	,,
,,	16 ,, 17 ,, ,,	..	..	3/11	,,
,,	17 ,, 18 ,, ,,	..	..	4/5	,,
,,	18 ,, 19 ,, ,,	..	..	4/11	,,
,,	19 ,, 20 ,, ,,	..	..	5/5	,,
,,	20 ,, 21 ,, ,,	..	..	5/10½	,,
Above	21 years of age	..	..	6/6½	,,

It is important for Colliers to understand that while the above rates are the lowest they can legally pay to their helpers, they can pay 1/- per day more on any of the rates without consulting the Manager if they care to do so, that is to say, they can pay their helpers as follows—

Between	14 and 15 years of age	..	..	3/11	per day
,,	15 ,, 16 ,, ,,	..	..	4/5	,,
,,	16 ,, 17 ,, ,,	..	..	4/11	,,
,,	17 ,, 18 ,, ,,	..	..	5/5	,,
,,	18 ,, 19 ,, ,,	..	..	5/10½	,,
,,	19 ,, 20 ,, ,,	..	..	6/4½	,,
,,	20 ,, 21 ,, ,,	..	..	6/10½	,,
Above	21 years of age	..	..	7/6	,,

Any Collier who, after paying any of the above rates, has not earned 7/4 plus percentage (at present 9/7 per day), is entitled to have his wage made up to that figure, provided he has done a fair, reasonable day's work.

VERNON HARTSHORN,

September 15th, 1915.   *MINERS' AGENT.*

98   Circular from Vernon Hartshorn, 'Miners Agent', explaining the new daywage rates operative in 1915

mattered. 'Frank Hodges regarded him as the greatest miners' leader the South Wales coalfield had ever had.' Lloyd George called him the 'statesman of the coal industry'.

He was the first president of the Mid Glamorgan Labour Party and was President of the South Wales Miners' Federation from 1922 to 1924. He later served on the Simon Commission, whose report resulted in the end of English domination in India, and contributed substantially to that report. Among the other members of that Commission were Sir John Simon (Chairman), Lord Burnham, Lord Strathcorna, The Hon. Edward Cadogan, Col. G. R. Lane-Fox and Clement Attlee. At the time of his death at the age of fifty-eight, he was Lord Privy Seal in the second Labour Government of 1929, having served as Postmaster General in 1924.

He was a man of aristocratic tastes and loved the good things of life. It was said that the difference between him and Lord Rhondda was that Hartshorn had the income of a peasant and the tastes of a duke, whereas Lord Rhondda had the income of a duke and the tastes of a peasant! Although Vernon Hartshorn was the idol of the miners, his closest friends were not among the miners' leaders. Two of the closest were Sir Harry Fildes (Conservative M.P. for Stockport) and Sir William Edge (Liberal M.P. for Bosworth). Both attended his funeral at Llangynwyd. He invariably called his local political associates by their surnames only, and none of them would ever dream of calling him by his Christian name. He was also impeccably dressed, and his waistcoats invariably displayed the then fashionable white slip. His fondness of cigars, when the workmen generally smoked 'Woodbines', was proverbial.

Although he declared in 1910, when beaten at the polls by a Liberal, that his object was to smash the capitalist system, he arranged for his elder son to be articled to his friend, Sir James German, as a stockbroker. By a twist of fortune, over which he had no control, his only daughter married the son of a local colliery agent, who had been one of his greatest antagonists.

Yet, he was justifiably the king of the Maesteg miners, and his funeral, attended by two Cabinet colleagues, C. R. Attlee and J. R. Clynes, was one of the three largest ever seen in Maesteg. There was a memorable memorial service at Llangynwyd Church, when Dr. Garfield Williams, Dean of Llandaff, and later of Manchester, read so effectively the 15th chapter of St. Paul's first Epistle to the Corinthians. Llangynwyd Churchyard is the last resting place of one of the outstanding leaders of the miners.

It is interesting to note that the Western Valley of the then Monmouth-shire, which produced Vernon Hartshorn, also produced four other M.P.'s from the same colliery—Alfred Onions (Caerphilly), William Brace (Abertillery), Charles Edwards (Bedwellty) and George Barker (also of Abertillery).

Publishers Note: The author's grave lies between those of Wil Hopcyn and Vernon Hartshorn near the entrance porch of Llangynwyd Church.

54. The Welsh Language

Sir Alfred T. Davies, in his booklet, *The Story of the National Anthem of Wales* (1941), confirms that 'Hen Wlad fy Nhadau' was publicly sung for the first time 'at a small entertainment in the vestry of the Welsh Calvinistic Methodist Church at Maesteg'. The building was formerly Tabor Chapel in Temple Street, Maesteg, the singer being a Miss John. The anthem was later sung at an Eisteddfod in Pontypridd in 1859. Miss Cissie Powell, a descendant of the composer, lived in Castle Street, Maesteg and was a well-known local pianist.

Throughout the last century the great majority of the Llynfi Valley spoke Welsh as their first language. When the district was entirely agricultural all the farms bore Welsh names, as they do to-day. The growth of Welsh Non-conformity contributed materially to the general use of the language.

The Welsh spoken was similar to that in use in the Rhondda and in the Western Valleys of Gwent, and known as *iaith y gloren*, being the language of the lower classes. At the time of the writing of this volume the best-known speakers of the old Llynfi Valley native language, in all its glorious imperfections and charm, are two ex-farmers, Richard Griffith Thomas, formerly of Caemabifor Farm and William David Thomas, formerly of Gilfach Farm, both of Llangynwyd. A list of the colloquial expressions used in the district is given by Cadrawd (History of Llangynwyd).

As the result of the Irish potato famine in the hungry forties of the last century many Irish immigrants found employment at the Llynvi Iron Works opened in 1839. By natural process, people bearing names such as O'Brien, Welch, Carey or Keefe became Welsh-speaking. Many English settlers followed the same pattern, and the Waldins, Gees and Martins soon learnt the language which was then in general use. When the district was far more Welsh than it is to-day there appeared to be less consciousness of Welshness. By 1864 Llynfi Valley children were almost all monoglot Welsh.

In 1889 the special rules to be observed under the Coal Mines Regulation Act, 1887, at North's collieries were published in Welsh as well as in English.

In 1906 Messrs. North's agreed to appoint a Dr. Thomas J. Cream as Medical Officer provided he would undertake to learn Welsh and be able to speak it within a year.

During the early days of the writer of these notes, Picton Street, Nanty-ffyllon, in which he lived, consisted of approximately 110 houses of which 90% were occupied by Welsh-speaking people. Caerau, which grew up much later than Nantyffyllon, was from the start, a cosmopolitan district, while Maesteg and Garth in the lower part of the valley, retained much Welshness until comparatively recently. When Vernon Hartshorn from Anglicised Monmouthshire became the local Miners' agent in 1905, he made an attempt to learn Welsh but found the mutations to be an insuperable obstacle.

Of the 16 members of the Maesteg U.D.C., when the writer became a member in 1930, one could not understand Welsh, another could follow a Welsh conversation while the remaining 14 could converse freely in Welsh.

Yet, a century ago, thoroughly Welsh Churches kept minutes of their meeting and their accounts in English, and even the minutes of the first meeting of the Tir Iarll Cymrodorion Society, formed in 1903, were in English. Records of subsequent meetings were in Welsh. Those who spoke to each other in Welsh would invariably correspond in English. Welsh traders called their shops Leicester House, Bristol House, London House, Westminster Stores, Liverpool House, Manchester Stores and Clara & Towy. A Welsh-speaking Nantyffyllon trader advertised himself as an 'English and Foreign Fruiterer'. The absence of consciousness of Welshness was exemplified by the fact that it was the father of the author of this volume who named Station Terrace in Nantyffyllon in 1902!

A major step in the decline of Welsh was the passing of the Education Act of 1870 making school attendance for children compulsory. The medium of instruction was English even in a 100% Welsh area. Children who were caught speaking their native language were invested with a 'Welsh not' and made the objects of derision and contempt. Those who complain to-day about 'ramming Welsh down children's throats'—a favourite phrase by opponents of Welsh language instruction—appear to have forgotten, or to have been unaware of that aspect of our history. The objection to compulsory teaching seemed to apply to Welsh only.

At the Nantyffyllon School, during the early days of the writer, there was a startling innovation. For the first time, term reports for boys from Welsh homes included remarks in Welsh by the teacher, Lewis John Clee, a native of Ystalyfera. The entire medium of instruction was English, and the pupils were unaware that the headmaster could speak Welsh. The local Secondary School followed the same pattern, and although many pupils came from Welsh homes during the writer's time, not a single Welsh hymn was then sung at the morning prayers.

The minute book of the first Maesteg Cymrodorion Society discloses that Welsh lectures had to be abandoned in 1904-5 owing to the impact of the Welsh revival at that time.

Early in 1906 the Rev. Glasnant Jones, minister of Siloh Welsh Congregational Church, Nantyffyllon, and one of the staunchest of Welshmen, accepted a call to a Cross Keys, Mon. Church to prepare for a bilingual congregation, as he could see the oncoming Anglicisation of the valley. Only the Nonconformist Churches held Welsh services at that time in the upper part of the valley.

Yet, Maesteg could vie with any valley of comparable size in South Wales in Welsh cultural activities, particularly in the first quarter of this century. Almost every Welsh Chapel had its flourishing Cwrdd Diwylliadol (Young People's Society), its penny readings and minor eisteddfodau. In 1920 Maesteg made an unsuccessful attempt to invite the National Eisteddfod to

99 Committee for the Siloh Eisteddfod which was held in Maesteg Town Hall
every Christmas
(Standing) William Fowler, Joshua Richards, Daniel Waldin, John Bevan, John
Brace, Morgan Anthony
(Sitting) Thomas Rees (Hen Blwyf), Daniel Harris, James Rees, Richard Williams
(Kneeling) Thomas Thomas (St. Helena), Thomas Morris, Benjamin Williams

Maesteg in 1922. The local deputation that appeared before the deciding
body consisted of the Rev. Iorwerth Jones (Iorwerth Ddu) of Bethania
Baptist Church, Maesteg, Evan Williams, assistant to Vernon Hartshorn,
M.P., and T. Richards, M.A., then Welsh master at the Maesteg Secondary
School. They were introduced by Sir Beddoe Rees, a native of Maesteg.

As far back as 1903, Welsh classes were held in Maesteg under the tutorship of the Rev. W. R. Watkin, minister of Tabernacle (B) Church,
Maesteg. Nearly 40 annual Welsh eisteddfodau for children were held in
Caerau under the auspices of Cymdeithas Gymraeg y Caerau (Caerau Welsh
Society) with D. Lloyd Evans as chairman and Miss Muriel Roberts as
secretary for several years. In 1932 the Caerau Urdd choir, under the conductorship of Miss Claudia Davies, won a prize at the Urdd National
Eisteddfod at Machynlleth. Incidentally, Richard Burton, when a young
lad, won the Champion Recitation Competition at a Christmas Eisteddfod
at the Maesteg Town Hall in 1938.

Urdd Gobaith Cymru became a force in the valley in the thirties, and held
its first annual eisteddfod in Nantyffyllon in 1931. Among the pioneers were

100   Cymanfa in Maes-y-Gân
       Park, Maesteg, 1938

Mrs. George Bowen and Miss Ena Grey, both of Maesteg, and also Miss Norah Isaac, who ultimately became the first head of the first Welsh School established at Aberystwyth, 25 September 1939. She was secretary of Aelwyd yr Urdd at Caerau, which was opened officially by Ifan ab Owen Edwards in 1938 with D. Lloyd Evans, Caerau, as chairman. A few years later a similar Aelwyd yr Urdd was opened at Commercial Street, Maesteg, by Mrs. Rhys Hopkin Morris, whose husband was a native of Caerau. Apart from weekly meetings, an annual cymanfa ganu and an annual service in one of the local chapels formed part of the activities of the Urdd in the thirties.

The valley has been visited by most of the outstanding Welsh scholars including Saunders Lewis, T. Gwynn Jones, Kate Roberts, Griffith John Williams, T. A. Levi, Elfed, Dyfnallt, and D. J. Williams (Fishguard). In 1931 the annual conference of the Union of Welsh Societies was held in Maesteg, and an address given by William George, brother of D. Lloyd

George. Debates were held with neighbouring Welsh societies, public Welsh lectures were popular, Welsh classes under the auspices of Cardiff University flourished and there was a spate of Welsh dramas, concerts, and nosweithiau llawen. The Urdd National Eisteddfod was held in Maesteg in 1953, and later in 1979, both events being outstandingly successful despite atrocious weather in the second event. In fact, the 1979 Eisteddfod made a record profit of approximately £32,000.

In addition, Gŵyl Werin yr Urdd, a folk dance and song festival, was held in Maesteg in 1970, with a folk dance party from Bavaria as guests.

Despite opposition, newly built houses in Maesteg and Caerau were given Welsh names and the Town Hall was re-named *Neuadd y Dref*. '*Maes-y-gân*' was preferred to the insipid 'The Arena' as the name of the amphitheatre in the Maesteg Park. Some of the difficulties encountered in seeking Welsh names are given by the author of this volume in a Welsh article on 'Bod yn Gymro Cymraeg' (Being a Welsh-speaking Welshman) in the Welsh periodical *Barn* (Opinion), February 1971.

However, the use of Welsh continued to decline, some contributing factors being the Anglicising influence of radio, T.V., and newspapers, apart from the long-term result of compulsory English education under the 1870 Education Act. The only weekly light literature available for Grammar School children were the *Magnet, Gem* and *Penny Popular*.

The 1971 census indicated that 3,360 out of 19,905, being 17% of the Maesteg Urban area, could speak Welsh. The pattern was that the father was thoroughly Welsh, the son bilingual and the grandson monoglot English. When the first voluntary Welsh nursery-school was opened at *Aelwyd y Llwyni,* it was estimated that only about 40 children in the valley were able to play in Welsh. According to an article in the Welsh weekly, *Y Cymro*, 18 May 1976, there were then about 1,000 valley children and young people who could speak Welsh, 284 of them being, at the time pupils at the Welsh School at Tyderwen, Nantyffyllon.

The realisation of the plight of the language in the forties impelled the Rev. Geraint Owen, then minister of Bethania Welsh Baptist Chapel, Maesteg, to establish a Welsh nursery school at Yr Aelwyd, Maesteg. Whatever success was ultimately achieved was due entirely to his initiative and perseverance. He was the pioneer of education through the medium of Welsh in the Maesteg Valley. When he left the district in 1956 he had taught the children of his Church to read in Welsh. In fact, the writer of these notes was asked to speak to about 40 of these children in Welsh, which they appeared to understand.

The first school catered for children between three and five, and by May, 1948, there were 15 pupils. In turn, 10 former teachers undertook voluntarily without pay to teach the children, the parents paying 10/- per child per quarter. The result of a questionnaire in the Maesteg area in 1948 indicated that the parents of 500 children wanted a Welsh School. By August 1949, £400 had been collected to help to maintain the nursery school. Concerts and dramas were held to aid the funds, all of the artists giving their services free.

On 2 May 1949 the Welsh School was opened at Bethania Chapel vestry, Maesteg, for pupils between four and eleven. The Llynfi Valley was one of the first districts in Wales to take advantage of the facilities provided for the teaching of Welsh under the Education Act of 1944, the first being at Aberystwyth by Miss Norah Isaac, as already stated, and the second at Llanelli, with Miss Olwen Williams as head. Maesteg became the third.

Two qualified teachers were appointed — Miss Nansi Roberts of Trefriw, North Wales, who died in 1972, and who, as head teacher, was assisted by Miss Enid Walters of Pontyberem, who later left for the U.S.A. They were helped by several voluntary workers from the various Welsh Churches of the valley. These two teachers deserve much praise as they had given up secure teaching appointments to undertake pioneering work at a school maintained by voluntary subscriptions of patriotic Welsh people implemented by the low fees paid by the parents of the pupils. In fact, £1,000 was collected locally in the first two years of the existence of voluntary Welsh instruction in nursery and primary schools of the valley.

After much hesitation and delay, the school was taken over by the Local Education Authority with accommodation at the former Nantyffyllon Junior Infants' School on 6 September 1949. Then, only children able to speak Welsh were allowed as pupils. The nursery school remained at Bethania vestry and Miss Beryl Evans was appointed teacher. The school provided a continuous intake for the Welsh Primary School. Mrs. Mary Mort was in charge from 1960 to 1973, the majority of the children being from non-Welsh homes.

In 1960 the Welsh School was given a home at the Tyderwen School, north of Nantyffyllon, the headmaster being Mr. Gerallt Jones with Mrs. Dilys Richards as deputy. By 1973 the number of pupils had increased to 240. Under the conductorship of Mrs. Dilys Richards, the school choir won major prizes at the National Eisteddfod and the Miners Annual Eisteddfod and also took part in T.V. and radio broadcasts.

Mr. Gerallt C. Jones (headmaster) announced in the Welsh press (*Y Faner*, 2 July 1964) that at an exhibition of books for children held at Tyderwen School in November 1963, in preparation for Christmas, over 500 Welsh books were sold for children under eleven.

The success of the school affected adversely the grading of other schools with the understandably unfavourable reaction from some of those schools. The 25th anniversary of the school was celebrated in July 1973.

To further Welsh nursery school teaching, an empty hotel in Bridgend Road, Maesteg, was bought in 1967 and officially opened in September 1968 by Professor Jac L. Williams, Aberystwyth. The cost of renewing and repairing came to approximately £5,000 and the 50 children who then attended were conveyed to the centre by a minibus bought through voluntary subscriptions. The maintenance has been helped by Christmas fairs, walking tours and concerts. A local tradesman, Edward James, contributed £500. Teachers of the Welsh School agreed to become guarantors for the purchase of the minibus, and the parents also helped. It was paid for within twelve months. In 1973, it had to be replaced by another minibus, at a cost of £1,500, without the help of a State grant.

In order that their education should not cease at primary level, pupils received secondary education in Welsh in Bilingual Schools at Rhydfelen, Ystalyfera and Llanhari. For some years pupils travelled daily by bus to Rhydfelen (near Pontypridd), involving two hours of travelling each day. On the opening of the Ystalyfera Bilingual School, about 100 pupils travelled daily by bus from Maesteg, and there are now 120 (in 1981) Maesteg pupils at the Llanhari Bilingual School, which was opened in 1974.

In 1964 Victor Hampson-Jones, Maesteg, on behalf of Undeb Cenedlaethol Athrawon Cymru (The National Union of Welsh Teachers) prepared a Memorandum on the legal status of the Welsh language, and the local branch of Plaid Cymru, in December 1966, gave £26 to the local Council towards the cost of bilingual signs. In 1975 owing to the refusal of the Ogwr Borough Council to contribute towards the Welsh National Eisteddfod, £500 was collected locally from Welsh- and English-speaking residents to make up for what could justifiably have been anticipated as a Council contribution. Although the Mid Glamorgan County Council also refused to contribute towards the Eisteddfod, it gave £1,000 towards the Urdd National Eisteddfod held in Maesteg in 1979.

In addition a Ulpan course for Welsh adult learners was commenced at Y Diwlith centre in 1976. All these activities indicate that the Llynfi Valley Welsh people did not accept the pronouncement of *The Times* in 1848: 'The Welsh language is . . . the curse of Wales . . . and is simply a foolish interference with the natural process of civilisation and prosperity'.

However, nearly a century and a half later, owing to overwhelming influences beyond their control, the decline in the use of the language has become obvious, resulting in former completely Welsh Churches becoming bilingual. Yet, the language that supplanted the native language has failed to shake off the influence of the one it overtook, and we still hear in the valley of the weather being *diflas* (disagreeable), of a woman who is *didoreth* (shiftless), of someone's house being full of *annibendod* (untidiness), of somebody who is *wit-wat* (fickle), that Mrs. Jones has no *cewc* (regard) for Mrs. Evans and that a certain young lady was a proper *Shoni-hoi* (tomboy).

55. Sport

Much has been written about sport in the Llynfi Valley. The authority on the history of local cricket was the late G. R. Glover. It was Gwyn Daniel of

101   Tennis courts and pavilion, Maesteg Park

Bryn and Victor Hampson-Jones of Maesteg who first mentioned the possibility of having Welsh rugby terms.

There are early accounts of bando-playing in Margam and Llangynwyd. Contemporary verses to the Margam bando boys indicate that the Margam team included players from Llangynwyd. It appears that in the early days of the Maesteg and Llynvi Iron Works, when there was an influx of Irish immigrants, hurling matches were held on a 120 yards pitch below the site now occupied by St. John's Colliery, Cwmdu.

There are parks at Caerau, Maesteg and Garth containing tennis courts and bowling greens.

Cricket. G. R. Glover states that cricket was introduced to Maesteg in 1826 by the surveyors of the Maesteg Iron Works. This is quite possible as it was in May of that year that clay was first cut to provide bricks for the construction of the works. The Good Templars' team fielded a good side. The Maesteg Cricket Club was formed in 1846. At the centenary celebrations in 1946, an informative brochure on the history of the Club was produced.

The earliest cricket matches were played on a meadow behind Cavan Row, Maesteg, on part of the former Maesteg Uchaf Farm. When the Llynfi branch of the G.W.R. was constructed, involving a track running through the ground, the Club found a new home in the town centre in 1860. Messrs. North's Collieries presented the Club with a new pavilion in 1920, whilst the N.C.B. leased the ground at a nominal rent. Part of the ground, on which

102   Maesteg Cricket Team, early 1900's

103   Maesteg Cricket Club ground and open-air baths

104   Maesteg Cricket Club, First XI, Season 1961
Champions Division 1, South Wales and Monmouthshire Cricket Association
(Standing) L Thomas (Scorer), R Hopkins, B Lee, M Walters, A Durban, V Rees,
A John (Chairman)
(Seated) S Garnon, T Prosser, H Morgan, V Dixon (Captain), R J Hopkins, G James,
R Barry

tennis used to be played, was handed over to the Maesteg U.D.C. for the construction of a swimming pool.

The famous big hitter, G. L. Jessop, was a member of a team that visited Maesteg in 1905, but to the great disappointment of local cricket lovers, rain prevented play. In the 1933-34 season, Maesteg were honoured with a visit from the Cambria Crusaders' team captained by F. R. Brown, the former Test captain. A former member of the Maesteg team, R. Duckfield, played for the Glamorgan County team for several years. Cyril Smart, who first played for Glamorgan in 1927, became a professional player for Maesteg in 1932-3-4. It was during his stay at Maesteg that he attracted much attention as a forceful batsman. He resumed playing for Glamorgan. In one over against Hampshire in 1935, he scored 32 runs and became known as the biggest hitter of his day in County cricket, being effectively assisted by R. Duckfield in several County matches, the latter having scored 286 runs in one innings.

The Maesteg Celtic cricket club has become one of the best known in Glamorgan. It celebrated its golden jubilee in 1976, having developed, out of an eyesore of a site, a swimming pool, tennis courts, bowling greens, cricket and rugby pitches. The ground was ultimately taken over by the Maesteg U.D.C. The praises of the Garth Social Service Club and its varied

105   Maesteg Cricket Club, Management Committee, Centenary year, 1946
(Back row) R Williams, A John, J Hitchings, H Couling, R M Lake, O Davies,
T C Treharne, H S Llewellyn, Con Sutton
(Middle) E Thomas, G R Glover, G Thomas, C H Brothers, C Jenkins, T Loveland,
T Thomas, J Carey
(Bottom) B I Davies, P Isaac, H Chappell (Gen. Sec), D Cambettie (Chairman)
A E Lockyer (J.P.), G Rees (Vice-Chairman), T B Lockyer (Ass't Sec.)
D D Jones (Treasurer)

activities have been justifiably sung on many occasions by Mr. Garfield
Thomas, one of the Club's pioneers, who has organised many local sporting
events and has been instrumental in bringing some of the best-known
sporting personalities to Maesteg.

Among the records of the Celtic club can be listed: seven times South
Wales Cricket Association champions, seven times winners of the Dan
Radcliff Cup (including four seasons in succession) and the O. L. Harris
Trophy Cup, the South Wales Daily Post Cup (1946), and the Glamorgan
County Supporters Cup (1957). The club is proud of its association with the
Hopkins brothers, the eldest of the sons, John Anthony Hopkins, being the
successful opening batsman of the senior Glamorgan County team. Some
years ago the club was privileged to have Sir Leonard Hutton as guest at a
celebration dinner. It could also boast of an excellent rugby team.

Rugby Football. Owing to limitations of space, one cannot hope to do
justice to this subject. One must rely on the separate publications of local
authors who have specialised in the history of sport in the valley. Maesteg is

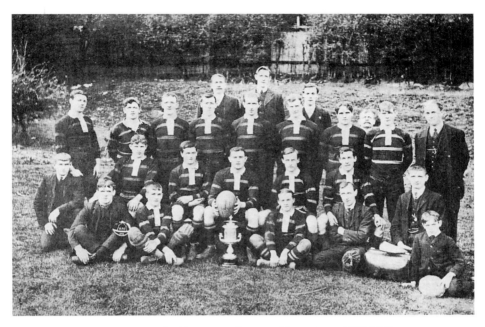

106 Maesteg RFC, Glamorgan League Champions, 1912-13 Season
(Top row) D Waters (Treasurer), A Lockyer (Committee), W Barnes (Committee),
W Howell (Committee)
(Third row) D Davies, S Bayliss, W J Davies, J Griffiths, D Watts, M Coleman,
E Jones, S Ackerman, R J Pole (Chairman)
(Second row) R Stradling, G Thomas, J Brennan, A Rees (Captain), A Griffiths,
J Richmond, J Jones
(Front row) R Bowen (Vice-captain), E Davies, W J Cooke, T Davies (Secretary)

clearly a town of rugby enthusiasts and it would be far too comprehensive a task to attempt to provide details of every one who has brought honour to the valley in this branch of sport, or list all the International players, the outstanding ones who had 'gone north', and the competent International referees.

The Maesteg R.F.C. will celebrate its centenary in 1982. The present ground was created from a tip of the Llynvi Iron Works and was first used in 1900. The present president, Windsor Major, is himself a Welsh International. During the 1949-50 season the team, under the captaincy of Trevor Lloyd, was unbeaten. A former player, Ray (Chico) Hopkins, toured Australia and New Zealand with the Lions team in 1971, having played a major part in a Welsh win at Twickenham the previous year, when he replaced Gareth Edwards, who was injured.

Although he played only a few games for the Maesteg team, the exploits of J. J. Williams of Nantyffyllon, a Lions and Wales wing-three-quarters of renown, have ensured him a secure place in the record book. He had

107   Ray (Chico) Hopkins with the author at a Civic Reception on the former's
return from New Zealand as a British Lion in 1971

previously been a Welsh Secondary School International player. Windsor
Lewis was also capped as a schoolboy and as a member of the senior Welsh
team, and later captained the Cambridge University, Guy's Hospital and
Barbarian teams. In all, the Maesteg Club has produced ten Internationals,
including two British Lions, whilst nine players have represented the Welsh
'B' team.

The doyen in rugby administrative circles was Enoch H. Rees, Maesteg, a
life member of the Welsh Rugby Union, a former President of the International Rugby Board, and a selector of the Welsh Rugby Union, of which
he was President in 1957-58. Denzil Lloyd, a former International referee
from Nantyffyllon is a former Vice-president of the Welsh Rugby Union.

During the last War the Maesteg R.F.C. pavilion was destroyed by fire
and the grandstand blown down during a gale. The stand was rebuilt by
voluntary labour by local craftsmen, and later a social club was added to its
amenities. Many of the club's best players, including 'Chico' Hopkins, 'went
North' and became professionals. Rees Thomas, a former Maesteg scrum-
half, was adjudged to be the outstanding Rugby League Player of the year
in 1958. Other local clubs that made their mark were the Maesteg Celtic
R.F.C., the Nantyffyllon R.F.C. (the ground and club-house having been
opened in 1963) and the Harlequins (Tir Iarll) R.F.C. Maesteg has provided
ten youth Internationals, thirty-one Welsh School caps and twelve Welsh
Secondary Schools Senior Group caps.

In the 1981 season the status of the Maesteg R.F.C. was further enhanced
by the emergence of two of its players, Gwyn Evans and Rhodri Lewis (now
playing with the Cardiff R.F.C.) as regular Internationals, the former

having achieved much scoring success and proving himself a worthy successor, as full back, to J. P. R. Williams. In the final match of the centenary year of the Welsh Rugby Union between the Welsh National team and the President's International side, Maesteg was represented by three players in the National side — Gwyn Evans (the top scorer), Rhodri Lewis and Colin Donovan as wing-three-quarters, whilst Huw Davies, the English outside-half, has his roots in Cwmfelin, Maesteg, his father and grandfather having played for Maesteg.

Soccer. The first soccer team of the valley, named Caerau Albions, was formed in 1903 as a result of the influx of people from North Wales, Cornwall, Somerset and Forest of Dean. Mr. Len Withers, Caerau, who was Hon. Treasurer of the controlling body of soccer in Wales, tells us in the *Coronation Issue of the Official Guide to Maesteg and District* in 1953 that winners of sixteen international caps had played for the Caerau A.F.C., each of whom played against the international teams of England, Ireland and Scotland as well as Continental teams. He also names five amateur International players as well as a youth International player. A few also played for some of the major soccer teams of England and Wales.

Up to 1953 the Caerau team had won the Welsh Amateur Cup on four occasions, then a record, and had defeated Willington Town in 1950 in their challenge of the English Amateur Cup winners. The Club was promoted to the Premier Division of the Welsh Soccer League in 1969.

David Bowen, a native of Nantyffyllon, was former manager of Northampton Town team, captain of Arsenal and Wales teams as well as manager of the Welsh International team. Soccer has now invaded Maesteg. The Maesteg Park A.F.C., formed in 1927, achieved much success, becoming Champions in 1978-79 of Division I of the South Wales Amateur League, and winners of the South Wales Senior Cup.

Physical Culture. The pioneer was C. B. Thomas who set up a school of physical culture and boxing at the Navigation Hotel, Caerau, from 1909 to 1916. He instructed his pupils in wrestling, cycling, weight lifting, walking and running, and they won over 300 prizes. He produced twelve amateur champions and seven runners-up. Perhaps it was as a boxing referee that he established his fame. He first appeared as such in London in 1930 and there-after refereed major contests in England, Scotland, Wales and Ireland. He was in charge of eight chief contests of the first ten at the Wembley Stadium, including a world championship, an Empire championship, two Lonsdale Belt contests and two between Jack Peterson and the German, Walter Neusel.

Among boxers of note trained in the valley was Bill (Kid) Hughes, who died aged seventy in 1974. He was a former Welsh flyweight champion, and fought Benny Lynch and Jackie Brown, both of whom became World champions. He later became promoter, referee and manager of several

108   Mr C B Thomas

Welsh champions and was elected a member of the Welsh Area Council of the British Boxing Board of Control.

One of the best-known valley boxers was Harry Davies, Caerau, still with us. He was the amateur middleweight champion of Wales in 1912 and 1913. In 1916 he became the Welsh professional middleweight champion. Other well-known local boxers were Ivor Pickens, welterweight champion of Wales, who once fought Jack (Kid) Berg, the world champion, Ossie Davies (son of Harry Davies), amateur welterweight champion of Wales and later of Great Britain. He was also Army welterweight champion. W. H. Walters of Caerau became Welsh light-heavyweight champion in 1934 and 1935 and amateur heavyweight champion in 1936, 1937 and 1939. Mike McLuskie, also of Caerau, was amateur welterweight champion in 1969 and 1970 and middleweight champion in 1971, thereafter becoming Welsh professional middleweight champion in 1973. Norman Jenkins, Caerau, was Welsh amateur welterweight champion in 1952. Others were Glyn David, flyweight champion of Wales and Tommy Edmunds, Welsh amateur welterweight champion in 1931 and 1932. Glan Pitman, Nantyffyllon, and his son known as 'Lenny the Lion', the latter becoming Welsh featherweight champion in 1963 and 1964, were well known boxers — as well as Emlyn Lewis, Caerau, who was the N.C.B. national bantamweight champion for 1948 at Wembley. All the above came from the upper part of the valley.

In Maesteg we had P. C. Rees Howells who was Welsh amateur middle-weight champion in 1923, 1924 and 1925 and light-heavyweight champion from 1926 to 1930. Stan Jehu was Welsh professional bantamweight champion in 1930 and featherweight champion in 1933 and 1935. He twice fought Freddie Miller, the World champion. Many of these details are given

109, 110, 111 Three early Maesteg sportspeople

by Mr. Tudor Isaac in his article on sport in the souvenir brochure published on the occasion of the centenary of the Maesteg Town Hall.

The famous Welsh boxer, Tom Thomas of Penygraig (1880-1911), began to suffer from rheumatism after walking home over the mountains after a fight in Maesteg and getting lost in the mist. The world famous boxer, Jimmy Wilde, visited Caerau in 1956.

Mr. Isaac's article also deals with hockey, basketball, swimming, billiards and snooker, weightlifting, athletics, tennis, bowls and golf. The three bowls clubs of Caerau, Maesteg and Maesteg Celtic all belong to the Mid Glamorgan Bowling Association. In 1950 the Caerau club became winners of the Caruthers Shield of the Association. The local golf club was opened in 1913 at Mount Pleasant, between Maesteg and Bryn. Members have won several important prizes from time to time.

Athletics have not been ignored, as J. J. Williams, the well-known rugby player, was champion runner of the 100 and 200 yards competition for several years, being the Welsh Sprint Champion (1968-1972) and winner in the Commonwealth Games in 1970. He participated with credit in the World Student Games of 1971. John Elias became the Glamorgan Triple Crown champion in 1963, besides holding other records.

We find that there was a bicycle club in Maesteg as far back as 1881 and that the famous billiard players, Willie Smith and Sidney Smith, gave an exhibition game in Nantyffyllon in 1932.

On the occasion of the celebration of the centenary of the Maesteg R.F.C., in 1982, a book called *The Old Parish — 100 Years not Out*, is being published by the Club. It is written by Glyn Phillips and Gwyn James, assisted by a small publication committee consisting of Garfield Thomas,

112   Tennis courts and pavilion, Caerau, early 1950's (Coegnant Colliery in operation back left)

113   Maesteg park, showing sports fields

Maxi Thomas and David Richards. Glyn Phillips deals with the history from the Club's inception until the second World War, and Gwyn James with its history from 1945 onwards.

56. Art

The first name that springs to the mind is Christopher David Williams (1873-1934), who later eschewed his middle name. His mother died at his birth (in Maesteg), whilst his father, Evan Williams, was a local grocer and a former chairman of the Maesteg U.D.C. Mr. Jeremiah Williams claims, in his biography of the artist, to have been the one who first discovered his genius when the latter was his pupil at the Llynvi British School, Maesteg. Tuition followed at Monkton House Cardiff, the Oswestry High School, the London College of Art and the Royal Academy Art School. The artist also studied in Italy. When studying in London he won several medals, prizes and the Landseer Scholarship and got to know Lord Leighton, (whose *Perseus and Andromeda* at the Walker Gallery, Liverpool, had first inspired him to become an artist) and G. F. Watts.

He first exhibited at the Royal Academy in 1902 with his *Paolo and Francesca*. The painting, together with his *The Remorse of Judas*, a portrait of his father, Evan Williams (exhibited at the Royal Academy in 1903) and a portrait of Mrs. Sackville Evans now hang at the Maesteg Town Hall. The artist's portrait of Sir Alfred Lyall was exhibited at the Royal Academy in 1906 and the artist was invited to join the Royal Society of British Artists. He also exhibited his paintings at the Royal Society of Portrait Painters. In 1911 he was commissioned to paint the Investiture of the Prince of Wales at Caernarfon, and was a guest at Buckingham Palace for a fortnight.

His works appear at the National Museum of Wales, the Glynn Vivian Art Gallery, Swansea, and the Newport Art Gallery. Shortly before he died he presented a large painting of a night scene on the Thames Embankment to the headquarters of the Salvation Army.

At the Bridgend National Eisteddfod, 1948, about fifty of his paintings were shown. The artist had adjudicated art at this Festival many times during a period of thirty years. In 1949 a further exhibition was opened on 12 May by Mr. Jeremiah Williams for a period of three weeks.

A memorial plaque set in the building in which the artist was born (in Commercial Street, Maesteg), was unveiled on 19 September 1956 by Sir Ben Bowen Thomas, with Sir Rhys Hopkin Morris, a native of Caerau, acting as chairman. Mr. Jeremiah Williams, then aged ninety-two, also spoke.

114 Official party for unveiling of memorial plaque to Christopher Williams at
Commercial Street, Maesteg on 19 September 1956
(Front row) Jeremiah Williams, Morgan Jones, Tom Jenkins and Mrs Christopher
Williams
(Second row) J A Roderick, G F Davies, A King Davies, Mrs Hezekiah Thomas,
Mrs Ivor Williams, Ivor Williams and T J Jones
with Mrs E A Williams between Mr and Mrs Ivor Williams
(Third row) Gwynedd Maddock, D M Thomas, Hezekiah Thomas and John Evans
(Fourth row) D C Watkins, Mrs D M Thomas, Enoch Llewelyn, Stanley Lewis
(Top) Brinley Richards

To commemorate the centenary of the artist's birth, an exhibition of his
paintings, compositions and drawings — seventy-nine in all — was held at the
National Museum of Wales in 1973 for a month, followed by a similar
exhibition at the Swansea Art Gallery for a further month and later at the
Maesteg Town Hall for three weeks.

His subjects for portrait-painting included D. Lloyd George (one as
Chancellor of the Exchequer and two as Prime Minister), Sir John Morris-
Jones, Sir Henry Jones, Sir John Rhŷs and Hwfa Môn (the former
Archdruid). His landscapes had settings in North and South Wales, Italy,
Morocco, Spain and France. His painting of the Welsh at Mametz Wood, a
war scene of the first World War, received much praise.

Mr. Saunders Lewis thought that the artist's painting of Sir John Rhŷs,
the renowned Celtic scholar, of Jesus College, Oxford, was his masterpiece,
and that the half-dozen oil-paintings, including the one of the girl in red
clothing with a background of mountains and clouds, were among his best,
revealing the influence of Augustus John.

Among the other prominent Welsh literary figures who paid tribute to his genius were Dyfnallt, Cynan, Crwys, Wil Ifan (all former Archdruids), and Dewi Emrys. In August 1934 a simple ceremony was conducted by the Rev. Samuel Williams, former minister of Soar Welsh Congregational Church, Maesteg, on the slopes of the steep hill leading from Cerdin Square to Llangynwyd village, near the Lamb and Flag hotel, where his ashes were scattered in accordance with his wishes. The writer of these notes was present at the service.

Mr. Ivor Williams, son of the artist, is himself an artist of high standing, especially as a 'realist' painter. He was educated at the King Alfred School, London, and the Slade School of Art. The Ivor Williams Group of an extramural department of the University of Wales at Cardiff became well-known. His paintings included a notable one of his mother and was accepted by the Royal Society of British Artists. His War paintings included one of Field Marshal Montgomery receiving the freedom of Newport, and one of the Welsh Regiment receiving the freedom of Cardiff. Another outstanding painting was that of Sir Winston Churchill. Among his subjects for portrait painting, in which he excelled, were Ted Williams (former High Commissioner of Australia), Principal Sir Emrys Evans (Bangor), Principal Sir J. F. Rees (Cardiff) and Principal Richard Thomas (Normal College, Bangor).

During the Town Hall centenary celebrations this year there was a further exhibition of the paintings by father and son at the Maesteg Town Hall. It was officially opened on 16 July by Sir Cennydd Traherne, K.G., Lord Lieutenant of the Counties of Glamorgan. Forty-five paintings by Christopher Williams were exhibited, seven of which—'Danae', 'Margam Buildings', 'The Remorse of Judas', 'Paolo and Francesca', 'Evan Williams' (the artist's father), 'Mrs. Sackville Evans' and 'Now that I am a Judge, Daddy' had been previously donated to the former Maesteg U.D.C. for hanging in the Town Hall. Thirty works by Ivor Williams were also shown.

Sir W. Beddoe Rees, a former pupil at the Llynvi Iron Works School, Maesteg, was well-known as an architect, particularly of chapel buildings. He designed the following local Chapels: Bethania (B), Tabor (C.M.) and the Wesleyan Chapel (now demolished), all of Maesteg, and Hope (B), Caerau. Bethel Congregational Chapel, Penclawdd, also designed by him, is of the same design.

Miss Lilian Griffiths, daughter of the Rev. Samuel Griffiths (a former curate of St. Peter's Church, Nantyffyllon) was a well-known artist in sculptures, miniatures and paintings, the one of her father being very well known. Her works were shown at the Bridgend National Eisteddfod Exhibition in 1948.

Frank Grey, the invalid son of David Grey of the Llwydarth Tinplate Works, won a special prize at the Llanelli National Eisteddfod, 1873, for pen and ink drawings. He won the first prize in 1900 at West Kirby for portrait-drawings in chalk and monochrome. His paintings and etchings were purchased by Lord Tredegar, Lord Adare, the Misses Olive and Emily Charlotte Talbot. His forest scenes remained at Margam Castle for many years. Tom Hughes, Maesteg, who died aged eighty-seven in October 1969, studied at the St. John's Wood School of Art, but his stay there was cut short by the death of his father. He excelled in portrait-painting (with a notable one of himself) and still-life pictues.

Neil Davies, Maesteg, when a student at the Sheffield College of Art in 1969, won a scholarship to the Slade School of Art, London, with the intention of spending a further year at the Paris Studio of Nicholas Schoffe. Ann Gazzi and Pauline Harris were prize winners at the Cardiff College of Art. Amos Dunn, U.S.A., formerly of Garth, was also considered an excellent artist, whilst David Carpanini of Abergwynfi, who has excelled in black and white drawings, can be claimed as a local product.

On 10 and 11 July 1969 there was an exhibition of the works of local artists at the Maesteg Town Hall. When the Urdd National Eisteddfod was held in Maesteg in 1979, there was an exhibition at the Midland Bank, Maesteg, of further paintings by local artists.

An Exhibition of Local Arts, Crafts and Photography, again part of the Town Hall centenary celebrations, was opened by the Mayor of Ogwr (Councillor H. V. Chilcott) on 7 September 1981.

Among exhibits there, and worthy of mention, were paintings and charcoal drawings by Marion Smith, Llynfi House, Maesteg, and drawings by D. J. Griffiths, Ewenny Road, Maesteg — particularly of Llangynwyd Church and also of the Corner House and Old House at Llangynwyd. Etchings by Mark Griffiths of the same family, were welcome additions. Other commendable local artists included Caradog Duncan (a retired Coegnant miner whose collection of paintings and etchings was the most extensive in the exhibition), Frank Crompton aged seventy-nine, who worked fifty-one years at Cwmdu Colliery, and T. Kennedy (oil paintings).

In the crafts section were exhibits by John J. Jones (love spoons, necklaces enamelled on copper plate, brassware), Llyfnwy Walters (whose brother, D. J. Walters, is also a well-known local craftsman), Roy Davies (the Nantyffyllon choir conductor), Len Ellis, Elfed Rowlands, Stephen Treharne, Mrs. P. Matthews, Bernard Carroll, Ray Jones, and Delyth M. Parry. Not to be forgotten were the exhibits of French pen-painting by Mrs. M. Lougher, Nantyffyllon, and of tapestry by her daughter, Miss C. E. Lougher, whilst models in wood, of chairs, a lampost, Llangynwyd Church, Big Ben and Cwmdu Colliery, by Will John, who was employed at Cwmdu Colliery for forty-five years, exemplified the quality of our local culture.

The valley artists also included the late T. Edgar Miller, and Miss Norah Isaac, Carmarthen (formerly of Caerau). Unfortunately, details of a good number of other local artists worthy of mention have not been received in good time for the publication of this volume. The omission should be rectified. There should be sufficient data available to justify publication of additional information, in booklet form at least, regarding our local artists.

57. Music

In musical talent, it can safely be claimed that the Llynfi Valley has a record second to none of valleys of comparable size and population in Wales.

It was at the old Tabor (C.M.) Chapel, Temple Street, Maesteg, where the Welsh National Anthem was sung for the first time, that the eight children of Jenkin and Anne Thomas, who then lived at South Parade, Maesteg, where christened by the Rev. Lewis Jones on 20 January 1878. The sixth child, then named David, aged five, ultimately became known as Dr. D. Vaughan Thomas, the noted Welsh musician. The event was commemorated at a service at Tabor Chapel sixty years later. This is confirmed by Emrys Cleaver, the biographer of the composer. Jenkin Thomas, father of Dr. W. Vaughan Thomas, who conducted weekly classes in music at Spelters (Caerau) before he and his family moved to Llantrisant in 1878.

The grandfather of Kathleen Ferrier was a native of Maesteg, and the grandparents of Olive Gilbert, who died early in 1980, lived at Nantyffyllon. Both singers used to visit Maesteg, where relatives still live. Incidentally, it was the grandfather of Olive Gilbert who named the writer of this volume, as he knew the famous pianist and composer, Brinley Richards, composer of *The Songs of Wales*, including 'God Bless the Prince of Wales', for which the writer of these notes was sometimes either praised or blamed!

Samuel J. Powell, who was manager of Madame Patti's private theatre at Craig-y-nos, at the top of the Swansea Valley, for fifteen years, was a native of Maesteg. David Davies, the local historian, claimed that John Thomas, father of *Pencerdd Gwalia*, who was Court harpist to Queen Victoria, and played the harp in all the principal cities of Europe, had lived at Maesteg.

It is asserted that Dr. Joseph Parry's popular opera *Blodwen* was performed for the first time at Maesteg. On the copy of the score presented to Philip Morgan, conductor of Carmel Choral Society, Maesteg, Dr. Parry wrote from Aberystwyth on 28 March 1879: 'To Philip Morgan for his great kindness and labour in training his choir in the first performance at Maesteg and Bridgend on 24 and 25 February, 1879.'

However, Mr. Roderick G. Williams, Maesteg, had in his possession a letter dated 10 September 1878 received by his father from Dr. Parry, stating that the work would be performed without a band on 26 September 1878 at Taibach. The letter referred to losses on the Neath and Treherbert supplementary concerts, and stated that it was at a complimentary concert arranged by the Aberystwyth Masonic Lodge for their Lodge organist, Dr. Parry, that *Blodwen* was first performed. Maybe the misunderstanding arose as Dr. Parry, in his note, meant the first performance in Maesteg and not necessarily in Wales.

Several well-known local musicians emigrated to the U.S.A. in the last century They included George Marks Evans, a native of Nantyffyllon, who

later lived at Wilkesbarre and Shamokin, Pennsylvania, where he died in
1931. He had composed and arranged over 300 anthems and at least 30
male choruses, as well as 100 hymn tunes and 750 songs, and many duets.
He was music editor of *Y Drych*, the Welsh American periodical, and
possessed a rich bass voice, used to advantage as a soloist in the rendering of
the anthem *Teyrnasoedd y Ddaear*.

Another noted musician who left Maesteg for the U.S.A. in the last
century was Ap Madoc (1844-1916), who wrote the music of several St.
David's Day songs and was a contributor to the *Holiadur Cymreig* columns
of *Cyfaill yr Aelwyd* in the eighties of the last century. He was well-known in
Welsh-American circles as musician, bard, editor, adjudicator, lecturer,
eisteddfod conductor, soloist, and organist. On leaving Utica for Chicago,
he was appointed choirmaster of All Souls' Church, Chicago. He died at St.
Luke's Hospital, of that City, on 12 August 1916.

Professor T. Lovett, a native of Maesteg, became well-known as a pianist
and music teacher in the U.S.A., whilst Thomas Morgan (*Llyfnwy*), to
whom there are many references in this volume, was a noted eisteddfod and
cymanfa ganu conductor, although he was better known for his literary
output.

Josiah Thomas, brother of Mrs George Bowen, doyen of Welsh life in the
valley, a triple winner of the flute solo competition at the National
Eisteddfod, and former flautist with the London Philharmonic orchestra,
also emigrated to the U.S.A. His son, Thomas Llyfnwy Thomas, was born in
Maesteg and proud to be a Welsh-speaking Welshman. He became probably the most famous and popular Welsh-American singer of his day, and
was made a member of the *Gorsedd* at the National Eisteddfod at Cardiff in
1978. His voice was familiar to concert, radio and T.V. audiences
throughout the entire American continent. He took part in concert tours
from coast to coast and appeared as guest artist with the U.S.A.'s leading
symphony orchestras and as a singing star of top flight radio and T.V.
shows. It was stated that he had gained in America one of the widest and
most discriminating audiences of any singer of his day. His brother, Elwyn,
also became known throughout the U.S.A. as an outstanding baritone
singer. He played in 2,418 consecutive performances of 'My Fair Lady'
during its Broadway run in New York. He died, aged seventy-three, in
February 1981.

Dr. Daniel Protheroe, the famous Welsh-American composer and
musician, used to visit the Llynfi Valley from time to time before he
emigrated, as his mother's sister lived at Tynderi, Nantyffyllon. Madam
May Evans Dawe, herself a contralto of considerable standing, was born at
Nantyffyllon, having married Dr. Charles Dawe, the eminent conductor of
the famous Cleveland Orpheus Male Choir.

David John Davis, the celebrated tenor from Nantyffyllon and thrice
winner at the National Eisteddfod, left for the U.S.A. in 1931 and died in
1979 at the age of eight-seven. His father, Billy Davies, precentor of Saron

Church, Nantyffyllon, known as *Telorydd Llyfnwy,* was called 'the prince of Welsh tenors' at the Pontypridd National Eisteddfod in 1893. He died at the early age of thirty-three.

William T. Williams, better known as *Gwilym Taf* (1859-1924), of Maesteg, was an outstanding tenor and conductor who emigrated to South Africa in 1916, gaining further fame as a vocalist. He was precentor of Soar (C) Church, Maesteg, and won several prizes as a tenor vocalist at the National Eisteddfod. He lies buried in his adopted country.

Marie Novello, Gwilym Taf's daughter, had won over 100 eisteddfodic prizes by the time she was fifteen and later gave over thirty piano recitals in South Wales, in addition to recitals in London and at all the principal cities of England and Ireland. She had also three National Eisteddfod wins to her credit, competing with approximately sixty aspirants each time. She studied piano-playing in Vienna for three years until 1907. At the Cardiff Triennial Festival, October 1907, she was hailed by the critics as the greatest pianist that Wales had ever produced, ranking with the greatest English and foreign pianists of the day. On her tombstone at the Maesteg Cemetery are carved the words by Wil Ifan:

> Llonydd yw'r bysedd a hedfannai gynt
> Fel gwylain diflin uwch ystorm o gerdd.

(At rest are the fingers that once fluttered like untiring seagulls above a tempest of music). An informative article on her career by Willie T. Davies appeared in *The Llynfi Valley Messenger* in 1909.

T. Glyndwr Richards of Nantyffyllon was considered to be one of the best male-voice choir conductors of his age in South Wales. His Mountain Ash choir toured the U.S.A. on three occasions, having also sung before Royalty at Windsor Castle. His choir won a famous victory at the Swansea National Eisteddfod in 1891 with a rendering of Dr. Joseph Parry's test piece, 'The Pilgrims'. He was also the composer of anthems and hymn tunes. His father and two brothers were killed in colliery accidents locally.

Another equally capable conductor, but perhaps not so well-known, was John Powell *(Eos Cynwyd),* precentor of Saron Church, Nantyffyllon, who left the district to become precentor at Treharris. He was the composer of the anthem *Daeth yr Awr.*

During the second half of the last century and the first quarter of this century the Llynfi Valley was famous for its singers and choirs, mainly nurtured in the local Chapels. Sol-fa classes were popular, one of them being conducted in Llangynwyd in 1894 by Morgan Jones, Llety Brongu, who was also a commendable local poet. The modulator was a necessity in the weekly Band of Hope. Several chapels had their own choirs and orchestras and frequently held their own *eisteddfodau,* penny readings and *cymanfaoedd canu.* The favourites for chapel choirs were the anthems *Teyrnasoedd y Ddaear* and *Dyddiau Dyn sydd fel Glaswelltyn,* whilst they were also capable

115   Bethania Welsh Baptist Chapel, Bethania Street, Maesteg, built 1908

of doing justice to the works of Handel (especially 'The Messiah'), Mozart ('Twelfth Mass'), Haydn ('The Creation') and Mendelssohn ('The Hymn of Praise').

In his essay on the precentors of Bethania (B) Church, Maesteg, Samuel Davies, a one-time precentor of the Church, states that the Church choir, conducted by Isaac Howells *(Perdonydd y Dyffryn)* competed at a Mountain Ash eisteddfod held on Christmas Day over a century ago. The choristers walked over the mountains in pouring rain to and from the eisteddfod and were all soaked to the skin. They had the satisfaction of winning the first prize for their rendering of 'Worthy is the Lamb', despite the possible dire consequences of the journey to the health of the choristers.

Several Chapels produced cantatas based on biblical characters or themes, such as 'David the Shepherd Boy', 'The Moabitess', 'Joseph',

'Esther', 'Daniel'. 'Belshazzar's Feast'. Other cantatas had secular themes. The repertoire of the male-voice choirs included 'The Pilgrims', 'Crossing the Plain', 'Nidaros', 'The Fishermen', 'The Crusaders', 'Martyrs of the Arena, and 'Italian Salad'. Owing to the emphasis on temperance at the beginning of the century, an annual temperance cymanfa ganu *(Cymanfa Ddirwestol)* became a feature of the activities of the Welsh Baptists of the valley.

Hundreds of *cymanfaoedd canu* have been held in the district, and for many years several Churches were able to hold a cymanfa without outside help. The most famous series is still called *Cymanfa Tanymarian*, to commemorate the centenary in 1922 of the birth of the Rev. Edward Stephen *(Tanymarian)*. The first of the series was held in the Maesteg Town Hall under the conductorship of Dr. Caradog Roberts, when the Hallelujah Chorus and the Welsh Chorus, 'Dyna'r Gwyntoedd yn Ymosod' from *Storm Tiberias* by Edward Stephen, were sung with electifying effect. It is still being held. The Congregationalists have recently been joined by the other valley Welsh Nonconformists to make it a united cymanfa.

The Town Hall became the focus of the major musical events of the Valley. All the best known singers of South Wales in the present century have sung at the Hall, either in concerts, eisteddfodau, operas, cantatas or oratorios. Sir Adrian Boult and his London Philharmonic Orchestra were visitors in 1953. Previously, Coleridge Taylor had adjudicated at the Tir Iarll Eisteddfod at Maesteg.

Benefit Concerts to aid needy persons to further their careers, especially in music, were generously supported. Instrumentalists and pianists were called 'professors' and noted female soloists prefixed their names with *'Madame'*.

A concert held on Sunday was called a 'sacred concert'. Every Christmas an eisteddfod was held at the Maesteg Town Hall, Siloh Chapel, Nantyffyllon, being the organisers. A concert followed in the evening. These events were considered on a par with those held at Carmel, Treherbert, at Merthyr and at Morriston. Sometimes local male choirs competed at three eisteddfodau in one day, e.g., at Pembre, Clunderwen and Llanymddyfri on Easter Monday.

Of the valley private schools for piano-playing, one called the 'Beethoven School of Music' with Madam Anna Hughes Thomas as tutor, was the best known. Madam Thomas was the daughter of the Rev. Richard Hughes, Bethania (B) Church, Maesteg, and married Edward Thomas, known as *Cochfarf*, who was a former Lord Mayor of Cardiff. She was well-known as an organist and pianist, and conducted a successful ladies' choir at Maesteg. She died, aged ninety, at Detroit in 1954. By to-day there are few private piano teachers in the valley.

Although Isaac Howells *(Perdonydd y Dyffryn)*, precentor of Bethania Church, was well known as a choir conductor and instrumentalist, he was

116   Town Hall, Maesteg, *c.*1910

better known as the pioneer of piano-playing in the valley, being the first
local man to possess a piano. The best-known valley pianist in later days was
Professor Willie Evans, Nantyffyllon. He was accompanist to the famous
Glyndwr Richards Male Choir that toured America on three occasions, and
acted as such when the choir sang before Royalty at Windsor Castle in 1922.
He was also accompanist to the notable Nantyffyllon Children's Choir.
Among other local pianists who attained National honours were Maggie
Davies at Llanelli in 1895 and Vera Grey Davies at Caernarfon in 1935,
when she was only fifteen years of age. She was twice winner of the open

pianoforte competition at the Central Hall, Westminster, and won the John Curwen Prize for harmony at the Tonic Sol-fa College of Music. In 1940 she won a three years' Glamorgan Music Scholarship for tuition at the Royal Academy, and during her stay in London, she became organist of All Saints Church, Chiswick. She was highly praised as pianist and organist by Sir Julius Harrison, Dr. J. F. Staton and Warwick Braithwaite. Her husband was the brilliant local journalist, Donald B. Jones of the *Glamorgan Gazette*. For some years she has lived in Canada.

Of the valley instrumentalists, Professor Gomer Jones and Cynwyd K. Watkins are probably the best known. The former, a native of Nantyffyllon, taught the violin, viola, cello, piano and theory. Over thirty of his pupils obtained diplomas in various branches of instrumental music and over 200 passed the examinations of the R.A.M., R.C.M., L.C.M. and Trinity College. He died, aged sixty-one, at Bridgend in 1931.

Cynwyd King Watkins of Maesteg became famous locally as a brilliant violinist and as the conductor of the Maesteg Orchestral Society, but it was as music master at the Gowerton Grammar School that he became known further afield. At that school he conducted a boys' choir of 150 voices and also an orchestra of 50 members. As far back as 1946, of the 420 boys attending the school, 214 were instrumentalists. Professor Alun Hoddinot, the well-known composer, describes his former teacher as one of the finest teachers of instrumental music in Wales.

Incidentally, a relative of Cynwyd K. Watkins, David Eynon Jones, was the doyen of Llynfi Valley organists, having been a chapel organist for sixty-four years at Carmel and Canaan Churches, Maesteg, respectively. At the age of thirteen he was appointed one of the official accompanists to the old Tir Iarll Eisteddfod. The father of Cynwyd K. Watkins was a well-known choir conductor and chapel precentor. He was the composer of the hymn tune on the words *Os cul yw'r ffordd* which has been sung on hundreds of occasions in the valley.

It was in July 1847 that a local band was first formed by the employees of the Llynvi and Garth Iron Works. In 1880 there were two brass bands in Maesteg — (1) The Maesteg Volunteer Band conducted by W. Y. Davies and (2) The Second Welsh Volunteers under the command of T. B. Boucher, Captain Morris and Captain Harris (Star Hotel). Since then there have been several other bands — Llangynwyd, Maesteg Town, Caerau, Hibernian, Catholic Mission and Salvation Army, and also dance bands and cinema bands (in the days of silent films). T.V., but the development of canned music has accelerated the decline of dance bands. A drum and fife band was once formed by Tom Evans (Skewen) of Nantyffyllon. During the first quarter of this century a German Band used to tour the valley and play in open streets. In 1921 the Caerau Silver Band, conducted by H. Heyes, could claim eleven firsts, three seconds and one third in fifteen contests.

117   Maesteg Silver Band, *c*.1895

The attitude of local chapels was not always favourable to the use of musical instruments. When the Maesteg United Choir conducted by David Jenkins (The Stores) sang *The Twelfth Mass* in Salem (B) Church, Nantyffyllon — being the first oratorio sung in the valley — there was much objection to the use of an orchestra.

However it is on record that Edward Jones, a deacon of Saron (C) Church, Nantyffyllon, played the cello to aid the congregational singing in the fifties of the last century. Bethel (B) Church, Maesteg, claimed that their new harmonium was the first musical instrument of its kind used in any place of worship in the district. In later years, Churches that had previously objected to the harmonium have welcomed orchestras as a help to hymn-singing.

As for harp playing, William Morgan *(Ap Siencyn)* was a familiar figure at the Farmers' Hotel, Maesteg, having won first prize for harp playing at four National Eisteddfodau (1881, 1891-2-3), and also at the World Fair Eisteddfod at Chicago in 1893. He had also played before Royalty. He died, aged sixty-eight, in Maesteg in 1936.

The other best-known valley harpists were Claudia Jones, and Sylvia Walters (both of Caerau), and Ann Griffiths. Claudia Jones registered three first prizes and two second prizes for harp playing at the National Eisteddfod, whilst Sylvia Walters was first on four occasions, having won the John Thomas *(Pencerdd Gwalia)* Scholarship for three years' tuition at the R.A.M. — and also several silver and bronze medals for harp playing.

Ann Griffiths began playing the harp at the age of ten, and at the age of thirteen she won the harp solo competition for competitors under eighteen at the Bridgend National Eisteddfod in 1948. She was the first British

118   Claudia Jones Grey at the harp outside the *Old House Inn,* Llangynwyd in the
1960's, welcoming Mr L M Howells and friends back from Australia

musician to receive the coveted gold medal of the Paris Conservatoire (in
1958) where she studied for three years. She has given recitals in France,
Germany, Iceland, Holland, and Israel, and also at the Wigmore Hall and
Festival Hall, London, and has played with several major orchestras. Her
research work involved the study of seventeenth-century harps and her
knowledge of folk-music is extensive. She possesses a unique and numerous
collection of harps, and for years has run a Harp School *(Ysgol y Delyn)* at
Pantybeilïau, near Abergavenny.

Her sister, Mari, has won national honours for harp playing but has concentrated on folk-singing to the accompaniment of the guitar. She is a
familiar figure on the T.V. screen. Their father, T. H. Griffiths, was a
schoolmaster at Maesteg when his daughters were teenagers.

The writer's father could remember devotional meetings at Nantyffyllon
when the hymns were announced two lines at a time as no hymn-books were
then available. The doyen of local musicians who taught sol-fa to them was
Samuel Davies G. & L., precentor of Bethania (B) Church, Maesteg for over
fifty years. Besides being an enlightened conductor, he composed anthems,
hymn-tunes and a cantata, and wrote music to old traditional verses
remembered by Cadrawd, the local historian. He also published collections
of his own hymn-tunes, *Mawl y Saint,* for cymanfaoedd canu and *Odlau'r
Sabath* (1890) for the use of Sunday schools and also cymanfaoedd canu. He
was one of three Welshmen (with D. W. Lewis of Brynaman and L. J.

Roberts of Aberaeron) to be awarded a scholarship of the Tonic Sol-fa School and elevated as graduate of the College. His devotion to Bethania was such that he turned down the offer of Vicar Stephen Jackson to become the first precentor of St. Michael's Church, Maesteg, at the yearly salary of £25, then big money.

Samuel Davies was also a man of letters and wrote the history of Bethania Church as well as *in memoriam* verses for ten deacons of that Church. In addition, he competed at the Tir Iarll Eisteddfod, 1924, in an essay competition on *Beth sydd yn gwneuthur Dyn yn Ddyn?* (What makes Man a Man?). The essay involved much research work in order to cite examples. He also wrote *Arweinyddion Canu Bethania, Maesteg* (The Precentors of Bethania, Maesteg) containing much information of the musical traditions, not only of the Church, but also of the valley.

Daniel R. Waldin published in the *Glamorgan Advertiser*, in the twenties, a most informative account of the 'Conductors of the Past', but limitations of space will not allow us to quote in detail.

There have been many local choral successes at the National Eisteddfod, a notable one being the victory of the Gitana Ladies' Choir (Côr Merched Maesteg) under the conductorship of Miss Minnie Morgan (daughter of Philip Morgan) at the Llanelli National Eisteddfod of 1895. Evan Jenkins, who was precentor in turn of Salem and Siloh Churches, Nantyffyllon, in the last century, conducted cantatas such as Blodwen and 'The Bohemian Girl'. His male choir was adjudged jointly-first with that of Taibach at the Merthyr National Eisteddfod, 1881.

The Nantyffyllon Choral Society consisted mainly of Saron Church members and became well-known for its oratorio singing. The conductor was W. J. Watkins *(Cerddor Llyfnwy)* who had been precentor of Saron for over fifty years. The Church was noted as the breeding ground of a record number of Church precentors within and outside the valley.

Two of the best known male voice parties in Maesteg in the twenties were the one conducted by W. Myrnach Davies, a native of Llanfyrnach, Pembrokeshire, and the Maesteg Male Voice Party conducted (1918-1928) by Tom Thomas. There was much rivalry between the two parties and both achieved impressive eisteddfodic successes. Tom Thomas (1883-1959), a native of Llangynwyd, was also the precentor of Libanus (C.M.) Church, Garth. His male choir's main achievement was the winning (out of fifteen choirs) of the Lloyd George Gold Cup and £100 at the Cardiff Empire in 1920. Sir Walford Davies, the adjudicator, referred to him as the 'musical magician from Maesteg'. His choir was three-times winner of the Tir Iarll Silver Cup, and won other cups, batons and chairs at many major provincial eisteddfodau. Several oratorios were conducted by him at the Maesteg Town Hall. He became a popular cymanfa ganu conductor, one cymanfa programme consisting entirely of his own hymn tunes and anthems.

119   Silurian Gleemen, 1926
(Back row) Dai Edwards, Nat Edwards, T Brimble, Glyn Jones
(Middle row) G Howells, W Lewis, W Hughes, G Llywelyn, Ossie Evans, W John
(Front row) G Williams, D G Davies, D G Thomas (Accompanist),
Dan Jones (Conductor), D J Lewis, T Henry, Dan Parry

120   Garth Unemployed and Social Service Male Voice Party ready to make a
radio broadcast in 1937

121   Libanus Welsh Calvinistic Methodist Chapel, Garth, built 1871

During the depression the Silurian Gleemen were formed in Caerau, and were conducted by Dan Jones (Noddfa). They achieved fame throughout Wales and the Border Country.

Trefor Davies, L.R.A.M., of Nantyffyllon, was a conductor of great promise and a brilliant pianist who died in his thirties, in 1942. Famous singers who sang in Maesteg considered him one of the best pianists ever to have accompanied them. He gained National honours as a pianist, and after serving as such to the best local choirs, he became conductor of the Nantyffyllon Choral Society and of the Coegnant Gleemen. He conducted oratorios and operas in the Maesteg Town Hall, and his Mixed Choir earned high praise at the Port Talbot National Eisteddfod of 1932 for a rendering of Wolf's 'Fire Rider', when the choir was adjudged second.

Stephen H. Page, a native of Llangynwyd and precentor of Soar (C) Church, Maesteg, was the conductor of the Llynfi Valley Operatic Society and the local N.C.B. choir. He conducted the opera 'Y Ferch o Gefn Ydfa' with music by Dr. Haydn Morris, and many other works including 'Aïda' (Verdi). T. Edgar Miller, a native of Maesteg, conducted, in his early years, children's choirs, male glee parties and choral societies. Thomas Llyfnwy Thomas was an artist in one of his earliest opera productions. He became music director of the Maesteg Grand Opera Society and precentor of Tabernacle Welsh Baptist Church, Maesteg. In 1942 he became music director, and later producer as well, of the Maesteg Amateur Operatic Society. From the presentation of 'The Desert Song' to his production of 'La Vie Parisienne', he had conducted twenty-eight operas ranging from Gilbert and Sullivan to Rogers and Hammerstein. The only show that was repeated was 'Chu Chin Chow' in 1965. He became the honorary music director and producer of the Society and held the long-service medal and two bars of the National Opera and Dramatic Association (N.O.D.A.) for over fifty years' service in the furtherance of music and drama in Maesteg. He died in May, 1981, aged eighty-nine.

A product of the local Operatic Society was David Dennis Thomas, Maesteg—with his tremendous ability as an actor and singer, who would have made a mark on the London stage and beyond the seas had he so desired. His demise at an early age was a heavy loss to the valley musical community.

Incidentally, David Emanuel, who gained world fame in 1981 as a royal dress designer, was once a member of the cast of the Maesteg Junior Operatic Society and took the part of the Major General in a production of 'The Gondoliers'.

Unquestionably the best-known and most successful choir in the history of the valley was the Nantyffyllon Children's Choir. It was formed in 1915 with D. C. Watkins as conductor and Adwen Williams as pianist (later followed by Professor Willie Evans). At their first National Eisteddfod attempt at Neath in 1918, they were finalists, being fourth out of twenty-six choirs. The following year at Corwen they gained second prize in the children's chief choral competition. In the Barry National Eisteddfod of 1920 they gained first prize in the folk-song choir contest and were again second in the children's chief choral. At Caernarfon in 1921 and at Llanelli in 1930 they secured the top place in the children's chief choral, besides winning the first prize at Llanelli in the girls' chorus competition. In five National Eisteddfodau they gained four first prizes and two second prizes. They won

122   Nantyffyllon Children's Choir, 1933. Conductor Mr D C Watkins

hundreds of prizes in provincial eisteddfodau. In 1930 they could claim thirty-five successive wins. Included in the many concerts given by them were one at Brighton and one at the Queen's Hall, London.

D. C. Watkins had earlier won success as the conductor of the Blaenllynfi School, Caerau, Juvenile Choir and many years later he conducted the Nantyffyllon Male Voice Party. His daughter, Dilys Richards, is the highly successful conductor of the valley Welsh School choir. His father, Llewelyn Watkins, was a well-known local chapel precentor, whilst his mother, Madam Kate Watkins, was one of the valley's greatest sopranos.

A new conductor of promise is Dr. Haydn James, London, a native of Nantyffyllon. His Gwalia (London) choir secured first place in a competition for under forty voices at a recent National Eisteddfod, whilst his Dylan Ladies Choir has sung in Russia and several other countries. Limitations of space will not permit us to enlarge upon present day local conductors such as John Henry Davies, Aldwyn Humphreys, and Gwyn Watkins, the first named having been a member of a successful vocal quartette at the National Eisteddfod. Deceased conductors such as David John (Hughes), Nant-yffyllon, whose choir toured America, Richard Powell (also an accomplished pianist), Jack Williams, Maesteg, and others all deserve special mention.

It is dangerous to enumerate the famous singers of the valley owing to the possibility of omitting the names of worthy artists.

John Hocking (1849-1953) was a renowned bass singer and a versatile artist. He and *Gwilym Taf* (tenor) were the successful duet winners at the London National Eisteddfod of 1887. He was an excellent cello player, and was the conductor of the first orchestra in the Llynfi Valley, besides being the conductor of the then Maesteg Male Voice Party, being succeeded by

W. Myrreck Davies. He was the Wesleyan Church organist for nearly fifty years and a former chairman of the Maesteg U.D.C. A century ago his Eisteddfod Prize Choir toured Australia and America. He was also the conductor of a drum and fife band.

Among the well-known local singers of that generation were the soprano, Madam Bronwen Jones Williams, who, in 1899, was the first soprano to sing at the Oireachtas, the Irish National Festival, in Dublin; Madam Sambrook-Jones, the contralto, several times winner at the National Eisteddfod and whose husband, the Rev. Gwilym Jones, was one time minister of the English Congregational Church, Maesteg; and Jenkin Rees, the renowned bass singer of Garth, Maesteg. He and Billy Davies *(Telorydd 'Llyfnwy)* were winners of the vocal duet competition at the Pontypridd National Eisteddfod of 1893.

Another local soprano was Sarah Catherine Morris, Nantyffyllon, who would have reached the heights, according to Dr. Joseph Parry, had it not been for her untimely death at the age of twenty-five. She had already attained fame as a soprano who had sung in many oratorios in South Wales, and won a scholarship to the then Music College of Swansea to study under Dr. Parry, who attended her funeral at Maesteg.

Mary Llewelyn *(Gwenhwyfar)*, an outstanding soprano from Nant-yffyllon, who married Alaw Davies, emigrated with her husband to America where she died in 1926. In Welsh-American circles she was acclaimed as one of Wales's greatest sopranos. Her father, the Rev. William Rees, was the minister of Siloh Church, Nantyffyllon, from 1856 to 1874. Other soloists whose fame extended beyond the confines of the Llynfi Valley were Isaac Morris (tenor), W. E. Llewelyn (bass) and Olive Grey (contralto), daughter of David Grey of the Llwydarth Tinplate Works.

Richard Davies, Nantyffyllon, precentor of Soar Church, Maesteg, was known locally as a poet and composer of hymn-tunes, but his two daughters, Maggie and Annie, became famous nationally as the two choristers who sang at the Revival meetings of Evan Roberts throughout Wales in 1904 and 1905. Annie (Mrs. Roberts) died at an advanced age at the Llynfi Hospital, Maesteg, in 1980.

Glanville Davies, Maesteg, was known as one of Wales's greatest singers in his day, being the winner of the baritone solo competition at Birkenhead National Eisteddfod in 1917 and the bass solo competition at the Neath Eisteddfod of 1918. He won many prizes at provincial eisteddfodau and sang in innumerable concerts and oratorios throughout Wales. Known as an intelligent singer, he was the perfect stage artist.

Emlyn Burns of Nantyffyllon was another outstanding soloist. He had a record number of wins as a tenor at the National Eisteddfod — three times in the solo competition, five times in the duet competition and four times in the quartette competition. He sang for a session with the Glyndebourne Singers, and was a favourite tenor soloist in operas, oratorios and concerts throughout Wales.

Bessie Bevan, born and bred in Nantyffyllon, and later known as Madam Bessie Davies, Tonyrefail, who died on Christmas Eve 1980, was an outstanding colaratura soprano, excelling in folk-songs, ballads and operatic-arias. She was the winner of the folk-song competition at the Corwen National Eisteddfod in 1919 and also a member of the winning quartette at the Liverpool National Eisteddfod of 1929, the bass member being J. H. Davies, Maesteg.

Another Nantyffyllon singer of note was Mildred Howells, who first came into the limelight by winning the solo competition for girls under sixteen at the Birkenhead National Eisteddfod of 1917. She again succeeded in the contest for young sopranos at the Pontypool Eisteddfod in 1924 and achieved further National Eisteddfod successes in 1925 and 1927. She became a popular concert artist, having appeared at the Duke's Theatre, London, and several provincial towns and cities. Cadivor Davies of Maesteg, a native of Coetrehen, became an oratorio singer of note and was at one time the principal tenor of the Carl Rosa Opera Company. He sang extensively on the Continent, Russia and America but had to retire before he was forty owing to throat trouble. He died, aged seventy-five, in 1951.

Esme Lewis of Caerau, now Mrs. Dr. John Bradley-Jones, is one of the outstanding folk-singers of Wales. She gained her M.A. degree in 1976 and the L.R.A.M. the following year, having published two collections of folk-songs (Welsh University Press) arranged for schools. She began broadcasting when she was eight and has written innumerable scripts for the B.B.C. She is an acknowledged authority on arranging classical airs for guitar accompaniment and has given recitals at the Wigmore Hall, the Festival Hall and the Albert Hall, London. She has taken part in radio and T.V. programmes in France, Holland, Germany and Spain and is now senior lecturer at the Cardiff College of Education.

Moira Griffiths of Llangynwyd won a medal for acting at the Cardiff College of Music and Drama and gained a scholarship to the R.A.M. to study singing under Marjorie Thomas. At the Royal Academy she won the Blyth-Buesst Prize (out of forty-five) for opera-singing open to all voices, with Dame Eva Turner as the adjudicator. She left for Geneva in 1969 to be trained at the Opera House for a career in opera.

The foregoing details form but a brief outline of the careers of some of the foremost singers and musicians of the valley. Lack of space prevents us from referring to others less known but who have contributed substantially to the musical life of the district. The local people are very jealous of their traditions, as exemplified by the fact that Dr. Leigh Henry, the well-known musician and adjudicator, had to be escorted by six police officers from the Maesteg Town Hall to the local railway-station for having made insulting remarks regarding a local conductor.

Incidentally, Sir Samuel T. Evans, one time M.P. for the district and later Solicitor General and famous High Court Judge, composed a once-popular hymn tune which he named 'Maesteg'.

Before going to press, we note that the coveted blue riband prize at the Machynlleth National Eisteddfod, 1981, restricted to winners (male and female) of the chief solo competitions at that Eisteddfod, was won by Gwion Thomas, whose father, the Rev. David Arthur Thomas, is a product of the valley, son of the late Mr. and Mrs. David Thomas, Nolton Stores, Maesteg. This was the first time for him to compete at the National Eisteddfod. He is a student at the College of Music at Manchester. He has already appeared (as a baritone) in Alun Hoddinott's opera, 'The Trumpet Major'.

58. Religion

It would certainly need a separate volume to deal adequately, if that were possible, with this aspect of life in the Llynfi Valley. Histories of several places of worship have been written by various authors, and these contain much information regarding the origins of the various Churches, and of the priests, clergy and ministers who have either been nurtured locally or who have served the various valley Churches from time to time. The saintly characters of the district and the spiritual activities of each Church are worthy subjects that have to be excluded owing to lack of space.

The early history of some local Churches, e.g., Salem, Nantyffyllon, is contained in a bottle buried in the structure of the Church building in 1872. If a new Church is built as the result of a disagreement, commonly known as a 'split', then there is a possibility that the bottled Church history could be highly coloured in favour of the dissidents.

(a) Early History

Llangynwyd Church, the mother Church of the valley, has already been referred to. The earliest ascertainable incumbent is recorded at Canterbury as 'John de Bononia presented in 1288 by Matilda, Countess of Gloucester and Hereford to Llangynwyd Church, Diocese of Llandaff'. In 1550 'John Herbert, Clerk' held the living and ten years later John ab Morgan was Vicar of 'Lan-gun-wode'. In 1608, Sir Hugh Meredith was Vicar of 'Llan-gynoud'.

One of the most famous incumbents was Michael Roberts, who was Vicar for three months only in 1639, having previously served as Vicar of Margam. He was appointed successively Fellow and Bursar and ultimately Principal of Jesus College, Oxford in 1648, but after nine years he was removed by Cromwell at the request of the Fellows of the College after a tempestuous and controversial career. Dr. Thomas Richards, the historian, formerly of Maesteg, has provided us with much information concerning him in his

123 Line illustration of Llangynwyd Church before the 1893 restoration, reproduced from the frontispiece of T C Evans' (Cadrawd's) 'History of Llangynwyd Parish', published 1887

treatise: 'The Puritan Visitation of Jesus College, Oxford and the Principalship of Dr. Michael Roberts, 1648-1657' published in the Transactions of the Hon. Society of Cymmrodorion, 1922-23, pp. 1-111. In his volume *Rhagor o Atgofion Cardi* (More Recollections of a Cardi), Dr. Richards refers to Michael Roberts in very uncomplimentary terms. He was a native of Anglesey and was educated at Dublin, Oxford and Cambridge. He graduated B.A. and B.D.

After 1150, Glamorgan was divided into ecclesiastical parishes. Stone church buildings replaced Celtic wooden structures. At one time the Parish of Llangynwyd was about 11 miles long, stretching from Coetrehen (4 miles north of Bridgend) to Blaengwynfi. It was sub-divided to create the Parish of Avon Vale, consisting of Cymer and Abergwynfi, in 1907, with the Parish Church (St. Gabriel's) at Abergwynfi, and another (St. John's) at Cymer. The Caerau Parish, including Caerau and Nantyffyllon, was created in 1911. The Parish of Tondu was formed in 1923, and Coetrehen became part of that Parish. In 1924, the Garth Parish, known ecclesiastically as Troed-y-rhiw Garth was created, the Parish Church being dedicated to St. Mary the Virgin. The Churches now served by the Vicar of Llangynwyd are: (1) the Mother Church at Llangynwyd, (2) Eglwys Dewi Sant, Maesteg, (3) St. Michael's Church, Maesteg, (4) St. Stephen's Church, Pontrhydycyff, (5) St. Tydfil's Church, Bryn.

Malkin, who visited Marcroes (Marcross) about 1803 stated that there was a tradition in Marcroes and Llangynwyd that rude structures in those areas were formerly the place of worship of each village. There is no tradition of an abbey or monastery having been built in the valley, although there was a close connection with the Cistercian Abbey at Margam.

William Gamais (Gamage) stated at the beginning of the Tudor period that Jasper Tudor, Earl of Pembroke, who built the Jasper Tower of Llandaff Cathedral, gave an organ to Llangynwyd Church. It was removed during the Reformation Period because some reformers did not favour musical instruments as aids to divine service.

Before the Reformation, rectorial tithes of the Parish of Llangynwyd were administered by Margam Abbey. At the time of the Reformation, Henry VIII sold the rights to these tithes to the Dunraven family.

As previously mentioned, there was a tradition that a Welsh translation of the Bible had been found at Celydd (Celfydd) Ifan Farm, Llangynwyd, over a century before Bishop Morgan's translation was published in 1588. It was also asserted that at this farm was found the MS of a translation of the New Testament into Welsh, the translator being Thomas Llewelyn of Rhigos and based on the English version by Tyndale (1490-1536).

In his *Hanes Morganwg* (The History of Glamorgan), p. 223, Dafydd Morganwg states that at this farm Dr. Richard Davies, Bishop of St. David's, when he was a young man, saw the Pentateuch (the five books of Moses) translated into Welsh. The Bishop mentions this in a letter published with William Salesbury's translation of the New Testament into Welsh in 1547. Dafydd Morganwg thought that the translation from Latin was completed about 1470.

In 1795 the *Cambrian Register* published details of all collections and MSS known to them, and included the collection at Celydd Ifan in the Parish of Betws belonging to 'the widow, Evans, then living in Ystrad Havodwg'. It is, therefore, obvious that old manuscripts were kept at Celydd Ifan. If modern scholars reject the idea of an earlier translation of the Bible into Welsh prior to the days of Bishop Morgan, then it would be interesting to know why in the first place the farm became linked with such a tradition.

(b) The Rev. Samuel Jones

Much of what was written about the controversies over the Rev. Samuel Jones's ejection from the living of Llangynwyd now appears to be nothing but the dust of vanished collisions, to use a phrase coined by Cardinal Newman.

On the one hand, it was contended that Samuel Jones had not been episcopally ordained, as it was after a Presbyterian ordination at Taunton that he was admitted to the vicarage of Llangynwyd on 4 May 1657, during the Commonwealth Period — 'upon a presentation . . . from his highness, ye Lord Protector, under ye Great Seal of England'. As he had refused to con-

form to the requirements of the Act of Uniformity, 1662, which decreed
(1) unqualified acceptance of the Prayer Book and (2) the necessity of being
re-ordained, he was turned out of his living.

It was pointed out that his immediate predecessor, the Rev. Griffith
David, had been ejected by the Puritans to make room for Samuel Jones. In
any case, Samuel Jones suffered much persecution after 1662 and was
imprisoned seven times. Dr. Thomas Richards, in his *Bedyddwyr Aberafan
a'r Cylch*, 1925, stated that he used to travel on horseback to preach to the
Presbyterians at Margam. The Margam mansion issued a warrant for his
arrest and that of Stephen Hughes, for not attending Church services on
Sundays.

At a meeting at Llanymddyfri (Llandovery) of the Historical Society of
the Welsh Congregational Union in June 1981, Professor Glanmor
Williams, Swansea, gave an address on *Ffydd dan gysgod erledigaeth
Anghydffurfiaeth yn Ne-Ddwyrain Cymru, 1660-1680* (Faith under the
shadow of the persecution of Nonconformists of South-East Wales,
1660-1680). Details of the persecution of the Rev. Samuel Jones figured
prominently in the address, which will presumably be published in the next
issue of the *Cofiadur* (The Recorder).

The pupils at the Brynllywarch Academy included Rees Price (father of
the renowned Dr. Richard Price, Tynton), James Owen (1654-1706), who
himself opened an Academy at Oswestry and whose works are listed in the
Dictionary of National Biography, Jeremy Owen (1704-44), nephew of
James Owen and himself a famous Presbyterian minister, Samuel Price,
brother to Rees Price and successor, as minister, to his friend, Isaac Watts,
the hymn-writer, and Philip Pugh (1679-1760), another famous
Presbyterian minister and author. *The Red Dragon*, 1885, p. 586, contains
a list of over forty students educated at Brynllywarch. One of the Mansels of
Margam sent his children to be educated at the Academy, but Cadrawd
contended that the Mansels did not enjoy much dignity until the reign of
Queen Anne. Bicentenary and tercentenary celebrations were arranged in
the Llynfi Valley in 1862 and 1962 respectively, as a reminder of the ejection
of the Rev. Samuel Jones from his living. In 1883 a movement was set afoot
to provide a suitable memorial above his grave in Llangynwyd churchyard.

At the National Library of Wales (11022A) there is an incomplete note-
book containing notes of his sermons together with a catalogue of his books
and also particulars of receipts and disbursements (1664-65) with other
undated accounts.

(c) Early Church Administration

Apart from the services of the clergy, one of the key figures in Church
worship and administration at the beginning of the last century was the
parish clerk, the best known being Thomas Evan, father of Cadrawd, who
held that office for forty-five years. He was the Vicar's right-hand man,

keeping a register of graves and allocating and opening new ones, recording all notices and fees of banns of marriage, weddings, christenings and burials. He arranged for the pealing of the Church bells for services and funerals. On Sundays, the parish clerk led the responses from his official seat in the lowest pew of the three-decker pulpit, which disappeared when the Church was restored in 1893.

(d) Origins of Nonconformity

Before the building of chapels in the last century, prayer-meetings and preaching services were held in farms and private houses. The preachers travelled either on horseback or on foot. Walter Thomas of Groeswen, near Caerphilly, used to walk to Llangynwyd each week to minister from May, 1795 onwards to Nonconformist members who worshipped in the Long Room of the Old House. Later (in 1799) they began to worship in Bethesda Congregational Chapel, Llangynwyd, the year in which Walter Thomas died.

Owing to the influx of iron and coal workers in the first half of the last century, chapels were built to meet the demand for public worship. They became places of comfort and centres of society. Charles Bowring, brother of Sir John Bowring, stated in 1847: 'The largest portion of the work people are Dissenters'.

The plan of the site of the new Maesteg (Brithdir) cemetery, prepared in 1883, indicated that 430 grave-spaces had been reserved for Roman Catholics, 553 for Anglicans and 2,893 in unconsecrated ground. As 80% of the population at that time attended places of worship, it is safe to assume that the 2,893 grave-spaces in unconsecrated ground were in the main reserved for Nonconformists.

Owing to the lack of available buildings, worship usually commenced in public houses — Bethesda, Llangynwyd, as we have seen, in the long room of the Old House, Llangynwyd; Bethania (B), Maesteg, in the long room of the Coetrehen Arms; Carmel (C) Maesteg, in the store room of the Coetrehen Arms; Tabor (C.M.), Maesteg (i.e., some of those who had previously worshipped at y Graig Fach, Sychbant, Llangynwyd), in the long room of the Old House, Llangynwyd; Siloh (C), Nantyffyllon, in the loft of the Cambrian Inn near the Forge site of the Llynvi Iron Works, as well as at Ton-y-cwd Farm, Spelters (later Caerau); Salem (B), Nantyffyllon, in the long room of the then Gelli Arms, Hermon Road, Caerau; Saron (C), Nantyffyllon, in the long room of the White Lion Hotel, Maesteg; Dyffryn (C), Caerau, in the then Colliers Arms in Dyffryn Road, Caerau; Noddfa, Caerau, in the Blaenllynfi Hotel, Caerau, although it was carefully pointed out that the hotel had not then received a licence to sell intoxicants! Hebron, Cymer, first worshipped at Yr Hen Dafarn (the old public house at Cymer) whilst the Rock Church, Cwmafan, first worshipped at the Rock and Fountain, Cwmafan. It appears that the revelries of Gŵyl Mabsant at the Cambrian Inn once came to a sudden end under the effect of a prayer-meeting held in the loft of that inn.

The early records of some of these churches indicated what they paid for candles and also for fodder for the visiting preacher's horse. As the early pioneers were mainly lowly paid workmen, the building of chapels involved much sacrifice.

On the contrary, the Anglican Church benefited from the munificence of the Talbot family of Margam, particularly Miss Olive Talbot, who was a complete invalid for twenty years because of spinal and other complaints, and who died in 1894, a day short of her fifty-second birthday. She paid £3,500 towards the building of St. Gabriel's Church, Abergwynfi, and three-quarters of the cost of building St. Michael's Church, Maesteg. The Parish Hall, Maesteg was the gift of the Margam family in 1909. Of the cost of building St. Cynfelyn's Church, Caerau, £2,000 was paid by the same family. Miss Emily Charlotte Talbot contributed up to two-thirds of the cost of the new heating apparatus at St. Michael's in 1913. Her sister, Mrs. Fletcher, paid £400 in aid of the Church organ fund, the balance of £100 being paid by Mrs. Llewelyn of Baglan Hall. Miss Olive Talbot gave £2,500 in 1892 towards the building of St. Mary's Church, Garth, and she also paid for the building of St. Tydfil's Church, Bryn. The cost of the restoration of the Parish Church at Llangynwyd, over £3,000, was paid by her in 1893. The Margam family defrayed the cost of £25,000 for the building of St. Theodore's Church, Kenfig Hill, and bore most of the cost of building St. Theodore's Church, Port Talbot. It was Miss Olive Talbot who paid the cost of enlarging Betws Parish Church and of the restoration of Llangeinor Parish Church. At one time the stipend of a curate of the Llangynwyd Parish was paid by the Margam family, who also gave £50,000 towards St. Michael's College, Llandaff.

Nonconformists, who also contributed to the rents and ground-rents that formed the source of income from which these gifts were made, had to pay for every brick in their buildings and every slate in their roofs.

(e) The Church and Social Problems

At the turn of the last century and in the first two decades of the present century there was much antipathy between the local churches and the Independent Labour Party (the I.L.P.). During the miners' strike of 1898 a local colliery manager scoured the South Wales coalfield to make sure that no local striker would obtain employment in any other pit. The object was to starve the workmen into submission. As this manager was a prominent local Nonconformist, the relations between worker and chapel deteriorated. The father of the writer of this volume had to use a false name to avoid detection when applying for work at Maerdy colliery. It was understandable why some colliery managers became lonely and isolated once they had retired.

The miners felt that they could achieve their aspirations through their own industrial and political organisations, and ceased to consider the chapels as their political allies. Some chapels disowned members of trade-unions and refused the use of their vestries to workmen's committees, with the result that the miners held their meetings in the long-rooms of public-houses until they built their own institutes. Many turned their backs on the chapels and depended on the South Wales Miners Federation for help in their struggle for a minimum wage and for better conditions.

There was a cleavage between the political liberalism of chapel ministers and a section of the officers on the one hand, and Socialism, which was represented as being ungodly and immoral, even advocating free-love, on the other hand. It was contended that the Socialists' God was Mammon and that economics was their theology. Keir Hardie had supplanted chapel-going Mabon as their political leader. The products of Sunday Schools became leaders elsewhere. Economics classes held on Sunday afternoons, thus supplanting the Sunday schools, and the Sunday-evening forum established by Vernon Hartshorn, the then miners' agent, were condemned. Keir Hardie was reproved for addressing political meetings on Sundays. The only prominent local leader who remained a chapel-goer was Evan Williams.

However there remained a strong element of Labour support within the chapels. Congregationalists invited Socialists like Principal Tom Rees, Bangor and the Revs. D. D. Walters, Newcastle Emlyn, E. T. Owen, Cwmgwrach (who had opposed Sir Alfred Mond at Carmarthen), and T. E. Nicholas, the well known Communist, to officiate at their services, whilst the Revs. Herbert Morgan and James Nicholas were favourites with the Baptists. Of the major valley denominations, the Presbyterians (Calvinistic Methodists) were the least inclined towards Socialism. Their churches were Liberal strongholds.

In the first quarter of this century a big political issue was that concerning the Disestablishment of the Anglican Church in Wales. A meeting organised by the Caerau Free Church Council at Hermon Chapel in 1909 in support of the proposal was addressed by a Mr. Parry, a London lawyer and the Rev. John Matthews, Fabian's Bay, Swansea. However, in the Llynfi Valley as in other mining valleys, the struggle for better living conditions took precedence over that issue. It was looked upon as something non-relevant to the working classes. When the Rev. T. Rhondda Williams, then of Bradford, an avowed Socialist, lectured in the valley in 1910, he ignored the question of Disestablishment, and chose to speak on 'Christian Socialism'.

(f) Visiting Preachers

All the outstanding preachers of Wales—too numerous to mention—either preached or lectured in the Llynfi Valley. The world-famous Bible scholar, Dr. G. Campell Morgan of Westminster Chapel, London, lectured and preached at Bethlehem (C) Church, Nantyffyllon, in May 1910. Dean Howells of St. David's conducted a religious campaign in the valley at the beginning of the century, whilst Dr. W. E. Orchard, a convert to Catholicism and former minister of Kings Weigh House Church, London, conducted services for a week in September 1946 at the Church of Our Lady and St. Patrick, Maesteg. A frequent visitor was the outstanding evangelical preacher, Dr. Martin Lloyd Jones, London. However, the most internationally-known figures who favoured Maesteg with a visit were Dr. Kagawa of Japan (known as the twentieth-century St. Paul) in June 1950, and, in June 1953, Martin Niemoller, the former German U-boat commander who had defied Hitler when the latter reigned supreme in Germany. Both visiting speakers spoke at Bethania Chapel, Maesteg.

(g) *The Welsh Religious Revival of 1904-1905*

An early revival had swept Wales in 1859, initiated by the Rev. Dafydd Morgan, Ysbyty Ystwyth. Its effects on the Llynfi Valley were described dramatically in two articles by the Rev. Glasnant Jones, Siloh, Nantyffyllon, on *Y Llwyni ar Dân* (Maesteg Afire) in *Y Diwygiwr*, January and February, 1905. The revivalist and D. Evans, Ffos-y-ffin, visited Maesteg in 1859. The Number 9 level miners held prayer-meetings at the pit bottom and on the mountain slopes near Cwmdu, with Jack Piper conducting the singing.

The map in Eifion Evans's book, *The Welsh Revival of 1904*, shows Nantyffyllon as the centre of the Llynfi Valley associated with the Revival. It is the only valley place mentioned in the map. The reason is obvious. Next to Evan Roberts, the leader of the 1904 Revival, the best-known leaders then and thereafter were the brothers Stephen and George Jeffreys, whose father, Thomas Jeffreys, was a member of Dyffryn Church, Caerau. The two sisters, Maggie and Annie Davies, who were the soloists in Evan Roberts's meetings throughout Wales, also lived in Nantyffyllon. They became members of Bethlehem (C) Church, Nantyffyllon, and later left for London to become nurses. It was at their home that Evan Roberts stayed on his visits to the district. His brother, Dan Roberts, lived in the nearby village of Bryn.

The revivalists emphasised the certainty of eternal punishment (hell fire) for non-believers. They preached their belief in a geographical heaven and in a day of judgment for sinners. 'Are you saved?' became the all-important question. Conversion, or being 'saved' meant one single act of transition from darkness to light, as in the case of St. Paul. Years after the Revival, a saintly character known as Dafydd Jones, Llanrwst, used to visit local Churches on behalf of the Salvation Army and describe in graphic terms, much appreciated by the congregation, how, where and when (to the very second) he became saved.

The revivalists proclaimed that they were engaged in the blasting operations of the everlasting God. They wanted to leave Satan's barracks in order to fight evil and to shoot the devil at close range. The devil was a person.

124   Evan Roberts,
the great revivalist

One footballer declared that he had kept goal for the devil for many a year but that from that night onwards, he hoped to play centre-forward for his Saviour! The local Chapels were besieged day and night. Prayer-meetings were held almost every night for several months without thought for working the following day. Some known to the author of these notes spent a year after conversion in distributing pamphlets on the 'new life'. Open-air meetings were held at street corners. Football fixtures were cancelled whilst public-houses and billiard-halls were deserted. Playing cards, dominoes and billiards meant aiding the devil. The reading of novels was condemned. The walls of the homes exhibited framed Biblical verses or precepts, such as 'Christ is the Head of this House', whilst any Biblical scholar who questioned the literal interpretation of the Scriptures was looked upon as a heretic.

The Rev. John Morris, father of Sir Rhys Hopkin Morris, M.P., and minister of Seion (C) Church, Caerau, was unable to preach for twelve consecutive Sundays because of the religious fervour in his Church. On 18 December 1904 he received into membership seventy-one converts, four 'restored' members and a further three, being transfers from other Churches. At the first communion service of the same Church in 1905, thirty-one members were received and several restored to membership. At a Baptist missionary prayer-meeting in Caerau in 1904, thirty-four were baptized and ten restored to membership. On one Sunday evening, Saron Church, Nantyffyllon, received seventy-three members. The Saron Sunday School numbered 414, including twenty-seven teachers, the average attendance in 1905 being 266. Although the Church practised infant baptism, nine converts, at their request, were baptized by immersion on professing faith and repentance. On 12 December 1904, sixty-four were baptized at Salem (B) Church, Nantyffyllon, with a further six on Christmas

Day. In all, the membership increased by 101. During the height of the Revival period, the Rev. Iorwerth Jones, Bethania (B) Church, Maesteg, baptized, in all, 158, whilst forty-three were restored to membership. He baptized seventy-four on one night. Other Nonconformist Churches in the valley could claim similar increases in membership as the result of the Revival.

On 10 December 1904, prayer-meetings, in which local ministers took part, were held at Coegnant Colliery and continued every Monday morning. In the Baltic district of the colliery they lasted for eighteen months. Welsh hymns such as *Marchog Iesu yn llwyddiannus* were sung 'with great effect'.

In 1906 the recession began to set in after the intense fervour had ceased, and by to-day the events which had stirred the religious life of Wales, including the Llynfi Valley, are now a matter of history only. The Roman Catholic Church and the Anglican Church appeared unaffected by the events of 1904-05.

Pastor Stephen Jeffreys (1876-1943) of Nantyffyllon was a Siloh Sunday School scholar and a member of the Siloh Flute Band. He claimed to have been 'saved' by a sermon delivered by the minister, the Rev. W. Glasnant Jones, on 17 November 1904. He was then twenty-eight. His father-in-law, Joseph Lewis, was a deacon of Siloh.

On his conversion he became an evangelical pastor, and in one of his campaigns, he converted a complete football team. He conducted missions in Welsh and English throughout Wales and in almost every State in North America, as well as in Canada, Australia, New Zealand and South Africa. With the help of an interpreter, he campaigned in France, Switzerland, Italy, Germany and Scandinavia. He joined the Elim Pentecostal Alliance at the invitation of his brother, George, with whom he conducted faith-healing

125   Reverend and Mrs
Stephen Jeffreys

campaigns at Grimsby, Hull, Kensington, Barking, the Kingsway Hall (London), Bedford, Manchester, Sunderland, and Liverpool. He claimed many thousands of converts and also a large number of cures through faith. He became too unwell to conduct campaigns in the last eight years of his life and retired to live at Maesteg. He preached his last sermon at Elim Church, Pontarddulais, on 27 October 1943 and died on 17 November of that year. He was buried at Llangynwyd churchyard. The writer of this volume happened to be the executor of his will. His son, Edward, published a biography of his father, *Stephen Jeffreys, the Beloved Evangelist*, in 1946.

George Jeffreys, a younger brother, was a member of the Sunday School class of the father of the author of this volume. He could point to the seat in that Chapel where he also was converted under the ministry of the Rev. W. Glasnant Jones. On his visits to Nantyffyllon he used to call to see the writer's sister, who had been born a spastic.

Attached to an affidavit sworn by him, and filed in a certain High Court action in 1918, there is a copy of his first ordination certificate of 1917 relating to his pastorate of the 'Independent Apostolic Church, Emanuel, Christ Church, Maesteg'.

He was the founder of the Elim Four Square Gospel Church. The 'Elim' in the movement's name was taken from the oasis of Elim, mentioned in the Book of Exodus. 'Four Square' stood for the four points which Principal Jeffreys emphasised — Salvation, Healing, Baptism and the Second Coming.

The first Elim Church was founded by him in a disused laundry in a back street, Hunter Street, Belfast in 1915. He then organised a body of Elim ministers and established a resident Bible College, a correspondence school, a publishing office, a printing works, a foreign missionary branch and innumerable Sunday schools. He estimated having saved 10,000 souls and had personally baptized thousands of converts. He claimed to have cured, by faith, hundreds of afflicted people. R. E. Darragh, in his volume, *In Defence of His Word* (1932), has collected a number of selected testimonies of dire suffering 'healed by the power of Christ under the ministry of Principal George Jeffreys'. The index to the volume refers to fifty-one diseases cured by faith.

Principal Phillips of the Cardiff Baptist College stated that only two could then fill a chapel in Cardiff — George Jeffreys and Dr. Martin Lloyd Jones. According to a London daily, George Jeffreys was one of only three who could fill the Albert Hall with 10,000 people. It was as the result of his campaign that the Cardiff City Temple was built. There were overflowing congregations at the Bingley Hall, Birmingham, which had been booked for ten weeks and the great halls of other major cities in England were similarly packed and besieged. In 1928 Pastor Ernest C. W. Boulton published his book, *George Jeffreys; A Ministry of the Miraculous*, being a chronicle of the establishment and extension of the work of Elim Foursquare Gospel Alliance, with an introduction by John Leech, M.A., K.C. It contains a detailed account of his campaigns with many instances of healing by faith.

126   Miss Rosina Davies

However, after twenty-five years of leadership of the Elim Movement, George Jeffreys severed his connection therewith in 1940 as a protest against the totalitarianism of the Movement's Church administration, and formed the Bible Pattern Church Fellowship with an inaugural rally at Westminster Central Hall in 1941. The new Movement issued a magazine, *Pattern*, to which Dr. Francis Thomas, a native of Nantyffyllon and the then pastor of the Kensington Temple, London, contributed a series of Bible studies. The events that led to the formation of the Pattern Church are described in George Jeffreys's book, *Fight for the Faith and Freedom*.

Pastor Jeffreys had another brother, William, who also became an Elim Foursquare Gospel pastor. He died in 1945. Pastor Stephen Jeffreys's son, Edward, followed in his father's footsteps and conducted many campaigns. However, he left the Pentecostal movement and ended his life as the Vicar of a Bournemouth Church.

Probably the best known lady evangelist connected with the Welsh Revival was Miss Rosina Davies, who, at one time, lived at Nantyffyllon. She was a native of Treherbert, but was christened by the Rev. William Morgan, Carmel, Maesteg. For some years she was a member of Libanus (C.M.) Church, Garth. She used to address meetings at the Town Hall Square, Maesteg, every Saturday night. Her experiences as an evangelist throughout Wales are given in her autobiography, *The Story of my Life*.

(h) The Roman Catholic Church

On the consecration by the Archbishop of Cardiff (Dr. John Murphy) of the Church of our Lady and St. Patrick, Maesteg, on 14 March 1963, a most

127   Our Lady's and St Patrick's Roman Catholic Church, Maesteg

informative booklet was published giving details of the opening of the new Catholic Church in 1907 and of the priests who ministered there in this century, together with an account of the history of the Parish. Most of the information now given is drawn from that booklet, written by Father (later Canon) Reidy.

The Catholic Faith had almost disappeared from Wales by the eighteenth century, but it was still practised in remote parts of Margam and Llangynwyd. The scattered remnants were served by Father Hill, who administered the sacraments to them for about thirteen years up to about 1736. In the first quarter of the last century there were only four Roman Catholic Churches in Wales. Then followed an influx of agricultural workers from Limerick to work on the Dunraven Estate, then owned by the third Earl, who was a convert to Catholicism. After the Irish potato famine of 1845-1849 many Irish workers came from Cork, Kerry, Limerick and Wexford to work in the old and new Iron Works at Maesteg. Many settled in Bridgend, Aberafan and Maesteg. The nearest Catholic Churches were at Cardiff and Swansea. The Crowleys, O'Donovans and O'Sullivans from this valley used to walk to Swansea or Cardiff to attend Mass. For the big Feasts of the year, including Christmas and Easter, they walked in a body to Cardiff, beginning their journey in the afternoon. They were housed by their fellow Irish Catholics in Cardiff for the night, heard Mass and received the Sacraments at St. David's Church and then walked home to Maesteg.

The third Earl of Dunraven bequeathed, by his will, £2,000 for the building of a Roman Catholic Church, house and school in Maesteg, but the sum was reduced to £1,800 after payment of death duties.

In the fifties of the last century, a Polish priest, Father Genzwioski, served Maesteg and Aberafan. Mass was celebrated at the Three Horse Shoes Hotel, Maesteg.

The first Church, built at Ewenny Road, Maesteg, was on land leased from the Dunraven Estate on favourable terms. It was opened 3 November 1872, the whole project being completed in 1873.

With the increase in the Catholic population of the valley, more ample accommodation became necessary. The foundation stone of a new Church, the present one, was laid by Bishop Hedley on 25 June 1906. A local contractor, John O'Brien, whose parents were natives of Killarney, built the Church for £4,000, the school for £3,000 and the presbytery for £2,300. Mr. J. Harvey, general manager of Messrs. North's, donated the High Altar, the table being of Yorkshire stone supported by pillars of Connemara marble. Miss E. C. Talbot, Margam had previously offered another site for the Church but Canon Kelly, the ruling spirit at the time, thought the Church deserved a more prominent site. The new Church was opened by Bishop Hedley on 17 November 1907. Archbishop McGrath celebrated High Pontifical Mass on 27 November 1957 on the occasion of the golden jubilee of the Church. The Altar was consecrated by Archbishop Murphy on 7 November 1972.

For many years the Parish had been the responsibility of the Benedictine Order. It was the Abbot and Council of Douai that granted permission to build the new school. The Maesteg Church had been assigned in 1891 to the Monastery of St. Edmund, King and Martyr, then an exiled Church at Douai. The Abbey returned to England in 1903 and became known as Douai Abbey, which was near Reading. In 1945 Abbot Money of Douai and the Archbishop of Cardiff agreed that the Maesteg Church should be administered for some years by the Cardiff Archdiocese, though still belonging to Douai Abbey.

To accommodate Catholics in the upper part of the valley, Hermon Welsh Presbyterian Chapel, Caerau, was bought in 1967 and is now known as *Eglwys y Bugail Da* (The Church of the Good Shepherd).

Two prominent local Catholics, Dr. Norman Farrell and Victor Hampson-Jones, were awarded the high honour of being made Knights of the Order of St. Gregory the Great. The first-ever local ordination service, being that of Alphonsus Thomas Keane of Llangynwyd, took place in June, 1969. For a month in 1896 Father Bilsborrow served as rector. He later became Bishop of Mauritius and subsequently the first Archbishop of Cardiff. Bishop Mullins, a native of Limerick, was an Assistant Priest at Maesteg in 1957. He is the holder of a First Class Honours Degree in Welsh at the Welsh University. He was consecrated Auxiliary Bishop of Cardiff in 1970, with the title of Bishop of Sidnecestre, a former Saxon see based on Stowe, near Lincoln, whose last bishop was murdered by Viking invaders. It is worthy of note that the three daughters of Mr. and Mrs. Con Redmond, Maesteg, named Hilda, Connie and Anne, became nuns attached to the Order of the Sacred Heart, Regents Park, London. They were later moved to different convents. The three were educated at the local R.C. School.

The relations between the Catholic Church and other branches of the Christian Churches of the valley are most cordial. Joint religious services are held from time to time. Respect is shown for the Welsh language by means of *Y Cylch Catholig Cymraeg*. The local Church has witnessed a Welsh R.C. baptism and also a Welsh marriage ceremony, as well as a Requiem Mass in Welsh. A small Welsh hymn book, with the Epistles and Gospels translated into Welsh, have proved helpful. In 1951 services once a month in the native language were introduced, whilst the *Cylch Catholig* has been addressed by several priests and notable Welshmen.

(i) The Anglican Church

Reference has already been made to the mother Church at Llangynwyd, whilst Cadrawd and others have written of its history. Hereunder are a few brief notes regarding the other valley Anglican Churches.

Eglwys Dewi Sant. This is the only Welsh Anglican Church in the valley, although Welsh services are still held at Llangynwyd Church. In recent years Welsh services have been held once a month only, otherwise the services are conducted almost entirely in English.

During the centenary celebrations (1852-1952), an informative booklet was published by the then Vicar of Llangynwyd (Canon Daniel Richards) who states therein that the data had been provided by David Davies (the People's Warden) and David Thomas (the Vicar's Warden).

At first the services were bilingual until St. Michael's Church, Maesteg, was built in 1897. The Countess of Dunraven was the largest contributor towards the cost of building the Church, which was completed in 1853. The curate ministering to the English worshippers was paid by the Llynvi Iron & Coal Co. After the opening of St. Michael's Church, the services were for many years conducted in Welsh. At the closing of Holy Innocents Church, where the services were entirely in English, the members joined Eglwys Dewi Sant, thus making it difficult to maintain the Welsh services thereat.

Cadrawd states that the first service was held in an old Chapel called Ysgubor Wen, where Soar Chapel, Maesteg, was later built. The Church then worshipped at the Tywith Schoolroom. The first curate, the Rev. Thomas Hughes Jones, commenced duties in 1845 and started a mission service at an old dismantled engine-room at Spelters (Caerau). The building was occupied as a school during the week days. The Rev. John George

128 St David's Church and War
Memorial, Maesteg

followed as curate of the upper hamlet in 1855, serving Glyncorrwg at the
same time until he became Vicar of Aberpergwm eight years later — at the
time the building of Eglwys Dewi Sant was completed.

The Church of St. Mary the Virgin at Garth was built in 1892, the building
being of early English style.

St. Stephen's Mission Church, Pontrhydycyff, was opened during the stay of
Vicar T. C. Phillips (1926-1931).

Holy Innocents Mission Church, Bridgend Road, Maesteg, was built in 1916
and was demolished in 1958.

The Church of St. Michael's and All Angels. At the time of the celebration
of the Golden Jubilee of the Church (1897-1947), a souvenir booklet was
published by the then Vicar, Canon Daniel Richards.

In 1892 it was decided to erect a Church for the 'English Church Congregation' at Maesteg. Miss Olive Talbot, Margam, whose generosity has
already been referred to, had instructed a Cardiff architect to prepare
plans. Stones from the derelict Llynvi Iron Works were used and the
foundation stone was laid 7 October 1895. The Church (in early English
style), was opened and consecrated 19 January 1897. It is doubtful whether
a church building on such a scale would have been erected had it not been
for the beneficence of Miss Olive Talbot. In 1958 the Church tower (with
eight bells) was dedicated. Material from Furnace No. 1 of the derelict

129   The Church of St Michael and All Angels (Parish Church of Llangynwyd
Parish)

130   St Cynfelyn's Church, Caerau

Llynvi Iron Works was used to complete the undertaking. J. P. Beynon, California, a native of Maesteg, contributed £1,000 towards the cost.

In the upper part of the valley we have:

St. Peter's Church, Nantyffyllon, which is of Gothic style and was opened in 1887 at a cost of £1,200. It was designed by E. Bruce Vaughan of Cardiff. Although English has been the language of worship during this century at least, the evening service on the day of dedication was bilingual.

St. Cynfelyn's Church, Caerau, was formed in 1899, the old Church building being the present Church Hall. The worshippers had earlier gathered at the Blaenllynfi Hotel, Caerau. The present Church building was opened in 1910 and half the cost was paid by Miss Emily Charlotte Talbot, Margam. It is doubtful whether another Church in the valley attracts a bigger congregation today.

It was announced at the Easter Vestry of the Llangynwyd Parish in 1981 that, for the first time, £10,000 had been received in the previous year in direct giving from the five Churches which belonged to the Parish.

(j) Nonconformity

Although there can still be an understandable divergence of views between Church and Chapel regarding doctrinal matters, the old enmity has almost entirely disappeared. The sources of bitterness no longer exist. The Disestablishment issue is long forgotten. The Welsh Congregational monthly, *Y Diwygiwr*, for July 1865 contains a colourful account of a stormy meeting held at Llangynwyd on 5 June 1865, when Nonconformists succeeded, by a majority of three to one, in opposing the levying of the parochial tax. The opposition against the Church authorities was led by the Rev. W. Watkins of Saron Church, Nantyffyllon. The Anglicans looked upon the Nonconformists as the riff-raff or the *shoni hois* of society.

Much later, visiting ministers to the preaching services of Bethesda Welsh Congregational Church, Llangynwyd, were usually accommodated at Tŷ Cynwyd, the home of Cadrawd, a devout churchman. It was Cadrawd who first mooted the idea of erecting a suitable memorial above the grave at Llangynwyd of the Nonconformist, the Rev. Samuel Jones of Brynllywarch. The local Free Church Council has been enlarged to become the Llynfi Valley Federation of Churches and is no longer confined to Nonconformists. Roman Catholics and Anglicans unite with Nonconformists in joint services without surrendering their respective fundamental beliefs. When the Caerau R.C. Church (formerly Hermon C.M. Chapel) was opened in 1967, it was a Nonconformist who led the singing of the hymns. Possibly the position locally could be summed up by saying that all the religious bodies worked at the same farm but not in the same field!

The strict Puritanism of the past in the valley would appear to the modern youth to be strict, narrow and over-demanding. Games such as

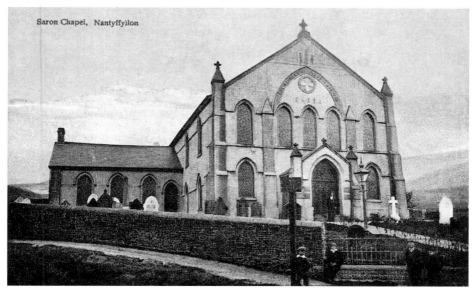
Saron Chapel, Nantyffyilon

131   Saron Chapel, Nantyffyllon

tennis, cricket and football were frowned upon. A local Church prayed for the soul of a minister of an adjoining Church who had desecrated his calling by playing tennis with the members of his Church. The main pleasures were picnics in the Sychbant Valley, Llangynwyd. The game of 'kiss in the ring' was sometimes discouraged. There was much correspondence in the *Glamorgan Gazette* a century ago regarding what was called 'the disgraceful and indelicate practice' of the kissing game, the duration of the kisses being about two minutes! The Whit Monday Sunday School tea party, the annual trip to the seaside and the Christmas or New Year's treat of a bun and four pence (of the old coinage) were permissible pleasures. One cannot find a record of any Welsh Nonconformist Church in the valley having held a whist-drive or dance. The winter entertainment for the children was the magic lantern in the Band of Hope. The social was ever popular. If fruit was included in the fare, it was called a 'fruit banquet'.

The minister was on a pedestal in the eyes of the congregation. He wore a top hat, frock coat and white tie, and if photographed, it was always in his 'study'. The older generation were Liberals (as opposed to Anglicans, who were Tories) and were expected to be total abstainers. A later generation became inclined towards Socialism, and more recently, the Welsh ministers were drawn towards Plaid Cymru. In the first half of this century, Non-conformist ministers were attracted to the Church in Wales, but in recent times they have turned to the teaching profession or have become full-time social workers.

In the last century the ministry was seldom considered a full-time calling in the valley. The Rev. William Rees, Siloh, Nantyffyllon (1856-1874), was a weigher at the Llynvi Iron Works, whilst the Rev. David Phillips, Tabor, Maesteg was a postmaster and kept a shop. He and the Rev. Thomas Levi (then of Swansea) joined the local industrialist, David Grey, in forming the Llwydarth Tinplate Company. The Rev. Rees Walters, Ebenezer, Garth, in the early years of his ministry had been a tinplate worker and a collier, and the Rev. David Morris, Bethesda, Llangynwyd, was also a weigher at a Pontrhydycyff coal level. The Rev. Howell Davies, the first minister of Salem, Nantyffyllon was a miner for several years whilst still a minister, and the Rev. W. Watkins, the first minister of Saron, Nantyffyllon, acted as part-time insurance agent. The Rev. D. Henry, Glyncorrwg, a product of Soar, Maesteg, worked as a tailor, whilst one of the most original preachers of Wales, the Rev. Robert Allen, Calfaria, Cwmfelin, indulged in opening coal levels. The Rev. Edward Roberts, Seion, Cwmafan, who had charge of about 500 souls, was a grocer. He was also architect of Saron Chapel, Nant-yffyllon. In more recent times a local minister became a part-time forestry worker. There is little evidence of local clergymen doing additional part-time work. However, we find that the Rev. John Parry, Vicar of Llangynwyd (1790-1829), was not only a parson but a farmer, a magistrate and a local coal-owner, besides being a huntsman of renown.

Some ministers became known as makers of wills for their Church members, whilst others took part in the activities of various Friendly Societies, such as the Ancient Order of Foresters. In the early part of this century it was an advantage to be a Baptist for the purpose of seeking an educational post as most members of the appointing body were Baptists!

Sermons seldom lasted less than an hour. Short sermons did not appear to satisfy the spiritual needs of the worshippers. The situation was once described thus – 'sermons for Christians and sermonettes for Christianettes'. On the other hand, those who were bored with lengthy sermons contended that there was a difference between preaching the everlasting Gospel and preaching the Gospel everlastingly! At the evening service, two or three deacons used to review the sermons of the day. From four to eight ministers from outside the valley would be engaged for the *cyrddau mawr* (annual preaching services) of a single Church. In 1863 eight ministers preached at the annual meetings of Saron Church, Nantyffyllon, one being in English. In some Welsh Baptist Churches a senior deacon read the hymns. There was also a spate of local preachers. The single cup used at communion services has been substituted (for health reasons) by individual cups in all the Nonconformist Churches of the valley.

Belief in eternal punishment was generally accepted. In fact, the Welsh Baptists of Glamorgan at their *Cymanfa Morgannwg* (annual conference) in 1888 passed a special resolution to the effect that eternal punishment for unbelievers was part of their faith. By accepting Jesus Christ as a Saviour they were insured against the torments of hell which were often vividly

132   Sunday School teachers at Siloh, *c.*1912
(Standing) May Evans (Bailey), Eunice Williams, Gertie Mort, Gwyneth Anthony
(Seated) Eunice Williams, Maggie Aberman, Owen John, Cassie Evans, Lily
Edwards

described. The Baptists and Congregationalist Churches were subject to the tenets of faith set forth in the various trust deeds of each Church. It is doubtful whether the main body of members were aware of the existence of such articles of belief. Local ministers were opposed to religious instruction in schools as it implied being tied to the State.

The practice of *adrodd pwnc* (reciting of catechisms) was very popular. *Y Diwygiwr* (February 1855) contains an account of a Christmas gathering of five Sunday Schools in Maesteg. There was a procession at 10 a.m. from Soar Chapel to Bethania Chapel—with Soar and Carmel Sunday Schools reciting the *pwnc* (catechism) and being questioned by the Revs. T. Lloyd (Soar) and William Morgan (Carmel). At 2 p.m. there was a further procession from Soar to Carmel, with Siloh and Tabor Sunday Schools being questioned by the Revs. D. Henry (Soar) and William Morgan (Carmel). Then at 6 p.m., Salem (Spelters) and Bethania Sunday Schools recited the 'pwnc' and were questioned by the Revs. Howell Davies (Salem) and Richard Hughes (Bethania). After the afternoon service, 200 children were given tea at Soar Chapel provided by a Mr. Evans, manager of the Forge Works, and others.

Every deacon was expected to be a total abstainer and capable of offering an extempore prayer *(o'r frest)*. In some local Churches the deacons in the main were colliery officials or tradesmen. They were appointed for life and were very primly attired. In one Congregational valley Church in the last century, all but one of the deacons wore a top hat. A seat in the *sêt fawr* (big pew) was much coveted and became the target for both ambition and satire. The two senior deacons sat immediately under the pulpit facing the congregation. If a big pew of deacons remained silent during the sermon without indulging in promptings to sustain the *hwyl*, they were considered as a 'set of waxworks'. A week-night prayer-meeting was looked upon as the power house of the Church. A *cwrdd paratoad* (preparatory meeting) was held on the Saturday night preceding the monthly communion service in order to allow as little time as possible to influence the spirit adversely in the meantime. The Rev. R. O. Hughes had a very flourishing Bible class on Saturday nights in 1911 in Siloh, Nantyffyllon, the session theme being the Sermon on the Mount.

Several local ministers became known for the *hwyl* of their preaching. They had no set pattern of worship as was practised in the Roman Catholic and Anglican Churches. The emphasis was on preaching the Gospel rather than on the sacramental aspect of the service. The pulpit was sometimes the sanctuary of the orator who could make the conscious sinner writhe in his pew. The desire to act and to entertain was an ever-present temptation. However, no-one could accuse the best-known valley ministers of this century, such as the Revs. T. H. Thomas (Tabor), W. R. Bowen (Carmel), Iorwerth Jones (Bethania) of anything but an enlightened presentation of the Gospel, whilst some of those who were inclined to indulge in the *hwyl*, such as the Rev. Rees Walters, Garth, were truly genuine and noble characters held in high esteem.

Church discipline was strict. One Church report in 1905 stipulated that any member found guilty of slander, drunkenness, swearing or using 'immoral' language would be denied communion participation and would only be 'restored' on the grounds of true repentance. Anybody causing intended offence to a co-member would be similarly dealt with. When four deacons were elected in Saron Church, Nantyffyllon, at the end of the last century, the minister expressed a hope in the Church annual report that they would be honest without idle words, not given to wining and exploiting, and able to discipline effectively their children in their own homes. Excommunication awaited those contracting a compulsory marriage. The term 'common law wife' was then unknown in the district.

Every Welsh Chapel from Garth upwards contained a gallery, which was occupied by the choir and *gwrandawyr* (non-members). The clock was either behind the pulpit or on the gallery front facing the pulpit. In the last century, farmer members of Bethesda Church, Llangynwyd, sometimes brought their dogs with them to the service. In most Chapels, mourners in deep black (kid gloves included) remained seated for about six months before they allowed themselves to stand and join in the singing. For the first month or two their bowed heads rested against the facing ledge of the pew.

At the end of the year in some valley Churches the Church secretary would read aloud details of what each member had contributed during the year, with special emphasis on the word *Dim* (nothing) if a member had failed to contribute at all. Many considered that having a church debt was a good thing as it was an incentive to more activity. Bazaars, concerts and dramas were frowned upon. In 1857, Bethania Church, Maesteg, decided to ask each member to pay his or her share of the church debt, which was cleared by each one paying 13/6.

The Maesteg Valley was also the scene of the activities of the Rev. Robert Allen, a local coal prospector, one-time minister of Calfaria Baptist Church, Cwmfelin, Maesteg, and one of the most original Welsh preachers in South Wales early this century. His imagination ran riot and knew no bounds. The torments of hell were described in very plaintive tones by *Allen bach*. All non-believers would be cast into a huge lake of slime and filth. The Almighty himself, armed with a truncheon, would keep watch to make sure that no transgressor's face would appear above the level of the lake. If anyone attempted to surface he would be clobbered back into the filth by the Almighty! His lectures (in Welsh) on 'The Garden of Eden', 'The Hen and her Brood' and 'The Plagues of Egypt' drew crowds, whilst lectures on him by the Rev. Ben Jones, his successor at Calfaria, were very popular. He was totally unaware of the fact that he was so original.

As a coal prospector, he maintained that he had observed the Coal Mines Regulations by affixing this notice to the mouth of the level: (1) No Smoking (2) No swearing (3) No Hartshorn (being Vernon Hartshorn, the then miners' agent).

(k) Sunday Observance

Sabbath-keeping was interpreted literally. Some housewives refrained from Sunday washing of dishes. A local minister was called to book by his Church for taking a bus to a preaching appointment in a village two or three miles away. The first Sunday excursion from Maesteg to Porthcawl on 15 August, 1909 caused consternation. Local ministers gathered at the Maesteg railway station to try to dissuade the offenders from travelling. One of them, the Rev. Iorwerth Jones, Bethania, Maesteg, shouted as the train was leaving: 'You are going head over heels to hell.' A passenger replied: 'Never mind, Mr. Jones, we've all got return tickets!'

An emergency meeting of the local Churches was called to request the G.W.R. to refrain from running the Sunday trains, rather than threaten the travellers. Forty Churches joined in the protest, not merely against trains, but against traps and brakes travelling to Porthcawl on Sundays, as it was contended that the railway employees and the drivers had been deprived of a Sunday break.

The editor of the *Llynfi Valley Messenger*, in referring to the first Sunday trip, said that some hundreds had returned as idiots under the condemnation of God. Porthcawl had been overrun by light-headed and thoughtless characters, and the Sabbath transformed into a day of dissipation and frivolity instead of a day of peace to the mind and rest to the body. The editor asked local ministers to urge their congregations (1) Not to neglect attending Sunday School, (2) Not to travel or join excursions to see friends on Sundays, (3) To accommodate preachers overnight to avoid Sunday travelling, (4) To oppose sacred concerts and Sunday political meetings, (5) To press for small shops to be closed and to oppose selling, buying or reading of Sunday newspapers, (6) Not to lease shops to be used for Sunday trading, (7) To oppose physical exercises on Sundays.

In this connection we note that in 1896 a summons was issued against a Rhondda man for selling newspapers in the Rhondda Valley on a Sunday. The Rev. John Evans (Eglwysbach), the most famous Welsh Wesleyan minister of the last century, had earlier stated that the district was worse than Sodom and Gomorrah.

(l) *The Drink Problem*

In the early days of Nonconformity in the valley, temperance did not necessarily imply total abstinence. In fact, a few ministers lost their pulpits owing to over-indulgence. In June, 1868, Richard Hopkins, the son of the reverend Thomas Hopkins, first minister of Bethania Church, Maesteg, applied for a licence to retail beer and cider at 11, Rock Street (later Commercial Street), Maesteg. The application was supported in writing by six Chapel members, including the applicant's father and Nicholas Dyer, one of the saintliest members of Bethania, despite the fact that beer and cider would be consumed on the premises from 5 a.m. onwards. Some of the foremost Chapel members used to call at public-houses after Sunday service and follow the precepts of St. Paul, in the 23rd verse of his first Epistle (Chapter 5) to Timothy.

W. Henry Buckland of Plasnewydd House, Maesteg, decreed in the early thirties of the last century that there should be no work on Sundays at the Maesteg Iron Works, of which he was a director. He became founder of Bethel English Baptist Church, Maesteg. He later built a brewery in the vicinity of Neath but continued to support the local cause at Maesteg. Before 1840 it was the custom in the valley to provide beer for preachers. The father of the Rev. Richard Hughes, Bethania, Maesteg, was a malster *(bragiwr)* but he later became a miner.

In 1830 the valley contained three public-houses, but in 1856, after the opening of the two local Iron Works, the number had increased to forty-nine. A public-house became the immediate neighbour of every colliery, particularly after 1889, when Col. North formed his Company to develop the local mining industry. In 1875 the only wine and spirit merchant listed in the valley was a prominent religious figure whose name appeared on the foundation stone of several local Chapels. On 27 January 1885 the Glamorganshire Working Men's Club — the first of its kind in the valley, was opened at 14, Bridge Street, Maesteg. Since then the district has followed the general pattern of the public-house being superseded by the club. John Lyons, Maesteg, has listed 107 public-houses in the Llynfi Valley. Of these thirty-seven are still open.

In the second half of the last century, running into the first quarter of this century, increasing drunkenness led to a mounting reaction, sometimes called the Nonconformist conscience. On Whit Monday, 10 June 1878, special trains carried Good Templars from Maesteg and Nantymoel to Porthcawl to attend a temperance rally. The procession, in full regalia, left the Porthcawl railway-station at 1 p.m. accompanied by three bands. Amusements were provided on the green until 4 p.m., and there were five speakers. The Amalgamated Good Templar Choir took part in the rally.

The two outstanding local advocates of total abstinence were the Revs. D. Phillips, Tabor (C.M.) Church, Maesteg, and T. Esger James, Saron, Nantyffyllon. Both equated temperance with total abstinence. In 1854 the Revs. D. Phillips and Thomas Levi (then of Swansea) took part in a big temperance rally at Cardiff. In *Yr Annibynwr* for April 1861, there is an account of a temperance campaign by the same two ministers for two weeks in Liverpool. The report testified that each night had improved on the previous night. The speeches were not of the milk-and-water type, but were 'strong, gripping and rousing'.

When the Rev. T. Esger James became the minister of Saron Church in 1894, he founded *Teml Rhosyn Saron*, being a temple of total abstainers. He organised a parade of 150 members of the Band of Hope through the main streets, each child wearing a blue ribbon. It was preceded by a banner bearing the words *Bendith Duw Arnom* (The Blessing of God be on us) and *Nac edrycher ar y gwin pan fyddo goch* (Look not upon the wine when it is red).

The Religious Revival of 1904-5 gave a big fillip to the doctrine of total abstinence. According to the Saron Church report for 1905 the *aelodau dirwestol* (temperance members), including the minister (the Rev. T. Esger James), twelve deacons (there were thirteen) and Sunday School officers, numbered 238. The 1908 Report gave the number of total abstainers (including the minister and *all* the deacons) for that year as 250. The minister stated that hundreds during his ministry had been convinced of the blessing of total abstinence in preference to alcoholism dubbed as moderation. Deacons were expected to be above suspicion. The Church performed the oratorio *God With Us* as a counter-attraction for young people who frequented eisteddfodau which led to drinking habits. The Rev. T. Esger James blamed the drink-trade for most of the secessions from his Church and added that the Church should fight to the last drop of blood against this enemy.

Almost every Church had its Band of Hope. The original purpose was the teaching of total abstinence. In 1909 the Rev. Teifi Davies, Garth suggested that all Church members should be total abstainers and form temperance societies known as Rechabites. Temperance rallies became frequent. The Good Templars opened a temple at Trinity Presbyterian Church at Nantyffyllon with fifty founder members. A temperance hotel was opened in Talbot Street, Maesteg. No intoxicating wine was to be used in the communion service. Total abstainers suffering from pneumonia would rather risk death than take a sip of whisky or brandy recommended by their doctors. When the local County Councillor, on the opening of a club some years ago, suggested that members should bring their wives to the club for a drink, there was much adverse comment. Previously, the provision of a room for women drinkers at a Maesteg public house was considered a scandal. No licensee was admitted to membership of a chapel.

By to-day, the Band of Hope and the Rechabites Lodges have disappeared and no eyebrows are raised when women join their husbands in clubs and public houses. Ministers and deacons seldom refuse a glass of sherry at weddings or at public functions, whilst one former Nonconformist minister in the valley within the last quarter of a century considered four pints of beer a night to be a reasonable supply of refreshment! The Rev. D. R. Davies, the author and former resident of Nantyffyllon, tells us in his autobiography *In Search of Myself* that on each of the several occasions he had preached at St. Paul's Cathedral, he had received a small cheque and half a bottle of sherry. Incidentally, Canon Collins of St. Paul's stated recently that when he took charge of a service at St. Paul's, his remuneration was £20 plus a bottle of sherry (presumably full).

(m) Biblical Names

The strength of the religious background of the valley can be gleaned from the Biblical names given to children.

The Christian names of some of the male members of Siloh Church, Nantyffyllon included Sephaniah, Nehemiah, Joshua, Joseph, Solomon, Shadrach, Elias, Ephraim, Simeon, Demetrie, Hiram, and Gideon. Those of the female members included Ruth, Naomi, Rebecca, Sephorah, Leah and Elizabeth.

The writer of this volume can remember in the valley men whose Christian names were Jesreel, Abraham, Isaac, Jacob, Timothy, Paul, Silas, Levi, Seth, Zachariah, Israel, Gabriel, Stephen, Moses, Aaron, Absalom, Peter, Reuben, Isaiah, Matthew, Mark, Luke, John, Jeremiah, Ezra, Abdon, Titus, Amos, Benjamin, Hezekiah, Jesse, Jonah, Josiah, Simon, Mordecai, Sylvanus, Urias, and Theophilus, whilst the ladies of the valley could sport the names of Deborah, Dorcas, Lydia, Priscilla, Lois, Sarah, Martha, Miriam, Magdalen, Melita, Rachel, Claudia and Elizabeth.

The most unusual Christian name of all was Maher-shall-lal-haz-baz (son of the prophet Isaiah). The holder lived at Nantyffyllon and was better known as 'Marshall'. His grandfather was likewise named.

(n) The Rise and Decline of Welsh Nonconformity

During the prosperous days of Nonconformity in the valley, the Rev. William Rees of Siloh Welsh Congregational Church, Nantyffyllon, had received into membership of his Church 969 in eighteen years (1856-1874). The Rev. John Jones, minister of Soar Welsh Congregational Church, Maesteg (now closed), had received 1,021 members in forty-six years (1851-1897). The Rev. Thomas Hopkins, the first minister of Bethania Baptist Church, Maesteg, had baptized by immersion approximately 500 between 1828 and 1845, whilst the Rev. Iorwerth Jones, who became minister of the same Church in 1894 had baptized 651 by 1924. The Rev. T. Esger James, Saron, Nantyffyllon (1894-1910), had received into membership 515 in sixteen years.

The churches in the lower part of the valley had a decided advantage over those in the upper reaches. Those employed in local government and the incoming members of the teaching profession in the higher schools seldom sought membership of a church or chapel beyond Maesteg itself where they lived.

The second half of this century has witnessed a decline in the influence of Nonconformity locally. After the 1939-45 War, each of the ten Welsh Congregational Churches had a resident minister. At the time of the writing of this volume, there are nine Churches with only one part-time minister. The Welsh Baptists had seven Churches. To-day, they have six without any resident minister. The Welsh Presbyterians had six Churches. The two in Caerau have ceased to exist, and the Chapel buildings have been sold to the Roman Catholic Church and the Pentecostal Church respectively, whilst the Nantyffyllon Chapel is now occupied by the Jehovah Witnesses. The remaining Welsh Presbyterian Churches have no resident minister, nor is there one available for the two local Welsh Methodist (Wesleyan) Churches. The one at Caerau was built to accommodate, in the main, former slate quarrymen from North Wales who had settled in Caerau as the result of depression in the slate industry at the beginning of the century. The other was built at Garth, Maesteg. There is now no full-time resident minister for any one of the Welsh Nonconformist Churches in the whole of the valley, whilst none of the Churches has a membership of over 100. With possibly one or two exceptions, the English Nonconformist Churches show a similar trend.

In 1981 there were in the Valley two Roman Catholic Churches, seven Anglican Churches as well as one or two Salvation Army Churches.

It was during the last century that the majority of the Nonconformist Chapels were built. The names of Church leaders (mainly laymen) can be seen on the foundation stones of many of these buildings, several having paid £10 for the privilege of having their names recorded for posterity.

In 1978 the Mid Glamorgan County Council, through its Planning Department, devised a scheme to measure, photograph and draw every

Chapel in Mid Glamorgan, which included the Maesteg Valley. A short history of each building was to be prepared, as it was considered that they represented a very important fabric of Welsh communities and were of great significance. It was stated that the County district had lost about ten Chapels a year, whilst others were being converted to secular use. The object was to preserve records of the 600 remaining Chapels in Mid Glamorgan before more disappeared, and to protect those of architectural or historical value from demolition. The information was to be placed in the County archives. By March 1981 it was announced that the work had been completed but that financial considerations had prevented immediate publication.

Church buildings have now become a burden and several churches worship in their respective vestries. The maintenance cost of central-heating has now become prohibitive, as some chapels have a seating capacity of 1,000 and over. Few miners are now church members whilst women constitute the big majority of the worshippers. It is only in the last few decades that women have been elected officers (deacons). Sunday Schools are now being held in the mornings as it appears difficult to compete with the afternoon attractions of T.V. and outdoor activities. The residual effects of two World Wars, the mass migration in the twenties and thirties caused by industrial depression, the growth of secularism, the advent of cars and caravans, and the comfort and entertainment provided by social clubs — all add to the difficulties of organised religion in the valley. The family pew of parents and children is now a thing of the past. Few laymen in the Welsh chapels can now offer an extempore prayer, and sisterhoods have taken the place of week-night prayer meetings.

Many more people attend the valley clubs than attend places of worship, whilst the officiating minister at a funeral service at the home of the deceased brings his own order of service as he is unlikely to find the former family Bible in evidence. Churches that used to be self-supporting are now compelled to think in terms of church unity with neighbours. Children collecting for the missionary cause is a thing of the past as is the reciting of Biblical verses by young and old at the weekly *cyfeillachau* (society meetings) of the various Welsh Churches.

(o) *The Various Valley Denominations*

There appears no record of Quakers having set up a Friends' Meeting House locally, neither do we know of any local Unitarian Church.

To Daniel R. Waldin (mentioned earlier) we are indebted for the following information regarding the Mormon cause. In the middle of the last century the Mormons had a branch Church at Garnlwyd, Maesteg, and also at Postman's Row (now High Street), Nantyffyllon, and at Caerau (then known as Spelters). The chief apostle at Garnlwyd was Rhys Williams (Rhys y Crydd), a shoemaker employed by a George Beynon. They met in a building belonging to a George Edwards. At Nantyffyllon, the chief apostle was a Richard Lewis (Dic y Sant), and, at Spelters, Evan Edwards. A big crusade was launched in the fifties and sixties of the last century and several families left for Salt Lake City in Utah, U.S.A.

However, T. H. Lewis, in his *Mormoniaid yng Nghymru* (The Mormons in Wales), 1956, quotes details given to *Cymanfa Morgannwg* (The Assembly of Glamorgan) towards the end of 1847. There had then been a big increase in Mormon membership. The Llwyni (Maesteg) branch, with Samuel Davies as president, had twenty-eight members, whilst the Cwmbychan (Cwmafan) and Bryn branch jointly, under the presidency of Thomas Pugh, could boast of sixty-three members. By the end of 1848 Llwyni had twenty-eight members, Cwmbychan thirteen and Bryn fifteen.

The Mormons of Aberkenfig met at the house of John Groves, those of Cwmafan at Tymaen Street and those of Y Llwyni (Maesteg) at the house of David Powell, opposite the Star Inn, Maesteg.

Thomas Pugh, president of the Cwmafan and Bryn Mormons, left his wife in Wales and took two other 'wives' with him to St. Louis. John Jeremiah of Maesteg wrote to the Mormon periodical *Yr Utgorn* (The Trumpet), January 1853, to express concern regarding the polygamy exercised by the Mormons. In a letter to *Y Diwygiwr* (The Reformer) in 1857, John Davies, formerly of Maesteg, who had emigrated with his parents to Utah two years earlier, gave his reasons for leaving Salt Lake City. He had been compelled to surrender his possessions to Brigham Young, head of the Mormons, and to pay a tithe of his income to him. Every male Mormon was expected to have two to ten 'wives'. Those who refused to conform were shot by Brigham Young's men.

By 1880 the Mormons had no branch in the Llynfi Valley and by 1890 had only 162 adherents in the whole of Wales. However, there was a Mormon Church in Bridgend in 1956, but we know of no local adherents.

The Salvation Army first formed a citadel in Maesteg in 1889. To mark the occasion, thirty-three were baptized by immersion in Bethania Chapel, Maesteg, in November of that year. They became known for their band, their Saturday evening open-air meetings at the Maesteg Town Hall Square, and for their welfare work and self denial.

As a result of the 1904-5 Religious Revival throughout Wales, Apostolic and Pentecostal Churches were formed locally, and three or four of these still remain. For several years the Pentecostal movement in South Wales held its annual Whit Monday Convention at Jerusalem (C.M.) Chapel, Nantyffyllon, where the exercise of the gift of tongues was much in evidence. In 1971 Peniel Apostolic Church building was taken over by a new Evangelical Church that had seceded on doctrinal and constitutional grounds from Bethlehem English Presbyterian Church, Maesteg.

133 Members of Maesteg Salvation Army Band, *c.*1910 including Councillors
T Jenkins, (seated), E Owens of River Street and Tom Haggar (Bandsman)

In the first few decades of this century there was a flourishing Spiritual
Church at Caerau, led by a Mr. Connolly, and also one at Maesteg. Two
local Churches still exist.

A religious sect known as Plymouth Brethren had a Church on a small
scale at Maesteg, whilst others, known as Exclusive Brethren, attended
services outside the valley. A Maesteg member of the latter sect used to
conduct religious services for high-ranking German prisoners of war, including Field Marshall Rundstedt, at the Island Farm Camp in Bridgend during
the last War.

A few local families were ardent Christian Scientists, but they worshipped outside the valley as there was no local Church.

As already stated, Jerusalem Chapel, Nantyffyllon has in recent years been acquired by Jehovah Witnesses. A new circuit minister, W. Stephenson, visited Maesteg in July 1958. At that time there were nineteen local 'witnesses'. Members from a wide area now attend services at Nantyffyllon.

(p) The Congregationalists (or Independents)

In 1939 the Congregationalists of the valley celebrated the tercentenary of their cause in Wales. A booklet was published giving the history of the Brynllywarch Academy and the background of the Llynfi Valley Congregational Churches.

Bethesda Church, Llangynwyd, the senior church, could trace its history from the time of the Rev. Samuel Jones, via Cildeudy (Coetrehen), Betws and Bridgend. The present Chapel was built in 1799. At a church meeting held at the beginning of the last century, it was decided that no member who kept a public-house should allow musical instruments to be played on his premises to lead young people to destruction. No member, old or young, was to indulge in courting on Sundays. The cup previously used at the communion service is now at the Welsh Folk Museum at St. Fagan's.

134   Bethesda Chapel, Llangynwyd

135   Carmel Chapel, Maesteg, built 1826

The following Welsh Congregational Churches are descended directly or indirectly from Bethesda: Carmel, Maesteg (1828), Siloh, Nantyffyllon (1841), Soar, Maesteg (1842 — closed until recently but re-opened in 1981 as a chapel of rest), Saron, Nantyffyllon (1852), Dyffryn, Caerau (1867), Ebenezer, Garth (1868), Seion, Caerau (1893), Noddfa, Pontrhydycyff (1894) and Canaan, Maesteg (1902). The English Congregational Church was established as a branch of Soar in 1869 and is now known as the United Reformed Church. Bethlehem English Congregational Church, Nantyffyllon, was founded in 1905 during the Revival fervour. For several years it could afford to keep a resident minister. At one time 150 children belonged to its Band of Hope. The Chapel building was demolished in the second quarter of the present century. The first minister of the Church was the Rev. J. T. Rhys, who ultimately became the private secretary for many years of Dame Margaret Lloyd George. Gosen Church, Caerau functioned for some years as a branch of Seion Church, Caerau.

If Bethesda, Llangynwyd, was the grandmother of the valley Congregational Churches, Carmel, Maesteg, could certainly claim to be their mother. Probably the Rev. William Morgan, Carmel, was the district Congregational minister best known nationally for his preaching. Professor John Evans, formerly of Brecon Memorial College, could remember him at a *cymanfa bregethu* (preaching festival) in Cardiganshire in 1868. He could recall his sonorous voice proclaiming *Edifarhewch* (Repent), heard with

136   Siloh Chapel, Nantyffyllon, built 1841

profound effect all over the vast cymanfa field. Hundreds of his holograph sermons are in the possession of the writer of these notes. When Carmel Church celebrated its centenary in 1928, a very informative paper on the history of the Church was read by the Rev. W. R. Bowen, the then minister, but unfortunately, the paper cannot be traced.

Siloh, Nantyffyllon, is the oldest of all religious bodies in the upper part of the valley. The early church-records were kept in English by the secretary,

137   Canaan Welsh Independent Chapel, St Michael's Road, Maesteg, built 1908

138   United Reformed and Methodist Church, Castle Street, Maesteg, Formerly
the English Congregational Church

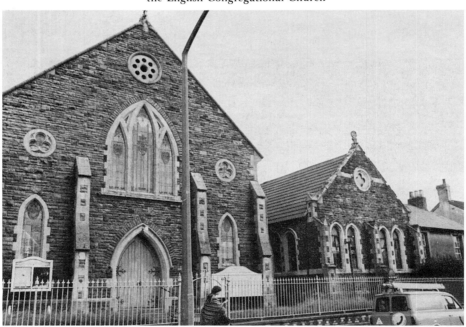

who was almost a monoglot Welshman. Owing to the depression in the iron industry in the last century, many members left for America. One former member of the church actually visited a Welsh Church in Maryland, U.S.A. named Siloh, as several of its members were former members of Siloh, Nantyffyllon. In its early days the Siloh Sunday School, on one occasion, formed a procession to Bethesda, Llangynwyd, to recite a catechism on a Sunday afternoon. They sang hymns all the way. The intense religious fervour lasted until almost midnight after returning home.

Soar Church, Maesteg, was looked upon as an enlightened Church but the most aristocratic of the local Nonconformist Churches. In 1854 it had 240 Sunday School members. It was converted into a Chapel of Rest in 1981. Saron Church became well known for its choir and its congregational singing. It provided at least seven precentors for other churches.

The first Dyffryn Chapel, known as Tŷ-cwrdd y Graig, was built in Dyffryn Road, Caerau, in 1868 after the congregation had been worshipping for a year in a room at the former Colliers' Arms. For several years Siloh, Nantyffyllon, and Dyffryn shared the ministry of the Rev. William Rees, and it is a happy omen that the two chapels that enjoyed separate ministries for many years are now re-united. It was during the ministry of the Rev. John Morris (father of Sir Rhys Hopkin Morris, M.P.) that Dyffryn established a branch chapel, later known as Seion, in Caerau Road. He ultimately devoted his full time to Seion. The foundation-stone of the new Dyffryn Chapel was laid in 1897. The centenary of the Church was celebrated in 1967 when the secretary, Herbert M. Davies, gave an address on the history of the chapel. One unusual feature was the fact that a former

139 Siloh Deacons 1941. The author's father, Joshua Richards, is sitting centre with his uncle, Tom, on his left

deacon, the Rev. James Davies, and his three sons, R. Anthony Davies, Granville Davies and Richard Gwynfi Davies, together with his grandson, Noel Davies, all became Congregational ministers, whilst another son, Herbert M Davies, became a local preacher.

Ebenezer Church, Garth, was noted for the long and dedicated ministry of the Rev. Rees Walters, and for its religious fervour and emphasis on temperance. The Church celebrated its centenary in 1968.

Noddfa, Cwmfelin, was built in 1891 with the aid of former members of Ebenezer Church. For many years, Noddfa and Bethesda, Llangynwyd, shared the same ministry.

Canaan Church was formed in 1901, and the present Chapel opened in 1904, Carmel Church being the mother Church. On the celebration of the first half-century of its existence, a full account of the Church's history was published. It remains a truly Welsh Congregational Church.

The Welsh Congregational Union, then representing nearly 900 Welsh Churches, held their annual conference, called *Yr Undeb*, at Maesteg in 1900 and in 1947.

The following two missionaries were brought up in local Churches:

Thomas M. Thomas (1828-1884) was a product of Bethesda, Llangynwyd. He became a missionary in Matabeleland, Central Africa. He wrote a series of articles to *Y Diwygiwr*, 1864-1870, on his travels in Africa where he met the famous missionary, Robert Moffatt. His publications included (1) An introduction to the alphabet, numerals, spelling and reading in the language of Matabeleland. (2) A book of hymns composed by him in the native language (3) A volume: *Eleven Years in Central Africa*, 1872. A full account of his career is given by the Rev. G. Penar Griffiths of Swansea in his essay containing the biographies of Welsh missionaries, published among the successful compositions of the Llanelli National Eisteddfod of 1895.

William Thomas Beynon (1860-1900) appears to be the only missionary martyr from the valley. His father was a policeman at Nantyffyllon. At ten years of age he became a member of Siloh Church and later became secretary of the Sunday School. He was educated at the Llynvi Iron Works School, Maesteg. After a short period at a local colliery office, he became a student at Allencliffe College, where he won a scholarship to the Welsh University College at Aberystwyth. From 1885 to 1895 he worked among Mongols in North China under the China Inland Mission, and later at Shanghai. He and his wife and three children were killed in the Boxer Riots in North China in July 1900. A memorial to the martyrs stands outside the South Gate of T'ai Yuan Fu and a tablet to his memory was unveiled at Siloh Church, Nantyffyllon, 26 March 1927, by his sister, Mrs. J. R. Evans, Nantymoel, when an address on the life of the martyr was given by David Evans, the Church Secretary. It is interesting to note that the famous China missionary, Dr. William Hopkyn Rees, who officiated at his wedding, was the nephew of the Rev. William Rees, who had received the martyred missionary into membership of Siloh Church.

(q) The Presbyterians (Calvinistic Methodists)

On the occasion of the centenary celebrations of Tabor C.M. Church, Maesteg, in 1940, a most helpful booklet, called *Preswylfeydd y Goruchaf*, on the history of the Church and Methodism in the valley generally was published by the Rev. J. Melville Jones, then minister of the Church.

The origins of the Methodist cause can be traced to Nant-y-crynwydd (near the present Maesteg R.F.C. grounds), Brynmawr Farm, Maesteg, Y Graig Fach Farm in the Sychbant Valley, Llangynwyd, and the long-room of the Old House, Llangynwyd, until Tabor Chapel was built. Preaching services and prayer-meetings were held at other local farms.

On the advent of the Methodist Revival of the 18th century, Howell Harris, one of the pioneers of the Revival, visited Llangynwyd on December 29 1740. He addressed his congregation from the mount above the steps adjoining the Church burial ground. The wife of the Vicar (the Rev. Morgan Thomas) alleged that he had polluted the place and demanded the removal of the mount to the site on the Square of the village where the memorial cross now stands. His visits gave rise to the beginnings of the C.M. cause in the valley. A Thomas John of Donat's used to walk 18 miles each way regularly to attend prayer meetings at Llangynwyd. Howell Harris also visited Caedu(?), Llangynwyd, on March 9 1742. His visits were implemented by the circulating schools of the Rev. Griffith Jones, Llanddowror, during the same period.

Other famous visiting preachers were Evan Phillips, Llangrallo (Coychurch), who lies buried near the Llangynwyd Church Tower, 1783, and David Jones, Llangan (1735-1810). Hopkin Bevan, Llangyfelach (1765-1839), preached behind Sgubor y Degwm (Tithe Barn), where the Corner House now stands. The noted preacher, William Evans, Tonyrefail, great-grandfather of Ivor Novello, preached at Llety Brongu in 1818. The original character, Siencyn Penhydd, Pontrhydyfen, was a regular visitor. Early worshippers up to 1811 used to walk to Gyfylchi, near Pontrhydyfen, to attend communion services occasionally conducted by the famous hymn-writer, the Rev. William Williams of Pantycelyn. Sometimes they would walk to Llangan in the Vale of Glamorgan for a communion service with the famous evangelist, the Rev. David Jones.

The Rev. Ebenezer Morris (1769-1825), one of the original subscribers to the *Cyffes Ffydd* (Confession of Faith) of the Methodists was invited to preach at a local farm-house before Methodism took root in the valley. He was a man of immense proportions and could not be seated on an ordinary chair. An open chair was constructed as a special mark of respect for him in

140   Tabor Chapel, Maesteg, built 1840

1809. This large square chair is now at the house of Mr. Ivor Davies, Maesteg, a former local Chief Health Inspector and a descendant of the maker.

All the greatest Methodist preachers of the past have officiated from time to time at Tabor Chapel. An indication of its early progress can be gleaned from the fact that in 1867 the Sunday School had 210 scholars, including 36 teachers, and had learned 30,399 verses.

The Welsh C.M. Churches of the valley consisted of Tabor (1840) with a new Chapel opened in 1908; Y Babell, Llangynwyd (1841), and now occupied as a dwelling-house; Hermon, Caerau (1851), with a new Chapel in 1872, now occupied by the Roman Catholic Church; Moriah, Pontrhydycyff (1901), the Chapel having been built in 1876; Jerusalem, Nantyffyllon (1904), now occupied by the Jehovah's Witnesses. Penuel Church, Caerau, seceded from Hermon Church and is now occupied by members of the Pentecostal Faith.

In addition, there were three English Presbyterian Churches: (1) Bethany, Caerau, occupying the old Hermon Chapel, built in 1851, (2) Trinity Church, Nantyffyllon, under the auspices of the Forward Movement during the fervour of the Religious Revival of 1904, and (3) Bethlehem Church, Maesteg, from which a number of members seceded to form Peniel Evangelical Church in 1971. The three Churches are all branches of Tabor

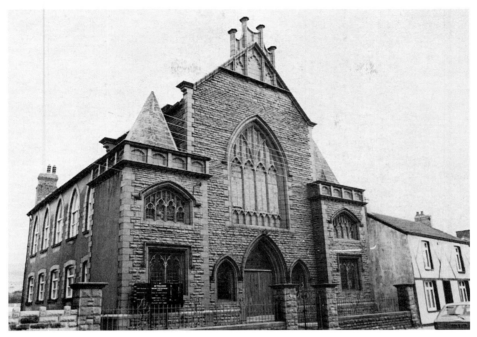

141   Bethlehem English Presbyterian Church, Bethania Street, Maesteg

Church, Maesteg. The seceding Church, Peniel, appears to be one of the most active Churches in the valley.

The religious controversy of half a century ago which centred around the Rev. T. Nefyn Williams, Tumble, regarding tenets of faith, affected rather deeply one local Welsh Presbyterian Church, but it now remains but a faint echo of past differences.

(r) The Baptists

Cadrawd, in his *History of Llangynwyd*, 1887, has referred to *Hanes y Bedyddwyr* (The History of the Baptists) by the Rev. Joshua Thomas, the Baptist historian, in whose book there are references to local Baptists in the days of Charles I, Cromwell and Charles II in the 17th century. In his synopsis of the history of the valley Baptist Churches, written on the occasion of the visit of the Welsh Baptist Union to Maesteg in 1926, Dr. Thomas Richards, former History master at the Maesteg Secondary School and later the celebrated Librarian of Bangor University, states that there were grounds for believing that the Rev. Howell Thomas of Glyncorrwg and the Rev. Thomas Joseph of Llangeinor were Baptists. By 1672 the former had moved to Nottage and the latter to Bridgend. Neither could be claimed by the Llynfi Valley. It was agreed that one of Cromwell's soldiers had lived

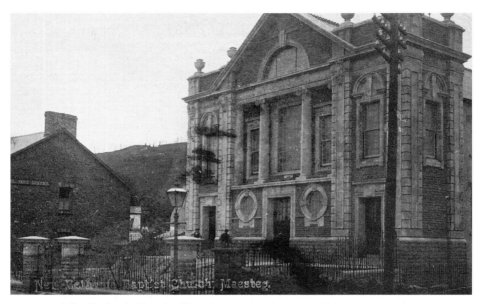

142   Bethania Baptist Church, Maesteg from an old post-card, *c.* 1910

at Nant-y-mwth on the borders of Betws, but that there was no proof that he was a Baptist. Dr. Richards testifies that there was but little history of the Baptists in Tir Iarll until the dawn of the Industrial Revolution at the beginning of the last century.

However, D. Rhys Phillips (Beili Glas) states that David Rees of Hengoed (1683-1748) was a student at Brynllywarch Academy. He was later ordained a Baptist minister at Limehouse in the East End of London, where he laboured for forty years.

Samuel Davies, precentor of Bethania Church, Maesteg, for over fifty years, wrote a comprehensive history of the Church during the last century. Much information is contained in Cadrawd's *History of Llangynwyd,* whilst Thomas Rees, Garnlwyd, a former secretary of the Church, added to the information provided by Samuel Davies. Some of the Rev. Iorwerth Jones's papers and also a number of the Church's annual reports are now at the National Library at Aberystwyth.

The practice of baptism by immersion began in the valley in 1827, when the Industrial Revolution began to develop. It took place in various parts of the Llynfi River, including a pool at Tŷ Candryll near the spot where Llwynderw schools were subsequently built. In that year Richard Evans and his wife, who kept a small grocery business at Maesteg, allowed their premises to be used as a place of worship for the Baptists.

The first to be baptized, *yn ôl dull Apostolaidd* (according to the Apostolic rites) was Thomas Davies, the father of William Dafydd bach, who was later a deacon at Salem Church, Spelters. According to David Jones in his *Hanes Bedyddwyr yn Neheubarth Cymru,* (The History of South Wales Baptists), 1839, the first baptism was conducted by a John Roberts. Bethania Church, the mother Baptist Church of the valley, came into being in 1828 with Thomas Hopkins of Hirwaun as its first minister. He was the grandson of Thomas Davies, the once famous *ffeirad coch* of Ystrad, Rhondda. The first Chapel was built in 1830-32 at a cost of £60. In 1838 the worshippers numbered thirty-two. The Church had previously been accepted as a member of the *Cymanfa* (Baptist Association) at Llanidloes in 1832. Among the early members was a Mrs Evans of Nant-tew-laeth, beyond Cymer, who used to walk to Bethania to attend Sunday and week-night prayer-meetings.

In 1829 the Rev. Thomas Hopkins baptized by immersion John Harry, a Congregational preacher, 'who had become convinced that such baptism was the only one mentioned in the Bible. He had followed the steps of our Saviour through the watery grave *(y dyfrllyd fedd).*

In 1830, with the influx of English workers at the Maesteg Iron Works, Henry Buckland, a director, joined the young Bethania Church. He could not understand Welsh, neither could the Rev. T. Hopkins preach in English. The Welsh and English worshipped in separate rooms in the same building. Visiting preachers to the English section included John James and William Williams, whilst George Thomas of Newton acted as a regular visiting preacher for some time. A convenient meeting-place was arranged and a call given to Edward Davies, formerly of Tredegar, who could preach in both languages. The Church, later called Bethel, was formed in 1831 and was received into membership of the *Cymanfa* (the Baptist Association) in 1833. However, as open communion, in which members of other denominations could join, was allowed in the young Church, its membership of the *Cymanfa* ceased in 1835, as strict communion, confined to Baptists, was enforced at the time. In 1837 the membership was restored. In 1839 the Church consisted of fifty-one members. The pioneer founder was undoubtedly Henry Buckland who had left the district before 1839.

The history of Bethel Church from 1847 to 1947 was published in a booklet in 1947 giving an account of one hundred years of Christian witness. In his reminiscences ('Eighty Years ago') published in the *Glamorgan Advertiser* in 1935, John Jenkins, Maesteg, who was then ninety years of age, states that before the days of fixed seats, some Bethel members used to bring their own chairs with them to the service for the day and return with them to their homes until required the following Sunday. It was after the coming of the Rev. Richard Davies that fixed seats became available to all.

The best known of the preachers nurtured in Bethel was the Rev. John Thomas M.A. (1873-1941) and better known as John Thomas, Liverpool, where he became famous as a preacher. At the age of fifteen he decided to enter the Christian ministry on the recommendation of Bethel Church. His home life was frugal and totally devoid of luxuries. When a young miner, he gained admission to the Baptist College at Pontypool, where he won a scholarship to the University College at Bangor. He came under the influence of Sir Henry Jones, who described him as the most brilliant student he had ever known. He took his M.A. degree, with a gold medal in Philosophy, at the University of London. He had hardly embarked on his first pastorate before the eminent authority, Professor A. B. Bruce, felt justified in describing him as the most brilliant preacher in the land. His fame throughout England was such that he was invited to become minister of Spurgeon's Tabernacle, London. Had he accepted he would unquestionably have been elected President of the Baptist Union of Great Britain.

When his former fellow student and friend in his Pontypool College days, the Rev. Edwyn Edmunds, died before delivering his presidential address to the Welsh Baptist Union in 1934, it was 'Johnny Thomas' of Maesteg who preached, with tremendous effect, the memorial sermon to his friend at Bethesda Chapel, Swansea. When returning to his home town, he used to preach to a well filled Town Hall. On resigning from Church oversight, he became tutor at the Swansea Bible College. He last visited Bethel on December 6, 1941 when in failing health, and died shortly after.

It is interesting to note that Bethel Vestry Hall (with classrooms, kitchen, minister's room and parlour) was designed by Sir Beddoe Rees. His father, Isaac Rees, was the Church secretary and brought up a distinguished family, including J. Tudor Rees, former Liberal M.P. for Barnstaple and later a County Court Judge. Another son, Col. Frederick Rees, was a well known doctor.

After meeting at various houses and at the then Gelli Arms in Hermon Road, Spelters, and also at the pot-room of the Spelter works, the Baptists of the upper part of the valley, despite much opposition from the higher authorities, formed Salem Church as a branch of Bethania Church, Maesteg, with Howell Davies, then a working miner, as the first minister, in 1850. In order to demonstrate their support, Bethania Sunday School, about 700 in all, at the time of the ordination of the Rev. Howell Davies, marched in procession to Spelters *i adrodd pwnc* (to recite a catechism) on *Dioddefaint Crist* (The Sufferings of Christ) by the Rev. J. M. Thomas, Cardigan. The Rev. H. W. Hughes (Arwystl), Bethania, asked the questions— all in the open air.

In 1859 the Rev. Howell Davies baptized by immersion in the River Llynfi forty-one persons in fifteen minutes in order to prove that the Apostles could easily have baptized 3000 on the day of the Pentecost! Samuel Davies, former precentor of Bethania Church, has testified that he saw the Rev. Richard Hughes, Bethania, baptize forty-eight in twenty minutes in the seventies of the last century. The record is surely held by the Rev. Dan Davies, Fishguard, who had near relations in Caerau. He claimed to have baptized by immersion ninety-eight in twenty-five minutes!

143   Salem Church, Nantyffyllon

Among the ministers of Salem in the last century was John Lewis who, as Dr. Gomer Lewis, later became famous as a lecturer and also as a public figure in Swansea. Another minister for a short period was the Rev. Dr. Fred Evans, one of five brothers who became Baptist ministers, one of whom, T. Valentine Evans, was the father of Sir D. Emrys Evans, former Principal of Bangor University. He was followed by the poet, the Rev. J. Ceulanydd Williams, who won the National Eisteddfod Chair at Pontypridd in 1893 for his ode *Pulpud Cymru* (The Pulpit of Wales). In 1903, John Evans, the Church secretary, published his prize essay on the history of Salem, containing much data regarding the early history. The Church had 407 members in 1876 and 409 Sunday School scholars (including 46 teachers) in 1879. The present secretary, Mrs. Mary Dixon, is a direct descendant of the first minister, the Rev. Howell Davies.

The branch Baptist Churches from Salem consist of Bethel, Glyncorrwg (1868), Caersalem, Abergwynfi (1881), Caersalem, Caerau (1890), closed some years ago and since destroyed by fire, and also Noddfa, Caerau (1897). On June 19 1898 eight members of Noddfa were baptised in the River Llynfi — being the first public baptism in Caerau.

144   Interior, Tabernacle Church, Maesteg

The Rev. Idris Williams, a product of Salem Church, informed the writer of this volume that Salem Church had, in 1872, refused the gift of a new chapel as the giver wanted to reserve the pulpit for Baptists only.

In the lower part of the valley, about sixty members seceded from Bethania in 1852-53 to form Tabernacle Church. They first worshipped in the former English Baptist Chapel in Galltcwm Row, Maesteg. The Church was fortunate in having the services of some outstanding ministers, two of whom excelled in the literary world — the Rev. W. R. Watkin (1900-1910), editor of *Seren Gomer*, and the Rev. E. Llwyd Williams (1931-36), who later won the Chair and Crown at the National Eisteddfod. There were centenary celebrations of the Church in October 1956, when a paper on the history of the Church was read by the Secretary, T. Edgar Miller. It does not appear to have been published.

Calfaria Church, Cwmfelin, Maesteg, was formed in 1877 at the suggestion of the Rev. Richard Hughes, Bethania, to cater for Baptists at the lower end of the valley. It remained under the care of Bethania until 1886, when Calfaria joined with Ainon, Pontrhydycyff (also under the care of Bethania) in arranging a joint ministry. The best known ministers of the Church were Robert Allen (1892-1907), famous in South Wales for his originality, and Ben Jones (1910-1950), who maintained his popularity and respect until the end of his forty years ministry. There were extensive centenary celebrations in 1977, when Miss Mary Powell recounted the Church history.

Ainon Church had its origins in prayer-meetings at Y Felin, owned by David Griffiths, and later at the house of Moses Thomas, Y Garth Fach. A lease of the site on which the Chapel building now stands was granted in 1875. Bethania released thirty-five members to form the Church in 1886. The Rev. Ben Jones combined the pastorate of Calfaria and Ainon for many years. In 1925 Ainon could boast of a Sunday-night congregation of about 150.

The Baptist cause had three English Churches in the valley, the oldest being Bethel, Maesteg, to which reference has already been made. Zion Church is within a stone's throw of Bethel and at the moment appears to be in a flourishing state. Hope Church, Caerau, was built in the early part of this century to meet the influx of workers upon the opening of the Caerau collieries. It would be well if the Church histories of Zion and Hope could be published in order to do justice to these worthy causes.

Up to comparatively recently, every Welsh Baptist Church in the valley practised *cymun caeth* (strict communion), which meant that no member of any other religious cause would be allowed to participate in their communion services unless he or she had been baptized by immersion. They went even further than that. No member of an English Baptist Church, although baptized by immersion, was allowed to participate in the communion service of a local Welsh Baptist Church, owing to the fact that the English Baptist Churches allowed non-Baptists, such as Methodists and Congregationalists to commune with them. The Rev. Iorwerth Jones, Bethania (1894-1930), once expressed a hope that no non-baptized preacher would ever be allowed to ascend the pulpit of his Church. This explains why his close friend, the Rev. W. R. Bowen, Carmel Congregational Church, Maesteg, would always preach from the *sêt fawr* (big pew), and not from the pulpit, whenever he took a service at Bethania. Believers in strict communion, confined to Baptists only, have now almost completely disappeared from the valley and there have been instances of a Baptist minister presiding over a local communion service in which ministers of other denominations have taken part. Baptism is no longer looked upon as a wholly essential requisite, even to Church membership.

In the early days, when people were baptized in the River Llynfi, some of those baptized would boast that they had broken the icy surface of the water in the depth of winter. Later the ceremony took place in the baptistry located under the big pew of the Church. A further development was the provision of a heating apparatus. By now, if the ceremony involves danger to the health of a delicate or elderly person, a certificate of exemption can be granted and associate members can be accepted.

The practice of *arddodiad dwylo* (the laying of hands) in Baptist ordination services was prevalent at one time, but when the Rev. Richard

Hughes, Bethania, was ordained minister of Bethania in 1851, he refused to take part in the ceremony. This resulted in much controversy in Baptist papers such as *Y Greal, Seren Gomer* and *Y Bedyddiwr,* but it had little, if any, effect on the local Churches. The Rev. Richard Hughes used to travel on horseback in the early days of his ministry. Among his many activities was the holding of Saturday night classes in Bethania to teach the geography of Canaan.

As a result of the Religious Revival of 1904, the Chapel became too small for the congregation. Even after the recession which followed the Revival, the members numbered 603 on December 31 1907, apart from the children and *gwrandawyr* (attendant non-members). The new (and present) Chapel, designed by Sir Beddoe Rees, was officially opened on March 28 1908. The minister, the Rev. Iorwerth Jones, insisted that the term, *Bedyddwyr Neilltuol* (Strict Baptists) should be inscribed on the front of the Chapel building. In all, sixteen meetings — surely a record — were held to mark the opening of the new Chapel. The secretary's salary was then fixed at £20 per annum. The treasurership of the Church was vested in the same family of four generations for a continuous period of over one hundred years, being Timothy James, his son of the same name, his grandson (Charles James) and great-grandson (Edward James). One member of the family, Mrs. Elizabeth James. was awarded the rare distinction of a Gee Medal for Sunday School service over a long period. The 150th anniversary of the Church was celebrated on December 4 1978, when Miss Phyllis Lloyd, the Church secretary, gave an address on the history of Bethania.

(s) *The Wesleyans (now called Methodists)*

An account of the early history of this branch of the Christian Church has been given by Cadrawd in his *History of Llangynwyd.* The English section first worshipped for 2 years (1839-41) in a cottage in McGregor Row, Maesteg, and was served in the main by local preachers. Later the Church was helped by ministers from Bridgend and Cowbridge, and worshipped at the old Calvinistic Methodist Chapel. The few adherents later held their meetings at the old English Chapel in Galltcwm Row, and later, success-ively, at Shoemakers' Row, the Swan Hotel club room, and afterwards in the Maesteg Iron Works Infants' schoolroom. A small Chapel was then built in Alfred Street, Maesteg, in the late fifties of the last century. When this became too small, a bigger Chapel, known as the Wesleyan Church, was built in Castle Street, Maesteg, adjoining the then G.W.R. station. This building was demolished in the seventies of this century and the adherents became scattered. The best known layman attached to the Church was A. Lockyer J.P., a prominent public figure of the town.

Owing to the influx of North Walians to the upper part of the valley in the early years of this century, Bethel Welsh Wesleyan Church was formed in Caerau. Another Welsh Church, called Horeb, was built in Duke Street, Maesteg. Both Churches were served by the same minister and later became part of a much bigger circuit of Churches. However, the Wesleyan Church does not appear to have taken root in the Llynfi Valley, possibly because its origins were outside Wales.

(t) High Office

High offices in their respective denominations have been attained by ministers with local associations.

The Rev. David Phillips of Tabor C.M. Church became *Llywydd y Gymanfa Gyffredinol* (President of the General Assembly) of the Welsh C. M. Churches in 1885. One of his successors at Tabor, the Rev. William H. Thomas (1887-1927), became President in 1931. A product of Tabor, the Rev. T. B. Phillips, a former missionary, occupied the same exalted position many years later.

The Rev. Iorwerth Jones, Bethania, Maesteg, became President of the Welsh Baptist Union in 1925, whilst his successor at Bethania, the Rev. Richard Edwards, who was elected President in 1955, died on April 18, 1956 before delivering his presidential address, which had been prepared by him and which was read by the Rev. John Thomas, Blaenwaun, Pembrokeshire. Mr J. P. Gibbon, a member of Bethania, became Treasurer of the Welsh Baptist Union.

The Rev. E. Gwyn Evans, a member of the Gelli Lenor family and a product of Tabor Church, minister of Charing Cross Welsh Presbyterian Church, London, became Moderator of the Free Church General Council of Great Britain in 1957, whilst the Rev. W. D. Rowlands, another product of Tabor, became President of Sasiwn y De (the South Wales Association of Welsh Presbyterian Churches).

The Rev. D. Hughson Jones, Liverpool, who decided to enter the Christian ministry when he was a member of Seion Welsh Congregational Church, Caerau, before the first World War, became the immediate predecessor of the writer of this volume as President of the Welsh Congregational Union in 1963, whilst the brother of the writer, Gwynfryn Richards, became Dean of Bangor.

The Rev. Idris Davies, a native of Pontrhydycyff and a former member of Ainon Baptist Church, became President of the English Assembly of the Baptist Union of Wales.

(u) Entrants to the Christian Ministry.

Lists have been prepared of local men raised to the Christian ministry or ordained to the priesthood. The details so far available are as follows: —

Congregationalists   58
Baptists   45
Anglican Church   28 + 1
Presbyterians (C. M.)   13
Elim Four Square &c.   6
R. C. Church   7
                           ─────
                           157
                           ─────

In addition, at least 50 local preachers, apart from lay readers and
unofficial pastors, have conducted religious services all along the years. It is
doubtful whether any valley of comparable size and population in Wales has
made a greater contribution towards the maintenance of the Christian
religion and the propagation of the Gospel.

The details given in this chapter constitute the merest outline of our
religious past and cannot possibly do justice to a subject that involves
something infinitely greater than a recital of the historical and mere factual
position.

59 Literature

(a) Early Traditions

The Llynfi Valley had a literary tradition second to none among the valleys
of Glamorgan prior to the Industrial Revolution.

The first known poem to the gentry of Glamorgan was written by
Casnodyn in praise of Madog o'r Goetref who lived at Nant-y-dylles,
Llangynwyd, and was buried at Margam. Madog was steward of Tir Iarll,
which was part of the Lordship of Glamorgan, about 1330. He was a figure
of sufficent importance to be praised by Casnodyn, who was looked upon as
the custodian of the cultural traditions of the Welsh when the poets of Tir
Iarll sang the praises of the descendants of the Welsh princes. The poem is
in a stately and majestic style and is included in the *Myvyrian Archaiology*.

Professor G. J. Williams states that all the major poets of Tir Iarll were
descendants of Einion ap Collwyn of the 12th century. Before 1282, a
Pencerdd (Master Poet) was one who had won a court chair, and a *Bardd
Teulu* was a Bard of the Household. After 1282, when Wales was conquered,
wandering minstrels appeared on the scene, the most famous of all being
Dafydd ap Gwilym of the fourteenth century. The bardic tradition was an
oral one, and transmitted from teacher to pupil, who later became teacher.

Dafydd Morganwg, in his *Hanes Morganwg* (The History of Glamorgan), 1871, asserts that the Tir Iarll Eisteddfod was held alternately at Cwmafan and Llangynwyd for many years, from 1261 onwards, under the patronage of the Lord of Morgannwg, and that the Morgannwg bards held their monthly meetings at Llangynwyd.

The Iolo MSS contain twenty poems which Iolo Morganwg attributed to Rhys Goch ap Rhiccert of Llangynwyd, who flourished in the mid-fourteenth century. These poems are accepted as genuine by Thomas Stephens in his *Literature of the Kymry,* and most of them are included in his book. Iolo stated that he had found them in a manuscript belonging to his bardic teacher, Siôn Bradford. However, Professor G. J. Williams contends that they were actually written by Iolo himself, but much doubt has arisen lately as to whether Professor Williams's assertions are supported by sufficient factual evidence to justify his conclusions.

Tir Iarll was the literary centre of Glamorgan for centuries until the mid-sixteenth century, the focal point of the tradition being Llangynwyd. The poets of that century looked upon Tir Iarll as the nursery of the literary traditions of Glamorgan. Testimony to the bardic life of the district and its neighbourhood in the fifteenth century can be found in a *cywydd* (a poem in the strict metres) by Dafydd Fychan, and a further *cywydd* by Llywelyn Goch y Dant (fl. about 1470), both poets being natives of Tir Iarll.

In an ode to Rhisiart Iorwerth of Llangynwyd, Dafydd Benwyn, one of the three most famous poets in the latter half of the sixteenth century and the beginning of the seventeen century, called Tir Iarll *Y plwyf gorau nwyf o'n iaith* (The most vivacious parish of our language). In the courts of the descendants of the old princes of Tir Iarll the bardic tradition of Glamorgan was maintained and remained unbroken until the seventeenth century when it finally disintegrated. By the end of that century, the Glamorgan gentry had lost all interest in the bardic tradition, and the standard became mediocre.

After the days of the patronage of the princes and gentry had ended, eisteddfodau were held in taverns, to which the poets would bring their compositions. The successful poet would sit in the chair of the following year's eisteddfod. The bards composed *tribannau* (the favourite type of Glamorgan verse) on subjects set at the time without previous notice.

(b) Early Poets up to the end of the 17th Century

Rhys Brydydd, whose family home was at Llangynwyd, ultimately moved to Llanharan and was considered the bardic teacher of the whole of the region towards the middle of the fifteenth century. According to Professor Ceri W. Lewis, he and his descendants were the most illustrious family of *Penceirddiaid* (Chief Poets) that ever lived in Glamorgan. He composed an *awdl* (ode in the strict metres) in praise of the Deity, and three poems *(cywyddau):* — (1) a complaint, as a farmer, of three molestations – the fox, the crow and the mole; (2) an address to the rood at Llangynwyd Church beseeching a cure after having been bitten by a snake; and (3) a request for the gift of a saddle and bridle from a John Twrel of Cardiff.

His great-grandfather, Rhys Fychan, lived at Gadlys Farm and also at Brynllywarch Farm. The descendants of Rhys Fychan once owned Maescadlawr and 'Keven Baydan,' whilst Rhys Brydydd's father lived at Cefn Ydfa. Rhys Brydydd himself was looked upon as a Tir Iarll poet, and became famous as the grandfather of Lewis Morgannwg and Thomas ab Ieuan ap Rhys. The three of them sang the praises of the rood at Llangynwyd Church. At one time this rood (crucifix) was as popular among pilgrims as was the shrine of Pen-rhys in the Rhondda Valley. An authoritative account of the poet is given by J. Morgan Williams in his *Gwaith Rhys Brydydd a'i Gyfoeswyr* (The Works of Rhys Brydydd and his Contemporaries).

Rhisiart ap Rhys Brydydd, son of Rhys Brydydd, was a *Pencerdd* (chief of song) and flourished between 1480 and 1520. He was the father of Lewis Morgannwg, described as the most learned *pencerdd* of the province in the sixteenth century. He was the bardic teacher of Iorwerth Fynglwyd. According to Professor G. J. Williams, the Llanstephan MS – 164 contains thirty of his poems, which include *awdlau* and *cywyddau* (poems in the strict metres) in praise of the Deity, two *cywyddau* to Catwg, and an elegy to Iorwerth Fynglwyd. He also composed an *awdl enghreifftiol* to prove that he had mastered the intricate rules of traditional strict metres in Welsh poetry. Dafydd, Abbot of Margam from 1500 to 1517, was one of his patrons, whilst Dafydd Benwyn in the latter half of the fifteenth century sang his praises in an elegy.

We are informed by Professor G. J. Williams that the two greatest poets of Tir Iarll in the latter half of the fifteenth century were Rhys Brydydd and Gwilym Tew, the latter, who flourished between *c.*1460 and 1480, being either the son or the brother of the former.

Gwilym Tew lived at Llangynwyd. He was described by Dafydd Benwyn, the famous Glamorgan poet, as *Gwilym Tew brydydd o dir jiarll* (Gwilym Tew, poet of Tir Iarll). He was a *pencerdd* (chief of song) and was steeped in the traditional lore of the Welsh bards. His experimental *awdl* (a poem in the strict metres) was included in the grammar of Siôn Dafydd Rhys. A Latin grammar translated into Welsh in the mid-fifteenth century was copied by him and studied by the Tir Iarll poets about 1470. He also copied a *dwned* (grammar) from the Latin, a book of lineage, triads, etc. A collection of his works, including his poems, gathered by J. M. Williams, is now at the National Library of Wales. He became known for his *cywydd* to the Virgin Mary shrine at Pen-rhys, Rhondda, in which poem he attempted to experiment with the many traditional metres then known to the bards. Among his other poems was a *cywydd* to the rood at Llangynwyd Church and *Cân y Mai* (May Song). He sang to the ladies of the hill districts of Glamorgan and to the gentry of Tir Iarll, and once owned the famous Llyfr Aneirin (The Book of Aneirin).

Llywelyn Goch y Dant (fl. circa 1470) was a native of Tir Iarll, but much of his work is lost. He wrote an *awdl* on the Abbey at Neath and a *cywydd* inviting Hywel ap Dafydd to visit the famous poets of Tir Iarll. He also sang the praises of Sir Roger Vaughan of Tretŵr (Tretower) and wrote an elegy to Sir Roger after he was beheaded at the instance of Jasper Tudor.

Gruffudd ap Dafydd Fychan of Betws, Tir Iarll, was a contemporary of Llywelyn Goch y Dant and composed an elegy to Henry VI in 1471, besides three poems of prophecy and three love songs.

Ieuan Du'r Bilwg was another contemporary, who composed three *cywyddau* — (1) A request to the Abbot for a copy of the anthems sung at Neath Abbey; (2) Thanks for a red gown; (3) An account of a conversation with a woman sifting barley. Another Ieuan Du, known as Ieuan Du ap Dafydd ab Owain, flourished during the same period and was the author of a poem to Ieuan Gethin of Baglan.

Lewis Morgannwg was closely connected with Tir Iarll although he lived at Cowbridge. His ancestors had lived for centuries at Llangynwyd and his father was looked upon as a Tir Iarll poet. He was a national figure of considerable standing, being the head of the bardic order throughout Wales (a *pencerdd*) from 1530 to 1560. He translated various historical chronicles and tracts and his advice was sought by John Leland, the antiquary. As an itinerant bard, he sang to the leading gentry of his day in Glamorgan and further afield in Wales. He was one of the most prolific of all Glamorgan bards who sang in the strict metres. Over one hundred of his poems are still available. They include a *cywydd* to Iorwerth Fynglwyd, a famous Tir Iarll poet, and another to Tudur Aled, one of the greatest Welsh poets, whom he had met at the Court of Sir Rhys ap Thomas. Further poems are his *awdl* in full 24 metres to Lleision ap Thomas (fl. 1513-41), the last abbot of Neath, praising the joys of monastic life, and a *cywydd* to the shrine of the Virgin Mary at Pen-rhys, Rhondda. He went on a pilgrimage to Rome and had an audience with the Pope. Incidentally, he later denounced the Pope and monastic life and sang the praises of Henry VIII. He was called *Athro'r Tair Talaith* (Teacher of the three Provinces of Wales), one of which, Dinefwr, included Glamorgan. He was an authority on genealogy. His literary output, called *Gweithiau Lewis Morgannwg,* was published by E. J. Saunders in 1922.

*Tomas ab Ieuan ap Rhys (c.*1510-*c.*1560), the other grandson of Rhys Brydydd, lived at Llandudwg (Tythegston), but he and his family were closely associated with Llangynwyd. He was a devout Catholic and resented the Protestant Reformation. He compared Queen Mary with the Virgin

Mary. He wrote *cwndidau*, a form of prosody frowned upon by North Wales poets such as Goronwy Owen even centuries later. They were poems in free verse, then popular in Glamorgan, containing a wide range of scriptural themes intended to be sung as carols. Although he was a professional poet, having received formal instruction in the bardic craft, he eschewed the traditional strict metres followed by his contemporaries. His poems include elegies to men of rank and also prophecies. They are included in *Hen Gwndidau* (1910) edited by Cadrawd and the Rev. Lemuel J. Hopkin James, a former curate of Llangynwyd (1898-1901).

Ieuan ab Ieuan ap Madog of Betws Tir Iarll (fl. 1547-87), a friend of Llywelyn Siôn and Antoni Powel of Llwydarth, had an important collection of prose works, and was a well-known copyist. In the Llanstephan MSS there is a copy in his handwriting in 1575 of *Y Marchog Crwydrad*, being a translation of the English version of a French text of the thirteenth century.

Tomas ab Ieuan ap Madog, a brother to the above, also composed *cwndidau* and poems praising the gentry, to whom he also composed elegies. He died before 1569.

Iorwerth Fynglwyd (fl. 1500-25). Although he lived in Sant-y-brid (St. Bride's Major) and was not a native of Tir Iarll, he was connected with Llangynwyd, where his son, Rhisiart Iorwerth, lived. Professor G. J. Williams states that all the Glamorgan bards had inherited the poetic traditions of Tir Iarll and that Iorwerth Fynglwyd was the greatest of Glamorgan poets writing in the strict metres. His bardic teacher was Rhisiart ap Rhys Brydydd who had close connections with Tir Iarll. His poems were addressed to the gentry of Glamorgan and were full of social comment and satire, exposing church and social evils. Lewis Morgannwg wrote an elegy to him. The two volumes — *Bywyd a Barddoniaeth Iorwerth Fynglwyd* (The Life and Poems of Iorwerth Fynglwyd) by Howell Ll. Jones (M.A. thesis, University of Wales, 1970) and *Gwaith Iorwerth Fynglwyd,* containing forty-four of his poems, edited by Howell Ll. Jones and E. I. Rowlands, 1975, contain much helpful information.

Rhisiart Iorwerth, son of Iorwerth Fynglwyd, was the last Glamorgan bard of any real significance who wrote in the traditional strict metres, and was the most important Glamorgan bard during the 1510-70 period. He lived at Llangynwyd and composed love songs and poems praising the gentry of Glamorgan, Carmarthen and Brecon. He was the bardic teacher of the noted Tir Iarll poet, Dafydd Benwyn, who wrote an elegy in praise of his tutor.

Dafydd Benwyn was a Llangeinor bard and flourished in the latter half of the sixteenth century. In addition to his elegy to Richard Iorwerth, he wrote an elegy to the father of Antoni Powel of Llwydarth, and a series of *englynion* (stanzas) describing the hospitality at Llwydarth. Two volumes of his poems to the gentry of Glamorgan still exist, one at the Cardiff Central Library and the other at Jesus College, Oxford.

Llywelyn Siôn (1540-*c*.1615) lived at Llangewydd, near Laleston, and was considered the greatest professional scribe of his day, being commissioned by the local gentry to copy documents, prose, poetry, etc. He remained loyal to the Catholic faith, and condemned the followers of Luther and Calvin.

In his *Traddodiad Llenyddol Morgannwg* (The Literary Tradition of Glamorgan), 1948, Professor G. J. Williams states that of Llywelyn Siôn's 13 MSS in our libraries, seven consist of *awdlau* and *cywyddau* (poems in the strict metres), one of *cwndidau* (religious songs in the free metres), one of genealogies and four of prose subjects. Some of his works were included in four other MSS. His three famous collections were *Llyfr Hir Amwythig* (Shrewsbury), *Llyfr Hir Llywarch Reynolds* and *Llyfr Hir Llanharan*.

Iolo Morganwg attributed *Cyfrinach Beirdd Ynys Prydain* (The Mysteries of the Bards of the Isle of Britain), the famous volume about which there has been so much controvesy, to Llywelyn Siôn and his bardic pupil, Edward Dafydd of Margam. T. O. Phillips, a former Welsh master at the Maesteg Grammar School, has written a detailed thesis (yet unpublished) on the works of Llewelyn Siôn.

Antoni Powel of Llwydarth, who was born *c*.1550-60, and who died in 1618, was a steward of the Mansels of Margam and a patron of the bards of Tir Iarll. He was under-sheriff of Glamorgan in 1594. His great-grandfather, his grandfather (Hywel ap Siôn Goch) and his father had occupied Llwydarth. Iolo Morganwg called the family *Y Poweliaid Doethion* (The wise Powels). At Margam Antoni Powel had access to a rare library which included *Llyfr Coch Hergest* (The Red Book of Hergest). Professor G. J. Williams suggests that he used to pay copyists, like Llywelyn Siôn of Llangewydd and others, for arranging collections of prose and poetry.

He is known for his *History of the Kings of Britain,* based on the writings of Caradoc of Llancarfan, and as the author of *Llyfr Du Pant-y-lliwydd,* being a holograph collection of some 700 pages written in Llangynwyd and now at the Cardiff Central Library (Hafod MS 22). The book is in two different handwritings, the major part having been written by Antoni Powel in the second half of the sixteenth century. We do not know what help was given by him regarding the Welsh translation, in the handwriting of a friend, of a portion of the *Ffestival liber ffestialis* (John Mirk), *c*.1400, a handbook for Sunday preaching and Church festivals.

In his handwriting are *Miraglau* (Miracles or Wonders) written in the form of *tribannau,* a popular form of verse in Glamorgan. Iolo Morganwg attributed to him a copy of *Brut y Saeson* (A Chronicle of the English) dealing with the troubles of Iestyn ap Gwrgant, a book on grammar and on *cerdd dafod* (bardic instruction), an account of old eisteddfodau, a collection of historical triads (in handwriting) of the old poets, a volume of

Cofion Llwydarth, being a collection of genealogies with an *englyn* at an eisteddfod at Craig y Dinas.

His praises were sung by a Ieuan Thomas, about whom little is known, whilst the elegy of Edward Dafydd of Margam is found in *Llyfr Hir Llanharan.* There was uncertainty as to what had happened to his collection of manuscripts. Edward Lhuyd (1660-1709) maintained that George Powel of 'pen y vay' (Penyfai), a nephew of Watcyn Powel, who in turn was a nephew of Antoni Powel, possessed the papers. Iolo Morganwg states that Siôn Bradford, Iolo's bardic teacher, once had them. According to Professor G. J. WIlliams, they later reached Thomas Wilkins, a Vale of Glamorgan antiquary. They are now in the Hafod collection at the Cardiff Central Library.

Watcyn Powel, who died in 1655, and was a nephew of Antoni Powel, lived at Penyfai. He was probably the last of the gentry of Tir Iarll to have mastered the bardic art. *Y Byrdew Mawr,* an extensive collection of poems gathered by Tomas ab Ieuan o Dre'r-bryn, includes six of his *cywyddau.* Iolo Morganwg stated that Watcyn Powel had a collection of reminiscences of many old Welsh poets, and that *Llyfreugell Tre Groes* (The Library of Tre Groes), near Pencoed, contained a hefty volume of *englynion* gathered by him throughout Wales. Iolo also asserted that he had dealt with a treatise on Welsh grammar prepared by Llawdden Fardd for Rhys ap Siôn — mentioned in documents of his ancestors at Llwydarth — and that he had a bardic copy of *Statut y Beirdd* (Statute of the Bards) in one of his books. He was the subject of two elegies, one by Edward Dafydd of Margam and the other by Dafydd o'r Nant, as well as two *englynion* by Dafydd Edward of Margam.

Edward Dafydd was a *clerwr* (an itinerant minstrel) in the mid seventeenth century and considered himself a sort of *bardd teulu* (family bard) to the Mansels of Margam. He sang the praises of the gentry, including the Powels of Llwydarth, whom he often visited. Professor G. J. Williams states that he was the last Morgannwg poet to live on his profession as a *clerwr.* He was an ardent Royalist. Much of his work is in *Llyfr Hir Llanharan,* copied by Llywelyn Siôn.

Tomas ab Ieuan o Dre'r-bryn, Llangrallo (Coychurch), was a scribe who flourished in the latter half of the seventeenth century, and one who spent his life collecting and copying old Welsh poetry. He had a vast collection of manuscripts, including six *cywyddau* by Watcyn Powel and some by Edward Dafydd. His main collection was called *Y Byrdew Mawr,* containing *cywyddau* from the Llywelyn Siôn MSS and works of seventeenth-century poets. In his *Traddodiad Llenyddol Morgannwg,* Professor G. J. Williams enumerates the contents of his collections, and calls him the last of the scribes of Morganwg. Iolo Morganwg stated that he was a descendant of Rhys Brydydd of the famous Llangynwyd family.

The Rev. *David Williams* (Dafydd o'r Nant) was vicar of Penlline, near Cowbridge, at the end of the seventeenth century and was very friendly with the Powel family. He composed elegies to Watcyn Powel (in 1655) and also to the Powels of Maesteg and Tondu, including Siôn Powel, as well as to the Rev. Samuel Jones and the gentry of Glamorgan. Professor G. J. Williams states that he was the only important poet of Glamorgan who sang at the end of the seventeenth century and was the first poet to use the printing press to publish his works. Some of his poems appeared in *Llyfr Hir Llanharan*. He was also a collector of old Welsh poetry, and died *c.*1693.

(c) Tribannau

Although the form of *triban* poetry can be traced back to the Tudor period, it was in the eighteenth century that it became a popular medium with the bards of Tir Iarll. Here is an example: —

> Pan fyddo'r Llan yn llawen
> Heb falais na chenfigen,
> Bydd mêl yn tarddu mas o'r cwar
> A ffigys ar y ddraenen.

(When Llan village will be cheerful, without malice or jealousy, honey will be found in quarries and figs will grow on thistles).

The last word in the third line had to rhyme with a word within the fourth line, e.g., 'cwar' and 'ar' in the above verse.

From these *tribannau* much information can be found regarding the social life of Glamorgan. Thousands of these verses were written, and many of them, attributed to Wil Hopcyn, had their setting in Tir Iarll, particularly in the Llangynwyd district.

Cadrawd's prize essay at the Aberdare National Eisteddfod, 1885, contained 224 examples, whilst the prize at the Bridgend National Eisteddfod, 1948, for a collection of unpublished Morgannwg *tribannau* was divided between Lewis Davies, the Cymer schoolmaster (with 224 verses) and Dan Herbert, Resolfen (with 1023 verses).

Tegwyn Jones of the National Library of Wales published his standard work on *Tribannau Morgannwg* in 1976, containing 677 verses, with helpful explanatory notes by Daniel Huws. Other well-known collectors were Jenkin Howell, Aberdare and Gwernyfed.

Many *tribannau* were published in the *Glamorgan Gazette* in the early part of this century, the main collectors being John Evans (Oenin), the Heol-y-cyw schoolmaster, and W. M. Rees, Brynmenyn, the Tondu station master.

By to-day, there seems little evidence of the continuing popularity of this type of Welsh poetry in the valley.

(d) Dafydd Nicolas

The two best-known local poets of the eighteenth century were Wil Hopcyn (1700-1741) and Dafydd Nicolas (1704?-1769). Reference to the former has already been made in a separate chapter. The latter was christened at Llangynwyd Church on July 1 1705 and kept a school at Llangynwyd. He ultimately became a family bard or tutor to the Williams family of Aberpergwm. He was a classical scholar and translated part of the *Iliad* into Welsh. Iolo Morganwg stated that he had learnt Latin, Greek and French. Professor G. J. Williams considered him to be the best Glamorgan poet of the eighteenth century before the days of Iolo Morganwg. He was the author of *Y Deryn Pur,* one of the most famous of Welsh folk-songs, and *Ffanni Blodau'r Ffair* (Fanny Blooming Fair), both songs being included in Miss Maria Jane Williams's collection of *Ancient National Airs of Gwent and Morgannwg* (1844). It is remarkable that the authors of two of the best-known Welsh airs should have had such a close connection with Llangynwyd.

Of the eighteenth-century Welsh poets, Lewis Hopkin (1708-1771) of Llandyfodwg should also be mentioned as he was the bardic teacher of Iolo Morganwg. He included in his book, *Y Fêl Gafod,* an account of an eisteddfod held at Cymer-Afan in 1735, attended by Wil Hopcyn.

Iolo Morganwg, in a letter, dated March 1800, to Owain Myfyr, London, stated that he had seen at Llangynwyd a collection of old printed works that were once at Margam Abbey.

(e) Literary Activity in the 19th Century

During the nineteenth century there was much local literary activity, most of which, unfortunately, remains unrecorded. Hundreds of eisteddfodau were held, thus implementing the tradition that competitive meetings of bards had taken place even in the Plantagenet Period (1154-1399) at Llangynwyd. However there was no longer a school of poets, and the old type of oral instruction by tutor to bardic pupils had long ceased. Yet, many local rhymesters remained in the Valley, e.g., *Y Drysorfa Gynulleidfaol* (The Congregational Treasury), August 1849, contains *tribannau* composed by an S. D. M. of Maesteg on the occasion of the marriage of two local people.

On May 26 in 1853 an eisteddfod was held in the long-room of the Old House, Llangynwyd. The vicar (The Rev. R. Pendril Llewelyn) presided. Prizes were awarded for poems on the bells of Llangynwyd Church, the new Welsh Church (Eglwys Dewi Sant) and the club box of *Yr Hen Gymry* (The Ancient Welsh).

At an eisteddfod held at Salem (B) Church, Spelters, in 1856, Thomas Morgan (Llyfnwy) won a prize for a detailed essay (in Welsh) on the industrial development of the Llynfi Valley, which was later published. Also published separately was *Lloffion Llenorol* (Literary Gleanings), being the successful literary compositions at the same eisteddfod.

In the same year, at an eisteddfod at Maesteg, an anonymous poet won a prize for a rather clever *englyn* on *Cysgu'n yr Oedfa* (Sleeping in Church). The literary adjudications of the Rev. Richard Morgan (Rhydderch ap Morgan) at an eisteddfod held at Llangynwyd, Christmas 1862, have survived.

The first eisteddfod under the auspices of Cymrodorion Dyffryn Llyfnwy was held under the presidency of J. T. Jenkins, squire of Gelly, Cymer at Bethania Chapel, Maesteg, on December 5 1864. There were three competitions for essays and five for poetry. A special prize was offered for the best picture of a *bwch gafr* (billy goat)! The following year the same society held another eisteddfod, when Rhydderch ap Morgan was chaired for a *pryddest* (lengthy poem) on 'Cefn Ydfa.'

The Glyncorrwg Eisteddfod of November 23 1868 became notable because the prize for an essay on the history of the Parish of Glyncorrwg was divided between Thomas Morgan (Llyfnwy) and the Rev. David Henry, Penygroes, Carmarthenshire, formerly of Maesteg. The successful compositions, including poetry, were published in 1869 under the title *Gardd Flodau Glyncorrwg* (The Flower Garden of Glyncorrwg) and were printed by Alfred Thomas & Co., Maesteg.

On September 20 1869 a famous local eisteddfod, under the presidency of Dr. W. H. Thomas, Maesteg, was held at Carmel Church, Maesteg. The successful compositions (in Welsh), including an informative essay on the botany of Llangynwyd Parish by Thomas Evans (presumably Cadrawd) and another essay of equal merit by David Bowen (Cynwyd) on the geology of the Llynfi Valley, together with much poetry on local topics and personalities, were published by Llyfnwy in a volume called *Y Berllan* (The Orchard) in 1870. Incidentally, a memorial to Dr. W. H. Thomas, who was held in great esteem locally, was erected at the Square facing the Maesteg Town Hall.

The poetical compositions of an eisteddfod held at Bryntroedgam (Bryn) near Maesteg were published in 1869 under the title *Rhosyn Frwdwyllt* (The Rose of Frwdwyllt).

Much deserved praise has been bestowed upon the National Union of Miners for initiating what they called the first miners' eisteddfod at Porthcawl after the second World War. However, the Maesteg miners have a prior claim to that distinction, as the miners of Oakwood Colliery, Maesteg, held an *Eisteddfod Fawreddog* (A Grand Eisteddfod) locally on May 18 1874. A local poet, S. Wilhelm Hennys (Enis Ddu), won the chair for an exceptional poem (an *awdl*) on *Yr Iawn* (The Atonement) when he was only twenty-three years of age. At another eisteddfod in the same year the author of an elegy to the Rev. D. Howells, Swansea, won the Tir Iarll chair and a medal worth £2.2.0.

The Tir Iarll Eisteddfod and the Mabon Day's Eisteddfod in the last century attracted many competitors of note who were not always pleased with the results. About a century ago, the poet, Dyfed, who later became Archdruid, and Brynfab, a noted Rhondda poet, failed to gain a prize at a Maesteg eisteddfod, whereupon the former composed the following *englyn* to Maesteg: —

> Nid Teg Faes, ond maes y mwg — maes o dips,
>> Maes o dai mewn tewfwg;
>> Diau gweled eu golwg
>> Sobrai drem yr ysbryd drwg.

(Not Fair Field, i.e., Maesteg, but a district of smoke, tips and houses in thick smoke — enough to sober the countenance of the devil himself).

Election songs, mainly in Welsh, generally composed by Cadrawd, contained much satire. Other poets wrote satirical and light verses on religious differences in the valley and on local events and characters. On the death of a local worthy or of a child, a local poet's tribute in verse would be printed, framed and hung at the deceased's home. Cadrawd wrote verses to be sung at a testimonial meeting to Dr. W. H. Thomas, Maesteg, on April 9 1890.

An anthology of poems called *Blodau'r Beirdd* (The Poets' Flowers) was published in 1871, being a collection of local Welsh poems edited by David Griffiths and Glan Afan, printers of Cwmafan and Maesteg, and containing poems by Llynfi Valley poets — Dewi Glan Llyfnwy, Iolo Tir Iarll, Enis Ddu and Thomas Morgan (LLyfnwy). The same editors in 1882 published *Oriel y Beirdd* (The Gallery of Poets), including poems by the Rev. Iorwerth Jones (Iorwerth Ddu), later minister of Bethania, Maesteg, and Iolo Tir Iarll of Nantyffyllon.

(f) Thomas Christopher Evans (Cadrawd), 1846-1918

The outstanding literary figure in the Llynfi Valley in the last century was Cadrawd, of Llangynwyd. It would require a volume on its own to do justice to his extensive activities and output as an antiquarian. In his early days he visited the U.S.A. twice, and worked as a blacksmith at Pittsburgh. It was when he was about forty years of age that he turned from being a blacksmith to being a quarryman. He stated that it was the vicar of Llangynwyd, the Rev. R. Pendril Llewelyn, who first introduced him to history and local lore.

His best known work is his History of the *Parish of Llangynwyd* (1887). He was the author of a book on Iolo Morganwg (*Cyfres y Fil*) and joint editor, with the Rev. Lemuel J. Hopcyn-James, of *Hen Gwndidau a Chywyddau* (Old religious songs and poems).

He won many prizes at the National Eisteddfod , one being at Aberdare in 1885 for an original collection of the folklore of Glamorgan. The collection included 224 *tribannau,* nursery rhymes, examples of weather prophecies, dialects, riddles, beliefs in the supernatural, phantom funerals etc. His first National Eisteddfod prize was for a collection of songs sung by local farmers when ploughing with oxen, and his last was for a collection of Celtic place names in the border Counties, for which he received the Eisteddfod Gold Medal, which is now at the National Museum. He also shared a prize with Jenkin Howell, Aberdare, at the Pontypridd Eisteddfod of 1893 for an essay on *Llên Gwerin Morgannwg* (The Folklore of Glamorgan). At the Llanelli Eisteddfod of 1895 he was awarded a twenty-five guineas prize for biographies of Welsh artists.

He was a regular contributor to the *South Wales Weekly News, Y Ddraig Goch* (The Welsh Dragon), *The Cardiff Times, Cymru* and several other Welsh periodicals. He was editor for fifteen years of *Yr Holiadur Cymreig* (Welsh Notes and Queries) in the monthly periodical, *Cyfaill yr Aelwyd*, and his contributions to that column showed his vast knowledge of Welsh literature and local lore. He was joint author, with Harry Evans, of Welsh nursery-rhymes, as well as joint-author with his son, C. J. Evans, of *Y Wyddor* (The Alphabet). Some of his papers are at The National Library, but most of his vast collection of papers can be seen at the Cardiff Central Library. The ten index cards, each listing several items, indicate the extent of his labours. Among the single items on the index cards are twelve volumes of his notes, letters and cuttings, seven volumes of correspondence, twenty-seven volumes of collections of old Welsh ballads, nine volumes of indexes to Welsh periodicals, and three volumes on the place names of Gwent. Other works not included in the Cardiff collection are an essay on the place-names of the parishes of Llangeinor, Glyncorrwg and Llanfihangel Afan, and other miscellaneous essays. He also collected all sorts of old furniture, and farming implements, many of which were presented to the Welsh Folk Museum at St. Fagan's.

(g) Thomas Morgan (Llyfnwy), 1835-1910

Next to Cadrawd, Llyfnwy was the best-known antiquary in the Llynfi Valley. He was born in the Vale of Glamorgan, but at an early age he moved with his family to Llangynwyd village. With his own large family, he emigrated to America, where he died. A tailor by trade, he was an essayist, poet, antiquarian, musician and eisteddfod conductor, and wrote prize essays, already referred to, on the early industrial development of the valley and on the history of the Parish of Glyncorrwg. As we have seen, he edited *Y Berllan*, 1870, containing much local history. In 1871 he published his *Geiriadur Lleol Plwyf Llangynwyd* (A Topographical Dictionary of the Parish of Llangynwyd) being a prize essay at a Maesteg Eisteddfod held at Christmas 1870, and published the following year. His booklet, *The Cupid*, 1869, contains the traditional story of the Cefn Ydfa romance and also the story of the Maid of Sker.

145 Thomas Morgan (*Llyfnwy*) and his family who emigrated to America. His son, Taliesin, (centre, standing) was for many years editor of a leading New York daily newspaper. Reproduced from a newspaper cutting of 27 December 1946

Llyfnwy also wrote brief histories of Llancarfan, Cynffig, Margam, the Chair of Glamorgan, Edward II in Glamorgan, St. Fagan's, and the castles of St. Donat's, Coety, Dunraven, Aberafan and Aberogwr. He wrote many poems on general and local topics and some appeared in the various anthologies of his day.

(h) 19th Century Valley Welsh Authors

The Rev. Evan Griffiths (1795-1873) was born at Gelli Eblig, near the Pontrhydycyff viaduct, Llangynwyd. After some college training he ministered to two Congregational Churches in Gower for four years until he moved to Swansea to translate into Welsh the *Commentaries of Matthew Henry*. He thereby became a printer and publisher.

He published over forty books, consisting of original works and translations, a biography of the Rev. William Jones, Bridgend, and a Welsh-English dictionary. He edited a book of 1042 hymns and several anthems, which reached its 4th edition, and also a collection of hymns for children and Sunday schools. He was a hymn-writer of note and is best known for his popular hymn: *Yn dy waith y mae fy mywyd.* He lies buried in Bethel Church graveyard, Sketty.

The Rev. Richard Hughes, Bethania, Maesteg, 1820-1885, who assumed the bardic name of Tremrudd, wrote many articles to Welsh religious periodicals such as *Seren Gomer* and *Y Greal* (The Grail). His biographer, the Rev. Dr. John Rowlands, Llanelli, states that he was a substantial poet, having composed many poems in the strict and free metres. Six years before his death he published *Y Pulpud ym Methania* (The Pulpit in Bethania) which includes thirty-one of his sermons.

David Bowen (Cynwyd), 1825-1873, who lived in Maesteg, contributed to several publications on subjects such as *Crefydd ac Offeiraid yr Aifft* (The Religion and Priests of Egypt), in 1845, and *Y Fodrwy Aur* (The Gold Ring) in 1849. Among his essays on local topics was one on the geology of the Llynfi Valley included in *Y Berllan* (1870) previously referred to. He died aged forty-eight and was buried in Llangynwyd.

William Madoc (ap Madoc), 1844-1916, left Maesteg for the U.S.A. He became editor of *Blodau'r Oes* and *Columbia.* He excelled as a writer of librettos for light opera, among them being 'The Maid of Cefn Ydfa' set to music by J. J. Mason, Mus. Doc., Wilkesbarre. Other works included 'Bethlehem,' 'Nazareth' and 'Bethany,' set to music by Dr. W. Rhys Herbert, of Resolfen. He was well-known in Welsh American circles as musician, bard, editor, adjudicator, lecturer, eisteddfod conductor, soloist and organist.

Benjamin Thomas (Alaw Dulais), 1846-1890, was a well-known essayist and at one time lived at Nantyffyllon, where his father-in-law, the Rev. William Rees, was the minister of Siloh Church. He later migrated to America, where he died. He won scores of prizes for essays on a variety of topics, including 'Marriage' (Treherbert Eisteddfod, 1877), science and theology, geology, facts about animals, the pitfalls of vanity, the civilizations of the East, including Babylon, Egypt and India, all of which appeared in *Y Diwygiwr.* In America he wrote many articles in Welsh on current affairs in the British Parliament, and many items for children in *Tywysydd y Plant.* He wrote an elegy to J. T. Jenkins, squire of Gelly, Cymer, who died June 11 1876. The Rev. T. Cynfelin Benjamin of Nanticoke, Pennsylvania, published in the Welsh American paper *Y Drych* an elegy of twenty-one *englynion* in memory of the essayist.

Edward Jones (1850-1914) was born at Garn Road, Maesteg, being the son of Richard Jones, a former secretary of Bethania Church, Maesteg. He intended becoming a Baptist minister but changed course after a visit to the continent. He later became a schoolmaster at Abergwynfi, Dolgellau and further afield, until he contracted arthritis through sleeping in a damp bed. Ultimately he became one of the down-and-outs on the Thames Embankment, where his constant friend was Francis Thompson, the poet. It was he who first discovered the poetic genius of Thompson. Edward Jones himself translated into Welsh the poem composed by Goronwy Owen to Anglesey — called 'In Praise of Mona.' He also translated into Welsh some of Milton's poems and portions of the New Testament direct from Greek. An article on him, written by D. R. Hughes, a well-known London Welshman, appeared in *John O'London's Weekly* many years ago and this was followed by a brief biography in Welsh in *Yma ac Acw* (Here and There) by the same author.

Evan Bevan (1803-1866) was a country poet born in Llangynwyd but who later moved to Ystradfellte. A short biography was written by the Rev. D. Glan-Nedd Williams and a collection of his works was published by William Morgan of Rhigos.

(i) 19th Century Welsh Authors connected with the Llynfi Valley

The Rev. Isaac Cynwyd Evans (1845-1910). who was minister of Bethesda Church, Llangynwyd, from 1876 to 1885, was a local poet of note and many of his poems appear in *Lloffion y Beirdd* (Gleanings of the Poets) collected by the Rev. T. Cunllo Griffiths in 1872. In his early days he won many eisteddfodic prizes for singing, reciting and poetry, and later he won a few bardic chairs. He later became minister of the famous Christian Temple Congregational Church, Ammanford. Amanwy, the Welsh poet and brother to James Griffiths M.P.. wrote a short biography: *Gweinidog fy Ieuenctid* (The Minister of my Youth) in 1945.

The Rev. T. Cunllo Griffiths was a congregational minister at Pontlotyn before coming to Maesteg in the seventies of the last century. He ultimately left for Cardiganshire. He edited *Lloffion y Beirdd* in 1879 and dedicated the volume to Lady Llanover. The anthology included some of his own poems. One of them was on the view from the summit of Pwll-yr-iwrch Mountain overlooking Nantyffyllon, from which he could see the Brecon Beacons and the Black Mountain. He wrote another poem, on 'Cleopatra's Needle', and also *In memoriam* stanzas to David Richards of Travellers' Rest, Nantyffyllon. A further poem describes the overflowing of the Rivers Llynfi and Ogmore in August, 1877. He also wrote an essay on *Glaniad y Ffrancod yn Abergwaun* (The Landing of the French in Fishguard).

S. Wilhelm Hennys (Enis Ddu), 1851-83, lived at Bethania Street, Maesteg, having been born in Cwmafan. At an early age he moved with his parents to Maesteg, which became the scene of all his literary activities. He was dogged by ill health and died. ͺed thirty-two, of tuberculosis, on July 6, 1883. His remains lie buried ͺ. the Cwmafan Parish churchyard.

Elegies to him were composed by Ieuan Dyfed, Robin Ddu Eryri and Gwilym Ffrwdwyllt. His main object in life had been to dedicate himself to the Christian ministry. In *Preswylfeydd y Goruchaf* (1940), published by the Rev. J. Melville Jones on the occasion of the centenary of Tabor Church, Maesteg, we are told that Enis Ddu was a leading member of the Tabor Young People's Society. However, in a volume of *Yr Haul* (a Welsh Anglican periodical, 1873-74, pp.354-6), there is a letter from Enis Ddu to the editor giving his reasons why he was an Anglican. One can only deduce that although he was a churchman, he also belonged to the Tabor young people's Welsh society in the absence of a similar society in his own Anglican Church.

Apart from the poem for which he was awarded the bardic chair at the early age of twenty-three at the Oakwood Miners' Eisteddfod in 1874, his published works were: (1) *Fy Mlaenffrwyth* (My First Fruits), being poems in strict and free metres on moral and religious subjects; (2) *Canonau'r Beirdd*. being a treatise on Welsh metrical rules; and (3) *Golud Gwalia* (The Wealth of Wales), which is a collection of Welsh proverbs. Several of his poems appeared in various anthologies and also in *Yr Haul,* 1873-74. He was also the author of *Y Blwch o Bleser* (The Box of Pleasure) and *Y Fwyalchddu* (The Blackbird). He would certainly have become an outstanding Welsh poet had he not died so early.

The Rev. David Henry (1816-73), known in bardic circles as Myrddin Wyllt, was a native of Carmarthenshire. His youth was spent at Maesteg as a local preacher connected with Soar Welsh Congregational Church. In 1849 he was ordained minister of Nebo Church, Glyncorrwg, and he also ministered at Bryn. In 1859 he left the district to take charge of Penygroes Church, Carmarthenshire. He won many prizes for poetry at various eisteddfodau, one prize being for a poem on the Llynfi Valley at the Salem, Spelters, eisteddfod of 1857. Among his poems is an elegy to the Rev. Henry Davies, Bethania and Llwynteg, near Llanelli, in 1871. His essay on the history of Glyncorrwg has already been referred to. At an eisteddfod in Maesteg in 1859 he won a prize and a silver medal for an essay: *Hanes Cymru o farwolaeth Llywelyn ein Llyw Olaf hyd Briodas Owen Tudur* (The History of Wales from the death of Llywelyn, our last Prince, to the marriage of Owen Tudur). In 1867, at a Carmarthen eisteddfod, he won a silver medal for an essay on *Hanes Enwogion Sir Gaerfyrddin* (The History of famous people of the County of Carmarthen) and in the same year, he was successful at a Treherbert eisteddfod for an essay on the history of Sir Rhys ap Thomas. He also shared a prize at another eisteddfod for an essay on the Town and County of Carmarthen. A short biography of the essayist was published by his son, the Rev. T. M. Henry, whilst another short biography, with details of his literary output are included in a volume called *Llwybrau Llafur* (The Paths of Labour) by the Rev. G. Brynmor Thomas, Penygroes.

The Rev. H. W. Hughes (Arwystl), a former minister of Bethania Church,

Maesteg, wrote *Cofiant Miss Mary David* (The Biography of Miss Mary David) of Siop-y-garreg, Dinas, as well as many articles between 1846 and 1883 for Welsh periodicals such as *Seren Gomer, Y Bedyddiwr, Y Greal,* and *Y Genhinen.*

The Rev. Evan Jones (1840-1903), known throughout Wales as *Gurnos*, was a Baptist minister at Betws, Tir Iarll, from 1882 to 1886. He won many bardic chairs, including two at the National Eisteddfod, one for an *awdl* on *Y Beibl* at Bangor in 1874 and another on *Y Cenhadwr* (The Missionary) at Rhyl in 1892. He was the runner up to Ceulanydd at the Pontypridd National Eisteddfod of 1893. His published works include *Caniadau Gurnos* (The poems of Gurnos) and *Caneuon, Llyfr III* (Cwmafan), 1890. He was buried at Groeswen Cemetery near Caerphilly.

The Rev. Aaron Morgan was minister of Bethania Church, Maesteg, from 1887 to 1892, when he left to take charge of a Baptist Church in Blaenffos, Pembrokeshire. He wrote on various topics in religious periodicals such as *Y Greal* and *Seren Gomer* and published *Salmau'r Ysgol,* being a collection of hymns set to music by W. T. Samuel, Swansea. Under the bardic name of Gwynrudd, he won several bardic chairs and prizes for poetry.

The Rev. Richard Morgan (1833-1882), known as Rhydderch ap Morgan, was a nephew of the Rev. William Morgan, Carmel, Maesteg, and became minister for a short period of Bethesda Church, Llangynwyd, in 1871. He composed a metrical play on the history of Job, which he called a 'chwaraegerdd gysegredig' (a sacred play). Some of his poems appeared in *Gemau Margam* (The Gems of Margam) in 1873, whilst a collection of his prize-winning poems in twelve eisteddfodau appeared in *Blodau Brynawen* (The Flowers of Brynawen)—122 pages in all. Other poems appeared in various anthologies. In 1883 David Evans, Aberdare, published his biography.

The Rev. John Williams (1847-1899) was a native of Ceulan, Talybont, Cardiganshire, hence the explanation why he assumed the bardic name of *Ceulanydd.* On leaving Llangollen Baptist College he became Baptist minister at Denbigh, Amlwch, Talysarn, Merthyr Tydfil and ultimately at Salem, Nantyffyllon, in 1881. He later became minister at Caersalem Church, Caerau, for the last five years of his life.

He won several chairs at provincial eisteddfodau and several prizes for poetry at the National Eisteddfod, in which he was chaired at Pontypridd in 1893 for his *awdl* (ode) to *Pwlpud Cymru* (The Pulpit of Wales). He later became adjudicator in the chief literary events of the Eisteddfod and published a treatise on *Athrylith Ceiriog Hughes* (The Genius of Ceiriog Hughes) and a collection of original hymns, *Mawl i'r Oen* (Praise to the Lamb). His poetry appeared in several Welsh periodicals. He lies buried at the Maesteg Cemetery.

146   Rev John Williams (*Ceulanydd*)

The Rev. T. J. Williams (1818-54) and known as *Myddfai,* lies buried in Llangynwyd churchyard. He died after serving only six months as curate of Eglwys Dewi Sant, Maesteg. He is best known as the author of the biography of John Evans, Llwynffortun. Islwyn, the greatest Monmouthshire poet of his day, sang a profuse and lengthy elegy to him. Cadrawd also wrote an article on him in *Cymru,* whilst James Morris refers to him in his *History of Methodism in Carmarthenshire.*

Among the lesser-known local authors of the nineteenth century, writing in Welsh, were (in alphabetical order): —

Benjamin Benjamin (Bardd Coch), who wrote on local topics and personalities including a poem in praise of Dr. Lewis, Maesteg, the founder of the Porthcawl Rest, October 1863, and a poem on the explosion at the Gin Pit, Maesteg, on December 26 1863. He was born at Llangeinor but later lived at 2, Bowrington Street, Maesteg, being a railway blocklayer by occupation.

John Bevan, who was born in Spelters, Caerau, and who was a member of Siloh Church, Nantyffyllon, became Congregational minister at Llangadog and Llansadwrn and wrote extensively to Welsh periodicals in the latter half of the last century. He wrote a series of ten articles to *Cyfaill yr Aelwyd* on the relationship between numbers up to ten and biblical events.

Ieuan Tir Iarll, author of several poems on local events, including an elegy to a William Isaac, who was killed in an explosion at the Llynvi Iron Works, Maesteg *(Y Diwygiwr,* January 1865).

J. T. Jones, Maesteg, was a writer of elegies, one of them commemorating the death of 15 miners in the Gin Pit explosion of 1863, and another on the death, by accident, of eleven miners and six pit ponies at Oakwood Colliery, Maesteg, on January 11, 1872.

Morgan Llewelyn of Blaencuneirion Farm, near Bryn, was known as the composer of *tribannau* and author of homely poems on local topics.

Myfyr Cynffig, who was born in the Parish of Llangynwyd on September 10, 1845, wrote a few published poems, some of which appeared in *Dail y Dolydd* (Meadow Leaves) edited by T. Tawenog Yorath, Porth.

John Price (Ioan Awst) was a popular local poet whose uncollected poems appeared in various periodicals. Further research could be worth while.

William Rees of Bryn, known as *Brynfab,* was the leading eisteddfodic and literary figure of the village, and composed several Welsh essays and poems which, unfortunately, remain uncollected.

Joseph Roderick (Iolo Tir Iarll) of Nantyffyllon, was a local poet of more than average ability, and could write commendable *englynion* showing that he had mastered the intricate measures of traditional Welsh poetry. As we have seen, some of his work appeared in several anthologies.

Morgan Thomas (Corsen Ysig), who died a young man in 1856, was bed-ridden for the last seventeen years of his life. His poem *Dynesiad Haf, neu Deimladau y Prydydd yn Ngwyneb ei Anallu i'w Fwynhau* (The approach of Summer, or the Poet's feelings owing to his inability to enjoy it) contains sincere pathos and merit. Shortly before he died he wrote an elegy to Mrs Hampton, the wife of a Llynvi Iron Works official. He also wrote articles to religious periodicals and was a member of Carmel Church, Maesteg.

William Watkins, of whom little is known except that he wrote *Hanes Merched Tŷ Talwyn* (The History of the Ladies of Tŷ Talwyn), Llangynwyd, which appeared in *Y Cymmrodor,* 1881.

David Williams (Dewi Glan Llyfnwy) appeared to be a popular local poet, but his works remain uncollected. An excerpt from his *pryddest* (lengthy poem) on Cefn Ydfa, 1869, appeared in the *Wil Hopcyn Souvenir Booklet,* 1927. Several of his poems appeared in various anthologies of local poetry.

Richard Williams of Llangrallo (Coychurch), published in 1874 a collection of poems mainly on religious themes called *Bartimeus ar Fôr Tiberias a Glenydd Ogwy,* which included the works of some Tir Iarll poets.

(j) Nineteenth Century Authors writing in English connected with the Valley

Sir John Bowring (1792-1872) was at one time owner of the Llynvi Iron Works at Maesteg. Apart from his status as an industrialist and a politician, he was a man of great culture and a famous linguist. He translated into English the works of Russian, Spanish, Polish, Magyar, Serbian, Danish, Hungarian and German poets. A privately-printed memoir lists upwards of thirty languages and dialects from which he had published translations. He learned French from a refugee priest and Italian from an itinerant vendor of barometers and musical instruments. Through the help of mercantile friends, he learnt many foreign languages. He was awarded an honorary Ll.D. by Gottingen University. His friends, including George Borrow and Tom Hood, referred to him as 'a man of many tongues.' A catalogue at the British Museum lists his translations of songs, hymns, original poems and other works, which are contained in fifty volumes. His fame as a hymn-writer was assured by his becoming the author of the famous hymn:

> In the Cross of Christ I glory,
>   Towering o'er the wrecks of time.

Among his published works were: (1) Specimens of the Russian Poets (1821-23) (2) A Batavian Anthology (1824) (3) Ancient Poetry and Romances of Spain (1824) (4) Specimens of Polish Poets (1827) (5) Servian Popular Poetry (1827) and (6) Poetry of the Magyars (1830).

James Motley was a director of the Maesteg (Old) Iron Works. In 1848 he published his *Tales of the Cymry,* a volume of blank verse with extensive explanatory notes. The tales are: (1) *Cwn Annwn;* (2) *The Torrent Spectre;* (3) *The Canwyll Corph;* (4) *The Ceffyl-y-dwfr;* (5) *The Legend of Cefn Castell,* and (6) *Arthurstone.* The poems refer to our druidical and mystical past and contain local references, e.g., to Tor Curig (Torcerrig), which he describes as a hill of stones, being 'a high mountain overhanging the vale of the Llynvi, immediately above the Maesteg and Llynvi Iron-Works upon the summit of which are the remains of an ancient encampment.'

According to Mr. Martin Phillips, the Port Talbot antiquarian, Motley left Maesteg for Borneo, where he was killed by the natives. It is thought that possibly the murdered man was the author's brother, Thomas Motley, who was also connected with the Maesteg Iron Works.

Mrs. Pendril Llewelyn (1811-74) was the wife of the Vicar of Llangynwyd. She gained fame as a translator of poems and hymns from Welsh into English and also as a preserver of the folklore and traditions of the district. Professor G. J. Williams claimed in *Y Llenor* (1927-28) that she was the originator of the story connecting Wil Hopcyn with the Maid of Cefn Ydfa. H. J. Randall, in his *History of Bridgend,* stated that Professor Williams had informed him that the Maid was made the heroine of the story, described as 'recently and deliberately manufactured.' We are still awaiting factual evidence, and not mere assumptions, to justify the accusation that a lady of such high repute had faked the story.

Mrs. Llewelyn's translation of *Y Gwenith Gwyn* appeared in *The Cupid* (Llyfnwy) in 1869, whilst translations of other poems appeared in *The Cambrian, The Merthyr Guardian, The Church of England Magazine* (1849-1858) and the *Archaeologia Cambrensis*. In 1857 she published her translations into English of some of the best known hymns of the Rev. William Williams, Pantycelyn. Thomas Stephens, the eminent scholar of Merthyr, in his *Literature of the Kymry,* p.47, refers to her 'faithful' translation of Hywel ab Owain Gwynedd, and to her translation of *Mabinogi Taliesin* as an 'elegant translation from the able pen of Mrs. Llewelyn' (p.173).

Rhys Dafydd Morgan (Ap Lleurwg), 1850-1933, was a pharmaceutical chemist at Maesteg for many years. He became known nationally as the translator of Welsh poems and hymns into English. Several translations were awarded first place at the National Eisteddfod by our best known adjudicators, including Sir John Morris-Jones, in the latter half of the last century. He translated into English the works of Hwfa Môn, the former Archdruid, who thanked him by letter, and famous Welsh poets such as Hiraethog, Ceiriog, Mynyddog, and Elfed, and was awarded a silver medal at Caernarfon in 1880. Various Anglo-Welsh periodicals, such as *The Red Dragon* (Vol. 1, 1882) published his translated poems. He wrote an effective satirical poem on *A Common Prayer Book for the Corph* (i.e., the Calvinistic Methodists) and published in the *Glamorgan Advertiser* in the twenties of this century his reminiscences of Maesteg, and an extensive essay on Llangynwyd, based on the works of David Jones (Wallington), John Howells (St. Athan's) and Cadrawd.

William Glover (1858-1920) was a native of Ossett, Yorkshire, and spent forty years as headmaster, mainly in Maesteg. He first took charge of the Llynvi Iron Works School in 1879. After nine years he left for school appointments in Yorkshire and Suffolk, returning to Maesteg in 1890 to become headmaster of the Higher Standards School. He later became headmaster of Plasnewydd School, Maesteg, until his death. The following are among his published works: (1) *Know your own Mind;* (2) *Hygiene and Temperance for Schools, old and new;* (3) *First Lesson in Coal Mining (1906);* (4) *Six Booklets on Welsh History;* (5) *A Little Book on the Cardinal Virtues, including the Good Citizen and Patriotism,* with an introduction by Philip B. Ballard; (6) *A European History;* and (7) *A Modern History.*

The Twentieth Century

(k) Deceased Welsh Writers

Lewis Davies (1863-1951) of Cymer. We can justify his inclusion, as Cymer was once part of the Parish of Llangynwyd, and as he was invariably involved in all Welsh movements in the Llynfi Valley. He was a schoolmaster, poet, lecturer, antiquarian, novelist (for adults and children), journalist, musician (composer of the well-known hymn-tune *Cymer*), an orchestra-pipe-band and choir conductor and chapel secretary and precentor, besides being a Justice of the Peace and a former chairman of the Glyncorrwg U.D.C. He won nearly thirty prizes at the National Eisteddfod for novels (historical and otherwise), short stories, literature for children, historical essays and a valuable collection of *tribannau*. All these are listed (in a chapter on his life and works) in *Hamddena* (1972) published by the author of these notes. They are also listed in a list of books, and articles written by authors connected with the Llynfi Valley.

The Rev. T. W. Llynfi Davies M.A., B.D., was born at Plasnewydd, Maesteg, and became a Congregational minister at Barham (Beaufort) for six years and at St. Thomas, Swansea, for twenty-eight years. For thirteen years he was lecturer in Hebrew, Greek and Church History at the Swansea Bible College. His M.A. thesis on *The Bardic Order in the sixteenth century* was presented after his death (in 1937) to the Maesteg Public Library in 1965. Many of his poems appeared in Welsh periodicals, whilst several gained prizes at the National Eisteddfod. He narrowly missed winning the Eisteddfod Crown on three occasions. His book, *Bili,* consisting of short stories, provides an insight into Welsh cultural and eisteddfodic life at the turn of the century. He also wrote the libretto for Dr. Haydn Morris's opera, *Y Ferch o Gefn Ydfa.* Among his publications were: (1) *Pauline Readjustments (1927);* (2) *St. Paul's Voyage to Rome;* (3) *Jesus and Society (a volume of sermons);* (4) *Studies in the Gospels of St. Mark and St. Luke;* (5) *A translation into Welsh of Professor Baird's* Acts of the Apostles; and (6) *Outlines of Welsh History* — and many articles on religious and literary topics in various Welsh periodicals. He was buried at Llangynwyd.

George Evans (Awenydd Tysul), who died aged fifty-six in 1948, was a native of Llandysul, but spent most of his life as a pharmaceutical chemist at Nantyffyllon. Composing lyrical poems in Welsh was his main hobby, enabling him to win some 400 prizes for lyrics at local and provincial eisteddfodau and sixteen bardic chairs — three times in succession at the Treorci Chair Eisteddfod. His works remain uncollected.

John Elias Hughes (1852-1925) was a native of Bala, North Wales, and was known by the bardic name of *Llwch Arian.* He lived for a considerable period in Tir Iarll and was at one time a colliery manager at Llety Brongu,

Llangynwyd, spending the remainder of his life at Abergwynfi. He composed a great deal of Welsh poetry, including *pryddestau* (lengthy poems), recitation pieces and sacred dramas. His drama (in four acts) called *Y Meddyg Llwyddianus* received much commendation. He was buried at Cymer Cemetery.

William John (1874-1947), a mining engineer, was born in Tondu and moved with his parents to Cefn Cribwr when he was two years of age. In 1912 he moved to Cymer, where he died. He lectured extensively on geology and mining, but was better known as a student of Druid lore, about which he published many articles, particularly in the *Glamorgan Gazette* and the *Glamorgan Advertiser*. He possessed a collection of rare Welsh literary and historical books and papers. He wrote three books of historical notes on Cefn Cribwr. One in Welsh is at the National Library of Wales. An article by the Rev. Gomer M. Roberts on *Llawysgrif William Siôn o Gefn Cribwr* appeared in *Y Genhinen,* Vol. XVI, Winter, 1965-66.

The Rev. T. Esger James, who was minister of Saron Church, Nantyffyllon, from 1896 to 1910, was the author of the biography of the Rev. William Jones, Pentretygwyn, Llanymddyfri, 1897, and of a published sermon *Duw ac Aderyn y To* (God and the Sparrow), 1908, in the *Pulpud Cymru* series. His other works include *Diana yr Oes Hon* (Diana of this Age), *Nodion Dirwestol* (Temperance Notes), *Oriau gyda'r Sêr* (Hours with the Stars) and *Oriau gyda'r Blodau* (Hours with the Flowers). He was also the Welsh editor in 1909-10 of the *Llynfi Valley Messenger,* a monthly magazine of the local Nonconformist Churches, and wrote other Welsh poems which remain uncollected.

David Jones was a native of Caerau, but spent the greater part of his life in Beckenham, Kent. Much information about the literary, religious and eisteddfodic life of the Llynfi Valley in the latter half of the century can be gleaned from his bilingual book of poems, *Fragments gathered at the Wayside,* 1925. He was adept at translating well-known Welsh hymns into English and English hymns into Welsh.

The Rev. D. Rhufon Jones, minister of Hebron Congregational Church for many years, mastered the intricacies of the Welsh metrical rules known as the *cynganeddion.* He won many prizes at various eisteddfodau, particularly for *englynion,* many of which were published in the local and denominational press.

The Rev. Iorwerth Jones (Iorwerth Ddu), who died in 1931 aged seventy-nine, was minister of Bethania Baptist Church, Maesteg, for over thirty years from 1894. His publications include (1) *Yr Epistolau at y Thesaloniaid* (The Epistles to the Thessalonians), 1910, a volume of 168 pages; (2) *Bedydd a Maddeuant* (Baptism and Forgiveness), being a series of sermons on Baptism; (3) *Gweddi Fawr yr Iesu a Phregethau Eraill* (The great Prayer of Jesus and other Sermons), 1894, consisting of 224 pages with laudatory comments by leading theologians of the day; and (4) *Yr Eglwys a'r Oes* (The Church and the Age), being his presidential address to the Baptist Union of Wales, 1926. He wrote scores of articles on religious themes to *Y Greal* and *Seren Cymru*. Some of his poems were included in *Oriel y Beirdd* (The Gallery of Poets), 1882, an anthology of the works of twenty Welsh poets. However his early promise as a poet did not materialise.

The Rev. W. Glasnant Jones, a native of Glanaman, was minister of Siloh Church, Nantyffyllon, from 1901 to 1906. He became known as a popular lecturer on Welsh topics and characters, and was a regular contributor to Welsh literary and religious periodicals. Although he shared a prize for a ballad at the Swansea National Eisteddfod in 1926 his literary strength lay in his entertaining style as a prose writer. In 1902 he wrote two arresting articles on *Y Llwyni ar Dân* (Maesteg Afire) giving a vivid account of the old religious characters of Nantyffyllon in the middle of the last century. His autobiography, *Cyn Cof Gennyf ac Wedyn* (Prior to Memory and Thereafter) contains interesting references to life in the Maesteg Valley at the beginning of the century.

The Rev. W. R. Pelidros Jones was minister of Noddfa Baptist Church, Caerau, from 1918 to 1924. His published works include the humorous volume on Isaac Lewis (1908), two volumes of poetry, *Cerddi Ieuenctid* (Poems of Youth), 1902 and *Tannau'r Wawr* (The Chords of Dawn), 1937. He was also the author of *Dilyn Llwybrau'r Iesu* (In the Steps of Jesus) and *Yr Ail Enedigaeth* (The Second Birth) in *Seren Gomer, 1922.*

John D. Miller was born in Maesteg and continued to live in the valley until his death, aged eighty-one, in 1979. He was headmaster of Nantyffyllon Boys' School for many years. His two published novels were *Bethel* and *Crysau Gwynion* (White Shirts) , both based on life in the Llynfi Valley. He could claim a record number of successes at the National Eisteddfod from 1931 onwards, especially for drama writing. Many of his dramas were published and performed — and produced by himself. He also produced many plays at the Maesteg Town Hall and further afield, and acted as adjudicator in and outside Maesteg on innumerable occasions. In addition he prepared many scripts, mainly in Welsh, for radio and T.V., one of them being a series for Welsh learners called *Carreg Filltir.*

T. Oswald Phillips, a native of Aberdare, succeeded Dr. Thomas Richards as Welsh master at the Maesteg Secondary School in 1926. He later taught at Gowerton County School and thereafter became deputy Director of Education for Cardiff. Many of his poems appeared in Welsh periodicals and in the *Western Mail* but they remain uncollected. He was the author of a very scholarly treatise on the poetical works of Meurug Dafydd, the Llanishen poet who flourished about 1580-93, and of Llywelyn Siôn, the professional copyist of Llangewydd.

Dr. Thomas Richards taught Welsh, Latin and History at the Maesteg Secondary School from 1912 to 1926, thereafter becoming the renowned Librarian of Bangor University. His literary output is truly staggering. On the centenary of his birth, March 15 1978, Derwyn Jones, of the Bangor University Library and Gwilym B. Owen (Dr. Richards's son-in-law) published a volume, *Rhwng y Silffoedd* (Between the Shelves), being a symposium of tributes to him, with an introduction by Sir Thomas Parry. The details given of his literary output indicate that he was one of the most dedicated authors of the century in Wales. Many of his profound and detailed volumes deal with the Puritan Movement in Wales, on which he was the recognised authority. The six best-known works on this subject were written by him when he lived at Maesteg. He wrote hundreds of authoritative articles to Welsh and English periodicals, and was the author of at least seventy short biographies of famous Welshmen up to 1940, in the *Bywgraffiadur Cymreig* (Dictionary of Welsh Biography) and its English counterpart. In his second volume of reminiscences, *Rhagor o Atgofion Cardi,* 1963, there is a highly entertaining chapter of forty pages on his stay at Maesteg, with another chapter, in the same vein, on the Rev. Robert Allen of Maesteg, one of the most original of Welsh preachers. In 1924, whilst at Maesteg, he received the degree of D. Litt. from the University of Wales, and in 1959 the honorary degree of Ll.D. In 1957 he became President of the Baptist Union of Wales, and a year later, received the rare honour of the Gold Medal of the Honourable Society of Cymmrodorion. He died June 24 1962 and was buried at Bangor public cemetery. Sir Thomas Parry gave a public lecture at Bangor on the occasion of the centenary of Dr. Richards's birth.

William M. Rees of Brynmenyn was formerly station-master at Tondu and an authority on the folk-lore of the district and of the Vale of Glamorgan. He contributed often to the Welsh column of the *Glamorgan Gazette* in the first half of this century. In 1931 he wrote a booklet, *O Frynllywarch i Frynmenyn* to prove that Betharan Church, of which he was secretary, had its origin in the Nonconformist Church founded by the Rev. Samuel Jones as a consequence of the passing of the Act of Uniformity in 1662.

The Rev. W. Rhys Watkin M.A. was a native of Clydach, Swansea Valley and minister of Tabernacle Welsh Baptist Church, Maesteg, from 1900 to 1910. He took an active part in the religious, literary and Welsh life of the valley and was tutor to a Welsh class arranged by the County Council in 1903. He was a frequent contributor to *Seren Gomer* and other periodicals and served as editor of that journal for many years. He was looked upon as a sound historian, particularly in matters relating to the Baptist cause. It was during his ministry at Maesteg that he graduated and gained his M.A. degree. An Obituary Appreciation (*Coffâd*) by Dr. Thomas Richards appeared in *Trafodaethau Cymdeithas Hanes Bedyddwyr Cymru* (The Transactions of the Welsh Baptist Historical Society), 1945-47, pp.67-89.

The Rev. E. Llwyd Williams (1906-1960) was a native of Efail Wen, North Pembrokeshire, and was minister of Tabernacle Church, Maesteg, from 1931 to 1936, after which he moved to Ammanford. He wrote a great deal about his native district in his volumes, *Hen Ddwylo* (Old Hands) and *Hanes Eglwys Rhydwilym* (The History of Rhydwilym Baptist Church), and was the author of *Cofiant Thomas Phillips,* the biography of Principal Phillips, also a native of Efail Wen, and former famous minister of Bloomsbury Baptist Church, London. His two volumes, *Crwydro Penfro* (Wanderings through Pembrokeshire) won much praise. With Waldo Williams, the famous Welsh poet, he wrote a book of Welsh poems for children, and won the National Eisteddfod Chair at Rhyl in 1953, and the Eisteddfod Crown in Ystradgynlais in 1954. He would have been Archdruid of Wales had it not been for his sudden death at a comparatively early age.

Other Welsh writers who deserve inclusion in a list of local authors are: —

The Rev. George Evans B.A., B.D., minister of Canaan Welsh Congregational Church, Maesteg, who was the editor of the booklet on the history of Congregationalism in the valley, published on the occasion of the visit of the Union of Welsh Independents to Maesteg in 1947. He had previously won a prize at the Aberafan National Eisteddfod in 1932 for a translation of a drama into Welsh, and wrote several articles to various religious periodicals.

The Rev. W. Cynon Evans of Blaencwm, Rhondda, was a member of Bethania Church when he decided to enter the Baptist ministry. He wrote many articles to journals such as *Y Greal* and *Seren Gomer* in the early part of this century and was a popular lecturer and an accomplished musician. His essay on *Cerddorion Bedyddiedig Cymru* (Welsh Baptist Musicians) was published in the transactions of the Baptist Historical Society of Wales, 1907-08. He refers therein to the three Maesteg brothers, Isaac Howells (*Perdonydd y Dyffryn*), John Howells and the Rev. Stephen Howells, then of Gilwern.

John Jenkins (Melinfab) of Garth, Maesteg who was a local poet of more than average ability, emigrated to Toronto, Canada. Unfortunately, his poems, including well-phrased *englynion*, remain uncollected, many of them having appeared in the *Glamorgan Advertiser.*

Thomas Jeremiah was also a native of Garth and wrote many uncollected poems on Welsh topics and local personalities that had appeared in the local press. He was an adept *englynwr*, and his *englyn* to the Rev. Robert Allen was much quoted.

The Rev. Edward Jones was minister of Tabernacle Church, Maesteg, in the latter half of the last century and was a frequent contributor to Welsh periodicals such as *Seren Gomer* and an active literary figure in the life of the valley.

G. Elfed Jones, who was a native of Forestfach, Swansea, was a Science master for many years at the Maesteg Grammar School. His unpublished *Lloffion y Llwyni* (Gleanings of Maesteg) is a collection of poems and nursery rhymes, heard at Aelwyd y Llwyni, Maesteg, in February, March and April, 1943. He was a keen collector of local lore.

The Rev. D. Brinley Pugh, a native of Blaengarw and a former minister of Soar Church, Maesteg, was the author of the volume *Triawd yr Ynys* (The Trio of the Island), 1954, being brief biographies of three missionaries in Madagascar — William Evans, D. O. Jones and J. T. Jones.

Thomas Rees (Ap Wengar) was a native of Nantyffyllon where he lived almost the whole of his life as a boot repairer. His poems on local topics and personalities remain unpublished and indicate that he could be more than a mere rhymester; he could also write in the traditional strict metres.

Nansi Roberts was a native of Brithdir, Meirionethshire, and was the first head-teacher of the Llynfi Valley Welsh School. She wrote extensively, mainly on religious subjects for young Welsh children, such as *Dyddiau Nasareth* (The Days of Nasareth) and *Y Grisiau* (The Steps). She was a regular contributor to Welsh periodicals.

The Rev. W. D. Roberts, a native of Bryncrug, North Wales, was minister of Saron Church, Nantyffyllon, for many years from 1926. He published two books of Welsh recitations for children — *Llyfr Adrodd i Blant* (1952) and *Ail Lyfr Adrodd* (1956).

David Thomas, formerly of Nolton Stores, Maesteg, wrote on Maesteg's *Evolution from Farming to Collieries (Glamorgan Advertiser,* September 20 1946) and also on the industries of Maesteg, included in a booklet published when the Union of Welsh Independents visited Maesteg in 1947. He also wrote on the religious and literary aspects of the valley, and addressed the Maesteg Rotary Club on these topics.

The Rev. Philip R. Thomas, a native of St. Clears, was curate of St. Peter's Church, Nantyffyllon (1927-35) during the depression period of the thirties. Although known for his care of the poor, he is remembered also as the author of a volume *Gwas yr Arglwydd* (The Servant of the Lord and Other Essays), 1924.

William Thomas, Caerau, was a native of Ystradgynlais and the author of scores of very homely poems. He excelled as a writer of *tribannau* and composed many elegies to departed friends. He was a deacon of Seion Congregational Church and an uncle to Mel Thomas, himself a man of culture and a former prominent N.U.M. official.

The Llynfi Valley was the home of at least twenty locally-known Welsh minor poets and rhymesters in the last and present century, but owing to limitations of space, they cannot be named.

William Evans, Cadrawd's brother, could recite from memory the Welsh metrical version of the Psalms by the Archdeacon Edmund Prys and scores of Welsh verses from *Canwyll y Cymry* by the famous Vicar (1579-1644) castigating the Welsh for their sinfulness. D. Arfor Williams, Nantyffyllon, a friend of the writer of these notes, was a local poet of distinct promise. He was dogged by ill-health and died in his twenties. His early poems, including one to the four seasons, remain uncollected. Sam Davies of Pontrhydyfen was a popular local rhymester, and possessed a valuable collection of *caneuon gwerin* (folk-songs), some of them relating to the Llynfi Valley.

(l) Deceased Local Authors of the 20th Century, writing in English

Before giving a few details of these authors, we recall that Vernon Watkins, close friend of Dylan Thomas and himself a major poet was born in Maesteg, the son of a Lloyds Bank clerk. His first volume of collected poems (1941) included his 'Ballad of the Mari Lwyd.' He won the Guinness Poetry Award of £300 out of 3,000 competitors for the three best poems in English published in Great Britain and Ireland during the year ended June 30, 1957. The honorary degree of D. Litt. was conferred upon him by the University of Wales. He died in America in October 1967 when he was a visiting English Professor at the University of Washington, Seattle.

Although the Rev. T. Maerdy Rees, Neath (one of three brothers who entered the Christian ministry) did not actually reside in the Llynfi Valley, his father was born in Grove Street, Nantyffyllon. He wrote five plays, three in Welsh and two in English, and was the author of several poems in both languages. His literary output included Welsh short stories, a Welsh novel, *Morris Owen,* bilingual articles to periodicals and two books — *Hiwmor y Cymro* (The Humour of the Welshman) and *Hanes y Crynwyr yng Nghymru* (The History of the Quakers in Wales). His volume *Notable Welshmen, 1700-1900,* contained much interesting information. He was the great uncle of Dr. Jill Evans, Caerau.

Hereunder are brief details of authors (in alphabetical order) who were either natives of the valley or connected therewith by a term of residence, however brief: —

Philip Boswood Ballard was a native of Maesteg and once lived at Llwydarth Road. He ultimately became Chief Inspector of Schools for the Greater London Authority and was an acknowledged authority on the art of teaching. Among his published works are: (1) *Teaching the Essentials of Arithmetic;* (2) *The New Examiner;* (3) *Mental Tests;* (4) *Group Tests of Intelligence;* (5) *Fundamental Arithmetic—Pupils' Book, 1-7;* (6) *Teachers' Book with Answers and Teachers' Notes, 1-5;* (7) *Thoughts and Language* (University of London Press), *1934;* (8) *Handwork as an Educational Medium;* (9) *Obliviscence and Reminiscence (for which he was awarded a D. Litt. and the Carpenter Gold Medal);* (10) *Teaching the Mother Tongue;* and (11) *The Changing School,* being a public lecture, then called 'Schools Old and New', delivered at the Maesteg Town Hall on June 15 1928. He was proud of his association with the Llynfi Valley and there are local references in his well known books, *Things I Cannot Forget* and *Some Schoolmasters I Have Known.* He also excelled as a public lecturer.

David Davies was known locally as 'the historian', and although born in Aberafan, he spent the major part of his life in the Llynfi Valley. His book, *Tŷ'r Llwyni* (1961) contains historical notes on the town of Maesteg. He wrote innumerable articles on local history to the *Glamorgan Gazette* and the *Glamorgan Advertiser,* dealing with the old tenements, including the Old House and the Corner House of Llangynwyd, the public houses of the valley, the iron, tinplate and coal industries. He was joint author, with David Thomas (the former headmaster of Garth School), of the history of Eglwys Dewi Sant, Maesteg, whilst his general survey of Maesteg in the Maesteg Coronation brochure of 1958 contained much useful information. Despite his initial educational disadvantages, he contributed much to our knowledge of the past.

The Rev. D. R. Davies was born in 1889 in Pontycymer. When he was eight years of age the family moved to Clydach, near Swansea, and after living there for three or four years, they finally settled down at 7, Station Terrace, Nantyffyllon. His father, Richard Davies, was the cultured precentor of Soar Church, Maesteg. During his formative years in the Llynfi Valley, D. R. Davies became a rebel against social conditions. Ultimately he became a Congregational minister, and whilst at Southport, he contested the Southport Division as an I.L.P. parliamentary candidate. In 1941 he was ordained deacon in the Anglican Church and wrote weekly articles to *The Record.* He held various livings as Vicar on the south-east coast of England, including Brighton and St. Leonards-on-sea, and finally South Downs in West Sussex. He often preached in St. Paul's Cathedral and Westminster Abbey.

D. R. Davies's two sisters, Maggie and Annie, were the singers who accompanied Evan Roberts the Revivalist, during his Revival campaigns of 1904-1905. His autobiography, *In Search of Myself* (1961), contains an account of his life at Maesteg (pp.34-58) and gives his reasons why, as a former rebel, he had become an orthodox Christian. Some assertions in this volume are open to question.

The author's other published works include (1) *On to Orthodoxy* (1939);

(2) *The Two Humanities* (1940), being 'an attempt at Christian interpretation of History in the light of the War'; (3) *Secular Illusion or Christian
Realism* (1943); (4) *Down, Peacock's Feathers,* a book about general
confession; (5) *Divine Judgment in Human History;* and (6) *The Record,*
being a volume of sermons preached at Holy Trinity Church, Brighton.

The Rev. William Edwards M.A., who was minister of Hermon Church,
Caerau, for forty to fifty years, was editor of the souvenir booklet published
in 1927 on the romance of Cefn Ydfa. He wrote articles on literary, religious
and historical subjects such as Iolo Morganwg (*Yr Ymofynydd,* 1927) etc.,
and translated into Welsh *Angels Unaware,* a play by Enoch H. Rees. As a
sub-editor of the *Glamorgan Advertiser* he wrote hundreds of humorous and
satirical articles on various topics to that local weekly paper, under the nom-
de-plume of *Sam the Haulier.* The Welsh column of that paper was edited
by him for many years, his bardic name being Llenor y Llwyni. His poems
included several translations from Welsh into English and remain
uncollected. He succeeded A. J. Lloyd as editor of the *Glamorgan
Advertiser* in 1931. His death at the age of eighty occurred in February
1964, and his remains are buried at Llantwit Major Cemetery.

Christopher John Evans was Cadrawd's eldest son, who died, aged seventy,
in March 1948. He was a head-teacher at Barry until his retirement in 1942.
He was the winner of numerous prizes for literary and historical essays at the
National Eisteddfod and was a lecturer and broadcaster on subjects such as
Castles of Wales and Welsh folklore. He was contributor and book reviewer
to the *Western Mail* and his articles appeared in *The Cambrian, The
Guardian* and *The Archaeologia Cambrensis.* Some of his historical works
were published in the County Series of the Cambridge University Press. At
the Mountain Ash National Eisteddfod of 1905, he was highly praised for his
essay on 'The Story of Glamorgan,' consisting of 316 pages, including 92
plans and pictures. Sir Marchant Williams, the adjudicator, said the essay
was worth three times the prize offered. In 1908 he published his *Place
Names of Glamorgan,* an appendix to the prize essay of 1905. He was also
the author of *The Story of Caernarvonshire* (1910), *The Story of Brecon*
(1912) and *A List of Monmouthshire Place Names* (1924).

Frederic Evans was Cadrawd's youngest son, who died, aged 69, at his
Sussex home on February 24 1958 and was buried at Llangynwyd
Churchyard. When a qualified teacher at Oakwood School, Maesteg, he
volunteered for service in the first World War, and thereafter studied at
Cambridge, where he graduated with 1st class honours in the Geography
Tripos. After a short period as schools inspector in Glamorgan, he became
director of education at Erith, Kent.

   As far back as 1910 he won a chair and a monetary prize out of thirty
competitors at the Tir Iarll Eisteddfod for a Welsh essay on *Datblygiad
Cymeriad* (The Development of Character). He also prepared a map of

147   Frederic and Llewellyn Evans pictured during the 1939-45 War

Wales showing the birth places of famous Welshmen. At the age of twenty-two he published his volume, *Tir Iarll*, in 1912, which contained much information regarding the history of the Llynfi Valley. He was joint author (with Rhys Evans) of a Welsh drama based on Croes Efa (The Cross of Eve) and also joint author (with Dr. Emrys Jones) of a drama on the Cefn Ydfa romance. Several of his articles appeared in the *Western Mail*, the *Glamorgan County Magazine*, and the Maesteg U.D.C.'s brochure of the Festival of Wales, 1958.

In 1943 he assumed the name of Michael Gareth Llewelyn as author, and his five novels published between 1943 and 1949 were: (1) *Sand in the Glass*, his autobiography; (2) *Aleppo Merchant*, retailing his experience as a pupil teacher, college student and qualified assistant; (3) *White Wheat* relating to the romance of Cefn Ydfa; (4) *Angharad's Isle* describing the Maesteg Valley during the wars of Napoleon — the last two novels having been translated into German; and (5) *To Fame Unknown*. In addition he published *Holiday Adventure for Children of all Ages*.

Llewelyn Evans was Cadrawd's third son, who died, aged eighty-six, in 1974, the last of Cadrawd's seven children. He was on the staff of Pentre (Rhondda) School up to the time of his retirement. His literary output consisted mainly of about twenty articles in the *Western Mail* on topics such as old Welsh customs, the seven wonders of Glamorgan, the dialects of the district, Llangynwyd Churchyard, ploughmen's songs, weather prophecies, Mari Lwyd, superstitions, Dafydd Nicolas (author of *Y Deryn Pur*), and Wil

Hopcyn's poetry. In addition, he wrote an article on his grandfather, Thomas Evan, the parish clerk, and a guide to Llangynwyd Church. In his later years he became secretary of the Old People's Welfare Committee of the Council of Social Services, and in that capacity wrote about forty articles on the problems of old people.

It may be added that Miss Celia Evans, the youngest of Cadrawd's children, was of literary bent, and wrote an occasional English poem such as *Plygain*, as well as articles on the Welsh-South African connection during her stay as teacher in Johannesburg.

The Rev. John Griffiths was curate of Llangynwyd from 1907 to 1914, having previously served as curate of Llangeinor (1903-07). He ultimately became Vicar of Llangwm, Monmouthshire, from 1922 to 1934, and died at his home in Bridgend on March 10 1942. His publications included (1) *The Astronomical and Archaeological Value of the Welsh Gorsedd* (reprinted from *Nature,* May 2 1907; (2) *Edward II in Glamorgan* (1904); (3) *Encilion: Nodiadau Hynafiaethol am Went a Morganwg* (Retreats: Antiquarian Notes re Gwent and Glamorgan), 1905; (4) *The Gorsedd of Britain Archaeologically Considered* (reprinted from the *South Wales Daily* News, 1906); (5) *The Kingdom of Llan,* the Llan Pageant play as performed at the annual reunion of the parishioners of Llangynwyd — 54 pages and printed by James James, Maesteg, in 1913; (6) *The Orientation of the Churches:* a lecture to the Sidmouth Observer; (7) *Pont ar Fynach: Mediaeval Tradition and Native Folklore* (reprinted from the *Welsh Gazette,* January, 1930); (8) *Rhondda: the History of the Name* (1900); (9) *Some Rhondda Cairns* (reprinted from the Transactions of the Cardiff Naturalists' Society, 1903-1904); (10) *Talcen y Byd:* the Alps of Glamorgan or the Greater Pennant Scarp (1907); (11) *Y Wenhwyseg:* a Key to the Phonology of the Gwentian Dialect (1902); and (12) Prehistoric London: its Mounds and Circles by E. O. Gordon with Appendices by John Griffiths (1925).

He also wrote on the Margam Chapter House, and whilst at Llangynwyd, he arranged a visit by Sir Norman Lockyer to the Llangynwyd district in 1907 to start the astronomical work of the survey of old monuments. His two papers of notes on the Caligny Calendar earned high praise from Sir John Rhŷs, the famous Celtic scholar, who was his cousin.

Victor Hampson-Jones B.A., Ll.B., (1909-1977) came to live at Nantyffyllon shortly after the end of the second World War. He was an extra-mural lecturer under the University of Wales and lectured on Welsh literature, history, economics and law, but it is not known how many of these lectures are available. They would be of a quality to justify publication. At the request of the Government, he lectured on law to the armed forces in Aden. His lectures included one on *Law and Individual Liberty* and among his publications was *Memorandum on the Legal Status of the Welsh Language* (1964) prepared on behalf of the National Union of Welsh Teachers. His Welsh articles on general topics in *Y Faner* were profound, and his knowledge of Welsh and English literature was extensive. A devout Roman Catholic, he received, as we have already seen, the signal honour of being made a Knight of the Order of St. Gregory the Great. His wife, Edna Hampson-Jones, has written on Welsh crafts and is the cultured author of English poems.

The Rev. L. J. Hopkin-James (1874-1937) was curate of Llangynwyd Church from 1898 to 1901 and was a direct descendant of Lewis Hopkin, bardic teacher to the famous Iolo Morganwg. His main publications were (1) *Hopkiniaid Morganwg* (1909); (2) *Hen Gwndidau*, a collection of carols and religious songs edited by him and Cadrawd (1910); (3) *Old Cowbridge* (1922); and (4) *Celtic Gospels* (1934). At the time of his death he was Chancellor of Llandaff Cathedral and his numerous articles were mainly in defence of the Anglican Church. They are enumerated in the list of authors connected with the Llynfi Valley.

A. J. Lloyd was the first editor of the *Advertiser* launched June 6 1919. It was later called *The Glamorgan Advertiser* (with offices at Maesteg) and mirrored the many-sided activities of local life. Mr. Lloyd was a man of deep culture, and one of the founders of the local Astronomical Society. At the Llanelli National Eisteddfod, 1930, he won high praise for his prize essay: *Women in Municipal Affairs.* He was an outstanding journalist, with a wide knowledge of English literature. He moved to Shrewsbury in 1931.

The Rev. W. Meredith Morris was curate of Eglwys Dewi Sant, Maesteg, 1907-08. His published works were: (1) *British Violin Makers, Ancient and Modern* (1904); (2) *The Effect of the Renaissance upon Welsh Literature;* (3) *A Glossary of the Demetian Dialect of North Pembrokeshire* (1910); (4) *The Life of Walter Henry Mayson;* (5) *The Church Bells of the Diocese of Llandaff;* (6) *Guiseppe Guareni;* and (7) *Y Delyn Gymraeg* (The Welsh Harp).

   In 1894 he presented to Cadrawd a home-made fiddle which is now at the *Oriel* (Gallery) of the Welsh Folk Museum at St. Fagan's.

Martin Phillips was a railway clerk who lived at Port Talbot, but was a keen collector of records of the past relating to the Llynfi Valley. The writer of these notes received several valuable documents from him. Much of what he wrote can be seen in the *Transactions* of the Aberafan and Margam Historical Society and includes: (1) *The Folklore of the Afan and Margam District* (1930) containing references to Maesteg and Llangynwyd, and (2) *Early Mining Records of the Maesteg District* (1932). In 1931 he published a valuable list of books, pamphlets and contributions to periodicals relating to the Port Talbot District, and also a list of the early published views of the same district. This includes many books, booklets and articles that have a bearing on the past of the Llynfi Valley.

Enoch Howell Rees, who died January 7 1969, was a native of

Cardiganishire and once lived in New Zealand. He settled down as a draper in Maesteg. A prominent administrator in rugby football circles, he devoted many years of his later life to the writing of novels and plays in English. They included: (1) *A Nazi Spy in Britain;* (2) *To Lighten their Darkness;* (3) *The Millers;* (4) *Death Ball* (1943); and (5) *Whose Sun is it?* His play in 3 Acts called *Dark O' the Moon,* formed the basis of an opera called *Gwyneth* with music by Dr. Haydn Morris, whilst his play, *Angels Unaware,* based on *Whose Sun is it?* was translated into Welsh as *Angylion yn Ddiarwybod* by the Rev. William Edwards M.A., Caerau.

Daniel R. Waldin (1844-1933) of Caerau, published many articles of interesting reminiscences in the *Glamorgan Advertiser* in the twenties of this century. They included (1) *Caerau's March of Progress;* (2) Four articles called *Seventy Years Ago—a Stroll through the Llynfi Valley;* (3) *Conductors of the Past in the Maesteg Valley;* (4) *Healing Wells of the Llynfi Valley;* (5) *The Story of a Notable Llangynwyd man—Llyfnwy;* (6) *The Llynfi Valley and its Tributaries;* (7) *Old Farmsteads in the Llynfi Valley;* and (8) *Iron Works in the Llynfi Valley.* The writer of this volume gained much local information during his visits to D. R. Waldin's home in Metcalf Street, Caerau, his father and D. R. Waldin being co-deacons of Siloh Church, Nantyffyllon.

Roderick G. Williams was the son of W. R. Williams and a brother to Gwilym Williams, a pharmaceutical chemist of Garnlwyd, Maesteg. He was a keen and reliable antiquarian. He and the writer of these notes used to travel together daily in the late twenties on the old P.T.R. line from Maesteg to Port Talbot. The Transactions of the Aberafan and Margam Historical Society contain many of his informative articles, particularly on the Vale of Glamorgan, including Old Beaupre, St. Hilary, Llantrithyd, Penlline, Flemingston, Llanfrynach, St. Athan, Merthyr Mawr and Ewenny. In 1932 he published his *Guide to the Vale of Glamorgan.* He also wrote on the romantic career of the 'great bard and scholar'—Dr. Siôn Dafydd Rhys.

Owing to limitations of space, only brief references can be made to the following deceased persons: —

Thomas Evans, Gelli Lenor Farm, Maesteg, wrote from time to time on farming matters. His articles on *Agriculture, Farming and Farm Names* appeared in the Maesteg Souvenir Brochure of the Festival of Wales, 1958. He had also a very wide knowledge of the cultural and religious life of the valley.

G. Rudolph Glover, Maesteg, son of William Glover, was an authority on local sport. Among his interesting articles in the *Glamorgan Gazette* were

Memories of Old Maesteg (1954) and *Reminiscences of Old Maesteg* (1960).

John Jenkins, Garn Road, Maesteg, whose series of reminiscences in the *Glamorgan Advertiser,* August, 1935 provided interesting information regarding past customs.

David Jones, Wallington, whose holograph copy of the history of Llangynwyd (1882?) is now at the Cardiff Central Library.

E. Verley Merchant, formerly of Garth, Maesteg, who published a novel, *Under the Hills* in 1944.

William Thomas of Galltcwm Farm, near Bryn, who wrote *Gleanings from the Fields of Past Years,* 1913.

David Williams, Ogmore Vale, was the author of several articles in the *Glamorgan Advertiser* in the thirties, including *Maesteg Sixty Years Ago,* and *Some Worthies of Mid-Glamorgan.*

Jeremiah Williams was a native of Nantyffyllon and former headmaster of Abergele County School, who edited and contributed to the biography of Christopher Williams, the artist. Some of his reminiscences regarding early education in the valley and Salem Chapel appeared in the local press.

J. Pentrevor wrote *The Kingdom of Llan* — a Llangynwyd pageant play in 1913.

(m) Contemporary Welsh Authors

The Rev. Herbert Hughes, a native of Flintshire and minister of Siloh Church, Nantyffyllon, in the sixties, now lectures in religious instruction at Trinity College, Carmarthen. His early poems showed promise of major achievement, but he decided to concentrate his efforts on work among young people and religious teaching in schools, upon which he wrote a major work a few years ago. He has written extensively on varied topics to the Welsh press in particular.

Norah Isaac was born in Caerau and attended the local elementary school and the Maesteg Secondary School, ultimately becoming Head of the Welsh, Drama and Bilingual Education at Trinity College, Carmarthen, from which position she retired a few years ago. Apart from being the pioneer of teaching through the medium of Welsh, her published works include: (1) A contribution to *Credaf,* setting forth her beliefs; (2) *Symud a Siarad* (Movement and Speech), 1968 — a book for teachers; (3) The Editor of *Storiau Awr Hamdden i Blant* (Leisure-time Stories for Children); (4) *Syr Ifan ab Owen Edwards* (1972); (5) *Iolo Morganwg,* a play, 1974; and (6) *Crwydro Gorff a Meddwl* (Wanderings in Mind and Body), 1980, being a vivid account of a visit to Patagonia. She has won National Eisteddfod honours for reciting and literature and is an honorary M.A. of the Welsh University. She has adjudicated on innumerable occasions at local and national level and is one of the best-known drama and pageant producers in Wales. Her radio and T.V. scripts and appearances are legion. Her other works include scripts for children's pageants at six National Eisteddfodau and for the Urdd National Eisteddfod, nine booklets for children in the series *Cyfres y Glöyn Byw* (The Butterfly Series) and innumerable articles to Welsh periodicals.

Allan James, a native of Maesteg, became tutor of Welsh at the Barry Training College. He is the author of *Y Geiriau a Genir ar Alawon Gwent a Morgannwg,* an M.A. thesis on the words sung to the airs of Gwent and Glamorgan, and *Y Gân Werin a'r Traddodiad Llafar* (The Folk Song and the Oral Tradition).

Myrddin Jenkins of Nantyffyllon was in charge of the Welsh literature department of the Welsh Joint Education Committee. Some years ago he published a book on the teaching of Welsh in schools.

Gareth W. Jones of Maesteg was awarded a £50 prize at the Dyffryn Clwyd National Eisteddfod of 1973 for a satirical farce.

Gerallt C. Jones, the headmaster of the Llynfi Valley Welsh School, is the author of the National Eisteddfod prize handbook, *Llyfr i Athrawon ar Sut i Arwain Dysgwyr i Siarad Cymraeg,* 1960, a handbook for teachers of Welsh to learners. In 1962 he published *Profion Un-ar-ddeg,* a book of Welsh examination questions with answers to help pupils and children to master good Welsh quickly. He was also responsible for the booklet published on the occasion of the 25th anniversary of the Welsh School. In 1974 he won a National Eisteddfod prize for a Welsh novel for children between 9 and 13 years, with its setting outside Britain.

The Rev. Ieuan S. Jones M.A., B.D., a minister of Siloh Church Nantyffyllon, in the forties, and now in charge of the Missionary Department of the Welsh Congregational Union, wrote commendable poems and hymns that remain uncollected. He was the author of a series of learned articles on the Dead Sea Scrolls *(Y Tyst,* May-June, 1952).

Morgan D. Jones M.A., the successor (now retired) to T. O. Phillips as Welsh master at the Maesteg Grammar School, is the author of (1) *Geiriadur Daniel Silvan Evans* (The Dictionary of Canon Daniel Silvan Evans), being his M.A. thesis, 1955); (2) *Y Cywiriadur Cymraeg,* 1965 (A Guide to Correct Welsh), praised by Mr Saunders Lewis and followed by an English version in 1977; (3) *Cerddi'r Trai,* 1976, being a collection of Welsh hymns composed by him; (4) *Advanced Welsh Test Papers,* 1975; (5) *Termau Iaith a Llên* (Terms of language and literature), 1972; (6) *Cymwynaswyr y Gymraeg* (Benefactors of Welsh), 1978, and (7) *Perlau'r*

Beirdd (the Pearls of the Poets), 1981. He is the author of the school song *Ein Hysgol ar y Bryn*, set to music by Dr David Evans, Cardiff.

Howard Lloyd, a native of Maesteg, a lecturer in physical education at Trinity College, Carmarthen, has published 2 books on sport with interesting local references: *Crysau Cochion* (Red Jerseys), 1958, a collection of articles by various authors, mainly on rugby football, and *Chwarae Teg* (Fair Play), 1967, written by the author on a variety of sports, with a foreword by Professor T. J. Morgan, Swansea. He has translated the rules of rugby, soccer and hockey into Welsh. His main hobby is the collection of details of old Welsh games. His prize essay at the Aberdare National Eisteddfod, 1956, contained a detailed account of three traditional games of Wales — (1) Fives (2) *Crafau* (wood ball game) and (3) *Bando.*

Siân Lloyd of Neath has her roots in Caerau, where her mother was born, whilst her grandparents, Mr and Mrs Mel Thomas, live at Nantyffyllon. She was crowned as author of a short story at the Urdd National Eisteddfod, 1975, at a very early age. Much is expected from her.

The Rev. L. Alun Page, a native of the Llynfi Valley and a Congregational minister at Carmarthen, has written 2 volumes: *Lle Bo'r Gwreiddyn* (Where the Roots lie), 1972, depicting his early days in Maesteg and (2) *Arwyddion Amserau* (Signs and Times), 1979, being a collection of his articles on many themes. As a weekly contributor, he wrote numerous articles to *Y Faner* and has lately developed as a poet of much merit. He was one of the founders of *Dock Leaves* and the *Anglo-Welsh Review.*

The Rev. J. Derfel Rees was born in Nantyffyllon, the son of the Rev. T. J. Rees, former minister of Saron Church, Nantyffyllon. In 1980 he published a volume of his reminscences, *Blas ar Fyw* (A Taste for Living), giving an account of his early days and of the places where he had ministered.

The Very Rev. Gwynfryn Richards is a native of Nantyffyllon. Gaining his B.Sc. (Wales) at the age of 18 and a 'first' at Oxford at 20, he proceeded to a first-class degree in theology at Boston University, Massachusetts, USA. He ultimately became the most prolific writer of all the Church dignitaries of his time in Wales. His published works include: (1) *Ffurfiau Ordeinio Holl Eglwysi Cymru* (The Forms of Ordination of all Welsh Churches), 1943, a National Eisteddfod Prize Essay; (2) *Ein Hymraniadau Annedwydd* (Our Unhappy Divisions), 1962; (3) *Gwir a Diogel Obaith* (Sure and Certain Hope), his expanded Pantyfedwen Lecture of 1967; (4) *Ar Lawer Trywydd* (On Many Tracks), a miscellany; and (5) *A Fyn Esgyn, Mynn Ysgol,* 1980, which traces the development of education in the Nantlle Valley.

His booklets include (1) *A Guide to the Church of St. Mary and All Saints, Conway,* 1951; (2) *Yr Hen Fam — Ei hanes bore* (The Mother Church — its early history), 1952; (3) *Bangor Cathedral, —* a souvenir booklet, 1967,

1971 and 1975; (4) *The Diocese of Bangor during the Rise of Welsh Methodism*, 1979. His numerous historical and miscellaneous articles have appeared in the *Journal of the Historical Society of the Church in Wales*, the *Transactions of the Caernarvonshire Historical Society, The Journal of the National Library of Wales, Y Llan, Yr Haul, Province,* Diocesan Gazettes (Bangor and St. David's), *Pan Anglican, Yr Ymofynnydd, Y Gangell, Cymry'r Groes, Country Quest, Bangor Diocesan History.* He wrote two plays for children. Many of his voluminous papers have already been deposited at the National Library of Wales and the Bangor University Library.

T. T. Richards of Llety Brongu Farm, Llangynwyd, and a native of the Vale of Glamorgan, was at one time a regular broadcaster in Welsh on farming matters. In recent years he has written, from time to time, articles published in the Welsh weekly periodical *Y Tyst* on religious themes based on his experience as a farmer.

The Rev. David Arthur Thomas, now of Tregaron, was born and bred in Maesteg and wrote commendable poetry, particularly in his early days. His poems remain uncollected.

William David Thomas of Gilfach Farm, Llangynwyd, is about the last survivor of the traditional embodiment of Welsh rural native culture for which the valley was once famous. His many uncollected poems, some in English, on local events, personalities, etc., make homely reading. They become highly entertaining when sung by him, and act as a welcome antidote to the synthetic din which is sometimes called 'music' to-day.

The Rev. Meurig Walters of Tondu has for several years contributed a weekly Welsh column, *Ar y Bont* to the *Glamorgan Gazette,* the only local paper circulating in the Llynfi Valley. He is also well-known as a writer of Welsh novels and as an authority on Islwyn, the greatest Monmouthshire poet of the last century. His standard work on Islwyn's epic poem *Y Storm,* recently published by the University of Wales Press in the Welsh Academy series of classics, has been most favourably reviewed. It is based on a lecture given by him at the poet's old Church, Y Babell (C.M.), Ynysddu, Gwent.

It is well to recall that in 1949, John Port of Garth published a collection of 17 Welsh hymns of his own composition, dedicated to Ebenezer Church, Garth.

We recollect that the former Vicar of Llangynwyd, the Rev. M. J. Mainwaring, lectured on *Hanes Plwyf Llangynwyd* to the annual meeting of the Church in Wales Welsh Society in 1978 and that he was responsible for the brochure on the Church of St. Michael's and All Angels, Maesteg, published in 1973, on the 75th anniversary of the Church. His monthly notes in the *Llangynwyd Parish Magazine* were a pattern of clarity and exposition.*

There are still young poets, born in the valley, people like Magdalen (Thomas) Jones (now of Benllech, Anglesey, and conductor of Côr y Traeth male voice choir), Menna Thomas and Ceri Wyn Richards, whose early Welsh poems give promise of the ability to excel as writers. Menna Thomas has also been successful as a folk-singer at National Eisteddfod level, and also at important folk-song festivals. Much is expected of Carol Hughes of Garth, who gained a 1st class honours degree in Welsh, and who is now engaged in research work in Welsh literature. Those who have written histories of local Churches also deserve honourable mention.

In the first half of the present century there was much activity in *Aelwyd yr Urdd,* Maesteg, whilst the St. David's Day children's eisteddfod at Caerau was a tremendous success for many years. Under the leadership of Mr Lloyd Evans, headmaster of Blaenllynfi Boys' School, and Gwynedd Maddocks, classes were held to teach the *cynganeddion,* being the traditional Welsh strict metres, and public debates in Welsh were arranged between various Cymrodorion societies. The Urdd National Eisteddfod was held in Maesteg in 1953 and 1979, the budget for 1953 being £2,500 and that for 1979, £65,000. In spite of atrocious weather and consequent ground conditions, aided by unfavourable T.V. and press reports on the state of the Eisteddfod field, the 1979 venture produced a financial profit of £33,000, being the highest in the history of the Eisteddfod whilst the competency of the competitors was of the highest standard.

Brief references to the literary tradition of the valley are contained in *Crwydro Blaenau Morgannwg* (Wanderings in the Uplands of Glamorgan), 1962 by the Rev. Gomer M. Roberts, the well-known historian, and in *A Literary Tour of Afan and Tir Iarll,* 1974, by Sally Roberts Jones in the series *Writers of West Glamorgan* edited by Prys Morgan.

Well-known Welsh literary figures had close connections with the district. The daughter of Trebor Aled, the Denbighire poet, lived at Maesteg, whilst Ben Bowen, the young Rhondda poet who died, aged 24, in 1903, had a sister who lived at Bryn. She was buried at the Maesteg Cemetery. Ben Bowen himself was a regular visitor to Bryn. A nephew of Dewi Wyn o Esyllt, a member of the famous *Clic y Bont* circle of poets of Pontypridd, lived at Nantyffyllon, and so did the son of the Pembrokeshire poet, Arianglawdd, whilst Dewi Môn (Profesor David Rowlands), the theologian, hymn-writer and poet, had two sons who settled in Maesteg — Dr. Cobden Rowlands as a medical practitioner and Wilfred Rowlands as a solicitor. A kinswoman of Thomas Lewis of Talyllychau (Talley), author of the famous Welsh hymn *Wrth gofio 'i riddfannau'n yr ardd* lived at Caerau.

Publishers Note. The Rev. M. J. Mainwaring officiated at the funeral of the author on 25 September 1981, but, sadly, died himself not long afterwards. Both their graves are side by side near the entrance to Llangynwyd Church.

Incidentally, the contemporary poet and novelist, Dannie Abse (brother to Leo Abse M.P.), had a tenuous connection with the valley as his grandparents once lived at Bridge Street, Maesteg. His *Collected Poems, 1948-76* were highly praised. His first novel, *Ash on a Young Man's Sleeve,* was published in 1952. (It was later that he developed as a poet). A new collection of his poems, *Way Out in the Centre,* was published last year (1981).

(n) Contemporary Authors writing in English

John Ackerman, born in Maesteg in 1934 and senior lecturer in English literature at Avery Hill College, has done a great deal of research work regarding Dylan Thomas, including interviews with the poet's widow and mother and with his friend, Vernon Watkins, the Swansea poet. In 1964 he wrote, *Dylan Thomas, Life and Work,* published by the Oxford University Press, whilst his articles on Dylan and R. S. Thomas appeared in the *Encyclopaedia Britannica.* In 1973 he organised a Welsh Arts Council exhibition portraying the Welsh Dylan and prepared the catalogue. Then in 1979 he published *Welsh Dylan* based on the 1964 volume with textual additions and new photographs. Other works by John include: (1) *The Sixties,* 1961, being a short collection of poems, including two of his own, being *Er Cof* (for Aneurin Bevan) and *A Heritage*; (2) *A Poetry Anthology* — Poems '72; (3) *The Image of the Dark,* 1975, a further collection of poems. He has also written a novel, *Bad Penny Blues.* His poems have appeared in *Poetry Wales, The Anglo-Welsh Review, Mabon, Planet* and *The Lilting House.*

Gloria Evans Davies was born in Maesteg in 1932 and moved with her parents to Bristol during the depression years. The family returned to Wales in 1955 and ultimately settled down in the Newcastle-Emlyn district. After living in England and Wales, Gloria says 'I feel I belong to neither. I have always felt a stranger wherever I have gone.' In 1962 her first volume of poems, *Words—for Blodwen* (being her mother) was published by Chatto and Windus in conjunction with the Hogarth Press. The blurb of the publishers states that the writer had struggled against poverty and ill-health and that her poems had a purity and originality which commanded serious respect. Robert Graves stated that her language was impeccable and that she never cheated. Herbert Read thought her poems were original and 'delicately beautiful', whilst Andrew Young said he was struck by her fine sense of rhythm and the quality of the verse and also by a number of 'beautiful things.'

By 1974 she had composed 250 poems. More were published in America than here. Some had appeared in the *New York Times,* whilst 25 were published in the *Adam International Review.* Other poems appeared in the *P. E. N. Anthology,* 1957, *The New Poetry Anthology, 1958 issue, The*

Times Literary Supplement, The Listener, Time and Tide, Spectator, The National and English Review, etc. During 1974 she published a further volume of poems — *Her Names like the Hours.*

Tudor John, a native of Maesteg and a former prisoner-of-war in Germany, now lives in Germany. He wrote much unpublished poetry in his early days in Maesteg, when his favourite poet was Ezra Pound. He established his reputation as a poet by composing a lengthy poem of approximately 60 pages from the text of Heidegger, which occupied the time of one of the professors at the Johann Wolfgang von Goethe University for several months. He started writing this poem when he was a boy, in the Sychbant Valley, Maesteg. In 1976 Tudor told the writer of these notes that there were not more than six people in Wales with any real knowledge of what he had written. In Japan, one or two academics at Kyoto knew that he had written 100 variations on a theme of Matsuo Basho. In Germany, his cycle on Dresden was praised by the academics, Tudor being actually in that city as a prisoner-of-war when it was mercilessly bombed for three days towards the end of the last War. His works, including an attack on the Urban myths, have been studied in London, Chicago and Los Angeles. He is much influenced by the enigma and mysteries of Africa, and has spent much time with the Shona and Matabele. His unpublished volume of poems called *The Basanos Poems* would appear to justify the assertion that his poetry is far more profound than popular.

Robert Minhinnick is the grandson of A. T. Minhinnick, who was formerly general manager of the N.C.B. colliery group which included the Llynfi Valley pits and who took an active part in the social life of the district. The poet's Triskel pamphlet *A Thread in the Maze* appeared in 1978, followed in 1980 by his volume of poetry *Native Ground,* which was awarded an Arts Council Literature prize. It is based on life in the Penyfai district of his childhood. The literary critic, Roland Mathias, described him as a young poet to watch. In 1980 he was awarded £3,000 by the Society of Authors as part of the Eric Gregory Trust Award for poets under the age of 30.

Iain Sinclair is a native of Maesteg, the only son of Dr. and Mrs. Henry Sinclair, now of Bridgend. His published works include: (1) *Back Garden Poems,* 1970; (2) *The Kodak Mantra Diaries* (1971), a documentary account of Allen Ginsberg in London, 1967; (3) *Muscata Würm,* 1972; (4) *The Birth Rug,* 1973; (5) *Lud Heat,* 1975; (6) *The Penances,* 1977; (7) *Brown Clouds,* 1977; and (8) *Suicide Village,* 1979.

His anthologies include *Ten English Poets* (New Direction New York), 1978, and *Anthologie de la Nouvelle Poesie Anglaise* (Paris, 1980. In *The Guardian,* October 1979, Jeff Nuttall stated that vitality was one of the main qualities radiating from the poet's superb collection of *Suicide Bridge* and that his powerful rhythmic lines were as masterful as those of Motram.

Writers who have written on general topics include:-

Glynne H. J. Ball, Llangynwyd, who has learnt Welsh, and has written a yet unpublished thesis on *Llangynwyd Tir Iarll: Some Aspects of an Upland Manor and Parish, 1570-1670.* As a keen student of the past, he has discovered many interesting facts concerning early surveys of the district, Llangynwyd Castle, pre-historic stones, ancient local wills, early Charters etc., and has assisted in the preparation of a card index of the valley to be published in 1981 for use in schools. He was the first chairman of the recently-formed Maesteg Historical Society.

Walter Haydn Davies of Bargoed, who was in charge of a commercial course at the Maesteg Grammar School from 1935 to 1941. His works include:- (1) *Ups and Downs,* 1935, being an autobiography (2) *The Day of the Explosion, Senghenydd, 1913* (Gelligaer Historical Society, Vol VIII, 1971) (3) *The Right Tune, the Place,* 1972 (4) *The Blythe Ones,* 1980 and an hour-long cassette featuring 20 songs from the South Wales coalfield in both English and Welsh, 1980.

Dr. Graham Humphrys, a native of Maesteg, and a senior lecturer in Geography at the University of Wales at Swansea, delivered a lecture at Llwynderw School, Maesteg, on March 19 1969 on the place of Maesteg in the Seventies. Among his published works are *Industrial Britain, Industrial South Wales* (1972), *Geographical Excursions from Swansea* (1978), Co-author of the *The U.K. Space* (1973), *Dealing with Dereliction* (1979), a contributor to *Swansea and its Region* (1972) and *Wales—a New Study* (1977). He is the author of innumerable articles in industrial and geographical publications, dealing mainly with South Wales districts.

Dr. D. R. L. Jones (Lyn Jones), Maesteg, a graduate of the Universities of Wales and Leicester, is a lecturer in mathematics at the Polytechnic of Wales, and a keen student of local history, our industrial background, instrumental and vocal music, pipe-organ construction, astronomy and particularly local ecclesiastical history. He has written on William Thomas, an eighteenth-century Vicar of Llangynwyd, and also on 'Doddington v. Mansel: a seventeenth-century dispute concerning the Parish of Margam' *(Glamorgan Historian,* Vol. 12).

Other writers still alive are Canon Daniel Richards, who retired in 1966 as Vicar of Llangynwyd after 35 years' service. After writing his autobiography, *Honest to Self,* he achieved unusual success by gaining the degree of Master of Theology (M.Th.) at the age of 88 at the Geneva College of North Carolina for a thesis on aspects of St. Paul's conversion. In May, 1981 he received the Archbishop of Canterbury's Lambeth Diploma for theological learning.

Edith Adams of Maesteg wrote her novel *The Honourable Philip* when she was only 16 years of age.

Charles Gwyn Kinsey, who emigrated with his family to Canada in 1930, wrote, when a schoolboy at Caerau in 1929, an exercise-book full of poetry which was praised by Wil Ifan in the *Western Mail,* July 30 1929. It is not known whether the poems were later published. He also wrote to the *Glamorgan Advertiser* on his adventures in Canada.

Cyril Golding, a Caerau product, is the author of poems, including *The Valleys* based on his early days in the Llynfi Valley. Incidentally, as a scientist with a 1st class honours degree, he achieved success with his thesis, *Electricity in Modern Coal Mining,* 1959, under the Technical Prize Paper Scheme of the Metropolitan Vickers Apprentice Association, and gained his M.Sc. Degree of the University of Wales in 1965 for his thesis on *Speed Control of Slipring Induction Motors.*

Dr. Islwyn Thomas of New York left Maesteg with his parents for the U.S.A. at the age of 11 years. Besides being an international authority on the Plastics Industry, on which he published his *Injection Molding of Plastics,* he is the author of *Our Welsh Heritage* giving details of the influence of Welsh people on American affairs. He has done much research work regarding the tradition that Prince Madoc, a Welshman, discovered America before the arrival of Columbus. He is a past President of the St. David's Society of New York and was recently honoured with the Robert Morris Award of the Welsh Society of Philadelphia.

Dr. Gareth Thomas of Heolfain, Garth, Maesteg, and now in the U.S.A., is known internationally as an authority on Metallurgy. By 1978 he had published 2 volumes, several book chapters and about 200 research articles on that subject.

The Rev. Mervyn M. Davies, a native of Nantyffyllon, when Vicar in the Garw Valley, wrote *The Young Valley* in 1967, being the history of the Anglican Church in the Garw Valley.

The Rev. James Dole, Llwynhendy, former minister of Bethania Church Maesteg was awarded in 1976 the degree of master of Theology (M.Th.) by the Southeastern College, Waste Forest, North Carolina for a thesis on *The Attitude to Death of the Geriatric Patient.*

The writers on the industrial side include *Thomas Getrych Davies,* the author of a treatise on the Llynfi and Rhondda Mineral District, 1932; *William Henry Evans,* a native of Nantyffyllon, who wrote (in conjunction with B. Simpson) an M.Sc. thesis on the *Coal Measures of the Llynfi Valley,* 1934; *D. G. Lewis,* the author of *The Maesteg Corn Stores* (connected with the Llynfi Iron Works) *Measured and Drawn,* 1962; *S. Richards* who wrote on the Rhondda & Swansea Bay Railway in 1976, the Llynfi & Ogmore Railway and the Port Talbot Railway (P.T.R.) in 1977.

In 1979 *Richard G. Keen* published his *Old Maesteg and the Bridgend Valleys in Photographs,* whilst Peter Cavalier and Geoff Silcock provided us with *A Chapter on Photographs of Maesteg.*

On the occasion of the golden jubilee of the Maesteg Celtic Cricket Club, 1926-1976, *Garfield Thomas,* Maesteg, wrote a detailed account of the history of the club. With G. Evans he published the account of '50 Glorious Years.'

Catherine Jones, formerly of Coed-y-garth, Maesteg, and now living in Paris, is producing a film about miners and it is assumed that it will contain references to the Llynfi Valley.

Ann Jones, of Maesteg, published in 1920 *Thoughts of Friends Far and Near,* being a collection of favourite quotations of mostly local people, whilst books of poetry by local writers include *Poetic Miscellany,* 1951, by Rona Davies, Nantyffyllon, *Simply a Tapestry* by Robert Harris of Maesteg, *Comforting Thoughts,* 1979, by Beryl Griffiths, Nantyffyllon, whilst Joan O'Connor of Maesteg has also written a number of poems of local interest. In 1980 *Janice Smith* of Pontrhydycyff published *Screwshot Suzy,* being a selection of her 250 poems of a light and satirical nature. A year later she published her second book of poetry called *Thoughts of a Welsh Girl,* containing more serious poems, while *T. Witts* has composed a poem called *Llangynwyd, the Village of Inspiration.*

(o) Cultural Activities Generally

It would be impossible in the space at our disposal to do justice to the cultural activities of the valley in the present century. In the first quarter, Welsh Nonconformist Churches were brimming with activities like lectures, penny-readings, eisteddfodau, concerts, young peoples' societies and drama companies. The annual Tir Iarll Eisteddfod, held in a marquee on the Maesteg rugby football ground, was famous for the quality of the competitors and the standard and status of the adjudicators. It became known later as the Maesteg Cottage Hospital Eisteddfod, held on August Bank Holiday, but ceased to be held in the early twenties. As many as sixty to seventy under sixteen years of age would compete on writing Welsh by dictation, and thirty to forty under twelve in a similar competition. Scores of children under 16 took part in a general knowledge competition. In the thirties, as many as sixty to seventy members of the Maesteg Cymrodorion Society would travel by 'bus to Cwmafan to take part in a debate on Welsh topics, whilst at Maesteg, the Cymrodorion would promote drama competitions, lectures, internal debates, mock trials and concerts, throughout the winter months.

In the annual report of Saron Church, Nantyffyllon, for 1902, the Rev. T. Esger James stated that copies of the following publications were bought by members of his Church: *Y Celt Newydd, Y Tyst, Tywysydd y Plant,*

Dysgedydd y Plant, Y Cennad Hedd, Y Cronicl Cenhadol, Y Diwygiwr, Y Dysgedydd, Ieuenctid Cymru, Pulpud y Cymry, The Examiner and *The British Weekly*, apart from un-denominational weeklies.

Sir O. M. Edwards was a big admirer of the culture of the valley and visited Cadrawd at Llangynwyd in 1911, after the latter had spent much time at Llanover inspecting Iolo Morganwg's vast collection of papers and manuscripts.

Most of the outstanding Welsh scholars, lecturers and preachers visited the Llynfi Valley, including Dr. T. Gwynn Jones (one of the greatest of Welsh poets), Dr. Elfed Lewis (many times), Sir Ifor Williams (Bangor), Dr. R. T. Jenkins (the historian), Dr. Iorwerth Peate, Professors W. J. Gruffydd, Henry Lewis, G. J. Williams, Stephen J. Williams, Sir Marchant Williams, Sir Ifan ab Owen Edwards, the Archdruids Dyfed, Gwili, Crwys, Wil Ifan, Dyfnallt, Sir Samuel Evans (The High Court judge), Principal Maurice Jones and scores of other well-known literary men too numerous to mention. Incidentally, Dyfnallt, in his published lecture *Awen y Rhondda* (The Muse of the Rhondda) in 1943, to the Honourable Society of Cymmrodorion, was pessimistic enough to assert that no Welsh poet had arisen to the east of the River Nedd (Neath) since Ben Bowen, the Rhondda poet, had died in 1903.

Among the hundreds who spoke in English were Judge Gwilym Williams, Dr. Philip B. Ballard, Principal Ivor B. John (Caerleon College) and a host of outstanding scholars, politicians and preachers.

The best known reciters in the valley included James Rees (Iago Goch), Nantyffyllon, who recited before Queen Victoria, Zachariah Jenkins, Urias Richards, Miss Daniels (Llaethferch), a native of Llanelli and a thrice National Winner who taught at Blaencaerau School, Caerau, Edwin John Thomas, Garth, Eiddwen Roderick, William Thomas, Norah Isaac, Gwyneth Latcham, Caerau and Meinir Tawe and her two daughters, Ann (the harpist) and Mary, who all won National honours. In fact, Meinir Tawe won at least four firsts in the main recitation competitions at the National Eisteddfod, apart from being awarded first prize out of thirty-four at the Bridgend Eisteddfod of 1948 for a short Biblical play for children.

Holding the fort in recent times is Huw Walters, Cemetery Road, Maesteg, who won the first prize out of fifty competitors between twelve and fifteen for a recitation from the Scriptures at the Wrexham National Eisteddfod, 1977.

The best known test pieces for recitations in the first quarter of the century were *Arwerthiant y Caethwas* (Auction sale of a Slave), *Ymson y Llofrudd* (Soliloquy of the Murderer), *Trychineb Johnstown* (the Tragedy of Johnstown), *Carlo, Y Baban ar fin y dibyn* (the Child on the Precipice) and *Ti wyddost beth ddywed fy Nghalon*, whilst the English favourites were *Casabianca, Smiting the Rock, The Amen Corner, The Women of Mumbles Head, The Charge of the Light Brigade* and *Where is my Boy To-night?*

A public lecture in Welsh would fill a spacious Chapel, as when the Rev.

W. Glasnant Jones gave a concert lecture on the poet, Watcyn Wyn, at Siloh, Nantyffyllon, in 1906. Another Welsh lecture, lasting two hours to a full house in Siloh Chapel in 1910, was delivered by the famous conductor, T. Glyndwr Richards, on his return from America with his male voice party. Most Welsh weeklies, denominational and literary (several from North Wales), would be provided at the local miners' libraries.

However, the Religious Revival of 1904-05 halted temporarily the Welsh literary activities of the valley. In the minute-book of the re-formed Maesteg Cymrodorion Society, Cadrawd, the secretary, stated that the famous Welsh poet, the Rev. Ben Davies, Ystalyfera, had cancelled his engagement to lecture in January, 1905. He could not leave his people in view of the many revival meetings in his district. Another lecture by the Rev. W. R. Watkin, Maesteg, had to be cancelled for the same reason. In September 1905, Cadrawd threatened to resign as secretary as it was easier to get speakers than to get listeners.

Before the Revival, Cadrawd had stated that the object of the Society was to attract young people to the clover fields of the culture of the mind, to breathe fresh air a thousand times more refreshing than that on the football field or the pleasure ground, and to encourage them to study the pure literature of our dear country and drink of the clear and pure springs to refresh the moral constitution of a Welsh man or woman. However, it appears that the tidal wave of the Revival had swept away those literary ideals!

It is doubtful whether any other Welsh valley of comparable size could boast of greater cultural and social activity. In a drama competition at the Maesteg Town Hall in January 1929, six local drama companies competed, whilst there were seven in 1933. In 1943 the valley could boast of two Welsh, and eight English, drama companies, two opera companies and seventeen youth clubs. The writer was privileged in 1940 to extend a civic welcome to Dame Sybil Thorndike and her Company at the Maesteg Town Hall. We can merely mention the activities of the Maesteg Little Theatre, the N.U.T. drama performances, and the annual drama festivals of the British Legion, each series for seven successive nights, drama sponsored by the Arts Council of Great Britain in co-operation with the Miners' Welfare Commission, local literary debating societies, particularly the one in Nantyffyllon, the Maesteg Contact Society founded in 1948, and Grammar School magazines.

With the closing of the Miners' Institutes and Libraries, the Maesteg branch library, opened by the County Council in 1955, now issues approximately 3,000 books a week, whilst the aggregate number borrowed from its inception to the end of 1980 was 3,800,000. The present librarian, Miss Gillian John, has herself, with others, published useful notes on the history of Tir Iarll. She and her staff played a major part in the forming of the local Historical Society in 1979.

Among the local weeklies that served the valley in the last century were *The Swansea and West Glamorgan Herald, The Maesteg Times and Llynvi*

Vale Advertiser published at 9 Commercial Street, Maesteg, and *The Evening Express*. About a century ago, *The Maesteg Weekly News* was being printed by James James, Printer, Bridge Street, Maesteg, whilst the *Bridgend Chronicle* of 28 October 1881 contained a full account of the official opening of the Maesteg Town Hall.

The two local weekly newspapers of the present century have been the *Glamorgan Gazette*, (the successor to the *Bridgend Chronicle*), which celebrated its centenary in June 1966, and *The Glamorgan Advertiser* launched in 1919, which ceased publication in 1962.

60. The Maesteg Town Hall

148   The earliest known representation of Maesteg Town Hall reproduced from a handbill captioned 'The New Town Hall Maesteg 1881, presented by E Rees, Family Grocer, Maesteg', who owned Gadlys Farm

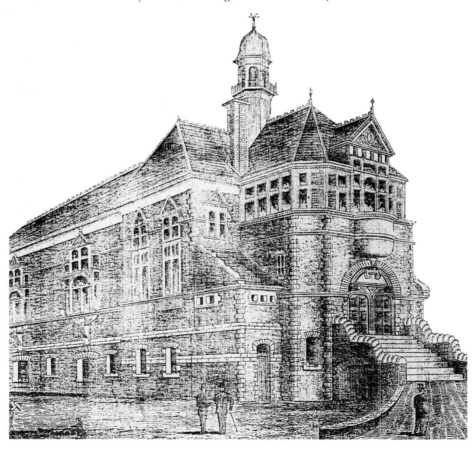

In his *History of Llangynwyd*, 1887, Cadrawd quotes 31 October 1881 as the date of the laying of the foundation-stone of the Town Hall by C. R. M. Talbot, M.P., but the year in question was 1880. Mr. Talbot gave £500 towards the building fund, and the miners of the valley agreed to levy themselves a day's wages towards the cost. Full reports of the opening, on 22 October 1881, by Mr. Chadwick, Chairman of the Llynvi and Tondu Company, were published in the *Western Mail*, 24 October 1881, and in the *Bridgend Chronicle*, 28 October, 1881. The original estimate of £3,000 of the cost of the building was exceeded, hence the reason why the miners' levy became necessary.

The original structure was of the Queen Anne style and hád an imposing frontage. It was reached from the street by a double flight of steps, and was considered one of the finest halls of South Wales. It was the venue of what residents called 'living pictures' or 'flicks', and of concerts, plays, operas and public meetings, cultural, religious and political.

In 1913-14 it was 'renovated', but unfortunately its outward appearance lost most of its charm. The re-opening ceremony took place on 25 November, 1914 with a performance of the 'Hymn of Praise' by the Nantyffyllon Harmonic Society, with W. J. Watkins as conductor.

In 1981 the centenary of the opening of the original building was celebrated in grand style with a series of many performances and functions mainly by local artists. A brochure prepared for the occasion under the auspices of the Leisure Services Department of the Ogwr Council contains articles by local contributors on the various aspects of the past of the Llynfi Valley.

149   A later and more conventional post-card view of Maesteg Town Hall, 1940's

In 1965, consultants advising the Maesteg Council on the re-planning of the centre of the Town, suggested demolishing the Town Hall and building a hall on another site. Had the Council accepted the suggestion, there would have been a campaign for the sacking of the Councillors guilty of such sacrilege.

61. The Changing Scene

Owing to the divisive mountains that separated the mining valleys, there was little social intercourse between the Llynfi Valley and, say, the Garw or Afan or Rhondda Valleys. Merthyr was considered beyond the pale! There was a local tradition that law transgressors fled to Merthyr (*cilio i Ferthyr*) to avoid capture. Of the Llynfi Valley itself, Nantyffyllon was by far the most clannish, as so many of the old families were inter-related. Years ago, the author of this volume knew the grown-ups of Nantyffyllon from their children. To-day, he knows the children from the grown-ups!

As in other mining valleys, the changes in the last 100 years have been phenomenal.

The Rev. T. Esger James, during his ministry at Saron Church, Nantyffyllon (1894-1910), had buried 116 children, and also a number of young men suffering from consumption. In 1902 he buried three members in their early twenties who suffered from that complaint. A daughter of the Rev. Richard Hughes, Bethania, Maesteg, died, aged eighteen, from the same illness. Much earlier, the Parish Register had disclosed deaths from small pox and 'decline', whilst Dr. Brock Thomas of Maesteg had died, aged forty-six, in a small-pox epidemic in the middle of the last century. However, Dr. John Davies reported to the Maesteg Local Board in October, 1894, that there had been no case of typhoid for four months.

In the first decade of this century the most common school complaints were whooping cough, ringworm and 'St. Vitus dance'. Presumably rock 'n' roll has supplanted the latter complaint. Sennapods for constipation and bread poultice for extracting poison have long ceased to be considered remedies.

A most informative article by Dr. Ralph W. H. Thomas, M.O.H. to the Maesteg U.D.C. from 1937 to 1946, on *Health in the Maesteg Area* appears in the brochure published during the centenary celebrations of the Maesteg Town Hall.

He states that up to 1939, tuberculosis was the second highest cause of death in Maesteg, the first being heart disease. Owing to better housing and improved nutrition, tuberculosis was now a rare event. And yet, an entry in the log book of Blaenllynfi Girls' School, Caerau, on 9 June 1932 states that three school managers, Councillors John Hughes, Howell Davies and D. O. Davies, had visited the school that day and had testified that no children at the school were considered to be undernourished. This was at the height of the industrial depression and in one of the worst affected spots — and before the provision of school meals had become compulsory.

At one time, infantile mortality rose to 220 per 1,000 live births, and scarlet fever was very prevalent. For some years after 1903, when the Maesteg Isolation Hospital was built, parents preferred to have their children 'isolated' in their own homes. Ambulance vans were then unheard of, and the Maesteg General Hospital had not then been built. By to-day, there is no need for a local hospital for infectious diseases.

Prior to the second World War, diphtheria among children was greatly feared. In 1938-39, 316 cases were notified in the valley. Owing to immunisation, the disease is non-existent locally.

In the same article we are given details of the progress of medical research to combat these diseases and are told that many hundreds of Maesteg people owe their lives to the discovery of penicillin and antibiotics.

It was between the two World Wars that a health visitor was first appointed in Maesteg. By now there is a highly-trained Home Nursing Service with nurses visiting the homes of the sufferers. Previously, there was no provision for handicapped children, whilst deaf children were sent to the Institute of the Deaf and Dumb at Swansea, the parents paying 2/- a week per child. By to-day there is provision at the local schools for handicapped and slow-learning pupils.

Years ago, mentally-ill persons were sent to the Asylum (an unfortunate name) near Bridgend, whilst extreme cases were sent to Parc Gwyllt (another unfortunate name). The former is now known as the Penyfai Hospital and the latter as the Parc Hospital, which is now a home for nearly 700 patients who receive highly-skilled medical and psychiatric treatment. Mental health troubles are treated like physical health complaints. The patient is no longer considered as an outcast.

Operations were carried out in private houses. An injured collier in Grove Street, Nantyffyllon, had his leg amputated at night in the parlour of his home — lit with an oil lamp. To-day, doctors, radiologists and nursing sisters are employed by the N.C.B.

Up to the first decade of this century, doctors extracted teeth, until a J. W. Cooper became a two-days-a-week dentist at Maesteg. A Henry Seline, Swansea, called every Monday for ten years at the Plasnewydd Hotel, Maesteg, to extract teeth 'painlessly' and brought with him 'Prize medal artificial teeth'. Children were invariably born at home. Many miners died of what was called *mociant* (asthma) now known as pneumoconiosis and silicosis, and gravestones provide ample evidence of the early deaths of such sufferers.

The dead were exhibited in open coffins in the parlour before burial. Even in the first quarter of this century, many coffins were carried on a heavy bier by relays of four bearers in funerals from all parts of the valley up the steep hill leading to Llangynwyd Churchyard. One can imagine the effort involved if the deceased was an obese person. Infants were buried in small white coffins. After the funeral service, the mourners would gather at the Corner House or the Old House at Llangynwyd, where they could temporarily forget their sorrows in a convivial evening. There was a repertoire of suitable Welsh hymns to be sung at the graveside, but by now the number has been reduced to only 'O Fryniau Caersalem.' Sometimes, even the precentor of a Welsh Chapel would need the help of the printed word to enable him to conduct the singing of this hymn. Formerly, various hymns were sung by the funeral cortege on the route to the burial ground.

Incidentally, the *Red Flag* was sung as a funeral 'hymn' outside the home of one of the first Communist members of the Maesteg U.D.C. in 1936, whilst 'Hen Wlad fy Nhadau' was sung in 1977 at the graveside service at the Maesteg Cemetery of an outstanding local Welsh scholar and patriot. It was during the last War that walking funerals ceased in the Valley. Even earlier, the custom of carrying coffins had ended. In 1909, William Davies and Sons, Posting Masters, Plasnewydd, Maesteg, announced in a local advertisement that they wished to inform their customers and the public that they had purchased a hearse and suitable carriages, and that they were prepared for all kinds of funeral arrangements. Incidentally, the four biggest funerals witnessed in the valley were those of the Rev. Richard Hughes, Bethania, Maesteg, Dr. W. H. Thomas, Maesteg, Dr. J. Harris Jones, Caerau, and Vernon Hartshorn.

Reference has already been made to the hardships suffered in the mining community. Sometimes, on the death of the wage-earner, the widow would open a parlour shop to maintain the family rather than suffer the 'stigma' of accepting parish relief. The writer of these notes knew a widow who used to walk to Neath to buy goods to sell in her parlour shop. Her young son would meet her half-way on her return journey to help her to carry the goods. Mrs. Elizabeth James, Llwydarth Road, Maesteg, a local nonagenarian, remembers local shopkeepers acting likewise. They asserted that their feet had been given to them before men gave them a railway! Incidentally, the barbaric killing of animals for human consumption by means of a pole-axe is happily a thing of the past. Illegal cock-fighting exhibitions, such as those at the rear of the White Hart Inn, Bridgend Road, Maesteg, in the late nineteenth century, ceased many years ago.

The streets reminded one of the uniformity of eggs or cement. They were internally lit by a paraffin lamp, usually with one wick. In Nantyffyllon, the paraffin was supplied from a pumping-machine set in the front room of a house in one of the oldest streets of the village. The dear old soul, a former minister of the Gospel in America, who was in charge, used to prepare home-made toffee for his young customers. The hand that handled the paraffin also dispensed the uncovered toffee to the eager children. To them, despite the taste of the paraffin, it was truly toffee-de-luxe!

The lavatories were at the far end of a lengthy garden. In most kitchens could be seen a dresser displaying china ornaments. On the mantelpiece were brass and china candlesticks, and below were the fender and stand, the hob, and the spills container. There was an oven on each side of the fire and this involved much blackleading. A Dutch oven supplemented the cooking, whilst the bakestone over the fire baked the delicious little cakes known as 'picks'. Bread was toasted with a fork in front of a coal fire. A bellows hung alongside one of the ovens. As there were no electric kettles or stoves, the water was boiled in an iron kettle, which meant much waiting, especially in the morning when a coal fire had to be lit first. In many houses, sand was spread over the kitchen floor so that it could assimilate the dirt when the floor was swept.

Before the days of pithead baths, the father, and sometimes as many as five or six collier sons, took their turn in bathing in a tin or zinc bath in front of the fire. For the wife, it meant untold drudgery in providing fresh water for each one, in mending their working clothes, in preparing a heavy meal for the hungry workers and also in preparing a box of food and a jack of tea for each one in readiness for the following morning's shift. The sight of a collier returning home unwashed in his working clothes is a thing of the past. Even as late as 1910, many streets of houses without baths were built in the valley. Central-heating of houses is only a recent development. The washing machine has eliminated the primitive and slavish 'rubber and tub' method of washing.

Most women baked their own bread, and about fifty years ago, there were twenty-eight public bakeries in the valley. Tinned fruit and tinned meat were luxuries. There was no soup before the main dish, but *cawl*, or broth, containing a variety of vegetables, with *sêr* (stars) 'swimming' on the surface, was a distinct favourite. Cured hams, gammons and sides of bacon hung from hooks in the kitchen. Many people kept pigs. In one district council election in Nantyffyllon before the first World War, the main election issue was the distance to be allowed between the pig-sty and the private houses. The favourite home drink was *diod fain* (small beer). In the pre-Welfare State period, the usual purchased drink was dandelion burdock, not forgetting lemonade, known as 'pop'. Home-made wine made of elder flower, elder berry, parsnip, celery, potato and rhubarb, became a later development.

Refuse was deposited in an ash bucket bought by the occupant and collected by Council employees known by the inelegant name of scavengers. A glance at the contents of the bucket would indicate the way in which the owner lived, particularly if it contained an abundance of empty tins. It is now collected in plastic bags provided by the local authority and seldom contains ashes. The windows of most houses had white linen blinds, which would attract much attention when drawn on the occasion of a family death. The better class sported Venetian blinds. A smell of camphor permeated the parlour atmosphere, and a pot of geraniums usually adorned the parlour window-sill.

150 Bill from the days when labourers cost 5½d per hour and master masons 9d

Overcrowding was prevalent. One street in Nantyffyllon contained about half-a-dozen families of ten to twenty children. Another street was unofficially called Incubator Row owing to the large families living there. On the opening of Caerau Colliery at the end of the last century, there was an influx of lodgers, and some houses accommodated as many as four to six at a time.

As miners spent most of their working days underground, particularly before the passing of the Eight Hours a Day Act, and saw daylight in the winter on Sundays only, their opportunity of following sartorial fashions was very limited, except that they would reserve their best suit, known as *dillad parch*, for the Sabbath Day. A suit or overcoat often lasted thirty years. Every man wore headgear — a cap, a bowler-hat, a trilby, a straw hat or a top hat. Every lawyer in the valley at one time wore a top hat. By to-day, the wearing of any sort of headgear is considered exceptional. Incidentally, about a hundred years ago, a native of Nantyffyllon, called Johnny Day, won much fame as the inventor of an ingenious diving suit that brought him much praise.

Men wore flannel shirts during the week days, and boots rather than shoes. In 1909, the Maesteg Boot Factory, owned by W. Daniel, advertised boots made to measure for colliers, farmers and railwaymen at 8/11, 10/6 and 12/6. In the same year, W. Isaac, Maesteg, advertised men's suits at 18/11 to 42/- and youth's suits at 12/9 to 27/6. The women wore flannel underwear, high bonnets, chignons (to emphasise their posteriors), elastic-sided boots and high-necked blouses. The tighter the waist — the better. The annual flannel fair was held in May, and sellers brought their wares to the Maesteg market from Pembrokeshire, Carmarthenshire and Cardiganshire.

Schoolboys wore collarettes, and later, Eton collars. They began to wear long trousers at the age of thirteen or fourteen. It was a sign of manhood. Shop assistants, particularly in the drapery business, dressed well, as they considered themselves a cut above the ordinary miner. The 'masher' wore spats, a bow tie, a wing (Lloyd George) collar, cuffs (with the cuff links in sight) and had a white slip bordering the top of his waistcoat. A pince-nez would indicate a state of superiority. Schoolboys who wore glasses were called 'Four eyes' by their playmates. Before the days of the wristlet watch, the watch was located in the higher left waistcoast pocket and was connected with the waistcoat by means of a guard, usually gold, as it was visible. The watch, out of sight, was usually of silver. The once democratic bowler hat is now the reserve of the middle class. A few men took to wearing earrings. Patches on trousers were then a matter of necessity and not of choice. In the *Llynfi Valley Messenger* in 1909, the Rev. T. Esger James, Saron, Nantyffyllon, emphasised that clothes should be bought for the sake of *gwedduster* (propriety) and not for show.

A Nantyffyllon grocer advertised his brown bread thus:

> Before you can swing with ease and perfection
> You must have a sound and healthy digestion.

He also wrote a limerick, using his own name to publicise his wares as a grocer and baker. Most grocers had flour lofts and rows of caddies, treacle taps, bacon-slicing machines and cash registers. In the Nantyffyllon district alone there were four private tailors, and several dressmakers who went from house to house to engage in their work. Before the first World War, there were two booksellers in the village and several smithies between Caerau and Llangynwyd.

Staff of Millinery Department, Messrs Laviers, *c.* 1912

152 Staff of Caerau and Maesteg Co-operative Society Ltd outside their well-stocked shop, *c.* 1910

With the advent of multiple shops and super-markets, private grocers in the valley are fast disappearing. The private tailors and the peripatetic dressmakers are with us no more. There is no longer a bookseller (apart from newsagents) in the upper part of the district. This is probably due to the fact that the County library service is such an excellent one.

In 1909, a Maesteg grocer, the recipient of a silver medal and a diploma by the South Wales Grocers' Exhibition, Swansea in 1907, advertised himself as a judge of tea: '. . . Buy the finest tea the world can produce.' It was sold at 1/4, 1/6, 1/8 and 2/- per lb. A Nantyffyllon ironmonger claimed to be the sole local agent for the Royal Daylight Lamp Oil.

The only valley pawnshop, which was in Commercial Street, Maesteg, disappeared many years ago. The Chinese laundry closed when collars ceased to be starched. However there is now a Chinese fish fryer's shop even in Nantyffyllon.

When young people had their hair cut regularly, there were barbers available to meet their needs. A Caerau barber in 1909 advertised his business, which consisted of haircutting and 'quick and easy shaving'. Ladies' combings were made up into 'tails and coils'. Young boys used to 'wobble' the faces of the customers in readiness for the sweep of the barber's razor. To-day, there is no barber to do the shaving, and there has been a complete revolution in the technique of dealing with women's tresses.

In 1907, Howell Beynon, a shipping agent of Maesteg, advertised locally for emigrants to Canada. Applicants were also given the choice of an assisted passage to New South Wales, Australia, the fare being £7 and upwards. There was much poverty in the mining valleys at the time. In the

153 A busy Commercial Street, *c.*1910

Rhondda, a committee was formed at the Treorchy Hotel in 1882 to set up a society to assist miners to emigrate, as it was contended that they had been 'reduced to slavery' by their masters. Applicants paid 1/- a month. Going to America then meant being lost for ever.

When old age pensions first became payable, the weekly pension was 5/-payable to the husband only. There were no widows' pensions. In fact, the then Marquis of Lansdowne predicted that the country would become bankrupt if 5/- were paid even to the husband only. However, the typical Welsh people of the valley were frugal, and always had in mind the need to save up for a rainy day, without the prospect of an index-linked pension to make that unnecessary. The provision of a 'bottom drawer' in anticipation of marriage was considered a necessity. The holiday travels were limited to an occasional excursion to the Belle Vue Gardens at Manchester, or to a day's outing to Ilfracombe. The father of the writer of these notes could boast that he had gone as far as Barmouth in North Wales!

A child's weekly pocket money seldom exceeded a few pence (of the old coinage) for the simple reason that the parents could not afford to pay more. Lollies and crisps each morning for young school children were unheard of. However, it would be fair to say that in the old days, toffee could be bought at 4 ounces a penny, which meant that in modern terms, a pound of toffee could be bought for just under 2 pence of present coinage. In 1936, non-miners could buy 2 cwts of coal for 3/- (15 pence of present money). In 1938 the price per cwt had reached 1/10.

Proud parents, who wanted some assurance regarding the future careers of their children, arranged to have their heads read by a well-known Swansea phrenologist, Professor Williams, whose diagnosis was usually a favourable one.

There were no grants for extending the education of promising pupils and they were often supported by benefit concerts to which the whole community contributed liberally. If a Club or Friendly Society member died, a black banner was displayed with an inscription *Brawd wedi marw* intimating that a brother had died. Sometimes, help for the needy would be in the nature of a raffle. On Saturday, 14 May 1892, a clock was raffled at a house in Dyffryn Row, Maesteg, for the benefit of the occupant. Printed tickets were sold at 6d each.

Female shop assistants were paid only nominal wages for the first year or two, as they were rated as apprentices. Before the passing of the Shops Hours Act, many shop assistants worked from 8 a.m. to 8 p.m. and up to 11.30 on Saturday nights. Tramps slept near the old coke ovens in the Cwmdu area.

Prior to the advent of cars it was usual for people to gather horse manure from the roads for use in their gardens or allotments.

Before there was a resident Registrar of Births and Deaths in the district, an officer used to tour the area from time to time and shout at the bottom of the street, *A oes ragor o fabis yma heddi?* (Are there more babies here to-

To be Raffled for,

On Saturday, May 14th & 28th, 1892,

A CLOCK,

At No. 16, Dyffryn Row, Maesteg, for the benefit
of Daniel Jones.

TICKETS, SIXPENCE EACH.

JAMES, PRINTER, MAESTEG

154   Raffle ticket from 1892 issued 'for the benefit of Daniel Jones' of Dyffryn Row,
Maesteg

day?) An elderly native could remember his mother relating how mothers of Union Street, Nantyffyllon, in response to the call, would have their babies registered at the Bell Inn, now known as the Masons Arms. Babies were carried in a shawl wrapped around the mother. The cost of prams was prohibitive.

As far as surnames are concerned, the influx of industrial workers created a variety of names. The late Rev. J. C. Beynon, Vicar of St. Cynfelyn's Church, Caerau, stated that he had on his electoral-roll list the surnames of Ham, Duck, Pheasant, Pye and Veal—as if they had been drawn from a hotel menu card! Maesteg could boast of surnames such as Brothers, Uncles, Husbands and Cousins! The valley had ceased to be a district of Joneses, Davieses, Willamses and Thomases only. Some named their children after their favourite politicians, resulting in Vernon Hartshorn Lewis and Snowdon Lewis. Several sported the Christian name of Gladstone. The son of a well-known Baptist minister was born on the day the famous Baptist preacher, Charles Haddon Spurgeon, died, and the son was consequently called Charles Haddon Williams. Hundreds of nick-names could be quoted. Gomer, wife of the prophet Hosea, was used as a male Christian name.

Men formerly walked many miles to their places of employment and to various meetings. The father of the writer of these notes walked to and from Aberafan on a Saturday evening to hear a famous preacher, the Rev. Dr. Herber Evans, described by Lloyd George as the greatest Welsh orator of his day. Nantyffyllon, Garth and Llangynwyd pupils used to walk each day to the Maesteg Secondary School. Women of the upper and lower parts of the valley used to walk to Llwyni (the old name for Maesteg) to do their shopping. Then came the horse-driven brakes and wagonettes, followed later by a conveyance known as Dan Gipsy's bus, and later by cars used as taxis, charging 1/- (in the old coinage) from Caerau to Maesteg. Messrs. Brewers, after the first World War, began their Caerau-Maesteg bus service with a fourteen-seater Maxwell bus, the single fare being 2½d and the return fare 4d in the old coinage. Petrol was then sold at the rate of 2 gallons

for 1/10 (9p. in present money). There was no time-table, and thirteen
operators were licensed by the Maesteg U.D.C. to travel along the same
route. A time-table later became a necessity, and the service was extended
to Garth, Llangynwyd and the Park Housing Estate. The route from
Maesteg to Port Talbot was first operated jointly with the South Wales
Transport Co. and the Llynfi Bus Co. (W. G. Thomas). The latter
Company has been the sole operator for many years. All services are now
subject to the jurisdiction of the Traffic Commissioners.

A century ago, letters arrived at Maesteg from Bridgend at 8 a.m. and
were dispatched at 5.15 p.m. the same day, whilst letters arriving at Spelters
(Caerau) at 10 a.m. were dispatched at 4 p.m.

The 'cheap jacks' who sold china and crockery at street corners have
disappeared. Games such as scotch (for girls) and marbles and cat-and-dog
(for boys) are no longer played. In the early days, when the leather ball
could not be afforded, boys played football with a pig's bladder. 'Bacco'
chewing and clay-pipe smoking of Franklin's shag have long ceased. No-one
has followed the example of Dr. Hector Jones of Nantyffyllon in distributing
new pennies to children on New Year's Day. The Town Crier, Benjamin
John, who used to awaken us with the call 'Take Notice' and end with 'God
save the King' has been mute for many years. His son took on the function
for a few years. Others who proclaimed their wares in a loud voice from their
roving carts were an old lady called Mari Wlanen, who used to sell salt in
big bars, whilst the high-pitched voices of the local fish vendor shouting
'Hake, lemon sole and flatfish', and the sand vendor with his 'Sand-o' from
their respective carts, are merely echoes of the long past. The colliery hooter
that sounded every morning at 5, 6 and 7 a.m. and at 2.30 p.m. at the end

155   Peace Day at Caerau, 1918

of the miners' day shift is no longer heard. The school bell which rang twice for every school session has been silent for many years.

There is now no local lady whose services were in great demand for preparing bodies for their last journey. In Welsh it was called *troi corff*. Another lady was known as one who was often consulted by single girls who found themselves 'in trouble'. It was satirically stated that she could tell when a girl was 20 minutes pregnant! The writer knew a lady in the upper part of the valley who could claim that she was a grandmother at the age of thirty-one. Richard Hopkins, son of the Rev. Thomas Hopkins, first minister of Bethania Church, Maesteg, had a collection of recipes for the curing of such afflictions as cancer and lockjaw.

Although the industrial revolution meant the obliteration of the rural scene, the badger and the rabbit were seen in the garden of the writer of this volume comparatively recently. However, the valley is no longer noted for its poachers who were active when the Llynvi Iron Works operated. Many kept a gun and a ferret. The story of Joe Lewis, who was hanged at Swansea goal in 1898 for shooting Scott, the Margam gamekeeper, was a much-repeated saga for many years. At the beginning of this century, children who misbehaved were threatened by their parents with a confrontation with a rough local character, Dai Lewis, who had been convicted of the murder of a Mrs. Charles at a shop in Talbot Street, Maesteg.

The years of depression in the mining valleys have been recounted and analysed by countless writers. Local shopkeepers also suffered by giving credit to the unfortunate sufferers, without too much hope of repayment in many instances. However, one local grocer encouraged people to buy at his shop but insisted upon production of the deeds of the customer's house as a security against default. Ministers of the Gospel voluntarily agreed to a reduction in their already low stipends which their unemployed members could not afford to meet, and cheerfully shared their hardships.

Of those who swarmed into the valley in search of work, the North Walian appeared to be the least popular. It is on record that T. L. Roberts, a native of North Wales and a local headmaster, once stated in Welsh: *Y mae nerth mil yn y North-man* (There is the strength of a thousand in the North Walian) and that a Lynfi-ite had replied *A saith mwy yn y South-man*. (And seven times more in the South Walian). A Mr. Matthews, manager of the Ffaldau Colliery in the adjoining Garw Valley, would refuse employment to a North Walian. Happily, the antagonism has long ceased, as no particular part of Wales has a monopoly of either virtues or vices.

However, Maesteg is not different from any other provincial Welsh town in the cultivation of élitism in which people prefer to be called British rather than Welsh—except on the rugby football ground. However, the tremendous improvement in the standard of houses generally throughout the valley has eliminated the idea of a so-called West End for the *crachach*.

Over a period of many years, anyone deemed worthy of public recognition was usually presented with an illuminated address, but such a practice has long since lost its favour and the worthy person is recognised in a more tangible way. The Maesteg Community Centre Committee has recently initiated a practice of honouring those considered worthy of recognition by presenting them with a replica of the Heraldic Shield presented to the former Maesteg Council by the Lord Lieutenant of Glamorgan (Sir Cennydd Traherne, K.G.) in 1970. The practice has its pitfalls as the entitlement of eminently worthy sons or daughters of the valley can be overlooked.

There have been three Royal visits to the valley, one by Edward II (as a fugitive) already referred to, another by Queen Mary, arranged by the Garth Social Service Centre in 1938, ending with a meeting in the Maesteg Town Hall, and the third by the present Prince of Wales, who descended the St. John's Colliery, Maesteg in February, 1974.

With increasing centralisation, Maesteg has lost many facilities. The tax collector's office and the branch offices of the main Assurance Companies were removed to Bridgend many years ago. The *Glamorgan Gazette* reported on 13 January 1977 that Maesteg had lost in one decade the administration offices of the Gas Board, the Electricity Board, the N.C.B., the Maesteg U.D.C. and the Departments of Employment and of Health and Social Security. We have already referred to the closure of the Maesteg Police Court. Previous to centralisation, the Maesteg Council received its supply of electricity in bulk from North's Collieries.

156   Gelli Hunt outside the *Old House,* Llangynwyd, *c.*1910
The hounds were owned originally by the Mansells of Margam, being taken over entirely by Thomas Jenkins of Gelli (Cymer) in 1832. They were known as the 'Cwm Duon' pack but were disbanded during the First World War

The industrial revolution eliminated most of the old-time customs of the district. The Gelli Hunt was once famous and the subject of a well-known Welsh ballad by the Rev. John Blackwell (Alun). At one time, the M.F.H. was Gwilym Treharne Jenkins of Llangynwyd. Changes in farming methods have meant the disappearance of the plough and the emergence of the tractor, together with a host of other changes. Much local information hereon has been provided by Tom Evans of Gelli Lenor Farm and Richard Griffith Thomas of Cae-mab-Ifor Farm, Llangynwyd. Shire horses have disappeared from the local farming scene and the farms have become mechanised. Some have been merged to become 'viable units', whilst other farm buildings have been demolished and the land planted with trees.

It was in 1880 that Messrs. B. Kaltenbach & Co. became the first watch makers, jewellers and opticians in Maesteg, whilst on 25 November 1927 the world-famous Woolworth's Stores secured a footing in the town.

The Maesteg Central Division of the St. John's Ambulance Brigade was formed in 1916 and held its first local examination in 1917. The Caerau Ambulance Station was opened on 19 March 1974. Its counterpart, the Red Cross, has performed equally effective service over a period of many years.

It was Dr. James Lewis, who was born in 1816 and became a resident doctor at Maesteg, who founded, over a hundred years ago, the Porthcawl Rest at which the aged and infirm people from the nearby mining valleys

157   Dr Bell Thomas with his two sons and members of his St John Ambulance
Brigade team, *c*.1919

could spend a fortnight in the summer. He sometimes arranged a day's excursion from the valleys to the Rest, and local Maesteg rhymesters sang his praises. A memorial tablet to his son can be seen in Eglwys Dewi Sant, Maesteg. Local Miners' Lodges later subscribed annually, through a special levy on its members, to the Rest and to the Cardiff and Swansea Infirmaries.

By to-day there are several rest-centres for elderly people throughout the district and a flourishing 'Over Sixties' club at Maesteg. An indication of the social activities of the valley can be gleaned from the fact that the writer of this volume, when he last served as chairman of the Maesteg Council (1969-70), received over fifty invitations to various functions at which he was to take part in the first three months of his holding office. This preceded a much heavier winter programme. Many of these functions were in aid of local charities. Innumerable charitable organisations have contributed to the welfare of the district. The local Rotary Club was formed in 1944, whilst the Inner Wheel (its female counterpart) was formed a year later. The Lions, the Samaritans, the Round Table, The Ladies Circle (whose charter was received in 1969) and many other similar bodies have all contributed to local welfare work.

The Freemasons have three local lodges in the valley—the Llynfi, the Maesteg and the Llangynwyd lodges. The foundation stone of the Maesteg Temple was laid in 1924, opposite Plasnewydd Schools, the members having previously attended at the White Lion Hotel, closed 1924-25. In 1980 a Welsh Masonic Lodge, the first of its kind, was formed for Mid Glamorgan members. The Maesteg lodge of the Loyal Order of Moose was formed in 1928.

In 1976, the idea of forming a community centre for the Maesteg Valley began to take shape. The cost was estimated at £350,000 and a fund was opened in January, 1977. Mr. Edward James, a local grocer, donated £500, and by 1978 over £3,000 had been received from personal subscribers. The centre was located at the lower end of the Forge site of the former Llynvi Iron Works in the immediate vicinity of the Maesteg rugby football ground. As the venture was being backed by a majority of the Ogwr Council members, there has been much opposition in other parts of the Borough owing to the financial aspect of the undertaking and the effect upon the rates caused by hefty Council borrowing. It is anticipated that the actual cost of financing the project will be far in excess of the original estimate. However, the proposed venture, despite financial difficulties, is an indication of the enterprise of the local residents in trying to secure a worthy future for their much loved valley.

There are now in Maesteg three Banks, the National Westminster, Lloyds and the Midland, and also a Trustee Savings Bank. The valley branches have been closed. It was during the last War that the Maesteg branch of Barclays Bank closed. H. J. Randall, in his *History of Bridgend*, reminds us

158 Staff in the entrance to the Caerau & Maesteg Co-operative Society Ltd store, 1923

that there was never a private bank in Mid Glamorgan as the district was not known for drovers or Quakers, who promoted banks. A sub-branch of the National Provincial and Union Bank, later known as the National Westminster Bank, was opened at Bridgend in May, 1835. Wages for the Iron Works at Maesteg were collected at Bridgend. The predecessor of Barclays, called the Bank of Wales, opened in Bridgend in the late 1860s. The Midland was a much younger institution, but it appears that Lloyds was the youngest of the three as it was in 1902 that the Bridgend branch was opened. Banks at Bridgend became the fore-runners of those we now know at Maesteg.

The local Co-operative Society was formed in 1864. It was after the Society had opened shops in Bryn, Glyncorrwg, Abergwynfi, Cymer, Caerau and Spelters that it began to operate from Maesteg. The local shops amalgamated into the Maesteg and District branch, and the Society later became one of the first to join the C.W.S. Retail Society. In 1974, the membership was over 7,000 and the Society operated ten grocery stores, including a self-service supermarket, four butchery shops and three small stores. A departmental store, containing the Society's own bank, was opened in Commercial Street in 1963.

159 This photograph, taken in August 1977, shows part of the Corn Stores, PTR Line, Nant-y-Crynwydd Farm, and NCB locomotive sheds. With the exception of the Corn Stores, this has all been demolished for the New Sports Centre. In the background on the left St Michael's Church is visible, the stonework for this church being from the furnaces of the new works

A hefty chapter would be needed to recount the achievements of sons and daughters of the valley who have excelled in the world of commerce, business, industry, the press, medicine, law, engineering, the stage, the Church, education, science, sport, the Air Force, local government and many other fields — activities that have brought credit to themselves and to the valley which is proud of having been their birthplace.

The task of collating these details would be an invidious, if not an impossible one, as facts continue to accumulate, and owing to the distinct possibility of overlooking the achievements (worth recording) of others. Although much material is already available, it is totally inadequate to do justice to such a wide field.

However, it is hoped that this volume, despite its inadequacy and unintended omissions, will cause us all to be proud of the splendid traditions of the past.

MAWR YW EIN BRAINT I BERTHYN I GWM LLYNFI
(Great is our privilege to belong to the Llynfi Valley)

Index

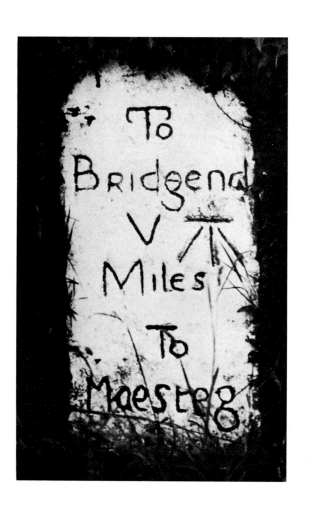